(in brackets) means relatively unimportant

et

ryday quality
erage
n. highly reputed
estigious, expensive
articularly good value in its class
al rating
nded years which may be currently available.
egarded as particularly successful for the property in question.
hold should be ready for drinking (the others should be kept). Where both reds and
e indicated the red is intended unless otherwise stated.
intages are codified by a different system.
on p. 104.
youngest available
ot normally shown on label. In Champagne, means a blend of several vintages for

erences are in SMALL CAPS
for extra explanation
eference vintage chart for France and Germany appears on p.199.

azley Publishers
n 1977, 1978, 1979, 1980, 1981, 1982, 1983, 1984, 1985, 1986, 1987,

d 1977
ished 1978, 1979, 1980, 1981, 1982, 1983, 1984, 1985, 1986, 1987, 1988
azley Publishers

& Schuster Inc.
ilding

Americas
10020

-6

shers will be grateful for any information which will assist them in keeping future
Although all reasonable care has been taken in the preparation of this book,
s nor the author can accept any liability for any consequences arising from the
the information contained herein.

vin, Nicola East, Lesley Crabb
nie Gill
tor    Chris Foulkes
Editor    Roger Walton
rt Bowling
Link Ltd, Welshpool, Powys, Wales
ou, China

# HUGH JOH

# POCKET ENCY

# OF WINE

# 1989

KEY TO SYM

r.    red
p.    ros
w.    wh
br.    bro
sw.    sw
s/sw.    ser
dr.    dry
sp.    spa
★    pla
★★    abo
★★★    we
★★★★    gra
▓▓▓▓    usu
( )    pro
83 84 etc.    rec
82′ etc.    Vin
**80** etc.    yea
   wh
N.B.    Ge
   See
D.Y.A.    drir
NV    vin
   cor
   Cro
   See
   A q

© 1977 Mitche
Text © Hugh Je
1988
First edition pub
Revised editions
© 1988 Mitche
A FIRESIDE BOO
Published by Sir
Simon & Schust
Rockefeller Cent
1230 Avenue of
New York, New

No part of this w
mechanical, incl
without prior wr

ISSN 0893-259

FIRESIDE and c

ISBN 0-671-66

The author and p
editions up to da
neither the publi
use thereof, or

Editors    Alison
Proof-reader
Senior Executive
Senior Executive
Production    St
Filmsetting by L
Printed in Sh

A FIRESIDE BOOK
PUBLISHED BY SIMON & SCHUSTE
NEW YORK LONDON TORONTO SY

# Contents

# Introduction

The task of revising this little book each year (this is the twelfth time I have pored over its minutiae) is also the occasion for a *tour d'horizon* of activity in the world's vineyards. One can see the trees all right, but how is the wood shaping up? Since its first edition in 1977 this encyclopediette has traced what amounts to a new image of the wine-growing world. The pages devoted to Italy, for example, have increased from 15 to 21; those listing Australia's wines from two and a half to nine; New Zealand did not appear at all in the first edition, and nor did the Pacific North-West. We are enjoying wines that were not available, or didn't exist, ten (or even five) years ago. And the competition engendered by so many new entries in the race has increased the quality of almost all the wines we buy today.

The 1989 edition has been redesigned and extended by eight pages to accommodate considerably more information than last year's. The 1977 edition had 142 pages. This has 200. More, I felt, would begin to threaten its claim to be a truly pocketable volume. But there is always more to say. So intense shoe-horning by the designer has somehow managed to squeeze the mass of new and updated information into a few more pages.

To new readers I should explain that this book is a continuing attempt to squeeze in as much up-to-date information about the wines of the world as possible. The information is gleaned from many sources through innumerable visits and tastings and via a perpetual spate of correspondence. The process of revision never stops, whether it involves a change of emphasis or fact or vintage or a new entry. There is a constant pressure by new producers for inclusion; newness itself, however, is not a qualification for entry ... old producers also do newsworthy things.

The arrangement of the book is intended to be as helpful as possible when you are buying a bottle, whether you are on the nursery slopes or an old hand with a bad memory. You are faced with a list of wines or an array of bottles in a restaurant, wine merchant's or bottle store. Your mind goes blank. You fumble for your little book. All you need to establish is what country a wine comes from. Look up the principal words on the label in the appropriate country's section. You will find enough potted information to let you judge whether this is the wine you want.

Specifically, you will find information on the colour and type of wine, its status or prestige, whether it is usually particularly good value, which vintages are good and which are ready to drink – and often considerably more ... about the quantity made, the grapes used, ownership and the rest. Hundreds of cross-references help you delve further.

# How to read an entry

The top line of most entries consists of the following information in an abbreviated form.

1. Which part of the country in question the wine comes from. (References to the maps in this book.)

2. Whether it is red, rosé or white (or brown/amber), dry, sweet or sparkling, or several of these.

3. Its general standing as to quality: a necessarily rough and ready guide based principally on an ascending scale:

    \* plain, everyday quality

   \*\* above average

  \*\*\* well known, highly reputed

 \*\*\*\* grand, prestigious, expensive

So much is more or less objective. Additionally there is a subjective rating: shading around the stars of any wine which in my experience is usually particularly good (which means good value) within its price range. There are good everyday wines as well as good luxury wines. The box system helps you find them.

4. Vintage information: which were the more successful of the recent vintages which *may* still be available. And of these which are ready to drink this year, and which will probably improve with keeping. Your first choice for current drinking should be one of the vintage years printed in **bold** type. Buy light-type years for further maturing.

The German vintage information works on a different principle: see the Introduction to Germany, page 104.

## Acknowledgements

This store of detailed recommendations comes partly from my own notes and partly from those of a great number of kind friends. Without the generous help and co-operation of every single member of the wine trade I have approached, I could not attempt it. I particularly want to thank the following for help with research or in the areas of their special knowledge.

| | |
|---|---|
| Rodrigo Alvarado | Miles Lambert-Gócs |
| Gerry Amdor | Tim Marshall |
| Burton Anderson | Patrick Matthews |
| Anthony Barton | Lindsay Messenger |
| Jean-Claude Berrouet | Christian Moueix |
| Tim Bleach | David Peppercorn M.W. |
| Bernhard Breuer | István Pusztai |
| Michael Broadbent M.W. | Alain Querre |
| Terry Dunleavy | Jan. Maite & Carlos Read |
| Len Evans | Belle Rhodes |
| Dereck Foster | Dr. Bernard Rhodes |
| Chris Foulkes | Dr. Bruno Roncarati |
| Rosemary George M.W. | Peter M.F. Sichel |
| James Halliday | Patrick Skinner |
| Peter Hasslacher | Steven Spurrier |
| Ian Jamieson M.W. | Serena Sutcliffe M.W. |
| Graham Knox | Bob Thompson |
| Matt Kramer | Peter Vinding-Diers |
| Tony Laithwaite | Manfred Völpel |
| John Lipitch | David Wolfe |

# Grape varieties

The most basic of all differences between wines is the flavour (or lack of it) of the grapes they are made of. Centuries of selection have resulted in each of the long-established wine-areas having its favourite single variety, or a group of varieties whose juice or wine is blended together. Red burgundy is made of one grape, the Pinot Noir; red Bordeaux of three or four: two kinds of Cabernet, Merlot, Malbec and sometimes others (the proportions at the discretion of the grower). The laws say which grapes must be used, so the labels do not mention them.

So in newer regions the choice of a grape is the grower's single most crucial decision. Where he is proud of it, and intends his wine to have the character of a particular grape, the variety is the first thing he puts on the label. Hence the useful, originally Californian, term "varietal wine" – meaning, in principle, *one* variety.

Familiarity with at least a few grape varieties, then, is the single most helpful piece of knowledge in finding wines you will like wherever they are grown. Learn to recognize the characters of the most important. At least seven – Cabernet, Pinot Noir, Riesling, Sauvignon Blanc, Chardonnay, Gewürztraminer and Muscat – have memorable tastes and smells distinct enough to form international categories of wine. To these you might add Merlot, Syrah, Sémillon . . .

Further notes on grapes will be found in the sections on Germany, Italy, central and south-east Europe, South Africa, etc. The following are the best and/or commonest wine grapes.

## Grapes for white wine

**Aligoté** Burgundy's second-rank white grape. Crisp (often sharp) wine, needs drinking young. Perfect for mixing with cassis (blackcurrant liqueur) to make a "Kir".

**Arneis** Traditional Piemontese grape being revived for high-quality, rich-textured whites.

**Blanc Fumé**
Another name for SAUVIGNON BLANC, referring to the reputedly "smoky" smell of the wine, particularly on the upper Loire (Sancerre and Pouilly). Makes some of California's best whites.

**Bual** Makes top-quality sweet Madeira wines.

**Chardonnay**
*The* white burgundy grape, one of the grapes of Champagne, and the best white grape of California and more recently Australia. Gives dry wine of rich complexity, especially when aged some months in new barrels. Italy, Spain, New Zealand, Bulgaria, Oregon, Washington, New York all also now make good Chardonnays.

**Chasselas** A prolific and widely grown early-ripening grape with little flavour, also grown for eating. Best known as Fendant in Switzerland (where it is supreme), Gutedel in Germany. Perhaps the same as Hungary's Leanyka and Romania's Feteasca.

**Chenin Blanc**
The leading white grape of the middle Loire (Vouvray, Layon, etc.). Wine can be dry or sweet (or very sweet), but always retains plenty of acidity – hence its popularity in California, where it can make fine wine, but is rarely so used. See also Steen.

**Clairette** A dull neutral grape formerly widely used in the s. of France.

**Fendant** See Chasselas.

**Folle Blanche**

High acid and little flavour makes it ideal for brandy. Known as Gros Plant in Brittany, Picpoul in Armagnac. Perhaps best in California.

**Furmint** A grape of great character: the trade mark of Hungary both as the principal grape in Tokay and as vivid vigorous table wine with an appley flavour. Called Sipon in Yugoslavia.

**Grecheto or Greco**

Ancient grape of central and s. Italy with vitality and style.

**Gewürztraminer (or Traminer)**

The most pungent wine grape, distinctively spicy to smell and taste, with flavours often identified as being like rose petals or grapefruit. Wines are often rich and soft, even when fully dry. Best in Alsace; also good in Germany, e. Europe, Australia, California, New Zealand.

**Grüner Veltliner**

An Austrian speciality. Round Vienna and in the Wachau and Weinviertel can be delicious: light but dry and lively. Drink young.

**Italian Riesling**

Grown in n. Italy and all over central eastern Europe. Much inferior to German or Rhine Riesling with lower acidity, but a fair all-round grape. Alias Wälschriesling, Olaszrizling (but no longer legally labelled "Riesling").

**Kerner** The most successful of a wide range of recent German varieties, largely made by crossing Riesling and Sylvaner (but in this case Riesling and [red] Trollinger). Early-ripening, flowery wine with good acidity. Popular in RHEINPFALZ, RHEINHESSEN, etc.

**Malvasia** Known as Malmsey in Madeira, Malvasia in Italy, Malvoisie in France. Alias Vermentino. Also grown in Greece, Spain, W. Australia, eastern Europe. Makes rich brown wines or soft whites with superb potential, not often realized.

**Müller-Thurgau**

Dominant variety in Germany's Rheinhessen and Rheinpfalz; a cross between Riesling and Sylvaner. Ripens early to make soft flowery wines to drink young. Makes good sweet wines but usually dull dry ones. Grows well in New Zealand, Austria, England.

**Muscadet (alias Melon de Bourgogne)**

Makes light, very dry wines round Nantes in Brittany. They should not be sharp, but faintly salty, savoury and v. refreshing.

**Muscat** (many varieties; the best is Muscat blanc à petits grains). Universally grown easily recognized pungent grapes, mostly made into perfumed sweet wines, often fortified (as in France's VIN DOUX NATURELS). Muscat d'Alsace is unusual in being dry.

**Palomino** Alias Listan. Makes all the best sherry but v. wishy-washy table wine.

**Pedro Ximénez**

Said to have come to s. Spain from Germany. Makes very strong wine in Montilla and Malaga. Used in blending sherry. Also grown in Australia, California, South Africa.

**Pinot Blanc**

A close relation of CHARDONNAY without its strength of character. Grown in Champagne, Alsace (increasingly), n. Italy (good sparkling wine), s. Germany, eastern Europe. Called Weissburgunder in German. California's "Pinot Blanc" is apparently actually Muscadet.

**Pinot Gris**

Makes rather heavy, even "thick", full-bodied whites with a certain spicy style. Known as Tokay in Alsace, Tocai in n.e. Italy and Yugoslavia, Ruländer in Germany.

**Pinot Noir**
> Superlative black grape (see under Grapes for red wine) used in Champagne and occasionally elsewhere (e.g. California) for making white wine, or a very pale pink "vin gris".

**Riesling** Germany's finest grape, now planted round the world. Wine of brilliant sweet/acid balance, flowery in youth but maturing to subtle oily scents and flavours. Successful in Alsace (for dry wine), Austria, parts of eastern Europe, Australia (where it is widely grown), California, South Africa. Often called White, Johannisberg or Rhine Riesling. Subject to "noble rot".

**Sauvignon Blanc**
> Very distinctive, aromatic, herby and sometimes smoky scented wine, can be austere (on the upper Loire) or buxom (in Sauternes, where it is combined with SÉMILLON, and parts of California). Also called Fumé Blanc or vice versa. Recently brilliant in New Zealand.

**Scheurebe** Spicy flavoured German Riesling × Silvaner cross, very successful in Rheinpfalz, esp. for Ausleses.

**Sémillon** The grape contributing the lusciousness to great Sauternes; subject to "noble rot" in the right conditions but increasingly important for Graves and dry white Bordeaux too. Makes soft dry wine of great potential. Traditionally called "Riesling" in parts of Australia. Old Hunter Valley Sémillon can be great wine.

**Sercial** Makes the driest Madeira; where they claim it is really Riesling.

**Seyval Blanc**
> French-made hybrid between French and American vines. Very hardy and attractively fruity. Popular and successful in the eastern States and England.

**Steen** South Africa's most popular white grape: good, lively, fruity wine. Said to be the Chenin Blanc of the Loire.

**Sylvaner (Silvaner)**
> Germany's workhorse grape: wine rarely better than pleasant except in Franconia, where it is savoury, and ages admirably and in Rheinhessen, where it is enjoying a renascence. Good in the Italian Tyrol and useful in Alsace. V.g. as "Johannisberg" in Switzerland.

**Tokay** See Pinot Gris. Also a table grape in California and a supposedly Hungarian grape in Australia. The wine Tokay is made of FURMINT.

**Traminer** See Gewürztraminer.

**Trebbiano** Important grape of central Italy, used in Orvieto, Chianti, Soave, etc. Also grown in s. France as Ugni Blanc, and Cognac as "St-Emilion". Thin, neutral wine, really needs blending.

**Ugni Blanc** See Trebbiano.

**Verdejo** The grape of Rueda in Castile, potentially fine and long-lived.

**Verdelho** Madeira grape making excellent medium-sweet wine.

**Verdicchio** Gives its name to good dry wine in central Italy.

**Vermentino** See Malvasia.

**Vernaccia** Grape grown in central and s. Italy and Sardinia for strong lively wine inclining towards sherry.

**Viognier** Rare but remarkable grape of the Rhône valley, grown at Condrieu to make very fine soft and fragrant wine.

**Welschriesling (or Wälschriesling)** See Italian Riesling.

**Weissburgunder** See Pinot Blanc.

# Grapes for red wine

**Barbera** One of several productive grapes of n. Italy, esp. Piemonte, giving dark, fruity, often sharp wine. Useful in blends in California.

**Brunello** S. Tuscan form of SANGIOVESE, splendid at Montalcino.

**Cabernet Franc**
> The lesser of two sorts of Cabernet grown in Bordeaux; the Cabernet of the Loire making Chinon, etc., and rosé.

**Cabernet Sauvignon**
Grape of great character; spicy, herby and tannic. The first grape of the Médoc, also makes the best Californian, Australian, South American and eastern European reds. Its red wine always needs ageing and usually blending. Makes v. aromatic rosé.

**Carignan** By far the commonest grape of France, covering hundreds of thousands of acres. Prolific with dull but harmless wine. Also common in North Africa, Spain and California.

**Cinsaut** Common bulk-producing grape of s. France; in S. Africa crossed with PINOT NOIR to make Pinotage.

**Dolcetto** Source of soft, seductive dry red in Piemonte.

**Gamay** The Beaujolais grape: light, very fragrant wines at their best young. Makes even lighter wine on the Loire and in Switzerland and Savoie. Known as Napa Gamay in California.

**Gamay Beaujolais**
Not Gamay but a variety of PINOT NOIR grown in California.

**Grenache (alias Garnacha)**
Useful grape for strong and fruity but pale wine: good rosé. Grown in s. France, Spain, California. Usually blended.

**Grignolino**
Makes one of the good cheap table wines of Piemonte.

**Malbec (also called Cot)**
Minor in Bordeaux, major in Cahors and Argentina.

**Merlot** Adaptable grape making the great fragrant and rich wines of Pomerol and St-Emilion, an important element in Médoc reds, soft and strong in California, lighter but good in n. Italy, Italian Switzerland, Yugoslavia, Argentina, etc.

**Mourvèdre (alias Mataro)**
Excellent, dark, aromatic, tannic grape used for blending in Provence (esp. in Bandol).

**Nebbiolo (also called Spanna and Chiavennasca)**
Italy's best red grape, the grape of Barolo, Barbaresco, Gattinara and Valtellina. Intense, nobly fruity and perfumed wine but very tannic, taking years to mature.

**Pinot Noir**
The glory of Burgundy's Côte d'Or, with scent, flavour, texture and body unmatched anywhere. Less happy elsewhere; makes light wines of no great distinction in Germany, Switzerland, Austria, Hungary. The great challenge to the winemakers of California and Australia. Shows great promise in Oregon.

**Sangiovese**
The main red grape of Chianti and much of central Italy. See also Brunello.

**Spätburgunder**
German for PINOT NOIR, but a v. pale shadow of burgundy.

**Syrah (alias Shiraz)**
The best Rhône red grape, with tannic purple wine, which can mature superbly. Very important as "Shiraz" in Australia.

**Tempranillo**
The characteristic fine Rioja grape, called Ull de Lebre in Catalonia, Cencibel in La Mancha. Early ripening.

**Zinfandel** Fruity, adaptable grape peculiar to California. Also makes "blush" white wine.

# Wine & Food

While there are no statutes or laws about what wine goes with what food, there is a vast body of accumulated experience which it is absurd to ignore, even while trying out new ideas.

This list of dishes and appropriate wines records many of the conventional combinations and suggests others that I personally have found good. But it is only a list of ideas intended to help you make quick decisions. Any of the groups of recommended wines could have been extended almost indefinitely, drawing on the whole world's wine list. In general I have stuck to the wines that are widely available, at the same time trying to ring the changes so that the same wines don't come up time and time again – as they tend to do in real life.

The stars refer to the rating system used throughout the book: see opposite Contents.

## Before the meal – apéritifs

The traditional apéritif wines are either sparkling (epitomized by champagne) or fortified (epitomized by sherry). They are still the best, but avoid peanuts with them, they destroy wine flavours. Eat almonds or walnuts instead. The current fashion for a glass of white wine before eating calls for something light and stimulating, dry but not acid, with a degree of character, such as:

**France:**
Alsace Edelzwicker, Riesling or Sylvaner; Chablis; Muscadet; Sauvignon de Touraine; Graves Blanc; Mâcon Blanc; Crépy; Bugey, Haut-Poitou, Côtes de Gascogne.

**Germany:**
Any Kabinett wine or QbA. Choose a "halbtrocken" – nearly dry.

**Italy:**
Soave; Orvieto Secco; Frascati; Gavi; Pinot Bianco; Montecarlo; Vernaccia; Tocai; Lugano; Albana di Romagna.

**Spain:**
Rioja Blanco Marqués de Caceres or Faustino V, or Albariño. But fino sherry, Manzanilla or Montilla is even better.

**Portugal:**
Any vinho verde; Bucelas.

**Eastern Europe:**
Leanyka, Welschriesling, Riesling, Chardonnay.

**USA:**
California "Chablis"; Chenin Blanc; Riesling; French Colombard; Fumé Blanc; Gewürztraminer, or a good "house blend"; Riesling from New York or Oregon, Sémillon from Washington.

**Australia:**
Barossa or Coonawarra Riesling; Houghton's "White Burgundy"

**South Africa:**
Steen is ideal. (The K.W.V. labels it Chenin Blanc.)

**England:**
Almost any English wine is ideal before a meal.

References to these wines will be found in national A-Z sections.

## First courses

**Aïoli**
A thirst-quencher is needed with so much garlic. ★→★★★ white Rhône, or Frascati, or Verdicchio, and lots of mineral water.

**Antipasto** (see also Hors d'oeuvre)
   ★★ dry or medium white, preferably Italian (e.g. Soave) or light red,
   e.g. Valpolicella, Bardolino or young ★ Bordeaux. Or fino sherry.

**Artichoke**
   ★ red or rosé.
   **vinaigrette** ★ young red, e.g. Bordeaux, Côtes-du-Rhône.
   **hollandaise** ★ or ★★ full-bodied dry or medium white, e.g. Mâcon
   Blanc, Rheinpfalz, or a California "house blend".

**Asparagus**
   A difficult flavour for wine, so the wine needs plenty of its own.
   ★★→★★★ white burgundy or Chardonnay, or Corsican rosé.

**Assiette anglaise** (assorted cold meats)
   ★★ dry white, e.g. Chablis, Muscadet, Sylvaner, Riesling; esp.
   Trocken wines from the Mosel.

**Avocado**
   **with prawns, crab, etc.** ★★→★★★ dry to medium white, e.g.
   Rheingau or Rheinpfalz Kabinett, Graves, California or Australian
   Chardonnay or Sauvignon, Cape Steen, or dry rosé.
   **vinaigrette** ★ light red, or manzanilla sherry.

**Bisques**
   ★★ dry white with plenty of body: Pinot Gris, Chardonnay. Fino or
   amontillado sherry, or Montilla.

**Bouillabaisse**
   ★→★★ very dry white: Muscadet, Alsace Silvaner, Entre-Deux-
   Mers, Pouilly Fumé, Cassis, Tuscan Trebbiano, Grechetto.

**Carpaccio**
   Seems to work well with the flavour of most wines, including ★★★
   reds. Top Tuscan vino da tavola is appropriate.

**Caviar**
   ★★★ champagne or iced vodka (or both).

**Cheese fondue**
   ★★ dry white: Fendant or Johannisberg du Valais, Grüner Veltliner,
   Alsace Riesling, NZ Sauvignon Blanc.

**Chicken liver pâté**
   Appetizing dry white, e.g. ★★ white Bordeaux or Pouilly-Fumé, or
   light fruity red; Beaujolais, Gamay de Touraine, young Chianti or
   Valpolicella.

**Clams and chowders**
   ★★ big-scale white, not necessarily bone dry: e.g. Rhône, Pinot Gris,
   Dry Sauternes, Napa Chardonnay. Or fino sherry.

**Consommé**
   ★★→★★★ medium-dry sherry, dry Madeira, Marsala, Montilla.

**Crudités**
   ★→★★★ light red or rosé, e.g. Côtes-du-Rhône, Beaujolais, Minervois, Chianti, Zinfandel.

**Eggs** (see also Soufflés)
   These present difficulties: they clash with most wines and spoil good
   ones. So ★→★★ of whatever is going. I can bear champagne with
   scrambled eggs.

**Empanadas**
   ★→★★ Chilean or Argentine Cabernet, Zinfandel.

**Escargots**
   ★★ red or white of some substance: e.g. Burgundy, Côtes-du-Rhône,
   Chardonnay, Shiraz, etc.

**Fish terrine**
   Rheingan Riesling, Trocken, Chablis, Washington Riesling, Rioja
   Blanco.

**Foie gras**
   ★★★→★★★★ white. In Bordeaux they drink Sauternes. Others
   prefer vintage champagne or a late-harvest Gewürztraminer.

### Gazpacho

Sangria (see Spain) is refreshing, but to avoid too much liquid intake dry Manzanilla or Montilla is better.

### Grapefruit

If you must start a meal with grapefruit try port, Madeira or sweet sherry with (or in) it.

### Gravlax

Akvavit, or Grand Cru Chablis, or ★★★ Californian or Australian Chardonnay.

### Haddock, smoked mousse of

A wonderful dish for showing off any stylish full-bodied white.

### Ham, raw   See Prosciutto.

### Herrings, raw or pickled

Dutch gin (young, not aged) or Scandinavian akvavit, and cold beer.

### Hors d'oeuvres (see also Antipasto)

★→★★ clean fruity sharp white: Sancerre or any Sauvignon, Alsace Silvaner, Muscadet, Cape Steen – or young light red Bordeaux, Rhône or equivalent. Or fino sherry.

### Mackerel, smoked

★★→★★★ full-bodied tasty white; e.g. Gewürztraminer, Tokay d'Alsace or Chablis Premier Cru. Or Manzanilla sherry.

### Mayonnaise

Adds richness that calls for a contrasting bite in the wine. Côte Chalonnaise whites (e.g. Rully) are good. Try NZ Sauvignon Blanc.

### Melon

Needs a strong sweet wine (if any) ★★ Port, Bual Madeira, Muscat, Oloroso sherry or Vin doux naturel.

### Minestrone

★ red: Grignolino, Chianti, Zinfandel, Shiraz, etc.

### Mushrooms à la Grecque

Robola from Cephalonia or any hefty dry white, or fresh young red.

### Omelettes   See under Eggs.

### Onion/leek tart

★→★★★ fruity, concentrated dry white, e.g. Alsace Pinot Gris or Riesling. Mâcon-Villages of a good vintage, Jurançon, California or Australian Riesling.

### Pasta

★→★★ red or white according to the sauce or trimmings, e.g.

**with seafood sauce (vongole, etc.)** Verdicchio, Soave, Pomino, Sauvignon.

**meat sauce** Chianti, Montepulciano d'Abruzzo, Montefalco d'Arquata.

**tomato sauce** Barbera or Sicilian or Yugoslav red or Zinfandel.

**cream sauce** Orvieto, Frascati or Italian Chardonnay.

### Pâté

According to constituents and quality e.g. chicken livers call for pungent white, a smooth red like a light Pomerol, or even amontillado sherry for simple pâté – ★★ dry white: e.g. Mâcon-Villages, Graves, Fumé Blanc.

### Peppers or aubergines (eggplant), stuffed

★★ vigorous red: e.g. Chianti, Dolcetto, Zinfandel.

### Pizza

Any ★★ dry Italian red or a ★★ Rioja, Australian Shiraz or California Zinfandel. Or Corbières or Roussillon.

### Prawns or shrimps

★★→★★★ dry white: burgundy or Bordeaux, Chardonnay or Riesling. ("cocktail sauce" kills any wine.)

### Prosciutto with melon

★★→★★★ full-bodied dry or medium white: e.g. Orvieto or Frascati, Pomino, Fendant, Grüner Veltliner, Alsace or California Gewürztraminer, Australian Riesling.

**Quenelles de brochet**
    ★★★ White Hermitage or white Châteauneuf-du-Pape, Grand Cru Chablis, Alsace Pinot Gris, Hunter Valley Sémillon.

**Quiches**
    ★→★★ dry white with body (Alsace, Graves, Sauvignon, Rheingau dry) or young red (e.g. Beaujolais-Villages), according to the ingredients.

**Ratatouille**
    ★★ vigorous young red, e.g. Chianti, Zinfandel, Bulgarian or young red Bordeaux.

**Salade niçoise**
    ★★ very dry not too light or flowery white, e.g. white (or rosé) Rhône or Corsican, Catalan white, Dão, California Sauvignon.

**Salads**
    As a first course, especially with blue cheese dressing, any dry and appetizing white wine. After a main course: no wine.
    N.B. Vinegar in salad dressings destroys the flavour of wine. If you want salad at a meal with fine wine, dress the salad with wine or a little lemon juice instead of vinegar.

**Salami**
    ★→★★ powerfully tasty red or rosé: e.g. Barbera, young Zinfandel, Tavel or Ajaccio rosé, young Bordeaux.

**Salmon, smoked**
    A dry but pungent white, e.g. fino sherry, Alsace Gewürztraminer, Chablis Grand Cru, Vernaccia di San Gimignano, vintage champagne.

**Soufflés**
    As show dishes these deserve ★★→★★★ wines.
    **Fish** Dry white, e.g. burgundy, Bordeaux, Alsace, Chard, etc.
    **Cheese** Red burgundy or Bordeaux, Cabernet Sauvignon, etc.

**Taramasalata**
    Calls for a rustic southern white of strong personality; not necessarily the Greek Retsina. Fino sherry works well.

**Terrine**
    As for pâté, or the equivalent red; e.g. Beaune, Mercurey, Beaujolais-Villages, fairly young ★★ St-Emilion, California Cabernet or Zinfandel, Bulgarian or Chilean Cabernet, etc.

**Tomato sauce (on anything)**
    The acidity of tomato sauce is no friend to fine wines. ★★ red will do. Try Chianti.

**Trout, smoked**
    Sancerre, Pouilly Fumé, or California or NZ Fumé Blanc. Or Rully.

**Vegetable terrine**
    Not a great help to fine wine, but Californian and Australian Chardonnays make a fashionable marriage.

# Fish

**Abalone**
    ★★→★★★ dry or medium white: e.g. Sauvignon Blanc, Chardonnay, Pinot Grigio, Muscadet sur Lie.

**Bass, striped**
    Same wine as for sole.

**Cod**
    A good neutral background for fine dry or medium whites, e.g. ★★→★★★ Chablis, Meursault, cru classé Graves, German Kabinett or dry Spätleses and their equivalents.

**Coquilles St. Jacques**
    An inherently slightly sweet dish, best with medium-dry whites.
    **in cream sauces** ★★★ German Spätlese or a Montrachet.
    **grilled or fried** Hermitage Blanc, Gewürztraminer, California Chenin Blanc, Riesling or champagne.

**Crab, cold, with salad**
    ★★★ California or Rheinpfalz Riesling Kabinett or Spätlese.

**Crab, softshell**
    ★★★ Chardonnay.

**Eel, jellied**
    NV champagne or a nice cup of tea.
    **smoked** Either strong or sharp wine, e.g. fino sherry or Bourgogne
    Aligoté. Or schnapps.

**Fish and chips, fritto misto (or tempura)**
    ★ white Bordeaux, Orvieto Secco, Koshu..

**Haddock**
    ★★→★★★ dry white with a certain richness: e.g. Meursault,
    California or Australian Chardonnay.

**Herrings**
    Need a white with some acidity to cut their richness. Burgundy Aligoté
    or Gros Plant from Brittany or dry Sauvignon Blanc.

**Kippers:** a good cup of tea, preferably Ceylon (milk, no sugar).

**Lamproie à la Bordelaise**
    ★★ young red Bordeaux, St-Emilion, Pomerol or Fronsac.

**Lobster or crab**
    **salad** ★★→★★★★ white. Non-vintage champagne, Alsace Riesling,
    Chablis Premier Cru, Condrieu, Mosel Spätlese.
    **richly sauced** Vintage champagne, fine white burgundy, cru classé
    Graves, California or Australian Chardonnay, Rheinpfalz Spätlese,
    Hermitage Blanc.

**Mackerel**
    ★★ hard or sharp white: Sauvignon Blanc from Bergerac or Touraine,
    Gros Plant, vinho verde, white Rioja. Or Guinness.

**Mullet, red**
    ★★ Mediterranean white, even Retsina, for the atmosphere.

**Mussels**
    ★→★★ Gros Plant, Muscadet, California "Chablis".

**Oysters**
    ★★→★★★ white. Champagne (non-vintage), Chablis or (better)
    Chablis Premier Cru, or Muscadet or white Graves.

**Salmon, fresh**
    ★★★ fine white burgundy: Puligny- or Chassagne-Montrachet, Meur-
    sault, Corton-Charlemagne, Chablis Grand Cru, California, Idaho or
    Australian Chardonnay, or Rheingau Kabinett or Spätlese, California
    Riesling or equivalent. Some like Beaujolais or a young ★★ red
    Bordeaux.

**Sardines, fresh grilled**
    ★→★★ very dry white: e.g. vinho verde, Dão, Muscadet.

**Scallops** See Coquilles St. Jacques.

**Shad**
    ★★→★★★ white Graves or Meursault or Hunter Semillon.

**Shellfish (general)**
    Dry white with plain boiled shellfish, richer wines with richer sauces.

**Shrimps, potted**
    Fino sherry, Chablis, Gavi or New York Chardonnay.

**Skate with black butter**
    ★★ white with some pungency (e. g. Alsace Pinot Gris) or a clean
    straightforward one like Muscadet or Entre-Deux-Mers.

**Sole, plaice, etc.**
    **plain, grilled or fried** An ideal accompaniment for fine wines: ★ up to
    ★★★★ white burgundy, or its equivalent.
    **with sauce** Depending on the ingredients: sharp dry wine for tomato
    sauce, fairly rich for sole véronique, etc.

**Sushi (and sashimi)**
    Sparkling wines, incl. Californian, or California or Australian Char-
    donnay or Sauvignon. Chablis Grand Cru.

**Swordfish**

★★ dry white of whatever country you are in.

**Tuna, grilled**

★★ white or red (or rosé) of fairly fruity character. NZ Sauvignon Blanc or a top Côtes-du-Rhône would be fine.

**Trout**

Delicate white wine, e.g. ★★★ Mosel.

smoked A full-flavoured ★★→★★★ white: Gewürztraminer, Pinot Gris, Rhine Spätlese or Australian Hunter white.

**Turbot**

Fine rich dry white, e.g. ★★★ Meursault or its California, Australian or New Zealand equivalent. Viognier from Condrieu. Mature Rheingau, Mosel or Nahe Spätlese or Auslese.

# Meat, poultry, etc.

**Barbecues**

★★ red with a slight rasp, therefore young. Shiraz, Chianti, Zinfandel, Turkish Buzbag.

**Beef, boiled**

★★ red: e.g. Bordeaux (Bourg or Fronsac), Côtes-du-Rhône-Villages, Australian Shiraz. Or good Mâcon-Villages white.

**Beef, roast**

An ideal partner for fine red wine. ★★→★★★★ red of any kind.

**Beef stew**

★★→★★★ sturdy red, e.g. Pomerol or St-Emilion, Hermitage, Shiraz, Calif. or Oregon Pinot Noir, Torres Sangre de Toro.

**Beef Stroganoff**

★★→★★★ suitably dramatic red: e.g. Barolo, Brunello, Valpolicella, Amarone, Hermitage, late-harvest Zinfandel.

**Cassoulet**

★★ red from s.w. France, e.g. Madiran, Cahors or Corbières, or Barbera or Zinfandel.

**Chicken or turkey, roast (or guinea fowl)**

Virtually any wine, including your very best bottles of dry or medium white and finest old reds. The meat of fowl can be adapted with sauces to match almost any fine wine (e.g. coq au vin with red burgundy). Avoid tomato sauces for ★★★ bottles.

**Chili con carne**

★→★★ young red: e.g. Bull's Blood, Chianti, Mountain Red.

**Chinese food**

Canton or Peking style ★★→★★★★ dry to medium-dry white: e.g. Yugoslav "Riesling", Mâcon-Villages, California Chardonnay. Or NV Champagne.

Szechuan style Very cold beer.

**Choucroute**

Alsace Pinot Gris.

**Cold meats**

Generally taste better with full-flavoured white wine than red. Mosel Spätleses, Hochheimer are v.g.

**Confit d'oie**

★★→★★★ rather young and tannic red Bordeaux helps to cut the richness. Alsace Tokay or Gewürztraminer matches it.

**Coq au vin**

★★→★★★★ red burgundy. In an ideal world one bottle of Chambertin in the dish, two on the table.

**Corned beef hash**

★★ Zinfandel, Chianti, Côtes-du-Rhône red.

**Curry**

★→★★ medium-sweet white, very cold: e.g. Orvieto abboccato, certain California Chenin Blancs, Yugoslav Traminer.

**Duck or goose**
    ★★★ rather rich white, e.g. Rheinpfalz Spätlese or Alsace Réserve Exceptionelle, or ★★★ Bordeaux or burgundy.
    With oranges or peaches, the Sauternais propose Sauternes.
    **Wild duck** ★★★ big-scale red: e.g. Hermitage, Châteauneuf-du-Pape, California. or S. African Cabernet, Australian Shiraz, Torres Gran Coronas.

**Frankfurters**
    ★→★★ German or Australian white, or Beaujolais. Or beer.

**Game birds**
    Young birds plain roasted and not too well hung deserve the best red wine you can afford. With older birds in casseroles ★★→★★★ red, e.g. Gevrey-Chambertin, Pommard, Grand Cru St-Emilon, Napa Cab. With very high game, Hermitage, Châteauneuf-du-Pape, Vega Sicilia.

**Game pie**
    (Hot) ★★★ red wine. (Cold) Equivalent white.

**Goulash**
    ★★ strong young red: e.g. Zinfandel, Bulgarian Cabernet.

**Grouse** See Game birds.

**Ham**
    ★★→★★★ fairly young red burgundy, e.g. Volnay, Savigny, Beaune, Corton, or a slightly sweet German white, e.g. a Rhine Spätlese, or a Tuscan red, or a lightish Cabernet (e.g. Chilean).

**Hamburger**
    ★→★★ young red: e.g. Beaujolais, Corbières or Minervois, Chianti, Zinfandel, Kadarka from Hungary.

**Hare**
    Jugged hare calls for ★★→★★★ red with plenty of flavour: not-too-old burgundy or Bordeaux. The same for saddle. Grange Hermitage would be an experience.

**Kebabs**
    ★★ vigorous red: e.g. Greek Demestica, Turkish Buzbag, Bulgarian or Chilean Cabernet, Zinfandel.

**Kidneys**
    ★★→★★★ red: Pomerol or St-Emilion, Rhône, Barbaresco, Rioja, California, Spanish or Australian Cabernet, Bairrada from Portugal.

**Lamb cutlets or chops**
    As for roast lamb, but less grand.

**Lamb, roast**
    One of the traditional and best partners for very good red Bordeaux – or its Cabernet equivalents from the New World.

**Liver**
    ★★→★★★ young red: Beaujolais-Villages, St-Joseph, Médoc, Italian Merlot, Zinfandel, Oregon Pinot Noir.

**Meatballs**
    ★★→★★★ red: e.g. Mercurey, Madiran, Rubesco, Dão, Bairrada, Zinfandel or Cabernet.

**Mixed grill**
    A fairly light easily swallowable red; ★★ red Bordeaux from Bourg, Fronsac or Premières Côtes; Chianti; Bourgogne Passe-tout-grains, Chilean Cabernet.

**Moussaka**
    ★→★★ red or rosé: e.g. Naoussa, Chianti, Corbières, Côtes de Provence, Ajaccio or Patrimonio, California Burgundy.

**Oxtail**
    ★★→★★★ rather rich red: e.g. St-Emilion or Pomerol, Burgundy, Barolo or Chianti Classico, Rioja Reserva, California or Coonawarra Cabernet or a dry Riesling Spätlese.

**Paella**
    ★★ Young Spanish r., dry w. or rosé, e.g. Penedès or Rioja.

**Partridge, pheasant**  See under Game birds.

**Pigeons or squabs**

★★→★★★★ red Bordeaux, Chianti Classico, Californian or Australian Cabernet. Silvaner Spätlese from Franconia.

**Pork, roast**

Pork is a good, rich, neutral background to very good white or red wine.

**Rabbit**

★→★★★ young red: Italian for preference.

**Ris de veau**  See Sweetbreads.

**Risotto**

Pinot Grigio from Friuli, Gavi, youngish Sémillon.

**Sauerkraut**

Lager.

**Sausages**

The British banger requires a 3-year-old n. Italian Merlot. (A red wine, anyway.) See also Salami.

**Shepherd's Pie**

★→★★ rough and ready red seems most appropriate, but no harm would come to a good one.

**Steak and kidney pie or pudding**

Red Rioja Reserva or mature ★★→★★★ Bordeaux.

**Steaks**

**Alligator**  Watch this space.

**Au poivre**  A fairly young ★★★ Rhône red or Cabernet.

**Tartare**  ★★ light young red: Beaujolais, Bergerac, Valpolicella.

**Filet or Tournedos**  ★★★ red of any kind (but not old wines with Béarnaise sauce).

**T-bone**  ★★→★★★ reds of similar bone-structure: e.g. Barolo, Hermitage, Australian Cabernet or Shiraz.

**Fiorentina (bistecca)**  Chianti Classico Riserva.

**Ostrich**  South African Pinotage.

**Stews and casseroles**

A lusty full-flavoured red, e.g. young Côtes-du-Rhône, Corbières, Barbera, Shiraz, Zinfandel, etc.

**Sweetbreads**

These tend to be a grand dish, suggesting a grand wine, e.g. ★★★ Rhine Riesling or Franken Silvaner Spätlese, or well-matured Bordeaux or burgundy, depending on the sauce.

**Tongue**

Ideal for favourite bottles of any red or white of abundant character, esp. Italian.

**Tripe**

★→★★ red: Corbières, Mâcon Rouge, etc., or rather sweet white, e.g. Liebfraumilch. Better: W. Australian "white Burgundy".

**Veal, roast**

A good neutral background dish for any fine old red which may have faded with age (e.g. a Rioja Reserva) or a ★★★ German white.

**Venison**

★★★ big-scale red (Rhône, Bordeaux of a grand vintage) or rather rich white (Rheinpfalz Spätlese or Tokay d'Alsace).

**Vitello tonnato**

Light red (Valpolicella, Beaujolais) served cool.

**Wiener Schnitzel**

★★→★★★ light red from the Italian Tyrol (Alto Adige) or the Médoc: or Austrian Riesling, Grüner Veltliner or Gumpoldskirchener.

# Cheese

Very strong cheese completely masks the flavour of wine. Only serve fine wine with mild cheeses in peak condition.

**Bleu de Bresse, Dolcelatte, Gorgonzola, Stilton**
Need emphatic accompaniment: young ★★ red wine (Barbera, Dolcetto, Moulin-à-Vent, etc.) or sweet white – or port.

**Cream cheeses: Brie, Camembert, Bel Paese, Edam, etc.**
In their mild state marry with any good wine, red or white.

**English cheeses**
Can be either mild or strong and acidic. The latter need sweet or strong wine.
**Cheddar, Cheshire, Wensleydale, Gloucester, etc.** If mild, claret. If strong, ruby, tawny or vintage-character (not vintage) port, old dry oloroso sherry, or a very big red: Hermitage, Châteauneuf-du-Pape, Barolo, Barbaresco, etc.

**Goat cheeses**
★★→★★★ white wine of marked character, either dry (e.g. Sancerre) or sweet (e.g. Monbazillac, Sauternes).

**Hard Cheese, Parmesan, Gruyère, Emmenthal, old Gouda**
Full-bodied dry whites, e.g. Tokay d'Alsace or Vernaccia, or fino or amontillado sherry.

**Roquefort, Danish Blue**
Are so strong-flavoured that only the youngest, biggest or sweetest wines stand a chance. Old dry amontillado or oloroso sherries have the necessary horse-power.

# Desserts

**Apple pie, apple strudel**
★★→★★★ sweet German, Austrian or Hungarian white.

**Apples, Cox's Orange Pippins**
Vintage port (55, 60, 63, 66, 70, 75).

**Bread and butter pudding**
10-year-old Barsac from a good château.

**Cakes**
Bual or Malmsey Madeira, Oloroso or cream sherry.

**Cheesecake**
★★→★★★ sweet white from Vouvray or Coteaux du Layon.

**Chocolate cake, mousse, soufflés**
Huxelrebe Auslese or California orange muscat.

**Christmas pudding, mince pies**
Sweet champagne or Asti Spumante, or cream sherry.

**Creams and custards**
★★→★★★ Sauternes, Monbazillac or similar golden white.

**Crème brûlée**
The most luxurious dish, demanding ★★★→★★★★ Sauternes or Rhine Beerenauslese, or the best Madeira or Tokay.

**Crêpes Suzette**
Sweet champagne or Asti Spumante.

**Fruit, fresh**
Sweet Coteaux du Layon white, light sweet muscat (e.g. California).
**Pears in red wine** A pause before the port.
**Raspberries** (no cream, little sugar) Excellent with fine reds.
**Rhubarb** Rhubarb wine, I suppose.

**Fruit flans (i.e. peach, raspberry)**
★★★ Sauternes, Monbazillac or sweet Vouvray or Anjou.

**Fruit salads, orange salad**
No wine.

**Nuts**
Oloroso sherry, Bual, Madeira, vintage or tawny port, Vinsanto.

**Sorbets, ice-creams**
No wine.

**Stewed fruits, i.e. apricots, pears, etc.**
Sweet Muscatel: e.g. Muscat de Beaumes de Venise, Moscato di Pantelleria or from Tarragona.

**Strawberries and cream**
★★★ Sauternes or Vouvray Moelleux.

**Wild strawberries**
Serve with ★★★ red Bordeaux poured over them and in your glass (no cream).

**Summer pudding**
Fairly young Sauternes of a good vintage (e.g. 75, 76, 79, 80, 82, 83).

**Treacle tart**
Too sweet for any wine but a treacly Malmsey Madeira.

**Trifle**
No wine: should be sufficiently vibrant with sherry.

**Sweet soufflés**
Sweet Vouvray or Coteaux du Layon. Sweet Champagne.

**Zabaglione**
Light gold Marsala.

# Savouries

Generally highly seasoned, these are not ideal partners for the last glass of a fine wine. A Bual or Verdelho Madeira would come to no harm. But **cheese straws** make an admirable meal-ending with a final glass (or bottle) of any particularly good red wine.

# Temperature

No single aspect of serving wine makes or mars it so easily as getting the temperature right. White wines almost invariably taste dull and insipid served warm and red wines have disappointingly little scent or flavour served cold. The chart below gives an indication of what is generally found to be the most satisfactory temperature for serving each class of wine.

| | | °F | °C | |
|---|---|---|---|---|
| | | 68 | 20 | |
| | | 66 | 19 | |
| Room | | 64 | 18 | |
| temperature | | 63 | 17 | Best red wines especially Bordeaux |
| | Red Burgundy | 61 | 16 | |
| | | 59 | 15 | Chianti, Zinfandel Côtes-du-Rhône |
| | Best white Burgundy | 57 | 14 | |
| | Port, Madeira | | | Ordinaires |
| | | 55 | 13 | |
| | | 54 | 12 | Lighter red wines e.g. Beaujolais |
| Ideal | Sherry | 52 | 11 | |
| cellar | Fino sherry | 50 | 10 | Rosés |
| | Most dry white wines | 48 | 9 | Lambrusco |
| | Champagne | 46 | 8 | |
| Domestic | | 45 | 7 | |
| fridge | | 43 | 6 | Most sweet white wines |
| | | 41 | 5 | Sparkling wines |
| | | 39 | 4 | |
| | | 37 | 3 | |
| | | 35 | 2 | |
| | | 33 | 1 | |
| | | 32 | 0 | |

# A little learning . . .

The last fifteen years have seen a revolution in wine technology. They have also heard a revolution in wine-talk – and the beginnings of a reaction. Attempts to express the characters of wine used to get no further than such vague terms as "fruity" and "full-bodied". Then came the demand for sterner, more scientific, stuff: the jargon of laboratory analysis. This hard-edge wine-talk is very briefly explained below.

The most frequent references are to the ripeness of grapes at picking; the resultant alcohol and sugar content of the wine; various measures of its acidity; the amount of sulphur dioxide used as a preservative, and the amount of "dry extract" – the sum of all the things that give wine its characteristic flavours.

The fashion today (French in origin) is for analogues with a quasi-poetic effect: "Scents of apricots, raspberries, leather; flavours of plum and truffle, shading to tar with a hint of fish-glue". Anybody can play. Few can play well.

The **sugar** in wine is mainly glucose and fructose, with traces of arabinose, xylose and other sugars that are not fermentable by yeast, but can be attacked by bacteria. Each country has its own system for measuring the sugar content or ripeness of grapes, known as the **"must-weight"**. The chart below relates the three principal ones (German, French and American) to each other, to specific gravity, and to the potential alcohol of the wine if all the sugar is fermented.

| Specific Gravity | °D °Oechsle | Baumé | Brix | % Potential Alcohol v/v |
|---|---|---|---|---|
| 1.065 | 65 | 8.8 | 15.8 | 8.1 |
| 1.070 | 70 | 9.4 | 17.0 | 8.8 |
| 1.075 | 75 | 10.1 | 18.1 | 9.4 |
| 1.080 | 80 | 10.7 | 19.3 | 10.0 |
| 1.085 | 85 | 11.3 | 20.4 | 10.6 |
| 1.090 | 90 | 11.9 | 21.5 | 11.3 |
| 1.095 | 95 | 12.5 | 22.5 | 11.9 |
| 1.100 | 100 | 13.1 | 23.7 | 12.5 |
| 1.105 | 105 | 13.7 | 24.8 | 13.1 |
| 1.110 | 110 | 14.3 | 25.8 | 13.8 |
| 1.115 | 115 | 14.9 | 26.9 | 14.4 |
| 1.120 | 120 | 15.5 | 28.0 | 15.0 |

**Residual sugar** is the sugar left after fermentation has finished or been artificially stopped, measured in grammes per litre.

**Alcohol content** (mainly ethyl alcohol) is expressed as a percentage by volume of the total liquid.

Acidity is both fixed and volatile. **Fixed acidity** consists principally of tartaric, malic and citric acids which are all found in the grape, and lactic and succinic acids, which are produced during fermentation. **Volatile acidity** consists mainly of acetic acid, which is rapidly formed by bacteria in the presence of oxygen. A small amount of volatile acidity is inevitable and attractive. With a larger amount the wine becomes "pricked" – i.e. starts to turn to vinegar.

**Total acidity** is fixed and volatile acidity combined. As a rule of thumb for a well-balanced wine it should be in the region of 1 gramme/thousand for each 10° Oechsle (see above).

**pH** is a measure of the strength of the acidity, rather than its volume. The lower the figure the more acid. Wine normally ranges in pH from 2.8 to 3.8. Winemakers in hot climates can have problems getting the pH low enough. Lower pH gives better colour, helps prevent bacterial spoilage, allows more of the $SO_2$ to be free and active as a preservative.

**Sulphur dioxide** ($SO_2$) is added to prevent oxidation and other accidents in wine-making. Some of it combines with sugars, etc., and is known as "bound". Only the "**free $SO_2$**" that remains in the wine is effective as a preservative. **Total $SO_2$** is controlled by law according to the level of residual sugar: the more sugar the more $SO_2$ needed.

## What makes a good wine glass?

Many of the traditional wine-growing regions of Europe have a design of glass considered ideal for enjoying their products. Some are based more on folklore than practicality. All good wine glasses are clear, thin, without cutting on the bowl, have a stem of moderate length and a relatively large bowl curving inwards towards the rim. The author is responsible for the design of the glasses illustrated. They constitute a matching set to do justice to all the main styles of wine. Left to right they are designed for: red Bordeaux and similar wines, champagne, red burgundy, white wine, sherry, port and brandy.

# France

*English Channel*

Le Havre

Caen

**NORMANDY**

Brest • **BRITTANY**

Tou

*R. Loire* **LOIRE**

Saumu

Nantes

La Rochelle

**COGNAC**

*Bay of Biscay*

Bordeaux

**BORDEAUX**

**S.W.
FRANCE**

Biarritz

The following abbreviations of regional names
are used in the text.

| | | | |
|---|---|---|---|
| **Al.** | Alsace | **Lo.** | Loire |
| **B'x.** | Bordeaux | **Prov.** | Provence |
| **B'y.** | Burgundy | **Pyr.** | Pyrenees |
| **Champ.** | Champagne | **Rh.** | Rhône |

France makes every kind of wine, and invented most of them. Tens of thousands of properties make wine of all complexions over a large part of her surface. This is a guide to the best known of them and their producers: the essential information in identifying wines that are authentic and good of their kind.

All France's best wine regions (producing about 20% of all her wine) have Appellations Contrôlées, which may apply to a single small vineyard or a whole large district. The system varies from region to region, with Burgundy on the whole having the smallest and most precise appellations, grouped into larger units by complicated formulae, and Bordeaux having the widest and most general appellations, in which it is the particular property (or "château") that matters. In between lie an infinity of variations.

An Appellation Contrôlée is a guarantee of origin and of

production method, of grape varieties and quantities produced, but only partially one of quality. All "AC" wines are officially tasted, but many of shoddy quality get through the net.

Appellations therefore help to identify a wine and indicate that it comes from a major area. They are the first thing to look for on a label. But the next is the name of the maker.

Wine regions without the overall quality and traditions required for an appellation can be ranked as Vins Délimités de Qualité Supérieure (VDQS), or (a third rank, created largely to encourage the improvement of mediocre wines in the south of France) Vins de Pays. VDQS wines are almost always good value, on the Avis principle. Vins de Pays are increasingly worth trying. They include some brilliant originals and often offer France's best value for money.

## Red Burgundy

**Côte d'Or** Côte de Beaune reds generally mature sooner than the bigger wines of the Côte de Nuits. Earliest drinking dates are for lighter commune wines: Volnay, Beaune, etc., latest for the biggest wines of Chambertin, Romanée, etc. Different growers make wines of different styles, for longer or shorter maturing, but even the best burgundies are much more attractive young than the equivalent red Bordeaux.

**1987**   Small crop with promising ripe fruit flavours. Will need time.

**1986**   A very mixed bag — few top-rate wines.

**1985**   A great vintage. Concentrated wines will be splendid. '89–2000.

**1984**   Lacks natural ripeness; tends to be dry and/or watery. Now–'96. Best aromatic and developing.

**1983**   Powerful, vigorous, tannic and attractive vintage, compromised by rot. The best are splendid, but be careful. Now–2000.

**1982**   Big vintage, pale but round. Best in Côte de Beaune. Drink soon.

**1981**   A small crop, ripe but picked in rain. Disappointing.

**1980**   A late, wet year, but attractive wines from the best growers who avoided rot. Better in the Côte de Nuits. Keep (only) the best another year or two.

**1979**   Big generally good ripe vintage with weak spots. Drink up.

**1978**   A small vintage of outstanding quality. The best will live 15 years.

**1977**   Very wet summer. Better than expected, but drink up.

**1976**   Hot summer, excellent vintage. As usual great variations, but the best (esp. Côte de Beaune) rich and long-lived — to 1995.

**1975**   Rot was rife, particularly in the Côte de Beaune. Mostly very poor.

**1974**   Another big wet vintage; even the best light and lean. Drink up.

**1973**   Light wines, but many fruity and delicate. Most are already too old.

**1972**   Firm and full of character, ageing well. Few need keeping longer now.

**1971**   Very powerful and impressive wines, not as long-lasting as they first appeared. Most now ready. The best have 3 or 4 years ahead.

Older fine vintages: '69, '66, '64, '62, '61, '59 (all mature).

**Beaujolais** 1987 was excellent, with Crus to keep. 1986 was highly satisfactory, but not great. 1985 was a wonderful vintage, with Crus to keep still. 1984 was fair, but should be drunk. 1983 was excellent, also now ready. Generally avoid older vintages except possibly 1976 Moulin à Vent.

## White Burgundy

**Côte de Beaune** Well-made wines of good vintages with plenty of acidity as well as fruit will improve and gain depth and richness for some years — anything up to ten. Lesser wines from lighter years are ready for drinking after two or three years.

**1987**   Mainly disappointing, though exceptions will emerge.

**1986**   Powerful wines with better acidity and balance than '85.

**1985**   Very ripe; many wines are too soft; be careful. Now–'95.

**1984**   Some well-balanced wines; most rather lean or hollow. Drink soon.

**1983**   Potent wines; some exaggerated, some faulty but the best splendid. -'95.

**1982**   Fat, tasty but delicate whites of low acidity, not for keeping.

**1981**   A sadly depleted crop with great promise. The best are excellent now.

**1980**   A weak, but not bad, vintage. Drink up.

**1979**   Big vintage. Overall good and useful, not great. Drink soon.

**1978**   Very good wines, firm and well-balanced. Keep only the best.

**1977**   Rather light; some well-balanced and good. Drink up.

**1976**   Hot summer, rather heavy wines; good but not for keeping longer.

**1975**   Whites did much better than reds. Chablis best, but all now ready.

**1974**   Never exciting. Avoid now.

**1973**   Very attractive, fruity, typical and plentiful. Drink up.

**1972**   High acidity, but plenty of character. All are now ready to drink.

**1971**   Great power and style. Top wines are now wonderful.

The white wines of the Mâconnais (Pouilly-Fuissé, St-Véran, Mâcon-Villages) follow a similar pattern, but do not last as long. They are more appreciated for their freshness than their richness.

**Chablis**   Grand Cru Chablis of vintages with both strength and acidity can age superbly for up to ten years. Premiers Crus proportionately less, but too many growers are stressing quantity, which results in wines that fade away without ever achieving the classic Chablis flavour. Only buy Petit Chablis of ripe years, and drink it young.

**1987**   Rain at harvest but balanced wines for the short term.

**1986**   A splendid, big vintage. Now-1995.

**1985**   Good but often low-acid wines. The best Grands and Premiers Crus will age 6 years.

**1984**   A small vintage. Most too feeble to last long.

**1983**   Superb vintage if not over-strong. The best will improve until '93.

**1982**   Charming soft wines. Good value. Not to keep.

**1981**   Small, concentrated and fine harvest. Keeping well. Now '90.

**1980**   More successful than the rest of Burgundy. Drink up.

**1979**   Very big crop. Good easy wines, not for storing. Drink soon.

**1978**   Excellent wines now passing their peak.

# Red Bordeaux

**Médoc/red Graves**   For some wines bottle-age is optional: for these it is indispensable. Minor châteaux from light vintages need only two or three years, but even modest wines of great years can improve for 15 years or so, and the great châteaux of these years need double that time.

**1987**   Difficult; at best sound. Strict selection necessary. Not for long keeping.

**1986**   Another splendid (and huge) heatwave harvest. Most will probably be superior to '85.

**1985**   Very good vintage, in a heatwave. Some great wines. '89-2010.

**1984**   Only fair. Little Merlot but good ripe Cabernet. Generally overpriced. -'95?

**1983**   A classic vintage: abundant tannin with fruit to balance it. -2010.

**1982**   Made in a heatwave. Huge rich strong wines which promise a long life. Only open petits châteaux now.

**1981**   Admirable despite rain. Not rich, but balanced and fine. Now-'98.

**1980**   Small, late harvest, ripe but rained-on. Many delicious light wines but few exciting ones. Drink now-'90.

**1979**   Abundant harvest of good average quality. Now-'95.

**1978**   A miracle vintage: magnificent long warm autumn saved the day. Some superb wines. Now-2000.

**1977**   Pleasant light wine, many better than 1974. Now-'87.

**1976**   Excessively hot, dry summer; rain just before vintage. Generally very good, maturing rather quickly. Now-'95.

**1975**   A very fine vintage, with deep colour, high sugar content (sometimes excessive) tannin. For long keeping. "Petits Châteaux" are now ready.

**1974**   Oceans of disappointing light wines. Be very careful.

**1973**   A huge vintage, attractive young and still give pleasure. Now or soon.

**1972**   High acidity from unripe grapes. Now.

**1971**   Small crop. Less fruity than '70 and less consistent. All are ready to drink.

**1970**   Big excellent vintage with scarcely a failure. Now-'95.

**1969/68**   Avoid them both.

**1967**   Never seductive, but characterful in its maturity. Drink soon.

**1966**   A very fine vintage with depth, fruit and tannin. Now-'90.

Older fine vintages: '62, '61, '59, '55, '53, '52, '50, '49, '48, '47, '45, '29, '28.

# St-Emilion/Pomerol

**1987**   Some very adequate wines but without great fruit and length.

**1986**   A prolific vintage; quality depends on the grower's restraint.

**1985**   One of the great years, with a long future. -2010.

**1984**   A sad story. Most of the crop wiped out in spring. Not for laying down.

**1983**   Conditions were ideal. Some growers prefer this vintage to 1982.

**1982**   Enormously rich and concentrated wines, most excellent. -2000.

**1981**   A very good vintage, if not as great as it first seemed. Now-'95+.

**1980**   A poor Merlot year; very variable quality. Choose carefully. Soon.

**1979**   A rival to '78, but not developing as well as hoped. Now-'95.

**1978**   Fine wines, but some lack flesh. Now-'92.

**1977**   Very wet summer. Mediocre with few exceptions. Drink up.

**1976**   Very hot, dry summer, but vintage rain. Some excellent. Drink from now on.

**1975**   Most St-Emilions good, the best superb. Frost in Pomerol cut crops and made splendid concentrated wine. Now-2000.

**1974/73/72**   All need drinking soon, if at all.

**1971**   On the whole better than Médocs but generally now ready.

**1970**   Beautiful wines with great fruit and strength. Very big crop. Now-'90s.

Older fine vintages: '67, '66, '64, '61, '59, '53, '52, '49, '47, '45.

**Abymes** Savoie w. dr. ★ D.Y.A.
Hilly little area nr. Chambéry known for light mild wine from Jacquère.

**Ackerman-Laurance** Champagne-method house of the Loire, at SAUMUR, said to be the first of the region. Fine CRÉMANT de Loire.

**Ajaccio** Corsica r. p. or w. dr. ★→★★★ 85' 86 87
The capital of Corsica. AC for some v. good SCIACARELLO reds.

**Aligoté** Second-rank burgundy white grape and its wine, often agreeably sharp and fruity and with considerable local character when young. BOUZERON (AC) makes the best.

**Aloxe-Corton** B'y. r. or w. ★★★ 69 71 76 78 79 80 82 83 84 85 86 87
Northernmost village of CÔTE DE BEAUNE famous for its Grands Crus: CORTON (red) and CORTON-CHARLEMAGNE (white). Village wines (called Aloxe-Corton) are lighter but can be v.g. value.

**Alsace** Al. w. or (r.) ★★ 76 81 83' 85' 86 87
Aromatic, fruity, often strong dry white of Germanic character from foothills of Vosges Mtns, bordering on the R. Rhine. Normally sold by grape variety (RIESLING, GEWÜRZTRAMINER, etc.). Matures well up to 5, even 10, years.

**Alsace Grand Cru** ★★★ 71 76 79 81 82 83' 84 85 86 87
Appellation restricted to about 45 of the best named v'yds.

**Alsace Grand Vin or Réserve** Wine with minimum 11° natural alcohol.

**Amance, Marcel** See Maufoux, Prosper.

**Ampeau, Robert** Dependable grower and specialist in MEURSAULT, POM-MARD, etc.

**Anjou** Lo. (r.) p. or w. (sw. dr. or sp.) ★→★★★ 76 78 82 83 85' 86
Very various Loire wines, incl. good CABERNET rosé, luscious COTEAUX DU LAYON. Maturity depends on style.

**Anjou-Coteaux de la Loire** AC for CHENIN BLANC whites, incl. the notable SAVENNIÈRES.

**Appellation Contrôlée** ("AC" or "AOC") Government control of origin and production of all the best French wines (see France Introduction).

**Apremont** Savoie w. dr. ★★ D.Y.A.
One of the best villages of SAVOIE for pale delicate whites, recently including CHARDONNAY.

**Arbin** Savoie r. ★★ Drink at 1-2 years
Deep-coloured lively red of Mondeuse grapes, rather like a good LOIRE Cabernet. Ideal après-ski wine.

**Arbois** Jura r. p. or w. (dr. sp.) ★★ On the whole, D.Y.A.
Various good and original light wines; speciality VIN JAUNE.

**l'Ardèche, Coteaux de** Central France r. (w. dr.) ★→★★ D.Y.A.
Light country reds, the best made of SYRAH. A useful change from BEAUJOLAIS. Also remarkable burgundy-like CHARDONNAY from Louis LATOUR – a bargain.

**Armagnac** Region of s.w. France famous for its sometimes excellent brandy, a fiery spirit of rustic character. The red wine of the area is MADIRAN.

**Auxey-Duresses** B'y. r. or w. ★★→★★★ 76 78 79 82 83 85 86 87
Second-rank (but v. pretty) CÔTE DE BEAUNE village: has affinities with VOLNAY and MEURSAULT. Best estates: Duc de Magenta, Prunier, Leroy, HOSPICES DE BEAUNE Cuvée Boillot.

**Avize** Champ. ★★★★
One of the best white-grape villages of CHAMPAGNE.

**Ay** Champ. ★★★★
One of the best black-grape villages of CHAMPAGNE.

**Ayala** NV "Château d'Ay" 75 76 79 and Blanc de Blancs 79
Once-famous Ay-based old-style champagne concern. To watch.

**Bandol** Prov. r. p. or (w.) ★★★ 76 78 80 81 82 83 84 85' 86 87'
Little coastal region near Toulon with strong tasty reds from the Mourvèdre grape; esp. Ch. Vannières, Domaine Tempier, Domaine Ott, Mas de la Rouvière, Domaine de Pibarnon.

**Banyuls** Pry. br. sw. ★★ normally NV
  One of the best VIN DOUX NATURELS (fortified sweet red wines) of the s. of France. A distant relation of port.

**Bar-sur-Aube** Champ w. (p.) sp. ★★★
  Secondary area to the s. Some good lighter wines and excellent Rosé des RICEYS.

**Barancourt** Cramant NV, Cramant Grand Cru 76 78 79 80 81, Bouzy Brut, Bouzy 81, Rosé NV  Grower at Bouzy making fine full-bodied champagnes. Pricey.

**Barsac** B'x. w. sw. ★★→ ★★★★ 70 71 75 76' 78 79' 80 81 82 83' 84 85 86'  Neighbour of SAUTERNES with similar superb golden wines, often less rich and more racy. Top ch'x: CLIMENS and COUTET.

**Barton & Guestier** Bordeaux shipper since 18th century, now owned by Seagram's.

**Bâtard-Montrachet** B'y. w. dr. ★★★★ 71 78 79 81 82 83 84 85 86 87
  Neighbour of MONTRACHET, the top white burgundy. Should be v. long-lived and intense in flavour. Top growers incl. LEFLAIVE, BOUCHARD PÈRE, Gagnard, Morey, Niellon.

**Baumard, Domaine des** Leading grower of Anjou wine, especially SAVENNIÈRES and COTEAUX DU LAYON (Clôs Ste Catherine).

**Béarn** s.w. France r. p. or w. dr. ★ D.Y.A.
  Minor appellation of growing local (Basque country) interest, esp. wines from the coop of Sallies de Béarn-Bellocq.

**Beaujolais** B'y. r. (p. w.) ★ D.Y.A.
  The simple appellation of the very big Beaujolais region: light short-lived fruity red of GAMAY grapes.

---

*Confusingly, the best wines of the Beaujolais region are not identified as such by their appellations. They are known simply by the names of their "crus": Brouilly, Côte de Brouilly, Chénas, Chiroubles, Fleurie, Juliénas, Morgon, Moulin-à-Vent, Regnié, St-Amour. See entries for each of these.*

---

**Beaujolais de l'année** The Beaujolais of the latest vintage, until the next.

**Beaujolais Primeur (or Nouveau)** The same made in a hurry (often only 4-5 days' fermenting) for release at midnight on the third Wednesday in November. Ideally soft, fruity and tempting but often crude and sharp. BEAUJOLAIS-VILLAGES *should* be a better bet.

**Beaujolais Supérieur** B'y. r. (w.) ★ D.Y.A.
  Beaujolais 1° of natural alcohol stronger than the 9° minimum. Since sugar is almost always added this means little or nothing.

**Beaujolais-Villages** B'y. r. ★★ 85 86 87
  Wines from the better (northern) half of Beaujolais, stronger and tastier than plain Beaujolais. The 10 (easily) best "villages" are the "crus": FLEURIE, BROUILLY, etc. Of the 30 others the best lie around Beaujeu. The crus cannot be released "en primeur" before December 15th. They are best kept until spring (or longer).

**Beaumes de Venise** Rh. (r. p.) br. sw. ★★★ NV
  Generally France's best dessert MUSCAT, from the s. CÔTES-DU-RHÔNE; can be high-flavoured, subtle, lingering (e.g. Domaine de Coyeux, Domaine Durban). The red and rosé from Ch Redortier and the cooperative are also good.

**Beaune** B'y. r. or (w. dr.) ★★★ 71 76 78' 80 82 83' 84 85 86
  Middle-rank classic burgundy. Négociants' "CLOS" wines (usually "Premier Cru") are often best, e.g. DROUHIN's "Clos des Mouches". "Beaune de Château" is a (good) brand of BOUCHARD PÈRE. V'yds incl: Grèves, Bressandes, Teurons, Marconnets, Fèves.

**Becker, Caves J.** Proud old family firm at Zellenberg, ALSACE.

**Bégadan** Leading village of the n. MÉDOC (appellation Médoc), with commendable coop (Cave St. Jean), and ch'x incl. LA TOUR DE BY, VIEUX-CH-LANDON, GREYSAC, LAUJAC, PATACHE D'AUX.

**Bellet** Prov. p. r. w. dr. ★★★

Fashionable, much above average, local wine from near Nice. Ch de Crémat is the one serious producer. Generally overpriced.

**Bergerac** Dordogne r. or w. sw. or dr. ░░ 82 83 84 85 86

Lightweight, often tasty, Bordeaux-style. Drink young, the white very young. See also Pécharmant, Montravel, Monbazillac. Growers incl. CH DE PANISSEAU, JAUBERTIE, Courts-les-Muts, Tiregand.

**Besserat de Bellefon** Cuvée Blanc de Blancs, NV, 75 79 82, Rosé 79, Brut Intégral 79 Rising champagne house for fine light wines, esp. CRÉMANT.

**Beyer, Leon** Ancient ALSACE family firm at Eguisheim making forceful dry wines that need ageing at least 2-3 yrs, esp. Comtes d'Eguisheim.

**Bichot, Maison Albert** BEAUNE-based grower and merchant. V'yds (Domaine du Clos Frantin) in CHAMBERTIN, CLOS DE VOUGEOT, RICHEBOURG, etc, and Domaine Long-Depauqit in CHABLIS.

**Billecart-Salmon** NV, 75 76 78 79 82, Rosé NV, Bl. de Blancs 79 82

Good small champagne house. Fresh-flavoured wines incl. a very tasty rosé.

**Bize, Simon** Admirable grower with 35 acres at SAVIGNY-LES-BEAUNE.

**Blagny** B'y. r. or w. dr. ░░→░░░ 76 78 81 w. 82 83 84 (w.) 85 86 87 Hamlet between MEURSAULT and PULIGNY-MONTRACHET; affinities with both and VOLNAY for reds. Ages well. Growers incl. LATOUR, AMPEAU, Matrot.

**Blanc de Blancs** Any white wine made from (only) white grapes, esp. CHAMPAGNE, which is usually made of both black and white. *Not* an indication of quality.

**Blanc de Noirs** White (or slightly pink or "blush") wine from black grapes.

**Blanck, Marcel** High-quality Alsace grower at Kientzheim.

**Blanquette de Limoux** Midi w. dr. sp. ░░ normally NV

Good bargain sparkler from near Carcassonne made by a version of the MÉTHODE CHAMPENOISE. Very dry and clean.

**Blaye** B'x. r. or w. dr. ★→★★★ 82 83 85 86

Your daily Bordeaux from e. of the Gironde. PREMIÈRES CÔTES DE BLAYE are better.

**Boisset, Jean Claude** Dynamic Burgundy merchant/grower at NUITS-ST-GEORGES.

**Bollinger** NV "Special Cuvée", Grande Année 69 70 73 75 76 79 82, Année Rare 73 75, Rosé 81 82 Top champagne house, at AY. Dry full-flavoured style. Luxury wines "RD" 73 75 76 and "Vieilles Vignes Françaises" 69 70 75 79 80 81 from ungrafted vines.

**Bommes** Village of SAUTERNES. Best ch'x: LATOUR-BLANCHE, LAFAURIE-PEYRAGUEY, etc.

**Bonneau du Martray, Domaine** Major producer (with 22 acres) of CORTON-CHARLEMAGNE of the highest quality; also admirable red CORTON.

**Bonnes Mares** B'y. r. ░░░░ 66 69 71 76 78' 79 80 82 83 84 85' 86 87 37-acre Grand Cru between CHAMBOLLE-MUSIGNY and MOREY-SAINT-DENIS. Sometimes (not often) better than CHAMBERTIN.

**Bonnezeaux** Lo. w. sw. ░░░ 76 78 81 82 84 85 86

Unusual fruity/acidic wine from CHENIN BLANC grapes, the best of COTEAUX DU LAYON. Esp. Ch de Fesles.

**Bordeaux** B'x. r. or (p.) or w. ★ 85 86 (for ch'x see p. 56)

Basic catch-all appellation for low-strength Bordeaux wine.

**Bordeaux Supérieur** ★→★★

Ditto, with slightly more alcohol.

**Bordeaux Côtes-de-Francs** B'x. r. or w. dr. ░░ 82 83 85 86

Fringe Bordeaux from east of ST-EMILION. Increasingly attractive light wines, esp. from Ch'x Puygueraud, de Belcier, Puyfromage.

**Borie-Manoux** Admirable Bordeaux shippers and château-owners, owned by the Castéja family. Ch'x incl. BATAILLEY, HAUT-BAGES MONPELOU, DOMAINE DE L'EGLISE, TROTTEVIEILLE, BEAU-SITE.

**Bouchard Ainé** Long-established burgundy shipper and grower with 62 acres in BEAUNE, MERCUREY, etc. Good, not top, quality.

**Bouchard Père et Fils** Important burgundy shipper (est. 1731) and grower with 209 acres of excellent v'yds, mainly in the CÔTE DE BEAUNE, and cellars at the Château de Beaune. Reliable quality.

**Bourg** B'x. r. or (w. dr.) ★★ 82 83 85 86 87
Meaty, un-fancy claret from e. of the Gironde. CÔTES DE BOURG are better.

**Bourgogne** B'y. r. (p.) or w. dr. ★★ 85 86 87
Catch-all appellation for Burgundy, but with theoretically higher standards than basic BORDEAUX. Light but often good flavour, best at 2-3 yrs. BEAUJOLAIS crus can also be sold as Bourgogne.

**Bourgogne Grand Ordinaire** B'y. r. (w.) ★ D.Y.A.
The lowest burgundy appellation for GAMAY wines. Rare.

**Bourgogne Passe-tout-grains** B'y. r. or (p.) ★ Age 1-2 years
Often enjoyable junior burgundy. ⅓ PINOT NOIR and ⅔ GAMAY grapes mixed in the vat. Not as "heady" as BEAUJOLAIS.

**Bourgueil** Lo. r. ★★★ 76' 81 82 83' 85 86
Normally delicate fruity CABERNET red from Touraine, the best from St. Nicolas de Bourgueil. Deep-flavoured and long-lasting in exceptional years. Growers incl. Caslot-Galbrun, Lame-Delille-Boucard, Audebert.

**Bouvet-Ladubay** Major producer of sparkling SAUMUR, controlled by TAITTINGER. Excellent CRÉMANT de Loire. "Saphir" is vintage wine, "Trésor" the top grade.

**Bouzeron** Village of the CÔTE CHALONNAISE distinguished for the only single-village appellation ALIGOTÉ.

**Bouzy Rouge** Champ. r. ★★★ 82 83 85 86
Still red wine from famous black-grape CHAMPAGNE village. Like light burgundy, ageing early but sometimes lasting well.

**Brédif, Marc** One of the most important growers and traders of VOUVRAY.

**Brouilly** B'y. r. ★★★ 85 86 87
One of the 10 best CRUS of BEAUJOLAIS: fruity, round, refreshing. One year in bottle is enough. Ch de la Chaize is top estate.

**Brut** Term for the driest wines of CHAMPAGNE until recently, when some completely unsweetened wines have become available as "Brut Intégrale", "Brut non-dosé", "Brut zéro" etc.

**Bugey** Savoie w. dr. or sp. ★→ ★★ D.Y.A.
District with a variety of light sparkling, still or half-sparkling wines. Grapes incl. Roussette (or Roussanne) and v.g. CHARD.

**Buzet** s.w. France, r. or w. dr. ★★ 81 82 83 85 86
Good Bordeaux-style wines from just s.e. of Bordeaux. Promising area with well-run cooperative. Best wine: Cuvée Napoleon.

**Cabernet** See Grapes for red wine.

**Cabernet d'Anjou** Lo. p. ★→★★ D.Y.A.
Delicate, grapey, often rather sweet rosé.

**Cahors** s.w. France r. ★→ ★★ 75 78 79 80 81 82 83 85' 86
Historically a hard "black" wine, now made more like Bordeaux, but can be full-bodied and increasingly distinct. Top growers: Baldès (esp. for "Prince Probus"), Jouffreau, Vigouroux (esp. Ch de Haute-Serre), Ch de Caix, Ch de Chambert, Ch Lagrezette.

**Cairanne** Rh. r. p. or w. dr. ★★ 83 84 85 86
Village of CÔTES-DU-RHÔNE-VILLAGES. Good solid wines, esp. from Domaine Rabasse-Charavin.

**Calvet** Famous old shippers of Bordeaux and Burgundy, now owned by Whitbread. Some reliable standard wines.

**Canard-Duchêne** NV Brut, rosé and Charles VII
NV, Vintage Charles VII and (sometimes) Coteaux Champenois. High-quality champagne house owned by VEUVE CLICQUOT.

**Canon-Fronsac**  B'x. r.  ★★ 70 75 78 79 81 82 83′ 85 86
Tannic, often full-flavoured reds of increasing quality and style from small area w. of POMEROL. Ch'x include Canon, Canon-Moueix, Canon de Brem, Coustolle, Junayme, Mazeris-Bellevue, Moulin-Pey-Labrie, Toumalin, Vraye-Canon-Boyer. Bottle-age is essential. See also Fronsac.

**Cantenac**  B'x. r. ★★★
Village of the HAUT-MÉDOC entitled to the appellation MARGAUX. Top ch'x include PALMER, BRANE-CANTENAC, etc.

**Cap Corse**  Corsica w. dr. br. ★★→★★★
The wild north cape of the island. Splendid muscat and rare dry VERMENTINO white. *Vaut le détour*, if not *le voyage*.

**Caramany**  Pyr. r. (w. dr.)  ★ 82 83 84 85 86
New appellation for part of CÔTES DE ROUSSILLON-VILLAGES.

**Cassis**  Prov. (r. p.) w. dr. ★★ D.Y.A.
Seaside village e. of Marseille known for its lively dry white, exceptional for Provence (e.g. Domaine du Paternel). Not to be confused with cassis, a blackcurrant liqueur made in Dijon.

**Castellane, de**  Long-established Epernay champagne house. Good wines incl. Maxim's house champagne.

**Cave**  Cellar, or any wine establishment.

**Cave coopérative**  Wine-growers' cooperative winery. Coops now account for 55% of all French production. 4 out of 10 of all French growers are coop members. Almost all coops are now well run, well equipped and making some of the best wine of their areas.

**Cépage**  Variety of vine, e.g. CHARDONNAY, MERLOT.

**Cérons**  B'x. w. dr. or sw. ★★ 79 80 81 83 84 85 86
Neighbour of SAUTERNES with some good sweet-wine ch'x, e.g. Ch de Cérons et de Calvimont.

**Chablis**  B'y. w. dr. ★★ 85 86 87
Distinctive full-flavoured greeny-gold wine. Made only of CHARDONNAY in n. Burgundy. Top growers incl. Raveneau, Dauvissat, LAROCHE, Long-Depaquit, Michel, Droin, Pic, Févre, etc. All the best Chablis is either Premier Cru or Grand Cru (see below). The coop, "La Chablisienne", has v.g. standards.

**Chablis Grand Cru**  B'y. w. dr.  ★★★★ 78 81 82 83 84 85 86 87
Strong, subtle and altogether splendid. One of the great white burgundies. There are seven v'yds: Blanchots, Bougros, Clos, Grenouilles, Preuses, Valmur, Vaudésir. See also Moutonne.

**Chablis Premier Cru**  B'y. w. dr.  ★★★ 81 83 84 85 86 87
Second-rank but often excellent and more typical of Chablis than Grands Crus. Best v'yds incl: Côte de Lechet, Fourchaume, Mont de Milieu, Montée de Tonnerre, Montmains, Vaillons.

**Chai**  Building for storing and maturing wine, esp. in Bordeaux.

**Chambertin**  B'y. r. ★★★★ 69 71 76 78 79 80 82 83 84 85 86 87
32-acre Grand Cru giving the meatiest, most enduring and often the best red burgundy, 15 growers, incl. ROUSSEAU, BOUCHARD PÈRE, Camus, Damoy, Tortochot, Rebourseau, Trapet, Ponsot.

**Chambertin-Clos-de-Bèze**  B'y. r. ★★★★ 76 78 79 80 81 82 83 84 85 86 87  37-acre neighbour of CHAMBERTIN. Similarly splendid wine. 10 growers incl. CLAIR-DAU, DROUHIN, DROUHIN-LAROSE, Damoy, ROUSSEAU.

**Chambolle-Musigny**  B'y. r. (w.) ★★★ 76 78 80 82 83 84 85 86 87
420-acre CÔTE DE NUITS village with fabulously fragrant, complex wine. Best v'yds: MUSIGNY, part of BONNES-MARES, Les Amoureuses, Les Charmes. Growers incl: DE VOGUE, DROUHIN, FAIVELEY, Roumier, Moine-Hudelot, Mugnier, Hudelot-Noëllat.

**Champagne**  Sparkling wine from 60,000 acres 90 miles e. of Paris, made by the MÉTHODE CHAMPENOISE. Wines from elsewhere, however good, cannot be champagne. (See also names of brands.)

**Champagne, Grande**  The appellation of the best area of COGNAC.

**Champigny**  See Saumur.

**Chandon de Briailles, Domaine**  Small burgundy estate at SAVIGNY. Makes v.g. CORTON.

**Chanson Père et Fils**  Growers (with 110 acres) and négociants at BEAUNE.

**Chante-Alouette**  A famous brand of white HERMITAGE from CHAPOUTIER.

**Chantovent**  Major brand of VIN DE TABLE, largely from MINERVOIS.

**Chapelle-Chambertin**  B'y. r. ★★★ 76 78 80 82 83' 85 86 87
13-acre neighbour of CHAMBERTIN. Wine not so meaty. Top producers: CLAIR-DAÜ, Drouhin-Larose, LEROY, Trapet.

**Chapoutier**  Long-established growers and traders of fine Rhône wines.

**Charbaut, A. et Fils**  NV, Blanc de Blancs, Rosé NV, 73 76 79 EPERNAY champagne house. Clean light wines. Good Rosé.

**Chardonnay**  See Grapes for white wine.

**Charmes-Chambertin**  B'y. r. ★★★ 71 76 78 79 80 82 83' 85 86 87
76-acre neighbour of CHAMBERTIN. Growers incl. Bachelet, Castagnier, Roty, ROUSSEAU.

**Chartron & Trebuchet**  Young company with delicate and harmonious white burgundies, esp. Domaine Chartron's PULIGNY-MONTRACHET, Clos de la Pucelle.

**Chassagne-Montrachet**  B'y. r. or w. dr. ★★★→★★★★  (reds ███ ★★★ )
76 78 80 (r.) 81 w. 82 (r.) 83 84 85 86 87  750-acre CÔTE DE BEAUNE village with superlative rich dry whites and sterling hefty reds. Best v'yds: MONTRACHET, BÂTARD-MONTRACHET, CRIOTS-BÂTARD-MONTRACHET, Ruchottes, Caillerets, Boudriottes (r. w.), Morgeot (r. w.), CLOS-ST-JEAN (r.). Growers incl. RAMONET-PRUDHON, Morey, MAGENTA, DELAGRANGE-BACHELET, Gagnard-Delagrange, Niellon, M. Colin-Deleger, J-N. Gagnard, Lamy-Pillot, Bachelet-Ramonet.

**Chasseloir, Domaine du**  The HQ of the firm of Chéreau-Carré, makers of several excellent domaine MUSCADETS, esp. Ch du Chasseloir.

---

**Château**  An estate, big or small, good or indifferent, particularly in Bordeaux. In Burgundy the term "domaine" is used. For all Bordeaux ch'x see pp. 56-75.

---

**Château-Chalon**  Jura w. dr. ★★★
Unique strong dry yellow wine, almost like *fino* sherry. Usually ready to drink when bottled (at about 6 years).

**Château Corton-Grancey**  B'y. r. ★★★ 76 78 79 81 82 83 85 86
Famous estate at ALOXE-CORTON, the property of Louis LATOUR. Recently rather disappointing.

**Château d'Arlay**  Major JURA estate; 160 acres in skilful hands.

**Château de Beaucastel**  Rh. r. w. dr. ★★★ 76 78' 79 80 81 83 84 85 86
One of the biggest (173 acres) and best-run estates of CHÂTEAUNEUF-DU-PAPE. Deep-hued wines intended for at least 10 yrs ageing.

**Château de la Chaize**  B'y. r. ★★★ 86 87
The best-known estate of BROUILLY, with 200 acres.

**Château de la Maltroye**  B'y. r. w. dr. ★★★
Sometimes excellent 32-acre estate in CHASSAGNE-MONTRACHET and SANTENAY.

**Château de Meursault**  B'y. r. w. ★★★
100-acre estate owned by PATRIARCHE with good v'yds in MEURSAULT, VOLNAY, POMMARD, BEAUNE. Splendid cellars open to the public for tasting. *Vaut le détour.*

**Château de Panisseau**  Dordogne r. p. w. dr. ★★ D.Y.A.
Leading estate of BERGERAC: good dry SAUV BLANC and Semillon.

**Château de Selle**  Prov. r. p. or w. dr. ██ ★★
Estate of the OTT family near Cotignac, Var. Well-known and typical wines.

**Château des Fines Roches**  Rh. r. ★★★ 78 79 80 81 83 84 85 86
Large (112 acres) and distinguished estate in CHÂTEAUNEUF-DU-PAPE. Strong old-style wine.

**Château du Nozet** Lo. w. dr. ★★★ 85 86 87
Biggest and best-known estate of Pouilly (FUMÉ) sur Loire. Top wine, Baron de L, can be wonderful (at a price).

**Château Fortia** Rh. r. ★★★ 79 80 81 83 84 85 86
First-class property in CHÂTEAUNEUF-DU-PAPE. Traditional methods. The owner's father, Baron Le Rcy, also fathered the APPELLATION CONTRÔLÉE system.

**Château-Grillet** Rh. w. dr. ★★★★ 82 83 84 85 86 87
3½-acre v'yd with one of France's smallest appellations. Intense, fragrant, over-expensive. Drink fairly young.

**Château-Gris** B'y. r. ★★★ 78 82 83 85 86
Well-known estate at NUITS-ST-GEORGES. Linked with BICHOT.

**Châteaumeillant** Lo. r. p. or w. dr. ★ D.Y.A.
Small VDQS area near SANCERRE. Light GAMAY and P NOIR.

**Châteauneuf-du-Pape** Rh. r. (w. dr.) ★★★ 78 79 80 81 82 83 84 85 86
7,400 acres near Avignon with standards steadily rising. Best estate ("domaine") wines are dark, strong, exceptionally long-lived. Others may be light and/or disappointing. The white can be heavy: most now made to D.Y.A. Top growers incl. Ch'x FORTIA, RAYAS, Doms. de BEAUCASTEL, VIEUX TELEGRAPH, Clos des Papes, etc.

**Château Rayas** Rh. r. (w. dr.) ★★★ 78 80 81 83 84 85 86
Famous old-style property of only 38 acres in CHÂTEAUNEUF-DU-PAPE. Concentrated wines are almost entirely GRENACHE. "Pignan" is 2nd label.

**Château Simone** Prov. r. p. or w. dr. ★★ Age 2-3 yrs
Well-known property in Palette; the only one with a name in this appellation near Aix-en-Provence. The red is best: herby and peppery.

**Château Vignelaure** Prov. r. ★★ 80 81 82 83' 84 85 86
135-acre Provençal estate near Aix making good Bordeaux-style wine with CABERNET, Syrah and Grenache grapes.

**Chatillon-en-Diois** Rh. r. p. or w. dr. ★ D.Y.A.
Small appellation e. of the Rhône near Die. Adequate GAMAY reds; white (some Aligoté) mostly made into CLAIRETTE DE DIE.

**Chauvenet, F.** Large commercial Burgundy firm linked with MARGNAT. Sound wines.

**Chave, Gérard** To many the top grower of HERMITAGE, red and white.

**Chavignol** Village of SANCERRE with famous v'yd, Les Monts Damnés. Chalky soil gives vivid wines that age 4-5 years.

**Chénas** B'y. r. ★★★ 85 86 87
Good Beaujolais cru, neighbour to MOULIN-À-VENT and JULIÉNAS. One of the weightier Beaujolais.

**Chenin Blanc** See Grapes for white wine.

**Chevalier-Montrachet** B'y. w. dr. ★★★★ 78 81 83 84 85 86 87
17-acre neighbour of MONTRACHET with similar luxurious wine, perhaps a little less powerful. Includes Les Demoiselles (LATOUR, JADOT). Growers incl. BOUCHARD PÈRE, LEFLAIVE, Niellon.

**Cheverny** Lo. r. p. or w. dr. (sp.) ★→★★ D.Y.A.
Loire VDQS from near Chambord. CHENIN BL or SAUV BL whites, GAMAY, P NOIR or CAB reds; generally light but fresh and tasty.

**Chevillon, R.** Little 21-acre estate at NUITS; outstanding wine-making since 1980.

**Chignin** Savoie w. dr. ★ D.Y.A.
Light soft white of Jacquère grapes.

**Chinon** Lo. r. ★★★ 76 82 83' 85 86
Delicate fruity CABERNET FRANC from TOURAINE. Drink cool when young. Exceptional vintages age like Bordeaux. Top growers: Couly-Dutheil, Joguet, Raffault.

**Chiroubles** B'y. r. ★★★ 86 87
Good but tiny Beaujolais cru next to FLEURIE; freshly fruity silky wine for early drinking.

**Chorey-lès-Beaune** B'y. r. ★★ 83 85 86 87
 Minor appellation on flat land n. of BEAUNE notable for one fine grower: TOLLOT-BEAUT.

**Chusclan** Rh. r. p. or w. dr. ▩ 85 86
 Village of CÔTE-DU-RHÔNE-VILLAGES. Good middle-weight wines from the cooperative.

**Cissac** HAUT-MÉDOC village just w. of PAUILLAC.

**Clair, Bruno** Recent little domaine at MARSANNAY. V.g. wines from FIXIN, MOREY-ST-DENIS, SAVIGNY.

**Clair-Daü** First-class 100-acre burgundy estate of the northern CÔTE DE NUITS, with cellars at MARSANNAY. Bought in 1986 by JADOT.

**Clairet** Very light red wine, almost rosé.

**Clairette,** Mediocre white grape of the s. of France. Gives neutral wine.

**Clairette de Bellegarde** Midi w. dr. ★ D.Y.A.
 Plain neutral white from near Nîmes.

**Clairette de Die** Rh. w. dr. or s./sw. sp. ★★ NV
 Popular dry or (better) semi-sweet rather MUSCAT-flavoured sparkling wine from the e. Rhône, or straight dry CLAIRETTE white, surprisingly ageing well for 3-4 years.

**Clairette du Languedoc** Midi w. dr. ★ D.Y.A.
 Plain neutral white from near Montpellier.

**La Clape** Midi r. p. or w. dr. ★→★★
 Full-bodied VDQS wines from limestone hills between Narbonne and the sea. The red gains character after 2-3 years, the white even longer. V.g. rosé. Some experiment with CHARDONNAY.

**Claret** Traditional English term for red BORDEAUX.

**Climat** Burgundian word for individual named v'yd, e.g. Beaune Grèves, Chambolle-Musigny les Amoureuses.

**Clos** A term carrying some prestige, reserved for distinct, usually walled, v'yds, often in one ownership. Frequent in Burgundy and Alsace. Les Clos is Chablis's Grandest Cru.

**Clos-de-Bèze** See Chambertin-Clos-de-Bèze.

**Clos de Bèze** B'y. r. ★★★ 71 76 78 79 80 82 83 84 85' 86 87
 38-acre Grand Cru at MOREY-ST-DENIS. Powerful complex wine like CHAMBERTIN. Producers incl. BOUCHARD PÈRE, Ponsot, DUJAC, ROUSSEAU, Rémy, Castagnier, Lignier.

---

*The Confrérie des Chevaliers du Tastevin is Burgundy's wine fraternity and the most famous of its kind in the world. It was founded in 1933 by a group of Burgundian patriots, headed by Camille Rodier and Georges Faiveley, to rescue their beloved Burgundy from a period of slump and despair by promoting its inimitable products. Today it regularly holds banquets with elaborate and sprightly ceremonial for 600 guests at its headquarters, the Cistercian château in the Clos de Vougeot. The Confrérie has branches in many countries and members among lovers of wines all over the world.*

---

**Clos des Lambrays** B'y. r. ★★★ 78 83 84 85 86 87
 15-acre Grand Cru v'yd at MOREY-ST-DENIS. Changed hands in 1979 after a shaky period. Young vines need time.

**Clos des Mouches** B'y. r. or w. dr. ★★★
 Splendid Premier Cru v'yd of BEAUNE owned by DROUHIN. The unusual white is particularly well-made and rewarding.

**Clos de Tart** B'y. r. ★★★ 71 76 78 79 80 82 83' 84 85 86 87
 18-acre Grand Cru at MOREY-ST-DENIS owned by MOMMESSIN. At best wonderfully fragrant, whether young or old.

**Clos de Vougeot** B'y. r. ★★★ 71 76 78 80 82 83 84 85 86 87
 124-acre CÔTE-DE-NUITS Grand Cru with many owners. Bewilderingly variable, occasionally sublime. Maturity depends on the grower's technique and his position on the hillside. Top growers incl: DROUHIN, CLAIR-DAÜ, DROUHIN-LAROSE, FAIVELEY, Gros, JADOT, Mugneret, Roumier.

**Clos du Roi** B'y. r. ★★★
Part of the Grand Cru CORTON. Also a Premier Cru of BEAUNE.

**Clos St Denis** B'y. r. ★★★ 76 78 79 80 82 83′ 84 85 86 87
16-acre Grand Cru at MOREY-ST-DENIS. Splendid sturdy wine. Growers incl. DUJAC, Lignier, Ponsot.

**Clos St Jacques** B'y. r. ★★★ 71 76 78 79 80 82 83′ 84 85 86 87
17-acre Premier Cru of GEVREY-CHAMBERTIN. Excellent powerful velvety wine, often better (and dearer) than some of the CHAMBERTIN Grands Crus. Main grower: ROUSSEAU.

**Clos St Jean** B'y. r. ★★★ 78 79 80 82 83′ 84 85 86 87
36-acre Premier Cru of CHASSAGNE-MONTRACHET. Very good red, more solid than subtle from e.g. CH DE LA MALTROYE.

**Coche-Dury** 16-acre MEURSAULT domaine (+1 acre CORTON-CHARLEMAGNE) with sky-high reputation.

**Cognac** Town and region of western France and its brandy.

**Collioure** Pyr. r. ■ 80 81 82 83 84 85 86
Strong dry RANCIO red from BANYULS area. Small production.

**Condrieu** Rh. w. dr. ★★★★ D.Y.A.
Outstanding soft fragrant white of great character (and price) from the Viognier grape. Only 35 acres of vines. The leading growers are Vernay, Ch du Rozay, Guigal, Pinchon and DELAS, CH-GRILLET is similar.

**Corbières** Midi r. or (p.) or (w.) ★→★★★ 85 86 87
Good vigorous bargain reds, steadily improving and now rewarded with AC. Rarely disappointing at their price. Most are from coops.

**Cordier, Ets D.** Important Bordeaux shipper and château-owner, including Ch'x GRUAUD-LAROSE, TALBOT, CANTEMERLE, MEYNEY, LAFAURIE-PEYRAGUEY and also SANCERRE, Clos de la Poussie.

**Cornas** Rh. r. ★★→★★★ 78′ 79 80 82 83′ 84 85 86
Expanding 400-acre district s. of HERMITAGE. Typical sturdy Rhône wine of v.g. quality from the SYRAH grape. Needs ageing. Growers incl. Clape, JABOULET.

**Corse** The island of Corsica. Strong wines of all colours. Better appellations incl. PATRIMONIO, Sartène, AJACCIO, CAP CORSE.

**Corton** B'y. r. ★★★★ 71 76′ 78′ 80 82 83 84 85′ 86 87
The only Grand Cru red of the CÔTE DE BEAUNE. 200 acres in ALOXE-CORTON incl. les Bressandes and CLOS DU ROI. Rich powerful wines should be long-lived. Many good growers.

**Corton-Charlemagne** B'y. w. dr. ★★★★ 78′ 79 81 82 83 84 85 86 87
The white section (one-third) of CORTON. Rich, spicy, lingering wine. Behaves like a red wine and ages magnificently. Top growers: BONNEAU DU MARTRAY, LATOUR, JADOT.

**Costières du Gard** Midi r. p. or w. dr. ★→★★ D.Y.A.
VDQS of moderate (improving) quality from the Rhône delta.

**Coteaux Champenois** Champ. r. (p.) or w. dr. ★★★
The appellation for non-sparkling champagne. Vintages follow those for Champagne. Do not pay inflated prices.

**Coteaux d'Aix-en-Provence** Prov. r. p. or w. dr. ★→★★★
An appellation on the move. The established CH VIGNELAURE is challenged by Ch'x Fonscolombe, de Beaulieu, Commanderie de la Bargemone.

**Coteaux d'Ancenis** Lo. r. p. w. dr. ★ D.Y.A.
Light CABERNET and GAMAY reds and pinks; sharpish whites from MUSCADET country.

**Coteaux de la Loire** Lo. w. dr. sw. ★★→★★★ 79 81 82 83 84 85 86
Forceful and fragrant CHENIN BLANC whites from Anjou. The best are in SAVENNIÈRES. Excellent as an apéritif.

**Coteaux de l'Aubance** Lo. p. or w. dr./sw. ★★ D.Y.A.
Light and typical minor ANJOU wines. The best are MOELLEUX.

**Coteaux de Pierrevert** Rh. r. p. or w. dr. or sp. ■ D.Y.A.
Minor southern VDQS from nr. Manosque. Well-made coop wine mostly rosé, with fresh whites.

**Coteaux de Saumur** Lo. w. dr./sw. ★★ D.Y.A.
Pleasant dry or sweetish fruity CHENIN BLANC.

**Coteaux des Baux-en-Provence** Prov. r. p. or w. dr. ★→ ★★
Neighbour of COTEAUX D'AIX, also gathering speed. N.B. Domaine de Trévallon (CABERNET and SYRAH).

**Coteaux du Giennois** Lo. r. w. dr. ★ D.Y.A.
Minor Loire area n. of SANCERRE. Light GAMAY and PINOT NOIR, SAUVIGNON and CHENIN BLANC.

**Coteaux du Languedoc** Midi r. p. or w. dr. ★→★★
Scattered better-than-ordinary Midi areas with AC status. The best (e.g. FAUGÈRES, St Saturnin, LA CLAPE, ST CHINIAN, Quatourze, St-Georges-d'Orques, Cabrières) age for 2-3 years.

**Coteaux du Layon** Lo. w. s./sw. or sw. ★★ 78 81 82 83 84 85 86
District centred on Rochefort, s. of Angers, making sweet CHENIN BLANC wines above the general Anjou standard. "C. du L-Chaume" is a higher appellation.

**Coteaux du Loir** Lo. r. p. or w. dr./sw. ★★ 78 82 83 84 85 86
Small region n. of Tours. Occasionally excellent wines. Best v'yd: JASNIÈRES. The Loir is a tributary of the Loire.

**Coteaux du Lyonnais** Rh r. p. (w. dr.) ★ D.Y.A.
Junior Beaujolais, and whites in keeping, from nr. Lyon. Best EN PRIMEUR.

**Coteaux du Tricastin** Rh. r. p. or w. dr. ★ 83 85 86
Fringe CÔTES-DU-RHÔNE of increasing quality from s. of Valence. Pierre Labeye is the chief producer. Attractive PRIMEUR red.

**Coteaux du Vendomois** Lo. r. p. or w. dr. ★ D.Y.A.
Fringe Loire from n. of Blois. Mainly GAMAY.

**Coteaux Varoís** Prov. r. p. w. dr. ★→★★
Substantial new VDQS zone with one California-style property, Domaine de St Jean de Villecroze.

---

**Côte(s)** Means hillside; generally a superior vineyard to those on the plain. Many appellations start with either Côtes or Coteaux, which means the same thing. In ST-EMILION it distinguishes the valley slopes from the higher plateau.

---

**Côte Chalonnaise** B'y. r. w. dr. sp. ★★→★★★
Lesser-known v'yd area between BEAUNE and MÂCON. See Mercurey, Givry, Rully, Montagny. Alias "Région de Mercurey".

**Côte de Beaune** B'y. r. or w. dr. ★★→★★★★
Used geographically: the southern half of the CÔTE D'OR. Applies as an appellation only to parts of BEAUNE.

**Côte de Beaune-Villages** B'yr. r. or w. dr. ★★ 78 80 83 85 86 87
Regional appellation for secondary wines of the classic area. They cannot be labelled "Côte de Beaune" without either "Villages" or the village name.

**Côte de Brouilly** B'y. r. ★★★ 85 86 87
Fruity, rich, vigorous Beaujolais cru. One of the best. Leading estates: Ch Thivin, Domaine de Chavanne.

**Côte de Nuits** B'y. r. or (w. dr.) ★★→★★★★
The northern half of the CÔTE D'OR. Nearly all red wine.

**Côte de Nuits-Villages** B'y. r. (w.) ★★ 78 83 85 86 87
A junior appellation, rarely seen but worth investigating.

**Côte d'Or** *Département* name applied to the central and principal Burgundy v'yd slopes, consisting of the CÔTE DE BEAUNE and CÔTE DE NUITS. The name is not used on labels.

**Côte Rôtie** Rh. r. ★★★ 78 79 80 82 83' 84 85' 86
Potentially the finest Rhône red, from just s. of Vienne; achieves complex, almost claret-like, delicacy with age. Top growers include JABOULET, CHAPOUTIER, VIDAL-FLEURY, Barge, Dervieux, Jasmin, Guigal, Jamet, Rostaing.

**Côtes d'Auvergne** Central France r. p. or (w. dr.) ★ D.Y.A.
Flourishing small VDQS area near Clermont-Ferrand. Red (at best) like light BEAUJOLAIS. Chanturgues is the best known.

**Côtes de Blaye** B'x. w. dr. ★ D.Y.A.
Run-of-the-mill Bordeaux white from BLAYE.

**Côtes de Bordeaux Saint-Macaire** B'x. w. dr./sw. ★ D.Y.A.
Run-of-the-mill Bordeaux white from east of SAUTERNES.

**Côtes de Bourg** B'x. r. ▆▶★★ 78 79 81 82 83 85 86
Appellation used for many of the better reds of BO . Ch'x incl. de Barbe, La Barde, du Bousquet, La Croix de Millorit, de la Grave, Grand-Jour, Font Guilhem, Guerry, Rousset, Lalibarde, La Grolet, Tayac, Lamothe, Mendoce, Falfas, Peychaud, de Thau.

**Côtes de Castillon** B'x. r. ▆▶★★ 78 79 81 82 83 85 86
Flourishing region just e. of St. Emilion. Similar wines, though a touch lighter. Ch'x incl. Fonds-Rondes, Haut-Tuquet, Lardit, PITRAY, Ste. Colombe, Moulin-Rouge, Rocher-Bellevue.

**Côtes de Duras** Dordogne r. or w. dr. ▆ 82 85 86
Neighbour to BERGERAC, dominated by its v. competent coop. Similar light wines.

**Côtes de Francs** See Bordeaux – Côtes de Francs.

**Côtes de Fronsac** See Fronsac.

**Côtes de Gascogne** s.w. France (r.) w. dr. ▆
Vin de pays gaining a name for deliciously floral SAUVIGNON whites.

**Côtes de Montravel** Dordogne w. dr./sw. ▆ NV
Part of BERGERAC; traditional medium-sw. wine, now often dry.

**Côtes de Provence** Prov. r. p. or w. dr. ★→★★
The wine of Provence; still often with more alcohol than character, though standards are rapidly improving. 60% is rosé, 30% red. See under Coteaux d'Aix, Bandol, etc.

**Côtes de Saint-Mont** s.w. France r. w. dr. p. ▆
Promising VDQS from the Gers, not unlike MADIRAN. The same coop as CÔTES DE GASCOGNE.

**Côtes de Thongue** Midi r. w. dr. ▆
Above-average *vins de pays* from the HÉRAULT.

**Côtes de Toul** e. France r. p. or w. dr. ★ D.Y.A.
Very light wines from Lorraine; mainly VIN GRIS (rosé).

**Côtes du Forez** Central France r. or p. ▆ D.Y.A.
Light Beaujolais-style red, can be good in warm years.

**Côtes du Frontonnais** s.w. France r. or p. ▆→★★ D.Y.A.
The local wine of Toulouse, gaining admirers elsewhere. Ch Bellevue-la-Forêt (250 acres) makes outstanding silky red.

**Côtes du Haut-Roussillon** s.w. France br. sw. ★→★★ NV
Area for VINS DOUX NATURELS n. of Perpignan.

**Côtes du Jura** Jura r. p. or w. dr. (sp.) ★ D.Y.A.
Various light tints and tastes. ARBOIS is theoretically better.

**Côtes du Luberon** Rh. r. p. or w. dr. sp. ▆→★★
Improving country wines from northern Provence. The star is Ch Val-Joannis, with good whites as well. Others incl. a good coop and Ch de Sannes.

**Côtes du Marmandais** Dordogne r. p. or w. dr. ★ D.Y.A.
Light wines from s.e. of Bordeaux. The coop at Cocumont makes most of the best.

**Côtes-du-Rhône** Rh. r. p. or w. dr. ★→★★★ 85 86
The basic appellation of the Rhône valley. Best drunk young – even as PRIMEUR. Wide variations of quality due to grape ripeness, therefore tending to rise with alcohol %. See Côtes-du-Rhône-Villages.

**Côtes-du-Rhône-Villages** Rh. r. p. or w. dr. ★→ ★★ 83 85 86 87
The wine of the 17 best villages of the southern Rhône. Substantial and on the whole reliable. Sometimes delicious.

**Côtes du Roussillon** Pyr. r. p. or w. dr. ★→★★ 82 83 84 85 86 87
Country wine of e. Pyrenees. The hefty reds are best and can be very tasty. Some whites are sharp VINS VERTS.

**Côtes du Roussillon-Villages** Pyr. r. ★★ 82 83 84 85 86 87
The best reds of the region, incl. CARAMANY and LATOUR DE FRANCE.

**Côtes du Ventoux** Prov. r. (w. dr.) ▓▓ 83 85 86
Booming appellation for tasty reds between the Rhône and Provence. La Vieille Ferme, owned by CH DE BEAUCASTEL, is top producer.

**Côtes du Vivarais** Prov. r. p. or w. dr. ★
Pleasant country wines from s. Massif Centrale. Like light CÔTES-DU-RHÔNE.

**Côtes Roannaises** Central France r. ▓▓ D.Y.A.
Minor GAMAY region high up the LOIRE.

**Coulée de Serrant** Lo. w. dr./sw. ★★★ 76 78 79 81 82 83 84 85 86
10-acre v'yd on n. bank of LOIRE at SAVENNIÈRES, Anjou. Intense strong fruity/sharp wine, good as an apéritif. Ages well.

**Crémant** In Champagne means "Creaming" – i.e. half-sparkling. Since 1975 an appellation for high-quality champagne-method sparkling wines from Alsace, the Loire and Bourgogne – often a notable bargain. e.g . . .

**Crémant de Loire** w. dr. sp. ▓▓ NV
High-quality sparkling wine from ANJOU and TOURAINE.

**Crépy** Savoie w. dr. ★★ D.Y.A.
Light, soft, Swiss-style white from s. shore of Lake Geneva. "Crépitant" has been coined for its faint fizz.

**Criots-Bâtard-Montrachet** B'y. w. ★★★ 76 78 79 81 82 83 84 85 86
4-acre neighbour to BÂTARD-MONTRACHET. Similar wine.

---

*Burgundy boasts one of the world's most famous and certainly its most beautiful hospital, the Hospices de Beaune, founded in 1443 by Nicolas Rolin, Chancellor to the Duke of Burgundy, and his wife Guigone de Salins. The hospital he built and endowed with vineyards for its income still operates in the same building and still thrives, tending the sick of Beaune without charge, on the sale of its wine. Many growers since have bequeathed their land to the Hospices. Today it owns 125 acres of prime land in Beaune, Pommard, Volnay, Meursault, Corton and Mazis-Chambertin. The wine is sold by auction every year on the third Sunday in November.*

---

**Crozes-Hermitage** Rh. r. or (w. dr.) ▓▓ 78 80 82 83 84 85 86
Larger and less distinguished neighbour to HERMITAGE. Robust and often excellent reds, but choose carefully e.g. Domaine de Thalabert of JABOULET.

**Cru** "Growth", as in "first-growth" – meaning vineyard.

**Cru Bourgeois** General term for MÉDOC châteaux ranked below CRU CLASSÉ.

**Cru Bourgeois Supérieur (Cru Grand Bourgeois)** Official rank one better than the last. Aged in barrels.

**Cru Classé** Classed growth. One of the first five official quality classes of the Médoc, classified in 1855. Also any classed growth of another district (e.g. GRAVES, ST-EMILION, SAUTERNES).

**Cru Grand Bourgeois Exceptionnel** Official rank above CRU BOURGEOIS SUPÉRIEUR, immediately below CRU CLASSÉ. Several fine châteaux are unofficially acknowledged (and labelled) as Exceptionnel, which makes them on a par with many CRUS CLASSÉS.

**Cruse et Fils Frères** Long-established Bordeaux shipper. Owner of Ch D'ISSAN.

**Cubzac, St.-André-de** B'x. r. or w. dr. ★ 82 83 85 86
Town 15 miles n.e. of Bordeaux, centre of the minor Cubzaguais region. Sound reds have the appellation Bordeaux. Estates include: Ch du Bouilh, Ch de TERREFORT-QUANCARD, Ch TIMBERLAY, Domaine de Beychevelle.

**Cussac**  Village just s. of ST JULIEN. Appellation Haut-Médoc.

**Cuve Close**  Short-cut method of making sparkling wine in a tank. The sparkle dies away in the glass much quicker than with MÉTHODE CHAMPENOISE wine.

**Cuvée**  The quality of wine produced in a "cuve" or vat. Also a word of many uses, incl. "blend". In Burgundy interchangeable with "Cru". Often just refers to a "lot" of wine.

**d'Angerville, Marquis**  Famous burgundy grower with immaculate estate in VOLNAY.

**Degré alcoolique**  Degrees of alcohol, i.e. percent by volume.

**De Ladoucette**  Leading producer of POUILLY-FUMÉ, based at CH DU NOZET. Luxury brand "Baron de L". Also SANCERRE Comte Lafond.

**Delagrange-Bachelet**  One of the leading proprietors in CHASSAGNE-MONTRACHET.

**Delas Frères**  Long-established and excellent firm of Rhône-wine specialists at Tournon, v'yds at CÔTE RÔTIE, HERMITAGE, esp. Cuvée de la Tourette CORNAS, CONDRIEU, etc. Owned by DEUTZ.

**Delorme, André**  Leading merchants and growers of the CÔTE CHALONNAISE. Specialists in sparkling wine and excellent RULLY.

**De Luze, A. et Fils**  Bordeaux shipper and owners of Ch'x CANTENAC-BROWN and PAVEIL DE LUZE; owned by Rémy-Martin of Cognac.

**Demi-Sec**  "Half-dry": in practice more than half sweet.

**Depagneux, Jacques et Cie**  Well-regarded merchants of BEAUJOLAIS.

**Deutz**  Brut NV and 75 76 79 81 82, Rosé 82, Blanc de Blancs 78 79 81 82. One of the best of the smaller champagne houses. Full-flavoured wines. Luxury brand: Cuvée William Deutz (75 79).

**Domaine**  Property, particularly in Burgundy.

**Domaine de l'Eglantière**  Important CHABLIS estate. See DURUP.

**Domaine du Vieux Télégraphe**  Rh. r. (w. dr.) ★★★ 76 78 79 81 83 84 85 86  A leader in fine modern CHÂTEAUNEUF-DU-PAPE.

**Dom Pérignon**  70 71 73 75 76 78 80 and Rosé 75 78 Luxury brand of MOËT & CHANDON, named after the legendary Abbey cellarmaster who "invented" champagne.

**Dopff "au Moulin"**  Ancient and top-class family wine-house at Riquewihr, Alsace. Best wines: Riesling Schoenenbourg, Gewürztraminer Eichberg. Pioneers of sparkling wine in Alsace.

**Dopff & Irion**  Another excellent Riquewihr (ALSACE) business. Best wines include Muscat les Amandiers, Riesling de Riquewihr.

**Doudet-Naudin**  Burgundy merchant and grower at Savigny-lès-Beaune. V'yds incl. BEAUNE CLOS DU ROI. Dark long-lived wines supplied to Berry Bros & Rudd of London.

**Dourthe Frères**  Well-reputed Bordeaux merchant representing a wide range of ch'x, mainly good Crus Bourgeois, incl. Ch'x MAUCAILLOU, TRONQUOY-LALANDE, BELGRAVE. "Beau-Mayne" is their reliable branded Bordeaux.

**Doux**  Sweet.

**Drouhin, J. et Cie**  Deservedly prestigious Burgundy grower (130 acres) and merchant. Offices in BEAUNE, v'yds in BEAUNE, MUSIGNY, CLOS DE VOUGEOT, CHABLIS, etc. Drouhin also owns Jaffelin et Cie and a v'yd in Oregon.

**Drouhin-Larose**  Prosperous little domaine in GEVREY-CHAMBERTIN, CLOS DE VOUGEOT, etc.

**Duboeuf, Georges**  Top-class BEAUJOLAIS merchant at Romanèche-Thorin. The leader of the region with a huge range of admirable wines.

**Dufouleur Frères**  Large-scale growers and merchants of burgundy at NUIT-ST-GEORGES and MERCUREY.

**Dujac, Domaine**  Fashionable burgundy grower at MOREY-ST-DENIS with v'yds in that village, ECHÉZEAUX, BONNES-MARES, GEVREY-CHAMBERTIN, etc. His best wines are splendidly vivid.

**Durup, Jean**  One of the biggest Chablis growers with 140 acres, including the DOMAINE DE L'EGLANTIÈRE and admirable Ch de Maligny.

**Echézeaux** B'y. r. ★★★ 76 78' 79 80 82 83' 84 85 86 87
74-acre Grand Cru between VOSNE-ROMANÉE and CLOS DE VOUGEOT. Can be superlative fragrant burgundy without great weight e.g. from Mugneret, Gouroux, DOM DE LA ROMANÉE-CONTI, Jacqueline Jayer.

**Edelzwicker** Alsace w. ★ D.Y.A.
Light white from mixture of grapes, often fruity and good.

**Engel, R.** Well-known grower of VOSNE-ROMANÉE and neighbourhood.

**Entre-Deux-Mers** B'x. w. dr. ★ D.Y.A.
Standard dry white Bordeaux from between the Garonne and Dordogne rivers. Often a good buy, esp. "La Gamage", Ch ST. BONNET.

**Eschenauer, Louis** Famous Bordeaux merchants, owners of Ch'x RAUSAN-SÉGLA and SMITH-HAUT-LAFITTE, DE LAMOUROUX and LA GARDE in GRAVES. Controlled by John Holt, part of the Lonrho group.

**l'Etoile** Jura w. dr./sw./sp. ★★
Sub-region of the Jura known for stylish whites, incl. VIN JAUNE like CHÂTEAU-CHALON and good sparkling.

**Faiveley, J.** Family-owned growers (with 182 acres) and merchants at NUITS-ST-GEORGES, with v'yds in CHAMBERTIN-CLOS-DE-BÈZE, CHAMBOLLE-MUSIGNY, CORTON, NUITS, MERCUREY (150 acres). Consistent high quality recently. Wines for serious ageing.

**Faller, Théo** Top ALSACE grower at the Domaine Weinbach, Kaysersberg. Concentrated firm wines need ageing.

**Faugères** Midi r. (p. or w. dr.) ★→★★ 85 86 87
Isolated village of the COTEAUX DU LANGUEDOC making above-average wine. Became Appellation Contrôlée in 1982.

**Feuillatte, Nicolas** NV Brut, Rosé
Champagne marque popular in restaurants. Rosé esp. good.

**Fèvre, William** Conservative Chablis grower with the biggest Grand Cru holding (40 acres). His label is Domaine de la Maladière.

**Fitou** Midi r. ★★ 82 83 84 85 86
Superior CORBIÈRES red; powerful and ages well. Mostly from coop at Tuchan.

**Fixin** B'y. r. ★★ 76 78 80 83 84 85 86 87
A worthy and under-valued neighbour to GEVREY-CHAMBERTIN. Often splendid reds. Best v'yds: Clos du Chapitre, Les Hervelets, Clos Napoléon. Top growers: Clair, Bertheau, Gelin.

**Fleurie** B'y. r. ★★★ 83 85 86 87
The epitome of a BEAUJOLAIS cru: fruity, scented, silky, racy.

**Frais** Fresh or cool.

**Frappé** Ice-cold.

**Froid** Cold.

**Fronsac** B'x. r. ★→★★ 75 78 79 81 82 83 85 86
Pretty hilly area of good reds just w. of St-Emilion. Ch'x incl. Dalem, La Dauphine, Mayne-Vieil, la Rivière, de Carles, La Valade, Villars, La Vieille Cure. See also Canon Fronsac.

**Frontignan** Midi br. sw. ★ NV
Strong sweet and liquorous muscat wine.

**Gagnard-Delagrange, Jacques** Estimable small (13-acre) grower of CHASSAGNE-MONTRACHET, including some LE MONTRACHET.

**Gaillac** s. w. France r. p. or w. dr./sw. or sp. ★
Ancient area showing signs of new life after generations of dullness. Slightly fizzy "Perlé" is good value. Reds can age well. Ch Larroze is the quality leader.

**Gallaire** B'x. r. ★★ D.Y.A.
Very attractive fruity young Bordeaux from SICHEL.

**Gamay** See Grapes for red wine.

**Geisweiler et Fils** One of the bigger merchant-houses of Burgundy: cellars and 50 acres of v'yds at NUITS-ST-GEORGES. Also 150 acres at Bevy in the HAUTES CÔTES DE NUITS and 30 in the CÔTE CHALONNAISE.

**Gevrey-Chambertin** B'y. r. ★★★ 76 78 79 80 82 83 85

The village containing the great CHAMBERTIN and many other noble v'yds, as well as a considerable number more commonplace. Top growers incl. Leclerc, ROTY, ROUSSEAU, DROUHIN-LAROSE, FAIVELEY.

**Gewürztraminer** The speciality grape of ALSACE: perfumed and spicy, whether dry or sweet.

**Gigondas** Rh. r. or p. ██ 78 80 81 83 84 85 86

Worthy neighbour to CHÂTEAUNEUF-DU-PAPE. Strong, full-bodied, sometimes peppery wine, e.g. Dom du Pesquier, Dom du Cayron, Dom les Pallières, Dom Raspail-Ay, and wines from MEFFRE.

**Gilbey, S.A.** British firm long-established as Bordeaux merchants at Ch LOUDENNE in the MÉDOC. Now owned by Grand Met.

**Gisselbrecht, Louis** High-quality Alsace shippers at Dambach-la-Ville.

**Givry** B'y. r. or w. dr. ██ 83 84 85 86 87

Underrated village of the CÔTE CHALONNAISE: light but tasty and typical burgundy from e.g. Baron Thénard, Clos Salomon.

**Gosset** NV, 73 75 76 78 79 80 81 82 83 85 "Grande Réserve" and Rosé NV Small, very old champagne house at Ay. Fine full wines (esp. Grande Réserve). Now linked with Philipponnat.

**Gouges, Henri** Worthy burgundy grower of NUITS-ST-GEORGES. Good reds and very rare white "La Perrière".

**Goulaine, Château de** The ceremonial showplace of MUSCADET; a noble family estate and its appropriate wine.

**Goulet, Georges** NV, rosé 76 79, Crémant Blanc de Blancs 79 and 71 73 75 76 79 81 High-quality Reims champagne house. Abel Lepitre is a cheaper range. Luxury brand: Cuvée du Centenaire 74 76 79.

**Goût** Taste, e.g. "goût anglais" – as the English like it (i.e. dry).

**Grand Cru** One of the top Burgundy v'yds with its own appellation contrôlée. Similar in Alsace but more vague elsewhere. In ST-EMILION the third rank of château, numbering about 200.

**Grand Roussillon** Midi br. sw. ★★ NV

Broad appellation for muscat and other sweet fortified wines ("Vins Doux Naturels") of eastern Pyrenees.

**Grands-Echézeaux** B'y. r. ★★★★ 69 71 76 78 79 80 82 83 84 85 86 87

Superlative 22-acre Grand Cru next to CLOS DE VOUGEOT. Top grower: Dom de la ROMANÉE-CONTI.

**Gratien, Alfred and Gratien & Meyer** Excellent smaller champagne house (fine, very dry, long-lasting wine 73 76 79 82) and its counterpart at SAUMUR on the Loire.

**Graves** B'x. r. or w. ★→★★★★

Large region s. of Bordeaux city. Most of its best wines are red, but the name is used chiefly for its dry whites.

**Graves-Léognan** New AOC for part of n. Graves, incl. six communes.

**Graves-Pessac** New appellation for the three northernmost GRAVES communes.

**Graves de Vayres** B'x. r. or w. ★

Part of ENTRE-DEUX-MERS; of no special character.

**Les Gravières** B'y. r. ██

Famous Premier Cru v'yd of SANTENAY. Incl. Clos des Tavannes.

**Griotte-Chambertin** B'y. r. ★★★ 69 71 76 78' 79 80 83 84 85' 86 87

14-acre Grand Cru adjoining CHAMBERTIN. Similar wine, but less masculine and more "tender". Growers incl. DROUHIN.

**Gros Plant du Pays Nantais** Lo. w. ██ D.Y.A.

Junior cousin of MUSCADET, sharper and lighter; made of the COGNAC grape also known as Folle Blanche, Ugni Blanc, etc.

**Haut-Benauge** B'x. w. dr. ★ D.Y.A.

Appellation for a limited area within ENTRE-DEUX-MERS.

**Hautes-Côtes de Beaune** B'y. r. or w. dr. ██ 83 85 86 87

Appellation for a dozen villages in the hills behind the CÔTE DE BEAUNE. Light wines, worth investigating.

**Hautes-Côtes de Nuits**  B'y. r. or w. dr.  ▓▓ **★★** ▓▓  78 83 85 86 87
    The same for the CÔTE DE NUITS. An area on the way up.

**Haut-Médoc**  B'x. r.  ★★→★★★  **66 70 75 76 78 79 80 81** 82 83 84 85 86
    Big appellation including all the best areas of the Médoc. Most of the
    zone has communal appellations (e.g. MARGAUX, PAUILLAC). Some fine
    ch'x (e.g. LA LAGUNE) are simply AC Haut-Médoc.

**Haut-Montravel**  Dordogne w. sw.  ★ 82 83 85 86
    Medium-sweet BERGERAC.

**Haut Poitou**  Lo. (r.) w. d.r.  ▓▓★→★★▓▓  D.Y.A.
    Up-and-coming VDQS area south of ANJOU. Cooperative makes v. good
    whites, incl. CHARDONNAY and SAUVIGNON BLANC.

**Heidsieck, Charles**  NV, rosé 81 and 73 75 76 79 81
    Major champagne house of Reims, family-owned, now controlled by
    Rémy-Martin; also includes Trouillard and de Venoge. Luxury
    brands: Cuvée Champagne Charlie 79 81.

**Heidsieck, Monopole**  NV, rosé and 73 75 76 79 82
    Important champagne merchant and grower of Reims now owned by
    MUMM. V.g. luxury brand: Diamant Bleu (76 79).

**Henriot**  NV, Blanc de Blancs Crémant Brut Souverain NV; Brut Rosé 81;
    Cuvée Baccarat 79; and 79  Old family champagne house now owned
    by VEUVE CLICQUOT. Very big dry style. Luxury brand: Réserve Baron
    Philippe de Rothschild.

**Hérault**  Midi
    The biggest v'yd *département* in France with 400,000 hectares of
    vines. Chiefly vin ordinaire but some good COTEAUX DU LANGUEDOC.

**Hermitage**  Rh. r. or w. dr.  ▓▓ **★★★** ▓▓  71 76 78′ 79 80 82 83′ 84 85 86
    The "manliest" wine of France. Dark, powerful and profound. Needs
    long ageing. The white is heady and golden; now usually made for
    early drinking, though the best wines mature for many years. Top
    makers: CHAVE, JABOULET, CHAPOUTIER, Guigal, Grippat.

**Hospices de Beaune**  Hospital in BEAUNE, with excellent v'yds in MEUR-
    SAULT, POMMARD, VOLNAY, BEAUNE, CORTON, etc. See panel on page 35.

**Huet, Gaston**  Top VOUVRAY grower and mayor of the commune.

**Hugel Père et Fils**  The best-known ALSACE growers and merchants.
    Founded at Riquewihr in 1639 and still in the family. Best wines are
    sweet: Cuvées Exceptionnelles, Selections de Grains Nobles.

**L'Ile de Beauté**  Name given to VINS DU PAYS from CORSICA.

**Imperiale**  Bordeaux bottle holding 8½ normal bottles (5 litres).

**Irancy**  B'y. r. or (p.)  ▓▓ **★★** ▓▓  78 83 85 86
    Good light red made near CHABLIS of PINOT NOIR and "César". The best
    vintages are long-lived and mature well. To watch.

**Irouléguy**  s.w. France r. p. (or w. dr.) ★★ D.Y.A.
    Agreeable local wines of the Basque country.

**Jaboulet, Paul**  Old family firm at HERMITAGE, leading growers of HERMITAGE (esp.
    "La Chapelle" ▓▓ **★★★★** ▓▓ ) and merchants in other RHÔNE wines.

**Jaboulet-Vercherre et Cie**  Well-known Burgundy merchant-house with
    v'yds (34 acres) in POMMARD, etc, and cellars in Beaune. Middling
    wines.

**Jadot, Louis**  Much-respected top-quality Burgundy merchant-house with
    v'yds (50 acres) in BEAUNE, CORTON, etc. See also Clair-Daü.

**Jaffelin**  See Drouhin.

**Jardin de la France**  Name given to VINS DU PAYS of the LOIRE valley.

**Jasnières**  Lo. (r.) (p.) or w. dr.  ★★★ 71 76 78 79 80 82 83 84 85 86
    Rare dry, rather VOUVRAY-like wine of n. Touraine.

**Jaubertie, Domaine de la**  Top BERGERAC estate of 114 acres, English-
    owned.

**Jayer, Henri**  Tiny VOSNE-ROMANÉE domaine acknowledged even by rivals
    as superlative.

**Jeroboam**  In Bordeaux a 6-bottle bottle, or triple magnum; in Cham-
    pagne a double magnum.

**Josmeyer** Family house at Wintzenheim, ALSACE. V.g. long-ageing wines, esp. GEWÜRZ and PINOT BLANC.

**Juliénas** B'y. r. ★★★ 85 86 87
Leading cru of Beaujolais: vigorous fruity wine.

**Jura** See Côtes de Jura.

**Jurançon** S.W. France w. sw. or dr. ★★ 78 79 81 82 83 84 85 86
Unusual high-flavoured and long-lived speciality of Pau in the Pyrenean foothills. Ages well for several years. Top growers: Barrère, Chigné, Guirouilh, Lamouroux, Ramonteu. Also the coop's "Grain Sauvage".

**Kressman, E.S. & Cie** Family-owned Bordeaux merchants and owners of Ch LATOUR-MARTILLAC in GRAVES. "Monopole Rouge" is a good standard blend.

**Kriter** Popular low-price sparkling wine processed in Burgundy by PATRIARCHE.

**Krug** "Grande Cuvée" (NV), 64 66 69 71 73 75 76 79 81, Rosé and Clos du Mesnil Blanc de Blancs 79 80 Small but very prestigious champagne house known for full-bodied very dry wines of the highest quality.

**Kuentz-Bas** Top-quality ALSACE grower and merchant at Husseren-les-Châteaux, esp. for GEWÜRZTRAMINER.

**Labarde** Village just s. of MARGAUX and included in that appellation. Best ch: GISCOURS.

**Labouré-Gontard** Producer of high-quality CRÉMANT de Bourgogne at NUITS.

**Labouré-Roi** Good little merchant at NUITS-ST-GEORGES, esp. for MEURSAULT.

**Lafon, Domaine des Comtes** 31-acre top-quality Burgundy estate in VOLNAY, MEURSAULT and LE MONTRACHET.

**Lalande de Pomerol** B'x. r. ★★ 75 76 78 79 81 82 83 85 86
Neighbour to POMEROL. Wines similar but considerably less fine. Top ch'x: Les Annereaux, Les Hauts-Conseillants, Les Hauts-Tuileries, Moncets, Tournefeuille, Belair, Siaurac.

**Langlois-Château** Producer of sparkling SAUMUR, controlled by BOLLINGER.

**Langon** The principal town of the S. GRAVES/SAUTERNES district.

**Lanson Père et Fils** Black Label NV, rosé NV, Red Label 75 76 79 81 82
Important Champagne house, cellars at Reims. Luxury brand: Noble Cuvée 81. Black Label is a reliable fresh N.V.

**Laroche** Important (160 acres) grower and merchant of CHABLIS, incl. Domaine Laroche, La Jouchère. Labels incl. Bacheroy-Josselin. Also owns the Château de PULIGNY-MONTRACHET.

**Latour, Louis** Top Burgundy merchant and grower with v'yds (120 acres) in CORTON, BEAUNE, etc. Among the best, esp. for white wines.

**Latour de France** r. (w. dr.) ★→★★ 82 83 84 85 86 87
New appellation in CÔTES DE ROUSSILLON-VILLAGES.

**Latricières-Chambertin** B'y. r. ★★★ 71 76 78 79 80 82 83 84 85′ 86 87
17-acre Grand Cru neighbour of CHAMBERTIN. Similar wine, but lighter and "prettier" e.g. from FAIVELEY, Ponsot, Trapet.

**Laudun** Rh. r. p. or w. dr. ★
Village of CÔTES-DU-RHÔNE-VILLAGES. Attractive wines from the cooperative incl. fresh whites.

**Laugel, Michel** One of the biggest ALSACE merchant-houses, at Marlenheim.

**Laurent-Perrier** NV, rosé brut and 71 73 75 76 78 79 81 82
Excellent and highly successful young champagne house at Tours-sur-Marne. Luxury brand: Cuvée Grande Siècle. Ultra Brut is the best buy.

**Leflaive, Domaine** Perhaps the best of all white burgundy growers, at PULIGNY-MONTRACHET. Best v'yds: Clavoillons, Pucelles, Bienvenue-, Chevalier-Montrachet.

**Leflaive, Olivier** Négociant at Puligny-Montrachet since '84, nephew of the above. Excellent whites and reds, incl. less famous appellations.

**Léognan** B'x.
Leading village of the GRAVES. Best ch'x: DOMAINE DE CHEVALIER, MALARTIC-LAGRAVIÈRE and HAUT-BAILLY.

**Leroy** Important négociant-élèveur at AUXEY-DURESSES with the finest stocks of old wines in Burgundy. Part-owners and distributors of the DOMAINE DE LA ROMANÉE-CONTI.

**Lichine, Alexis et Cie** Post-war Bordeaux merchants, proprietors of Ch LASCOMBES. No longer connected with the author Alexis Lichine (see Prieuré Lichine).

**Lie, sur** "On the lees." Muscadet is often bottled straight from the vat, without "racking" or filtering (or so its makers say), for maximum freshness.

**Limoux** Pyr. r. or w. dr. **★★** NV
The non-sparkling version of BLANQUETTE DE LIMOUX and a remarkable fresh claret-like red: Anne des Joyeuses.

**Lirac** Rh. r. p. or (w. dr.) **★★★** 81 83 84 85 86
Neighbouring village to TAVEL. Similar wine; the red becoming more important than the rosé, esp. Ch de Segriés, Dom St-Roch.

**Listel** Midi r. p. w. dr. **★→★★★** D.Y.A.
Vast estate on the sandy beaches of the Golfe du Lion. Owned by the giant Salins du Midi, making very pleasant light "vins des sables" incl. sparkling. Domaine du Bosquet is a light fruity red. Domaine de Villeroy is a fresh blanc de blancs "SUR LIE".

| | |
|---|---|
| MISE EN BOUTEILLES AU DOMAINE<br><br>**VOLNAY**<br>**LES CAILLERETS**<br><br>APPELLATION CONTROLEE<br>DOMAINE DE LA POUSSE D'OR<br>A VOLNAY, COTE D'OR | **Burgundy: a grower's own label**<br><br>Domaine is the burgundy equivalent of château.<br>The Appellation Contrôlée is Volnay.<br>The individual v'yd in Volnay is called Les Caillerets.<br>The name and address of the grower/producer.<br>(The word propriétaire is often also used.) |
| **GEVREY-CHAMBERTIN**<br>**CLOS ST JACQUES**<br><br>APPELLATION CONTROLEE<br><br>REMOISSENET PERE ET FILS<br>NEGOCIANTS A BEAUNE | **A merchant's label**<br><br>The village.<br>The vineyard.<br>The wine qualifies for the Appellation Gevrey-Chambertin Premier Cru.<br>Remoissenet Père et Fils is a négociant, or merchant, who bought the wine from the grower to mature, bottle and sell. |

**Listrac** B'x. r. ★★→ **★★★**
Village of HAUT-MÉDOC next to MOULIS. Best ch'x: FOURCAS-HOSTEN, FOURCAS-DUPRÉ, CLARKE.

**Long-Depaquit** V.g. CHABLIS domaine (esp. MOUTONNE), owned by BICHOT.

**Lorentz** Two small high-quality Alsace houses at Bergheim, Gustave L. and Jerome L, have the same management.

**Loron et Fils** Big-scale burgundy grower and merchant, specialist in BEAUJOLAIS and sound VINS DE TABLE.

**Loupiac** B'x. w. sw. ★★ 76 79 80 81 83 85 86
Neighbour to SAUTERNES with similar but less good wine. Top ch'x: Loupiac-Gaudiet, de Ricaud, Haut-Loupiac, Clos-Jean, Rondillon.

**Ludon** HAUT-MÉDOC village s. of MARGAUX. Best ch: LA LAGUNE.

**Lugny** ("Macon-Lugny") B'y. r. w. dr. sp. ★★ 85 86 87
Village next to VIRÉ with active and good co-operative. Wine of Les Genevrières v'yd is sold by Louis LATOUR.

**Lupé-Cholet et Cie** Merchants and growers at NUITS-ST-GEORGES controlled by BICHOT. Best estate wines: Château Gris and Clos de Lupé.

**Lussac-Saint-Emilion** B'x. r. ★★ 78 79 81 82 83 85 86
N.e. neighbour to ST-EMILION. Top ch'x incl. Lyonnat, Tour de Grenat, Bel Air, Villadière. Coop (at PUISSEGUIN) makes "Roc de Lussac".

**Macau** HAUT-MÉDOC village s. of MARGAUX. Best ch: CANTEMERLE.

**macération carbonique** Traditional technique of fermentation with whole bunches of unbroken grapes in a vat full of carbon dioxide. Fermentation inside each grape eventually bursts it, giving vivid and very fruity mild wine for quick consumption. Esp. in BEAUJOLAIS; now much used in the MIDI and elsewhere.

**Machard de Gramont** Burgundy family estate: cellars in NUITS and v'yds in NUITS, SAVIGNY, BEAUNE, POMMARD. Extremely well-made reds.

**Mâcon** B'y. r. (p.) or w. dr. ★★ 85 86 87
Southern district of sound, usually unremarkable, reds and tasty dry (CHARDONNAY) whites. Wine with a village name (e.g. Mâcon-Prissé) is better. POUILLY-FUISSÉ is best appellation of the region. See also Mâcon-Villages.

**Mâcon-Lugny** See Lugny.

**Mâcon Supérieur** The same but slightly better, from riper grapes.

**Mâcon-Villages** B'y. w. dr. ★★→★★★★ 85 86 87
Increasingly well-made and typical white burgundies. Mâcon-Prissé, MÂCON-VIRÉ, MÂCON-LUGNY, Mâcon-Clessé are examples.

**Mâcon-Viré** See Mâcon-Villages and Viré.

**Madiran** s.w. France r. ★★ 75 76 78 79 81 82 83 84 85 86
Dark, vigorous, fragrant red from ARMAGNAC. Well worth ageing. Top growers: Dom de Bouscassé, Peyros, Laplace, Barréjat.

**Magenta, Duc de** Burgundy estate (30 acres) based at CHASSAGNE-MONTRACHET, managed by JADOT.

**Magnum** A double bottle (1.5 litres).

**Mähler-Besse** First-class Dutch wine-merchants in Bordeaux, with a majority share in Ch PALMER. Brands incl. Cheval Noir.

**Maire, Henri** The biggest grower and merchant of JURA wines. Not the best.

**Marc** Grape skins after pressing; also the strong-smelling brandy made from them (cf. Italian "Grappa").

**Marcillac** s.w. France r. p. ★ D.Y.A.
Good rustic VDQS from the coop.

**Margaux** B'x. r. ★★→★★★★ 66 70 75 76 78 79 80 81 82 83' 84 85 86
Village of the HAUT-MÉDOC making the most "elegant" red Bordeaux. The name includes CANTENAC and several other villages as well. Top ch'x include MARGAUX, LASCOMBES, etc.

**Margnat** Major producer of everyday VIN DE TABLE.

**Marque déposée** Trade mark.

**Marsannay** B'y. (r.) or p. ★★★ 78 80 83 85 86 87 (rosé ·D.Y.A.)
Village near Dijon with excellent light red and delicate PINOT NOIR rosé, perhaps the best rosé in France. Growers incl. CLAIR.

**Mas de Daumas Gassac** Midi r. ★★★ 80 81 82 83 84 85 86
The outstanding estate of the MIDI, producing huge Bordeaux-like, largely CABERNET wines on apparently unique soil. Also "Rosé Frisant". Alarming quality.

**Maufoux, Prosper** Family firm of burgundy merchants at SANTENAY. Reliable wines with good keeping qualities. Alias Marcel Amance.

**Maury** Pyr. r. sw. ★→★★★ NV
Red VIN DOUX NATUREL from ROUSSILLON.

**Mazis (or Mazy) Chambertin** B'y. r. ★★★ 76 78 80 82 83 85 86 87
30-acre Grand Cru neighbour of CHAMBERTIN. Lighter wine. Best from LEROY.

**Médoc**  B'x. r. ★★ 78 79 81 82 83 84 85 86
Appellation for reds of the less good (n.) part of Bordeaux's biggest and best district. Flavours tend to slight earthiness. HAUT-MÉDOC is better.

**Meffre, Gabriel**  The biggest southern Rhône estate, based at GIGONDAS. Includes Ch de Vaudieu, CHÂTEAUNEUF-DU-PAPE.

**Ménétou-Salon**  Lo. r. p. or w. dr. ★★ D.Y.A.
Attractive light wines from w. of SANCERRE. SAUVIGNON white; PINOT NOIR red.

**Mercier et Cie**  NV, Extra Rich and Rosé 80 81 and 73 75 76 78 80 81
One of the biggest champagne houses, at Epernay. Controlled by MOËT & CHANDON. Commercial quality.

**Mercurey**  B'y. r. or w. dr  ★★ 78 83 84 85 86 87
Leading red-wine village of the CÔTE CHALONNAISE. Good middle-rank burgundy. Growers incl. Ch de Chamirey, FAIVELEY, Chanzy.

**Métaireau, Louis**  The ring-leader of a group of top Muscadet growers. Expensive well-finished wines.

**méthode champenoise**  The traditional laborious method of putting the bubbles in champagne by refermenting the wine in its bottle.

**Meursault**  B'y. (r.) w. dr. ★★★ 78 81 82 83 84 85 86 87
CÔTE DE BEAUNE village with some of the world's greatest whites: rich, savoury, dry but mellow. Best v'yds. incl. Perrières, Genevrières, Charmes. Top growers incl: AMPEAU, COCHE-DURY, Delagrange, LAFON, LATOUR, MAGENTA, Matrot, Michelot-Buisson, CH DE MEURSAULT, P. Morey, G. ROULOT. See also Blagny.

**Meursault-Blagny**  See Blagny.

**Midi**  General term for the south of France, where standards have risen consistently in recent years.

**Minervois**  Midi r. or (p.) (w.) or br. sw.  ★→★★★ 83 85 86
Hilly VDQS area with some of the best wines of the Midi: lively and full of flavour esp. from Ch de Gourgazaud. Also sweet MUSCAT de St Jean de M.

**mise en bouteilles au château, au domaine**  Bottled at the château, at the property or estate. N.B. dans nos caves (in our cellars) or dans la région de production (in the area of production) are often used although they mean little.

**Moelleux**  Mellow. Used of the sweet wines of VOUVRAY, etc.

**Moët & Chandon**  NV, rosé 81, Dry Imperial 71 73 75 76 78 80 81 82
The biggest champagne merchant and grower, with cellars in Epernay and sparkling wine branches in Argentina, Brazil and California. Consistent quality. Luxury brand: DOM PÉRIGNON.

**Moillard**  Big family firm of growers and merchants in NUITS-ST-GEORGES, making dark and tasty CÔTE DE NUITS wines.

**Mommessin, J.**  Major BEAUJOLAIS merchant. Owner of CLOS DE TART.

**Monbazillac**  Dordogne w. sw.  ★★ 71 75 76 78 79 80 81 83 85 86
Golden SAUTERNES-style wine from BERGERAC. Ages well. Ch Monbazillac is best known.

**Mondeuse**  Savoie r. ★★ D.Y.A.
Red grape of SAVOIE. Good, vigorous, deep-coloured wine.

**Mongeard-Mugneret**  40-acre VOSNE-ROMANÉE estate. Fine ÉCHÉZEAUX, VOUGEOT, etc.

**Monopole**  Vineyard in single ownership.

**Montagne-Saint-Emilion**  B'x. r.  ★★ 75 76 78 79 81 82 83 85 86
North-east neighbour of ST-EMILION with similar wines, becoming more important with each year. Top ch'x: Calon, St-André-Corbin, Vieux-Ch-St-André-Corbin, Vieux-Ch-St-André, Roudier, Teyssier, des Tours.

**Montagny**  B'y. (r.) w. dr. ★★→★★★ 85 86 87
CÔTE CHALONNAISE village between MÂCON and MEURSAULT, both geographically and gastronomically. A little red, too.

**Montée de Tonnerre**　B'y. w. dr.　***
　　Famous and excellent PREMIER CRU of CHABLIS.

**Monthelie**　B'y. r.　***　78 80 82 83 84 85 86 87
　　Little-known neighbour and almost equal of VOLNAY. Excellent fragrant reds. Best estate: Château de Monthélie.

**Montlouis**　Lo. w. sw./dr.　** 75 76 78 81 82 83′ 84 85 86
　　Neighbour of VOUVRAY. Similar sweet or dry long-lived wine.

**Montrachet**　B'y. w. dr.　****　69 71 76 78 79 80 81 82 83 84 85 86 87
　　19-acre Grand Cru v'yd in both PULIGNY and CHASSAGNE-MONTRACHET. Potentially the greatest white burgundy: strong, perfumed, intense, dry yet luscious. (The "t"s are silent.)

**Montravel**　See Côtes de Montravel.

**Mont-Redon, Domaine de**　Rh. r. (w. dr.)　*** 78 79 80 81 83 84 85 86
　　Outstanding 235-acre estate in CHÂTEAUNEUF-DU-PAPE. Relatively early-maturing wines.

**Moreau et Fils**　CHABLIS merchant and grower with 175 acres. Also major table-wine producer. Best wine: Clos des Hospices (Grand Cru).

**Morey, Domaines**　50 acres in CHASSAGNE-MONTRACHET. V.g. wines made by family members.

**Morey-Saint-Denis**　B'y. r.　***　71 76 78 79 80 82 83 84 85 86
　　Small village with 4 Grands Crus between GEVREY-CHAMBERTIN and CHAMBOLLE-MUSIGNY. Glorious wine, often overlooked. Growers incl. Amiot, DUJAC, Lignier, Ponsot, Serveau.

**Morgon**　B'y. r.　*** 83 85 86 87
　　The "firmest" cru of BEAUJOLAIS, needing time to develop its rich and savoury flavour.

**Moueix, J-P et Cie**　The leading proprietor and merchant of St-Emilion and Pomerol. Ch'x incl. MAGDELAINE, LAFLEUR-PÉTRUS, and part of PÉTRUS. Now also has a venture in California: see Dominus.

**Moulin-à-Vent**　B'y. r.　*** 83 85 86 87
　　The "biggest" and best wine of Beaujolais; powerful and long-lived, eventually tasting more like CÔTE D'OR wine.

**Moulis**　B'x. r.　**→***
　　Village of the HAUT-MÉDOC with its own appellation and several Crus Exceptionnels: CHASSE-SPLEEN, POUJEAUX-THEIL, MAUCAILLOU, etc. Wines are growing steadily finer.

**Mousseux**　Sparkling.

**Mouton Cadet**　Best-selling brand of blended red and white Bordeaux.

**Moutonne**　CHABLIS GRAND CRU *honoris causa*, owned by BICHOT.

**Mumm, G. H. & Cie**　NV "Cordon Rouge", rosé 79, Crémant de Cramant (NV) and 69 71 73 75 76 79 82　Major champagne grower and merchant owned by Seagram's. Luxury brand: René Lalou (79). The Cramant is superb.

**Muscadet**　Lo. w. dr.　** D.Y.A.
　　Popular, good-value, often delicious dry wine from round Nantes in s. Brittany. Should never be sharp. Perfect with fish.

**Muscadet de Sèvre-et-Maine**　Wine from the central and usually best part of the area.

**Muscat**　Distinctively perfumed grape and its (usually sweet) wine, often fortified as VDN. Made dry in ALSACE.

**Muscat de Beaumes de Venise**　One of the best French muscats (see Beaumes de Venise).

**Muscat de Frontignan**　Midi br. sw.　** D.Y.A.
　　Sweet Midi muscat. Quality improving.

**Muscat de Lunel**　Midi br. sw.　** NV
　　Ditto. A small area but good.

**Muscat de Mireval**　Midi br. sw.　** NV
　　Ditto, from near Montpellier.

**Muscat de Rivesaltes**　Midi br. sw.　* NV
　　Sweet muscat from a big zone near Perpignan.

**Musigny** B'y. r. (w. dr.) ★★★★ **69 71 76 78 79 80 82** 83 84 85 86
25-acre Grand Cru in CHAMBOLLE-MUSIGNY. Often the best, if not the
most powerful, of all red burgundies (and a little white). Best growers:
DE VOGÜÉ, DROUHIN, LEROY, Roumier, Mugnier.

**Nature** Natural or unprocessed, esp. of still champagne.

**Néac** B'x. r. ★★
Village n. of POMEROL. Wines sold as LALANDE-DE-POMEROL.

**Négociant-éléveur** Merchant who "brings up" (i.e. matures) the wine.

**Nicolas, Ets.** Paris-based wholesale and retail wine merchants controlled
by Rémy-Martin. One of the biggest in France and one of the best.

**Nuits-St-Georges** r. ★★→★★★ **69 71 76 78′ 80 82 83 84 85′ 86 87**
Important wine-town: wines of all qualities, typically sturdy and full-
flavoured. Name can be shortened to "Nuits". Best v'yds incl. Les St-
Georges, Vaucrains, Les Pruliers, Clos de Corvées, Les Cailles, etc.
Many growers and merchants esp. FAIVELEY, Chevillon, MACHARD DE
GRAMONT.

**Oisly et Thesée, Vignerons de** Go-ahead cooperative in e. TOURAINE
(Loire), experimenting successfully with superior grapes, esp. SAUV BL,
CAB, and (since '85) CHARD. Blended wines labelled Baronnie d'Aignan.
Good value.

**Ott, Domaine** The most important producer of high-quality PROVENCE
wines.

**Pacherenc-du-Vic-Bilh** s.w. France w. sw. ★ NV
Rare minor speciality of the ARMAGNAC region.

**Paillard, Bruno** NV, Crémant Blanc de Blancs, Rosé, **75 76 79**
Small but prestigious young Champagne house with excellent silky
vintage and NV wines at fair prices.

**Palette** Prov. r. p. or w. dr. ★★
Near Aix-en-Provence. Aromatic reds and good rosés from CH SIMONE.

**Parallèle 45** Excellent brand of CÔTES DU RHÔNE from JABOULET.

**Parigot-Richard** Producer of high-quality CRÉMANT DE BOURGOGNE at
SAVIGNY.

**Pasquier-Desvignes** Very old firm of Beaujolais merchants at St Lager,
BROUILLY.

**Patriarche** One of the bigger firms of burgundy merchants. Cellars in
Beaune; also owns CH DE MEURSAULT (100 acres), KRITER, etc.

**Patrimonio** Corsica r. w. dr. p ★★→★★★
Wide range from dramatic chalk hills in n. Corsica. Fragrant reds,
crisp whites, fine VDN. Top grower: Gentile.

**Pauillac** B'x. r. ★★→★★★★ **66 70 71 73 75 76 78 79** 81 82 83 84 85 86
The only village in Bordeaux (HAUT-MÉDOC) with three first-growths
(Ch'x LAFITE, LATOUR, MOUTON) and many other fine ones, famous for
high flavour but very various in style.

**Pécharmant** Dordogne r. ★★ 82 83 85 86
Usually better-than-typical light BERGERAC red, with more "meat". Top
estate: Ch de Tiregand.

**Pelure d'oignon** "Onion skin" – tawny tint of certain rosés.

**Perlant or Perlé** Very slightly sparkling.

**Pernard-Vergelesses** B'y. r. or (w. dr.) ★★★ 78 80 82 83 84 85 86
87 Village next to ALOXE-CORTON containing part of the great CORTON
and CORTON-CHARLEMAGNE v'yds and one other top v'yd: Ile des
Vergelesses. Growers incl. BONNEAU DE MARTRAY, Dubreuil-Fontaine,
Rapet, Chandon.

**Perrier, Joseph** NV, rosé and **71 73 75 76 79** 82
Family-run champagne house with considerable v'yds at Chalon-sur-
Marne. Consistent light and fruity style.

**Perrier-Jouet** NV, Blason de France NV, **71 73 75 76 79** 82
Excellent champagne-growers and makers at Epernay now linked
with MUMM. Luxury brands: Belle Epoque **79** (in a painted bottle),
Blason de France (NV). Also Belle Epoque Rosé **79** 82.

**Pétillant**  Slightly sparkling.

**Petit Chablis**  B'y. w. dr. ★★ D.Y.A.
Wine from fourth-rank CHABLIS v'yds. Lacks great character.

**Piat Père et Fils**  Important growers and merchants of BEAUJOLAIS and MÂCON wines at Mâcon, now controlled by Grand Metropolitan Ltd. V'yds in MOULIN-À-VENT, also CLOS DE VOUGEOT. BEAUJOLAIS, MÂCON-VIRÉ in special Piat bottles maintain a fair standard.

**Pic, Albert**  Fine CHABLIS producer, controlled by DE LADOUCETTE.

**Picpoul-de-Pinet**  Midi w. dr. ★ NV
Rather dull very dry southern white, best v. cold on the spot.

**Pineau de Charente**  Strong sweet apéritif made of white grape juice and Cognac.

**Pinot**  See Grapes for white and red wine.

**Piper-Heidsieck**  NV, Pink 79, Vintage 71 73 75 76 79 82, Année Rare 76, Brut Sauvage 79  Champagne-makers of old repute at Reims.

**Pol Roger**  NV, rosé 75 79, Blanc de Chardonnay 79 and 71 73 75 76 79  Excellent champagne house at Epernay. Particularly good non-vintage White Foil, Rosé and Chardonnay. Luxury cuvée: "Sir Winston Churchill".

---

*"Noble rot" (in French* pourriture noble, *in German* Edelfäule, *in Latin* Botrytis cinerea*) is a form of mould that attacks the skins of ripe grapes in certain vineyards in warm and misty autumn weather.*

*Its effect, instead of rotting the grapes, is to wither them. The skin grows soft and flaccid, the juice evaporates through it, and what is left is a super-sweet concentration of everything in the grape except its water content.*

*The world's best sweet table wines are all made of nobly rotten grapes. They occur in good vintages in Sauternes, the Rhine, the Mosel (where wine made from them is called Trockenbeerenauslese), in Tokaji in Hungary, in Burgenland in Austria, and occasionally elsewhere – California included. The danger is rain on pulpy grapes already far gone in noble rot. All too often, particularly in Sauternes, the grower's hopes are dashed by a break in the weather.*

---

**Pomerol**  B'x. r. ★★ →★★★★ 70 71 75 76 78 79 81 82 83 85 86
The next village to ST-EMILION: similar but more "fleshy" wines, maturing sooner, reliable and delicious. Top ch. PÉTRUS, LA FLEUR-PÉTRUS, VIEUX-CH-CERTAN, LATOUR À POMEROL, etc . . .

**Pommard**  B'y. r. ★★★ 69 71 76 78 80 82 83 84 85 86 87
The biggest and best-known village in Burgundy. No superlative wines, but many warmly appealing ones. Best v'yds: Rugiens, Epenots and HOSPICES DE BEAUNE cuvées. Growers incl: Courcel, Gaunoux, LEROY, Armand, Pothier-Rieusset.

**Pommery & Greno**  NV, NV rosé and 71 73 75 76 78 79 80 81 82
Very big CHAMPAGNE growers and merchants at Reims. Wines are v. dry, not v. charming. Luxury brand: Louise Pommery 80.

**Pouilly-Fuissé**  B'y. w. dr. ★★→★★★ 85 86 87
The best white of the MÂCON area. At its best (e.g. Ch Fuissé, Vieilles Vignes) excellent, but almost always over-priced.

**Pouilly-Fumé**  Lo. w. dr. ★★→★★★ 86 87
"Gun-flinty", fruity, often sharp pale white from the upper Loire, next to SANCERRE. Grapes must be SAUVIGNON BLANC. Good vintages improve for 2-3 yrs.

**Pouilly-Loché**  B'y. w. dr. ★★
Neighbour of POUILLY-FUISSÉ. Similar wine but little of it.

**Pouilly-Sur-Loire**  Lo. w. dr. ★ D.Y.A.
Inferior wine from the same v'yds as POUILLY-FUMÉ, but different grapes (CHASSELAS). Rarely seen today.

**Pouilly-Vinzelles**  B'y. w. dr. ★★ 86 87
Neighbour of POUILLY-FUISSÉ. Similar wine, worth looking for.

**Pousse d'Or, Domaine de la**  32-acre estate in POMMARD, SANTENAY and (esp.) VOLNAY, where its "monopoles", "Bousse d'Or" and "60 Ouvrées" are tannic, austere, powerful and justly famous.

**Preiss Zimmer, Jean**  Old-established Alsace wine-merchants at Riquewihr.

**Premières Côtes de Blaye**  B'x. r. w. dr.  |★—★★★|  78 81 82 83 85 86
Restricted appellation for better reds of BLAYE. Ch'x include Barbé, Charron, Bourdieu, Haut-Sociondo, La Tonnelle, l'Escadre, Segonzac, Le Menaudat.

**Premier Cru**  First-growth in Bordeaux (see page 54), but the second rank of v'yds (after Grand Cru) in Burgundy.

**Premières Côtes de Bordeaux**  B'x. r. (p.) or w. dr. or sw.  |★—★★★|
Large area east of GRAVES: a good bet for quality and value, though never brilliant. Ch'x incl. Laffitte [sic.] Gardera, Fayau, Haut-Brignon, REYNON, Tanesse.

**Prieur, Domaine Jacques**  35-acre estate all in top Burgundy sites, incl. Premier Cru MEURSAULT, VOLNAY, PULIGNY- and CHEVALIER-MONTRACHET. Recently disappointing.

**Primeur**  "Early" wine for refreshment and uplift; esp. of BEAUJOLAIS.

**Prissé**  See Mâcon-Villages.

**Propriétaire-récoltant**  Owner-manager.

**Provence**  See Côtes de Provence.

**Puisseguin-Saint-Emilion**  B'x. r.  ★★  81 82 83 85 86
Eastern neighbour of ST-EMILION; wines similar – not so fine but often good value. Ch'x incl. Laurets, Guibeau, Puisseguin, Soleil, Teyssier. Also "Roc de Puisseguin" from coop.

**Puligny-Montrachet**  B'y. w. dr. (r.)  ★★★  78 81 82 83 84 85 86 87
Bigger neighbour of CHASSAGNE-MONTRACHET with equally glorious rich dry whites. Best v'yds: MONTRACHET, CHEVALIER-MONTRACHET, BÂTARD-MONTRACHET, Bienvenue-Bâtard-Montrachet, Les Combettes, Clavoillon, Pucelles, Champ-Canet, etc. Top growers incl: AMPEAU, BOUCHARD PÈRE, CHARTRON, LEFLAIVE, SAUZET, L. Carillon.

**Quarts de Chaume**  Lo. w. sw.  ★★★  75 76 78 82 84 85 86
Famous 120-acre plot in COTEAUX DU LAYON. CHENIN BLANC grapes. Long-lived, intense, rich golden wine, esp. Ch La Suronde.

**Quatourze**  Midi r. (p.) or w. dr.  ★  83 85 86 87
Minor VDQS area near Narbonne.

**Quincy**  Lo. w. dr.  ★★  85 86 87
Small area making v. dry SANCERRE-style wine of SAUV BL.

**Ramonet-Prudhon**  One of the leading proprietors in CHASSAGNE-MONTRACHET with 34 acres. Sometimes excellent whites, and red Clos St-Jean.

**Rancio**  Term for the tang of wood-aged fortified wine, esp. BANYULS and other VINS DOUX NATURELS. A fault in table wines.

**Rasteau**  Rh. r. (p. w. dr.) or br. sw.  ★★  85' 86
Village of s. Rhône valley. Very sound reds. Good strong, sweet, dessert wine is the local speciality.

**Ratafia de Champagne**  Sweet apéritif made in Champagne of ⅔ grape juice and ⅓ brandy.

**Récolte**  Crop or vintage.

**Regnié**  Beaujolais village between MORGON and BROUILLY, promoted to "Cru" status in 1988. About 1,800 acres.

**Reine Pédauque, La**  Burgundy growers and merchants at ALOXE-CORTON.

**Remoissenet Père et Fils**  Fine Burgundy merchants (esp. for white wines) with a tiny estate at BEAUNE.

**Rémy Pannier**  Important Loire-wine merchants at SAUMUR.

**Reuilly**  Lo. (r. p.) w. dr.  ★★  85 86 87
Neighbour of QUINCY with similar wine; also good PINOT GRIS.

**Riceys, Rosé des**  Champ. p.  ★★  D.Y.A.
Minute appellation in southern Champagne for a notable PINOT NOIR rosé. Principal producer; A. Bonnet.

**Richebourg**  B'y. r. ★★★★ 66 69 70 71 76 78 79 80 81 82 83 84 85 86 87
19-acre Grand Cru in VOSNE-ROMANÉE. Powerful, perfumed, fabulously expensive wine, among Burgundy's best. Top grower: DOM DE LA ROMANÉE-CONTI.

**Riesling**  See Grapes for white wine.

**Rivèsaltes**  Midi r. w. dr. br. sw. ★★ NV
Fortified sweet wine, some muscat-flavoured, from e. Pyrenees. An ancient tradition still very much alive, if struggling.

**La Roche-aux-Moines**  Lo. w. dr./sw. ★★★ 75 76 78 79 82 83 85 86
60-acre v'yd in Savennières, Anjou. Intense, strong, fruity/sharp wine ages well.

**Rodet, Antonin**  Substantial Burgundy merchant and a well-known grower of MERCUREY (Ch de Chamirey).

**Roederer, Louis**  Brut Premier NV, Rosé 75 and 71 73 75 76 78 79 81
One of the best champagne-growers and merchants at Reims. V. reliable non-vintage wine with plenty of flavour. Luxury brand: Cristal Brut 79 (in white glass bottles) is sumptuous.

**La Romanée**  B'y. r. ★★★★ 71 76 78 80 82 83 84 85 86 87
2-acre Grand Cru in VOSNE-ROMANÉE just uphill from ROMANÉE-CONTI, distributed by BOUCHARD.

**Romanée-Conti**  B'y. r. ★★★★ 66 71 73 76 78 79 80 81 82 83 84 85 86
4⅓-acre Grand Cru in VOSNE-ROMANÉE. The most celebrated and expensive red wine in the world. Sometimes the best: '85 is astonishing.

**Romanée-Conti, Domaine de la**  The grandest estate of Burgundy, owning the whole of ROMANÉE-CONTI and LA TÂCHE and major parts of RICHEBOURG, GRANDS ECHÉZEAUX, ECHÉZEAUX and ROMANÉE-ST-VIVANT (under Marey-Monge label). Also a very small part of LE MONTRACHET. Aims for longevity in its wines.

**Romanée-St-Vivant**  B'y. r. ★★★★ 71 76 78 79 80 82 83 84 85 86
23-acre Grand Cru in VOSNE-ROMANÉE. Similar to ROMANÉE-CONTI but lighter and less sumptuous.

**Ropiteau**  Burgundy wine-growers and merchants at MEURSAULT. Specialists in MEURSAULT and CÔTE DE BEAUNE wines.

**Rosé d'Anjou**  Lo. p. ★ D.Y.A.
Pale, slightly sweet, rosé. Cabernet d'Anjou *should* be better.

**Rosé de Loire**  Lo. p. dr. ★→★★ D.Y.A.
Appellation for dry Loire rosé (Anjou is sweet).

**Roty, Joseph**  Small grower of classic GEVREY-CHAMBERTIN.

**Rousseau, Domaine A.**  Major burgundy grower famous for CHAMBERTIN, etc, of highest quality. Only avoid his '82s.

**Rousette de Savoie**  Savoie w. dr.  ▨▨ D.Y.A.
The tastiest of the fresh whites from s. of Geneva.

**Roussillon**  See Côtes du Roussillon. "Grands Roussillons" are VINS DOUX NATURELS.

**Ruchottes-Chambertin**  B'y. r. ★★★ 71 73 76 78 79 80 82 83 84 85
7½-acre Grand Cru neighbour of CHAMBERTIN. Similar splendid long-lasting wine.

**Ruinart Père et Fils**  NV, rosé 79 and Bl. de Blancs 71 73 75 76 78 79 81
The oldest champagne house, now belonging to Moët-Hennessy. Luxury brand: Dom Ruinart, Blanc de Blancs 79. N.B. the Rosé.

**Rully**  B'y. r. or w. dr. or (sp.).  ▨▨ 85 86 87
Village of the CÔTE CHALONNAISE famous for sparkling burgundy. Still reds and white light but tasty and good value. Growers incl. DELORME, FAIVELEY, Jacquesson, Dom de la Folie.

**Sablet**  Rh. r. (p.) w. dr.  ▨▨
Admirable CÔTE-DU-RHÔNE village, esp. Ch du Trignon.

**Saint-Amour**  B'y. r. ★★ 85 87
Northernmost cru of BEAUJOLAIS: light, fruity, irresistible.

**Saint-Aubin** B'y. (r.) or w. dr. ▓▓ 83 85 86 87
Little-known neighbour of CHASSAGNE-MONTRACHET, up a side-valley.
Not top-rank, but typical and good value. Also sold as CÔTE-DE-BEAUNE-
VILLAGES. Top grower: J. Lamy.

**Saint Bris** B'y. (r.) w. dr. ▓ D.Y.A.
Village w. of CHABLIS known for its fruity ALIGOTÉ, making good
sparkling burgundy, but chiefly for SAUVIGNON DE ST BRIS.

**Saint Chinian** Midi r. ▓←→▓▓ 85 86 87
Hilly area of growing reputation in the COTEAUX DU LANGUEDOC.
Appellation Contrôlée since 1982. Tasty reds.

**Sainte-Croix-du-Mont** B'x. w. sw. ▓▓ 71 75 76 79 80 81 82 83 84 86
Neighbour to SAUTERNES with similar golden wine. No superlatives but
well worth trying, esp. Ch Loubens, Ch du Mont, Clos des Coulinats. A
bargain.

**Sainte-Foy-Bordeaux** B'x. w. sw. ★ D.Y.A.
Part of ENTRE-DEUX-MERS, more akin to BERGERAC.

**Saint-Emilion** B'x. r. ★★→★★★★ 70 71 75 76 78 79 81 82 83 85 86
The biggest (13,000 acres) top-quality Bordeaux district; solid, rich,
tasty wines from hundreds of ch'x, incl. CHEVAL-BLANC, AUSONE, CANON,
MAGDELAINE, FIGEAC, etc. Also a v.g. coop.

**Saint-Estèphe** B'x. r. ▓▓ →★★★★ 75 78 79 80 81 82 83 84 85 86
Northern village of HAUT-MÉDOC. Solid, satisfying, occasionally superlative wines. Top ch'x: CALON-SÉGUR, COS D'ESTOURNEL, MONTROSE, etc,
and many notable CRUS BOURGEOIS.

**St-Gall** Brand-name used by Union-Champagne the very good
champagne-growers' Cooperative at AVIZE.

**Saint-Georges-Saint-Emilion** B'x. r. ▓▓ 81 82 83 85 86
Part of MONTAGNE-ST-EMILION with high standards. Best ch'x: ST-
GEORGES, Belair-Montaiguillon, Marquis-St-Georges, Tour-du-Pas-St-
Georges.

**Saint-Joseph** Rh. r. (p. or w. dr.) ▓▓ 76 78 79 80 82 83 85 86
Northern Rhône appellation of second rank but reasonable price.
Substantial wine often better than CROZES-HERMITAGE esp. from
JABOULET, Rostaing.

**Saint-Julien** B'x. r. ★★★ →★★★★ 70 75 76 78 79 80 81 82' 83' 84
85' 86 Mid-Médoc village with a dozen of Bordeaux's best ch'x, incl.
three LÉOVILLES, BEYCHEVELLE, DUCRU-BEAUCAILLOU, GRUAUD-LAROSE, etc.
The epitome of well-balanced red wine.

**Saint-Laurent** Village next to SAINT-JULIEN. Appellation HAUT-MÉDOC.

**Saint-Nicolas-de-Bourgueil** Lo. r. ★★ 82 83 84 85 86
The next village to BOURGUEIL: the same light but lively and fruity
CABERNET red. Top growers: Ammeux, Audebert, Cognard, Jamet.

**Saint-Péray** Rh. w. dr. or sp. ★★ NV
Rather heavy white from the n. Rhône, much of it made sparkling. A
curiosity worth investigating.

**Saint Pourçain** Central France r. p. or w. dr ▓ D.Y.A.
The venerable local wine of Vichy, rather chic in Paris. Made from
GAMAY and/or PINOT NOIR, the white from Tressalier, CHARDONNAY or
SAUVIGNON BLANC.

**Saint Romain** B'y. r. w. dr. ▓▓ 85 86 87
Overlooked village just behind the CÔTE DE BEAUNE. Value, esp. for
young whites. Top growers: LEROY, Thévenin.

**Saint-Sauveur** HAUT-MÉDOC village just w. of PAUILLAC.

**Saint-Seurin-de-Cadourne** HAUT-MÉDOC village just n. of SAINT-ESTÈPHE.

**Saint-Véran** B'y. w. dr. ▓▓ 85 86 87
Next-door appellation to POUILLY-FUISSÉ. Similar but better value: real
character from the best slopes of MÂCON-VILLAGES.

**Salins du Midi, Domaine Viticole** See Listel.

**Salon Le Mesnil** 61 64 66 69 71 73 76 79
The original Blanc de Blancs champagne, from Le Mesnil. Fine very
dry wine with extraordinary keeping qualities.

**Sancerre** Lo. (r. p.) or w. dr. ★★★ 86 87

Very fragrant and fresh SAUVIGNON white almost indistinguishable from POUILLY-FUMÉ, its neighbour over the Loire. Drink young. Also light P. NOIR red (best drunk at 2-3 yrs) and rosé. Top growers incl. Crochet, Delaporte, CORDIER, Gitton, Reverdy.

**Santenay** B'y. r. or (w. dr.) ★★★ 71 76 78 79 80 82 83 84 85 86 87

Very worthy, rarely rapturous, sturdy reds from the s. of the CÔTE DE BEAUNE. Best v'yds: Les Gravières, Clos de Tavannes, La Comme. Top growers: DOM DE LA POUSSE D'OR, Lequin-Roussot.

**Saumur** Lo. r. p. or w. dr. and sp. ★→ ★★

Big versatile district in ANJOU, with fresh fruity whites, v.g. CRÉMANT, pale rosés and increasingly good CABERNET reds, the best from Saumur-Champigny, esp. Ch de Chaintres.

**Sauternes** B'x. w. sw. ★★ →★★★★ 67 71 75 76 78 79 80 81 82 83 84 85 86 District of 5 villages (incl. BARSAC) making France's best sweet wine: strong (14%+ alcohol), luscious and golden, demanding to be aged. Top ch'x: D'YQUEM, SUDUIRAUT, COUTET, CLIMENS, GUIRAUD, etc. Also dry wines that cannot be sold as Sauternes.

**Sauvignon Blanc** See Grapes for white wine.

**Sauvignon-de-St-Bris** B'y. w. dr. ★★ D.Y.A.

A baby VDQS cousin of SANCERRE from near CHABLIS. To try.

**Sauvion et Fils** Ambitious and well-run MUSCADET house, based at the Ch de Cléray. Top wine: Cardinal Richard.

**Sauzet, Etienne** White burgundy estate at PULIGNY-MONTRACHET. Clearly defined, well-bred wines at best superb.

**Savennières** Lo. w. dr./sw. ★★★ 75 76 78 81 82 83 84 85 86

Small ANJOU district of pungent, long-lived whites, incl. COULÉE DE SERRANT, LA ROCHE AUX MOINES, Clos du Papillon.

**Savigny-lès-Beaune** B'y. r. or (w. dr.) ★★★ 78 80 82 83 85 86 87

Important village next to BEAUNE, with similar well-balanced middle-weight wines, often deliciously delicate and fruity. Best v'yds: Marconnets, Dominode, Serpentières, Vergelesses, les Guettes. Top growers incl: BIZE, Girard-Vollot, TOLLOT-BEAUT, CLAIR.

**Savoie** E. France r. or w. dr. or sp. ★★ D.Y.A.

Alpine area with light dry wines like some Swiss wine or minor Loires. CRÉPY, SEYSSEL and APREMONT are best known whites, ROUSSETTE is often more interesting. Also MONDEUSE red.

**Schlumberger et Cie** ALSACE grower-merchants of luscious wines at Guebwiller.

**Schröder & Schyler** Old family firm of Bordeaux merchants, owners of Ch KIRWAN.

**Sciacarello** Red grape of Corsica's best red and rosé, e.g. AJACCIO, Sartène.

**Sec** Literally means dry, though champagne so-called is medium-sweet (and better at breakfast and tea-time than Brut).

**Selection de Grains Nobles** Descriptions coined by HUGEL for Alsace equivalent to German BEERENAUSLESE. "Grains nobles" are individual grapes with "noble rot" (see page 46).

**Sèvre-et-Maine** The *département* containing the best v'yds of MUSCADET.

**Seyssel** Savoie w. dr. or sp. ★★ NV

Delicate pale dry white making admirable sparkling wine.

**Sichel & Co.** Two famous merchant houses. In Bordeaux owners of Ch D'ANGLUDET and part-owners of Ch PALMER. In Germany, maker of BLUE NUN and respected trader.

**Soussans** Village just n. of MARGAUX, sharing its appellation.

**Sylvaner** See Grapes for white wine.

**Syrah** See Grapes for red wine.

**La Tâche** B'y. r. ★★★★ 62 69 70 71 73 76 78 79 80 81 82 83 84 85 86

15-acre Grand Cru of VOSNE-ROMANÉE and one of the best v'yds on earth: dark, perfumed and luxurious wine. Owned by the DOMAINE DE LA ROMANÉE-CONTI.

**Taittinger** NV, Collection Brut 78 and 71 73 75 76 78 79 80 82
   Fashionable champagne growers and merchants of Reims with a light touch. Luxury brand: Comtes de Champagne 76 79 (also v.g. rosé 79).

**Tastevin, Confrèrie des Chevaliers du** Burgundy's colourful and successful promotion society. Wine carrying their Tastevinage label has been approved by them and will usually be of a fair standard. A tastevin is the traditional shallow silver wine-tasting cup of Burgundy. See panel, page 31.

**Tavel** Rh. p. ★★★ D.Y.A.
   France's most famous, though not her best, rosé, strong and dry, starting vivid pink and fading to orange. Avoid orange bottles.

**Tempier, Domaine** Top grower of BANDOL, with noble reds (incl. single-v'yd wines) and rosé.

**Tête de Cuvée** Archaic term vaguely used of the best wines of an appellation.

**Thénard, Domaine** The major grower of GIVRY, but best known for his substantial portion (4½ acres) of LE MONTRACHET.

**Thevenet, Jean** A master maker of white Mâcon-Clessé (Domaine de la Bon Gran) at Quintaine-Clessé, near LUGNY. Even some Botrytis wines.

**Thorin, J.** Grower and major merchant of BEAUJOLAIS, at Pontanevaux, owner of the Château des Jacques, MOULIN À VENT. Recently bought by Racke of Germany.

**Thouarsais, Vin de** Lo. r. ★ D.Y.A.
   Light GAMAY VDQS area south of SAUMUR.

**Tokay d'Alsace** See Pinot Gris under Grapes for white wine.

**Tollot-Beaut** Stylish burgundy grower with some 50 acres in the CÔTE DE BEAUNE, incl. CORTON, BEAUNE, Grèves, SAVIGNY (Les Champs Chevrey) and at Chorey-lès-Beaune where he is based.

**Tortochot, Domaine** 25-acre estate based at GEVREY-CHAMBERTIN. Classic wines.

**Touraine** Lo. r. p. w. dr./sw./sp. ★→★★★★
   Big mid-Loire province with immense range of wines, incl. dry white SAUVIGNON, dry and sweet CHENIN BLANC (e.g. VOUVRAY), red CHINON and BOURGUEIL, light red CABERNETS, GAMAYS and rosés. Cabernets, Sauvignons and Gamays of good years are bargains. Amboise, Azay-le-Rideau and Mesland are sub-sections of the appellation.

**Trimbach, F. E.** Distinguished ALSACE grower and merchant at Ribeauvillé. Best wines (incl. the austere Riesling Clos Ste. Hune) mature magnificently.

**Tursan** s.w. France r. p. w. dr. ★
   Emerging VDQS in the Landes. Sound reds.

**Vacqueyras** Rh. r. ★★ 78 80 82 83 84 85 86
   Prominent village of S. CÔTES-DU-RHÔNE, neighbour to GIGONDAS; comparable with CHÂTEAUNEUF-DU-PAPE but less heavy and more "elegant". Try JABOULET's version.

**Valençay** Lo. w. dr. ★ D.Y.A.
   Neighbour of CHEVERNY: similar pleasant sharpish wine.

**Val-Joannis, Ch de** Prov. r. p. w. dr. ★★
   Impressive new estate making v.g. CÔTES DU LUBÉRON wines.

**Valréas** Rh. r. (p. w. dr.) ★★
   Côtes-du-Rhône-village with big coop "Enclave des Papes" and good red wines.

**Varichon & Clerc** Principal makers and shippers of SAVOIE sparkling wines.

**Varoilles, Domaine des** Burgundy estate of 30 acres, principally in GEVREY-CHAMBERTIN. Wines with great keeping qualities.

**Vaudésir** B'y. w. dr. ★★★★ 78 81 83 84 85 86 87
   Arguably the best of the 7 Grands Crus of CHABLIS (but then so are the others).

**VDQS** Vin Délimité de Qualité Supérieure (see p. 23).

**Vendange**   Vintage.

**Vendange tardive**   Late vintage. In ALSACE equivalent to German AUSLESE.

**Veuve Clicquot**   NV ("Yellow label"), NV Demi-Sec (White Label) and (Gold Label) 73 75 76 78 79 80 and rosé   Historic champagne house of the highest standing, now owned by Moët-Hennessy. Full-bodied wines. Cellars at Reims. Luxury brand: La Grande Dame 79.

**Vidal-Fleury, J.**   Long-established shippers and growers of top Rhône wines, esp. HERMITAGE and CÔTE-RÔTIE.

**Vieilles Vignes**   "Old vines" – therefore the best wine. Used for such wine by BOLLINGER, DE VOGÜÉ and others.

**Viénot, Charles**   Grower-merchant of good burgundy, at NUITS. 70 acres in Nuits, CORTON, RICHEBOURG, etc.

**Vignoble**   Area of vineyards.

**Vin de garde**   Wine that will improve with keeping. The serious stuff.

**Vin de l'année**   This year's wine. See Beaujolais, Beaujolais-Villages.

---

### The Colour of Age

*One very easy way of gauging the maturity of a red wine without opening the bottle is simply to hold the neck of the bottle up to a bright light. If the colour of the wine in the neck is deep red the wine is almost certainly still young and vigorous. If it appears a light orange colour, the wine is fully mature and should be drunk. If possible, compare a very fine Bordeaux and a simple one at, say, ten years old to see the difference: the better wine will look much darker.*

---

**Vin de paille**   Wine from grapes dried on straw mats, consequently very sweet, like Italian passito. Especially in the JURA.

**Vin de Pays**   The junior rank of country wines. Well over 100 are now operational. Don't turn up your nose; there are some gems.

**Vin de Table**   Standard everyday table wine, not subject to particular regulations about grapes and origin. Choose the previous entry.

**Vin Doux Naturel ("VDN")**   Sweet wine fortified with wine alcohol, so the sweetness is "natural", not the strength. The most distinguished product of ROUSSILLON. A vin doux liquoreux is several degrees stronger.

**Vin Gris**   "Grey" wine is very pale pink, made of red grapes pressed before fermentation begins, unlike rosé, which ferments briefly before pressing. Oeil de Perdrix means much the same; so (though I blush to say it) does "blush".

**Vin Jaune**   Jura w. dr. ★★★
Speciality of ARBOIS: odd yellow wine like fino sherry. Normally ready when bottled. The best is CHÂTEAU-CHALON.

**Vin nouveau**   See Beaujolais Nouveau.

**Vin vert**   A very light, acidic, refreshing white wine, a speciality of ROUSSILLON and v. necessary in summer in those parts.

**Vinsobres**   Rh. r. (p. or w. dr.)   ★★   78 80 81 83 84 85 86
Contradictory name of good s. Rhône village. Strong substantial reds which mature well.

**Viré**   B'y. w. dr.   ★★   86 87
One of the best white-wine villages of Mâcon. Good wines from coop, Ch de Viré, Clos du Chapitre, JADOT.

**Visan**   Rh. r. p. or w. dr.   ★★ 83 85 86
One of the better s. Rhône villages. Reds better than white.

**Viticulteur**   Wine-grower.

**Vogüé, Comte Georges de**   First-class 30-acre burgundy domaine at CHAMBOLLE-MUSIGNY. At best the ultimate MUSIGNY and BONNES MARES. Avoid '83s.

**Volnay**   B'y. r.   ★★★ 71 76 78 79 80 82 83 84 85' 86 87
Village between POMMARD and MEURSAULT: the best reds of the CÔTE DE BEAUNE, not strong or heavy but fragrant and silky. Best v'yds: Caillerets, Clos des Ducs, Champans, Clos des Chênes, etc. Best growers: POUSSE D'OR, d'ANGERVILLE, Lafarge.

**Volnay-Santenots**  B'y. r. ★★★
  Excellent red wine from MEURSAULT is sold under this name. Indistinguishable from VOLNAY.

**Vosne-Romanée**  B'y. r. ★★★→★★★★  71 76 78 79 80 81 82 83 84 85 86  The village containing Burgundy's grandest Crus (ROMANÉE-CONTI, LA TÂCHE, etc.). There are (or rather should be) no common wines in Vosne. Many good growers incl: Arnoux, JAYER, Gros, Mongeard-Mugneret, Mugneret, DOM DE LA ROMANÉE-CONTI, Costagnier, Engel.

**Vougeot**  See Clos de Vougeot.

**Vouvray**  Lo. w. dr./sw./sp. ★★→★★★★  71 76 78 79 82 83 85 86
  Small district of TOURAINE with very variable wines, at their best intensely sweet and almost immortal. Good dry sparkling. Best producers: Huet, Foreau, Ch Moncontour, Brédif.

**Willm, A.**  Northerly ALSACE grower at Barr, with v.g. GEWÜRZ Clos Gaensbronnel.

**"Y"**  (Pronounced ygrec) 78 79 80 84
  Brand name of powerful dry wine of great character, occasionally made at Ch D'YQUEM.

**Ziltener, André**  Swiss burgundy merchant with cellars in Gevrey-Chambertin. Reds especially good.

**Zind-Humbrecht**  64-acre Alsace estate in Wintzenheim, Turckheim and Thann. First-rate individual v'yd wines (esp. Clos St. Urbain Riesling).

---

### Masters of Wine

*The Institute of Masters of Wine was founded in London in 1953 to provide an exacting standard of qualification for the British wine trade. A small minority pass its very stiff examinations, even after rigorous training, both theoretical and practical. (They must be able to identify wines "blind", know how they are made, and also know the relevant EEC and Customs regulations). In all, only 130 people have qualified to become Masters of Wine. Fourteen "Masters" are women.*

*In 1988 the Institute, aided by a grant from the Madame Bollinger Foundation, opened its examinations for the first time to non-British candidates. "Master of Wine" (or M.W.) should eventually become the equivalent of a Bachelor of Arts degree in the worldwide wine trade.*

# Châteaux
# of Bordeaux

Some 400 of the best-known Bordeaux châteaux are listed below, A-Z. The current state of the wine of each vintage of each château (whether it is ready for drinking or will still improve, whether it is a wine of which its proprietor is especially proud) has been discussed with the proprietor and compared with my notes and those of others.

This information is complete up to the 1986 vintage, the most recent to be bottled. 1986 and 1985 seem set to become one of those pairs of years that keep discussion going for a generation. Which was the better? As in 1982 and 1983 it is a question of style, location, luck and ultimately personal taste. Certainly for Sauternes 1986 was an exceptionally luscious vintage.

1987 offers no such promise, alas. Serious rain in June during the flowering was followed by a warm summer, but it rained almost continuously throughout the vintage. The result is diluted wine, from which good proprietors have had to make a very severe selection. Prices have been reduced by about 30% from the 1986, which was already slightly less expensive than 1985, reflecting the over-supply which Bordeaux has suffered since the 1984 vintage. It should always be remembered that in Bordeaux the making of a vintage is only the preface to its history: opinions and reputations continue to alter until the last bottle has been drunk.

MEDOC

R. Gironde

ST-SEURIN-DE-CADOURNE

ST-ESTEPHE  St Est

ST-SAUVEUR  St-Sau
ST-LAURENT  St-Lau
ST-JULIEN  St-Jul
LISTRAC-MEDOC
MOULIS

PAUILLAC  Pau

CUSSAC

SOUSSANS-MARGAUX  Sou-Mar

MARGAUX  Mar

LABARDE-MARGAUX  Lab-Mar
ARSAC-MARGAUX  Ar-Mar

CANTENAC-MARGAUX  Cant-Mar

HAUT MEDOC

FRONSAC
LALANDE
DE POMEROL
POMEROL

Libourne

ST-GEORGES  St-Geo
Castillon  ST-EMILION  St-Em

Bordeaux

R. Dordogne

GRAVES

R. Garonne

ENTRE-DEUX-MERS

BARSAC

SAUTERNES

Langon

**d'Agassac**  Haut-Médoc r.  ★★  75′ 78 79 80 81 82′ 83 84 85 86
  14th-century moated fort with 86 acres. Same owners as Ch'x CALON-SÉGUR and DU TERTRE. Very tasty wines.

**Andron-Blanquet**  St-Est. r.  ★★ 82 83 84 85′ 86
  Sister-château to COS LABORY. Rather "open" and easy wine. 40 acres.

**L'Angélus**  St-Em. r.  ★★ 75′ 76 78 79′ 80 81′ 82 83 85′ 86
  Well-situated classed-growth of 57 acres on the St-Emilion Côtes w. of the town. More steady than exciting, but worth watching.

**d'Angludet**  Cant-Mar. r.  ██ ★★  70′ 75 76′ 78′ 79 80 81′ 82 83′ 84 85′ 86
  75-acre Cru Exceptionnel of classed-growth quality owned by Peter A. Sichel. Lively fragrant Margaux of great style.

**d'Archambeau**  Graves r. and w. dr. (sw.)  ██ ██  (r.) 85 86 (w.) 84 85 86 87  Up-to-date 54-acre property at Illats. V.g. fruity dry white; since '84 fragrant barrel-aged reds.  **Bx**

**d'Arche**  Sauternes w. sw.  ★★ 78 79 80 81 82 83′ 85 86
  Substantial second-rank classed-growth of 88 acres rejuvenated since 1980. Ch d'Arche-Lafaurie was its second label until '81.

**d'Arcins**  Central Médoc r.  ★★
  185-acre property of the Castel family (cf. Castelvin); sister-château to neighbouring Barreyres (160 acres).

**l'Arrosée**  St-Em. r.  ██ ██  78 79 81 82 83 84 85 86
  Substantial 24-acre Côtes property. Seriously fine wine with "stuffing", despite its name (which means watered).

**Ausone**  St-Em. r.  ★★★★ 70 75 76′ 78 79′ 80 81 82′ 83′ 85 86′
  Celebrated first-growth with 17 acres (about 2,500 cases) in the best position on the Côtes and famous rock-hewn cellars under the vineyard. The firmest, most elegant and subtle St-Emilion. See also Ch Belair.

**Bahans-Haut-Brion**  Gr. r.  ★★★ NV and 83
  The second-quality wine of Ch HAUT-BRION.

**Balestard-la-Tonnelle**  St-Em. r.  ██ ██  70′ 75′ 76′ 78 79 81 82 83 85 86′
  Historic 30-acre classed-growth on the plateau near the town. Mentioned by the 15th-century poet Villon and still in the same family (which also owns Ch CAP-DE-MOURLIN). Big flavour; more finesse since '85.

**de Barbe**  Côtes de Bourg r. (w.)  ██ ██  79′ 81 82′ 83 85 86
  The biggest (148 acres) and best-known ch of the right bank of the Gironde. Good tasty, light but fruity, Merlot red.

**Bastor-Lamontagne**  Sauternes w. sw.  ██ ██  76 79 80 82 83′ 84 85 86′
  Large "bourgeois" Preignac property; excellent rich wines. 10,000 cases.

**Batailley**  Pauillac r.  ██ ★★★  61 70 71 75′ 78′ 79′ 80 81 82′ 83 84 85 86
  The bigger of the famous pair of fifth-growths (with HAUT-BATAILLEY) on the borders of Pauillac and St-Julien. 110 acres. Fine, firm strong-flavoured wine. Sold by BORIE-MANOUX.

**Beaumont**  Cussac, Haut-Médoc r.  ██ ██  78′ 79 81 82 83 84 85 86
  200-acre+ Cru Bourgeois, well-known in France for rather light but increasingly attractive wines. In new hands since '79. Second label: Ch Moulin d'Arvigny. 35,000 cases.

**Beauregard**  Pomerol r.  ██ ★★★  75′ 76 79′ 81 82′ 83 85 86
  32-acre v'yd with pretty 17th-century ch near LA CONSEILLANTE. Well-made delicate "round" wines to drink quite young.

**Beau Séjour-Bécot**  St-Em. r.  ★★★ 75′ 76′ 78 79 81 82′ 83 85′ 86
  Half of the old Beau Séjour Premier Grand Cru estate on the w. slope of the Côtes. Easy, tasty wines. 45 acres. Controversially demoted in class in '85. The Bécots also own Ch GRAND PONTET.

**Beauséjour-Duffau-Lagarrosse**  St-Em. r.  ★★★ 70 75 76 78 79 80 81 82 83 85 86  The other half of the above, 17 acres in old family hands, making well-structured (not heavy) wine for long maturing.

**Beau-Site** St-Est. r. ★★ 70′ 75′ 76 78′ 79 80 81 82 83 84 85 86′
55-acre Cru Bourgeois Exceptionnel in same hands as Ch'x BATAILLEY, TROTTEVIEILLE, etc. Regular quality and substance typical of St-Estèphe.

**Belair** St-Em. r. ★★★ 70 71 75′ 76′ 78 79′ 80 82′ 83′ 85′ 86′
Sister-ch and neighbour of AUSONE with 34.5 acres on the Côtes. Wine a shade heartier and less subtle. A very high standard in recent vintages (esp. '85 and '86). Makes an NV, "Roc-Blanquant", in magnums only.

**de Bel-Air** Lalande de Pomerol r. ★★ 75′ 76 79 81 82′ 83 85 86
The best-known estate of this village just n. of Pomerol, with very similar wine. 25 acres.

**Bel Air-Marquis d'Aligre** Sou-Mar. r. ★★ 70′ 75′ 76 78 79 80 81 82′ 83 84 85 Cru Exceptionnel with 42 acres of old vines. The owner likes gutsy wine.

**Belgrave** St.Lau. r. ★★ 81 82 83 85 86′
Obscure fifth-growth in St-Julien's back-country. 107 acres. Acquired by DOURTHE in 1979. '86 shows real promise.

**Bel-Orme-Tronquoy-de-Lalande** St-Seurin-de-Cadourne (Haut-Médoc) r. ★★ 70′ 71 75′ 76 78′ 79′ 81 82′ 83 84 85 86 Reputable 60-acre Cru Bourgeois n. of St-Estèphe. Old v'yd producing tannic wines. Same owner as Ch RAUZAN-GASSIES.

**Berliquet** St-Em. r. ★★ 79 81 82 83 85 86
Tiny Grand Cru Classé recently v. well run (by the coop).

**Beychevelle** St-Jul. r. ★★★ 61 66 70′ 75′ 78 79 80 81 82′ 83 84 85 86
170-acre fourth-growth with the Médoc's finest mansion. Wine of more elegance than power, patchy to '82, now steady.

---

**CHATEAU
LANGOA-BARTON
GRAND CRU CLASSE
APPELLATION ST-JULIEN
CONTROLEE
MIS EN BOUTEILLES AU
CHATEAU**

**A Bordeaux label**

A château is an estate – not necessarily with a mansion or a big expanse of vineyard.
Reference to the local classification. It varies from one part of Bordeaux to another.
The Appellation Contrôlée: look up St-Julien in the France A-Z.
"Bottled at the château" – now the normal practice with classed-growth wines.

---

**Bonnet** Entre-Deux-Mers r. & w. dr. ★★ (w.) D.Y.A.
Big-scale producer of some of the best Entre-Deux-Mers.

**Bon-Pasteur** Pom. r. ★★★ 70 75 76 78 79 81 82 83 84 85 86
Excellent very small property on the St-Emilion boundary. Concentrated, sometimes even creamy, wines.

**Le Bourdieu** Haut-Médoc r. ★★ 75′ 78′ 79 80 81 82 83 85 86
Cru Bourgeois at Vertheuil with sister-ch Victoria (134 acres in all) known for well-made St-Estèphe-style wines.

**Bourgneuf** Pomerol r. ★★★★★★★ 75′ 76 78 79 81 82 83 84 85′ 86
22-acre v'yd on chalky clay soil making fairly rich wines with good typically plummy Pomerol perfume. 5,000 cases.

**Bouscaut** Graves r. w. dr. ★★★ 70′ 75′ 78′ 79 80 81 82′ 83 85 86′
Classed-growth at Cadaujac bought in 1980 by Lucien Lurton, owner of Ch BRANE-CANTENAC, etc. 75 acres red (largely Merlot); 15 acres white. Never yet brilliant, but getting there.

**du Bousquet** Côtes de Bourg r. ★★ 78 79 81 82 83 85 86
Reliable estate with 148 acres making attractive solid wine.

**Boyd-Cantenac** Margaux r. ★★★ 75′ 76′ 78′ 79 80 81 82′ 83′ 84 85 86′ 44-acre third-growth regularly producing attractive wine, full of flavour and tending to improve. See also Ch Pouget.

**Branaire (Ducru)**  St-Jul. r.  **\*\*\*** 70′ 75′ 76 78 79′ 80 81 82′ 83 84 85
 86  Fourth-growth of 125 acres producing notably spicy and flavoury
 wine: attractive and reliable.

**Brane-Cantenac**  Cant-Mar. r.  **\*\*\*** 75′ 78′ 79 80 81 82′ 83 84 85 86′
 Big (211 acres) well-run second-growth. Fragrant, gamey wines of
 strong character. Same owners as Ch'x DURFORT-VIVENS, VILLEGEORGE,
 CLIMENS, BOUSCAUT, etc. Second label: Ch Notton.

**Brillette**  Moulis, Haut-Médoc r.  **\*\*** 75 78 79 80 81′ 82 83 84 85′ 86
 70-acre v'yd. Reliable and attractive; fulfilling high promise.

**La Cabanne**  Pomerol r.  71 75′ 76 78′ 79′ 81 82′ 83 85 86
 Highly regarded 25-acre property near the great Ch TROTANOY.
 Recently modernized; expect to hear more.

**Cadet Piola**  St-Em. r.  **\*\*** 70′ 71 75′ 76 78 79 81 82 83′ 84 85′ 86
 Distinguished little property just n. of the town of St-Emilion. 3,000
 cases. Ch Faurie de Souchard has same owner; slightly less fine wine.

**Caillou**  Sauternes w. sw.  **\*\*** 81 82 83 85 86
 Well-run second-rank 37-acre Barsac vineyard for firm, fruity wine.
 "Private Cuvée" is a top selection.

**Calon-Ségur**  St-Est. r.  **\*\*\*** 70 75 78′ 79′ 80 81 82′ 83 84 85′ 86
 Big (123-acre) third-growth of great reputation. A great classic for big
 hearty wines, but recently suffering in reputation.

**Cambon-la-Pelouse**  Haut-Médoc r.  **\*\*** 82 83 84 85 86
 Huge (145-acre) accessible Cru Bourgeois. A sure bet for fresh typical
 Médoc without wood ageing.

**Camensac**  St-Lau. r.  **\*\*** 75′ 78 79 80 81 82′ 83 84 85 86′
 149-acre fifth-growth, replanted in the '60s with new equipment and
 the same expert direction as LAROSE-TRINTAUDON. Good vigorous but
 not exactly classic wines.

**Canon**  St-Em. r.  **\*\*\*** 70 71 75′ 76 78 79′ 80 81 82′ 83′ 85′ 86
 Famous first-classed-growth with 44+ acres on the plateau w. of the
 town. Conservative methods; very impressive wine.

**Canon**  Canon-Fronsac r.  **\*\*** 78 79 80 81 82 83 85 86′
 Tiny property of Christian MOUEIX. Long-ageing wine.

**Canon-la-Gaffelière**  St-Em. r.  **\*\*** 75 79 81 82′ 83 85 86′
 47-acre classed-growth on the lower slopes of the Côtes in German
 ownership. Reliable lightish wines.

**Canon de Brem**  Canon-Fronsac r.  **\*\*** 78 79 80′ 81 82′ 83 84 85 86
 One of the top Fronsac v'yds for dark, tannic and vigorous wine.
 MOUEIX property.

**Canon-Moueix**  Canon-Fronsac r.  **\*\*** 83 85 86
 The latest MOUEIX investment in this rising appellation. V. stylish wine.

**Cantemerle**  Macau r.  **\*\*\*** 61 70′ 75′ 78 79 81 82 83′ 84 85 86
 Superb estate at the extreme s. of the Médoc, with a romantic ch in a
 wood and 150 acres of vines. Officially fifth-growth: potentially nearer
 second. Problems hampered quality in late '70s. A new broom
 (CORDIER) since 1981 is fulfilling potential.

**Cantenac-Brown**  Cant-Mar. r.  **\*\*\*** 70 75 76 78 79 80 81 82 83 84 85 86
 Formerly old-fashioned 77-acre third-growth, with very promising
 '82 and '83. Big wines. New owners since '87 investing heavily. 2nd
 label Canuet.

**Capbern-Gasqueton**  St-Est. r.  **\*\*** 75 78 79 80 81 82 83 84 85 86
 Good 85-acre Cru Bourgeois; same owner as CALON-SÉGUR.

**Cap de Mourlin**  St-Em. r.  **\*\*** 70′ 75′ 78 79′ 81 82′ 83 84 85 86
 Well-known 37-acre property of the Cap de Mourlin family, owners of
 Ch BALESTARD and Ch Roudier, Montagne-St-Em. Classic St-Emilion.

**Carbonnieux**  Graves r. and w. dr.  **\*\*\*** (r.) 78′ 79 81 82 83 85 86
 Historic estate at Léognan making good fairly light wines. The whites
 of eg. '83, '86, '87 have the structure to age 10 yrs. Ch'x Le Pape and
 Le Sertre are also in the family.

**La Cardonne**  Blaignan (Médoc) r. ★★ 78 79 81' 82 83 84 85 86
Large (300+ acres) Cru Bourgeois in the n. Médoc bought in 1973 by
the Rothschilds of LAFITE. A safe bet for early drinking.

**Les Carmes-Haut-Brion**  Graves r. ▓▓ 75 78 79 80 81' 82' 83 85 86
Small neighbour of HAUT-BRION with high bourgeois standards.

**Caronne-Ste-Gemme**  St-Lau. (Haut-Médoc) r. ★★→★★★ 75 76 78 79
80 81 82' 83 84 85 86  Cru Bourgeois of 100 acres. Steady quality
repays patience.

**du Castéra**  Médoc r. ▓▓ 75 78 79 81 82 83 84 85 86
Historic property at St-Germain in the n. Médoc. Recent investment;
to watch for tasty but not tannic wine.

**Certan de May**  Pomerol r. ★★★ 70 71 75 76 78 79 81 82' 83 84 85' 86
Neighbour of VIEUX-CHÂTEAU-CERTAN. Tiny property (2,000 cases) with
full-bodied rich and tannic wine recently flying very high.

**Certan-Giraud**  Pomerol r. ★★★ 71 75 76 78 79 81 82 83' 85 86
Small (17-acre) property next to the great Ch PÉTRUS.

**Chambert-Marbuzet**  St-Est. r. ▓▓ 78 79 80 81 82 83 84 85 86
Tiny (20-acre) sister-ch of HAUT-MARBUZET. Very good fruity wine aged
in new oak matures quite fast.

**Chantegrive**  Graves r. w. dr. ▓▓ 83 84 85 86
180-acre estate half white, half red; modern Graves of high quality.
Other labels incl. Mayne-Levéque, Bon-Dieu-des-Vignes.

**Chasse-Spleen**  Moulis r. ▓▓▓ 70' 75' 76 78' 79 80 81' 82' 83' 84 85
86  180-acre Cru Exceptionnel of classed-growth quality. Consistently good, usually outstanding, long-maturing wine. 2nd label:
Ermitage de C-S. One of the surest things in Bordeaux.

**Chéret-Pitres**  Graves r. w. dr. ★→★★
Substantial estate in the up-and-coming village of Portets.

**Cheval Blanc**  St-Em. r. ★★★★ 66 70 75' 76 78 79 80 81' 82' 83' 84 85 86
This and AUSONE are the "first-growths" of St-Emilion. Cheval Blanc is
richer, more full-blooded, intensely vigorous and perfumed, from 100
acres on the border of Pomerol.

**Chicane**  Graves r. ▓▓
Satisfying and reliable product of the Langon merchant Pierre Coste.
Domaine de Gaillat is another. Drink at 2-6 years.

**Cissac**  Cissac r. ▓▓ 70' 75' 76 78' 79 80 81 82' 83' 84 85 86
A pillar of the bourgeoisie. 80-acre Grand Bourgeois Exceptionnel
with a steady record for tasty long-lived wine.

**Citran**  Avensan, Haut-Médoc r. ★★ 70' 75 78' 81 82 83 85 86
Grand Bourgeois Exceptionnel of 178 acres bought by Japanese in
'87. Stylish wine.

**Clarke**  Listrac, Haut-Médoc r. (p.) ★★→★★★ 78 79 80 81 82 83 84
85' 86  Huge (350-acre) Cru Bourgeois Rothschild development, incl.
elaborate visitor facilities. Ch'x Malmaison and Peyrelebade are
second labels.

**Clerc-Milon**  Pauillac r. ★★★ 75' 76 78' 79 80 81 82' 83' 84 85 86
Once forgotten little fifth-growth bought by the late Baron Philippe de
Rothschild in 1970. Now 73 acres. Not normally thrilling, but a v.g.
'83, '85 and '86.

**Climens**  Sauternes w. sw. ▓▓▓ 71' 75' 76' 78' 79 80' 81 82 83' 85 86'
74-acre classed-growth at Barsac making some of the best and most
stylish sweet wine in the world for a good 10 years' maturing. A
superb '83. (Occasional) 2nd label: Les Cyprès. Same owner as Ch
BRANE-CANTENAC, etc.

**Clinet**  Pomerol r. ★★ 75 76 78 79 81 83 85
15-acre property in central Pomerol making tannic "Pauillac-style"
wine. Some more flesh would help.

**Clos l'Eglise**  Pomerol r. ▓▓▓ 71 75 76 78 79' 81 82' 83 85 86
14-acre v'yd in one of the best sites in Pomerol. Excellent wine
without great muscle or flesh. The same family owns Ch PLINCE.

**Clos Fourtet** St-Em. r. ★★★ 78 79 80 81 82' 83 85 86
Well-known 42-acre first-growth on the plateau with cellars almost in the town. Back on form after a middling patch. Same owners as CLIMENS, BRANE-CANTENAC, etc.

**Clos Haut-Peyraguey** Sauternes w. sw. ■■ 78 79 80 81 82 83 84 85 86' Tiny production of good medium-rich wine. The v.g. Cru Bourgeois Ch Haut-Bommes is in the same hands.

**Clos des Jacobins** St-Em. r. ■■ 75' 76 78 79 80 81 82' 83' 85 86
Well-known and well-run little (18-acre) classed-growth owned by the shipper CORDIER. Wines of notable depth and style.

**Clos du Marquis** St-Jul. r. ■■ 75 76 78 79 80 81 82 83 84 85 86
The second wine of LÉOVILLE-LASCASES.

**Clos l'Oratoire** St-Em. r. ★★ 78 79 80 81 82 83 85 86
Richly typical Grand Cru. See also Ch Peyreau.

**Clos René** Pomerol r. ■■■ 70 71' 75 78 79 80 81 82' 83 85 86
Leading ch on the w. of Pomerol. 38 acres making powerful wine; eventually delicate. Also sold as Ch Moulinet-Lasserre.

**La Closerie-Grand-Poujeaux** Moulis (Haut-Médoc) r. ★★
Small but respected traditional middle-Médoc. To keep.

**La Clotte** St-Em. r. ■■ 75' 76' 78 79 81 82 83' 85 86
Tiny Côtes Grand Cru with marvellously scented "supple" wine.

**Colombier-Monpelou** Pauillac r. ★★
Reliable small Cru Bourgeois made to a high standard.

**La Conseillante** Pomerol r. ★★★ 70' 75' 76 78 79 80 81' 82' 83 84 85 86
29-acre classed-growth on the plateau between PÉTRUS and CHEVAL BLANC. Some of the noblest and most fragrant Pomerol, worthy of its superb position.

**Corbin (Giraud)** St-Em. r. ★★ 75 76 78 79 81 82' 83' 85 86
28-acre classed-growth in n. St-Emilion where a cluster of Corbins occupy the edge of the plateau. Can be very rich.

**Corbin-Michotte** St-Em. r. ■■ 70 75 78 79 81 82 83 85 86
Well-run 19-acre property; "generous" Pomerol-like wine.

**Cos-d'Estournel** St-Est. r. ★★★★ 61 66 70 71 73 75' 76' 78' 79 80 81' 82' 83 84 85 86 140-acre second-growth with eccentric chinoiserie building overlooking Ch LAFITE. Always full-flavoured, often magnificent, wine. Now regularly one of the best in the Médoc. Maître d'Estournel is a good blend.

**Cos Labory** St-Est. r. ★★ 75' 78' 79' 80 81' 82' 83 84 85 86
Little-known fifth-growth neighbour of COS D'ESTOURNEL with 37 acres. Blunt fruity wines mature early. To watch.

**Coufran** St-Seurin-de-Cadourne (Haut-Médoc) r. ■■ 78' 79 81 82' 83 85 86 Coufran and Ch VERDIGNAN, on the northern-most hillock of the Haut-Médoc, are under the same ownership. Coufran has mainly Merlot vines; soft lightish wine. 148 acres.

**Couhins-Lurton** Graves w. dr. ■■ 82 83 84 85 86' 87'
Small quantity of very fine Sauvignon wine for maturing.

**La Couronne** Pauillac r. ★★ 75 76 78 79 81' 82' 83
Excellent (very) small Cru Exceptionnel made at Ch HAUT-BATAILLEY, though not since '83.

**Coutet** Sauternes w. sw. ★★★ 70' 71' 73 75' 76 79 81 82 83' 84 85 86
Traditional rival to Ch CLIMENS; 91 acres in Barsac. Often slightly less rich; at its best equally fine but recently less reliable. "Cuvée Madame" is a v. rich selection of the best. A dry GRAVES sold under the same name is not v. special.

**Couvent des Jacobins** St-Em. r. ■■ 75 78 79' 80 81 82' 83 85 86
Well-known vineyard of 22 acres adjacent to the town of St-Emilion on the east. Among the best of its kind.

**Le Crock** St-Est. r. ■■ 79 80 81 82 83 84 85 86
Well-situated Cru Bourgeois of 74 acres in the same family as Ch LÉOVILLE-POYFERRÉ. Among the many excellent C.B.s of the commune.

**La Croix** Pomerol r. ✶✶ 70′ 71′ 75′ 76 78 79′ 81 82′ 83 85 86
Well-reputed property of 32 acres. Appealing plummy Pomerol with a spine; matures well. Also La C.-St-Georges, La C.-Toulifaut and Clos des Litanies.

**La Croix de Gay** Pomerol r. ✶✶✶ 70′ 75′ 76′ 78 79 81 82′ 83′ 85 86
30 acres in the best part of the commune. Recently on fine form. Has underground cellars, rare in Pomerol. "La Fleur de Gay" is the best selection.

**Croizet-Bages** Pauillac r. ▓▓ 70′ 75′ 78′ 79 80 81 82′ 83 84 85 86
52-acre fifth-growth (lacking a ch) with the same owners as Ch RAUZAN-GASSIES. Wines with growing finesse.

**Croque-Michotte** St-Em. r. ✶✶ 75 78 79 80 81 82′ 83 85 86
35-acre Pomerol-style classed-growth on the Pomerol border.

**du Cruzeaux** Graves r. w. dr. ✶✶
100-acre GRAVES-LÉOGNAN v'yd recently developed by André Lurton of LA LOUVIÈRE etc. V. high standards; to try.

**Curé-Bon-la-Madeleine** St-Em. r. ✶✶✶ 71′ 75 76′ 78 79 81 82′ 83 85 86
Small (12-acre) property among the best of the Côtes; between AUSONE and CANON. Managed by MOUEIX.

**Dassault** St-Em. r. ▓▓ 78 79 81 82 83 85 86
Consistent early-maturing middle-weight Grand Cru. 58 acres.

**Dauzac** Lab-Mar. r. ▓▓→✶✶✶ 75 78 79′ 80 81 82′ 83′ 84 85′ 86
Substantial fifth-growth near the river s. of Margaux. In new hands and much improved since '79. 120 acres. 22,000 cases.

**Desmirail** Mar. r. ✶✶→✶✶✶ 81 82 83′ 84 85 86
Third-growth, now 45 acres. A long-defunct name recently revived by the owner of BRANE-CANTENAC. Gentle, easy wines for drinking young.

**Dillon** Haut-Médoc r. (w. dr.) ✶✶ 75′ 78′ 79′ 81 82 83 84 85 86
Local wine college of Blanquefort, just n. of Bordeaux. 85 acres. Dry white: Ch Linas (D.Y.A.) 15,000 cases.

**Doisy-Daëne** Barsac w. sw. and dr. ▓▓▓ 75 76′ 78 79 80 81 82 83′ 84 85 86 Forward-looking 34-acre estate making crisp dry white (incl. Riesling grapes) and red Ch Cantegril as well as notably fine sweet Barsac.

**Doisy-Dubroca** Barsac w. sw. ▓▓ 71′ 75′ 76 78 79 80 81 83 84 85 86
Tiny (8½-acre) Barsac classed-growth allied to Ch CLIMENS.

*Why do the Châteaux of Bordeaux have such a large section of this book devoted to them? The reason is simple: collectively they form by far the largest supply of high-quality wine on earth.*

*A single typical Médoc château with 150 acres (some have far more) makes approximately 26,000 dozen bottles of identifiable wine a year – the production of two or three Californian "boutique" wineries. The tendency over the last two decades has been for the better-known châteaux to buy more land. Many classed-growths have expanded by as much as 10 times since they were classified in 1855.*

**Doisy-Védrines** Sauternes w. sw. ▓▓▓ 71 75′ 76′ 78 79 80 81 82′ 83′ 85 86 50-acre classed-growth at Barsac, near CLIMENS and COUTET. Deliciously sturdy rich wines designed for a long life.

**Domaine de Chevalier** Graves r. and w. dr. ▓▓▓▓ (r.) 61 66 70′ 71 75′ 76 78′ 79′ 80 81′ 82′ 83 84 85 86 Superb small estate of 36 acres at Léognan. The red is stern at first, richly subtle with age. The white is delicate but matures to rich flavours. (w. 75 76′ 78 79′ 81 82 83′ 84 85 86). Changed hands (but not management) in 1983. Up to 9,000 cases red, 1,000 cases white.

**Domaine de l'Eglise** Pomerol r. ✶✶ 70 71 75 76 78 79′ 81 82′ 83 85 86
Small property: solid wine distributed by BORIE-MANOUX.

**Domaine la Grave** Graves r. w. dr. ▓▓ 82 83 84 85 86 (w. 87)
Innovative little estate at Portets. Lively medal-winning reds made for a long life. Oak-aged delicious whites.

**La Dominique** St-Em. r. ■■■ 70 71' 75 76 78 79 80 81 82' 83 85 86'
Fine 45-acre classed-growth next door to Ch CHEVAL BLANC, making wine almost as arresting.

**Ducru-Beaucaillou** St-Jul. r. ■■■ 61 66 70' 71 75' 76 78' 79 80 81 82' 83' 84 85' 86' Outstanding second-growth; 120 acres overlooking the river. The owner, M. Borie, makes classic "cedar-pencil" claret for v. long ageing. See also Grand-Puy-Lacoste, etc.

**Duhart-Milon-Rothschild** Pauillac r. ■■■ 75' 76' 78 79 80 81 82' 83 85 86 Fourth-growth neighbour of LAFITE under the same management. Maturing vines; increasingly fine quality. 110 acres.

**Duplessis-Fabre** Moulis r. ■■ 82 83 84 85 86
Small sister-château of FOURCAS-DUPRÉ, replanted since '74.

**Durfort-Vivens** Margaux r. ■■■ 78' 79' 80 81 82' 83 85' 86
Relatively small (49-acre) second-growth owned by M. Lurton of BRANE-CANTENAC. Recent wines (except '84) have real finesse.

**Dutruch-Grand-Poujeaux** Moulis r. ■■ 70 73' 75 76 78' 79 80 81 82' 83 84 85 86 One of the leaders of MOULIS; full-bodied, rich and tannic wines.

**L'Eglise-Clinet** Pomerol r. ■■■ 70 71 75 76 78 79 80 81 82' 83' 84 85' 86 11 acres. Highly ranked; full, fleshy wine. Changed hands in '82; '85 is noble. 2,000 cases.

**L'Enclos** Pomerol r. ■■ 70 71 75 76 78 79 80 81 82' 83 85 86
Respected 26-acre property on the w. side of Pomerol, near CLOS RENÉ. Big, well-made, long-flavoured wine.

**L'Evangile** Pomerol r. ■■■ 70' 71' 75' 76 78 79 80 81 82' 83' 84 85' 86 33 acres between PÉTRUS and CHEVAL BLANC. Impressive wines. In the same area and class as LA CONSEILLANTE.

**Fargues** Sauternes w. sw. ■■■ 70' 71' 75' 76' 78 79 80 81 83 85'
25-acre v'yd in same ownership as Ch YQUEM. Fruity and extremely elegant wines, maturing earlier than YQUEM.

**Ferrande** Graves r. (w. dr.) ■■ 82 83 84 85 86
Major estate of Castres with 100+ acres. Easy enjoyable red. Early drinking is fun; the proprietor prefers to wait.

**Ferrière** Margaux r. ■■ 70 75 78 79 81 82 83 85 86
Phantom third-growth of only 10+ acres. The wine is made at Ch LASCOMBES.

**Feytit-Clinet** Pomerol r. ■■ 70' 71' 75' 76 78 79 81 82' 83 85 86
Little property next to LATOUR-POMEROL. Has made some fine big strong wines. Managed by J-P MOUEIX.

**Fieuzal** Graves r. and (w. dr.) ■■■ 75' 78' 79 80 81' 82' 83 84 85' 86'
75-acre classed-growth at Léognan. Finely made memorable wines of both colours esp. since '84. Recent whites are keepers.

**Figeac** St-Em. r. ■■■ 61 70' 71 75 76 78 79 80 81 82' 83 84 85 86 Famous first-growth neighbour of CHEVAL BLANC. 98-acre gravelly v'yd gives one of Bordeaux's most attractive rich but elegant wines, maturing relatively quickly, but lasting almost indefinitely.

**Filhot** Sauternes w. sw. and dr. ■■■ 75 76' 79' 80 81 82' 83' 85 86'
Second-rank classed-growth with splendid 148-acre v'yd. Lightish sw. wines for fairly early drinking, a little dry, and red.

**La Fleur** St-Em. r. ■■ 75 76 78 79 80 81 82' 83 85 86
Very small Côtes estate producing luxuriously fruity wines.

**La Fleur-Gazin** Pomerol r. ■■ 78 79 80 81 82 83 85' 86
Tiny MOUEIX-run property. Appealing, not over-aweing wines.

**La Fleur-Pétrus** Pomerol r. ■■■ 70 75' 76' 78 79 80 81' 82 83' 84 85 86 18-acre v'yd flanking PÉTRUS and under the same MOUEIX management. Exceedingly fine plummy wines; Pomerol at its most stylish.

**Fombrauge** St-Em. r. ■■ 70' 75' 78 79 80 81 82' 83 84 85 86
Major property of St-Christophe-des-Bardes, e. of St-Emilion, with 120 acres. Reliable St-Emilion making great efforts.

**Fonbadet** Pauillac r. ★★ 70 75 78 **79** 80 81' 82' 83 84 85 86
  Cru Bourgeois of high repute with 38 acres next door to PONTET-CANET.
  Old vines and no oak give solid wine needing long bottle-age. Notable
  value.

**Fonplégade** St-Em. r. ★★ 71 75 76 78 79 81 82' 83 85 86
  48-acre v'yd on the Côtes w. of St.-Emilion in another branch of the
  MOUEIX family. Fragrant and appealing.

**Fonréaud** Listrac r. ★★ 78' 79 80 81 82' 83 84 85' 86'
  One of the bigger (96 acres) and better Crus Bourgeois of its area.
  New broom (and barrels) since '83. See also Ch Lestage.

**Fonroque** St-Em. r. ★★★ 70 71' 75' 76' 78 79 80 81 82 83' 84 85' 86
  48 acres on the plateau n. of St-Emilion, MOUEIX property. Big deep
  dark wine that needs lots of time.

**Les Forts de Latour** Pauillac r. ★★★ 70' 71 75 76 78' 79 80 81 82'
  The second wine of Ch LATOUR; well worthy of its big brother. Unique
  in being bottle-aged at least three years before release.

**Fourcas-Dupré** Listrac r. ★★ 70' 75 76 78' 79 80 81 82' 83' 84 85' 86
  A top-class 100-acre Cru Bourgeois Exceptionnel making consistent
  and elegant wine. To follow.

**Fourcas-Hosten** Listrac r. ★★→★★★ 70 75 76 78' 79 80 81 82' 83'
  84 85 86' 96-acre Cru Bourgeois currently considered the best of its
  commune. Firm wine with a long life.

**La Gaffelière** St-Em. r. ★★★ 70 79 81 82' 83' 85 86
  61-acre first-growth at the foot of the Côtes below Ch BEL-AIR.
  Justifying its reputation since '82.

**La Garde** Graves r. (w. dr.) ★★ 75' 76' 78 79 81 82' 83' 84 85 86
  Substantial ESCHENAUER property making reliably sound red.

**Le Gay** Pomerol r. ★★★ 70 71 75' 76' 78 79 81 82' 83' 85 86
  Well-known 14-acre v'yd on the northern edge of Pomerol. Same
  owner as Ch LAFLEUR, different management since '85. Splendid wine.

**Gazin** Pomerol r. ★★★ 71' 75' 76 78 81 82 83 85 86
  Large property (for Pomerol) with 56 acres. Not quite as splendid as
  its position next to PÉTRUS. 2nd label: Ch l'Hospitalet.

**Gilette** Sauternes w. sw. ★★★ 37 49 53 55 59 61 62
  Extraordinary small Preignac château which stores its sumptuous
  wines in cask to a great age. Only about 5,000 bottles of each. Ch Les
  Justices is the sister-château.

**Giscours** Lab-Mar. r. ★★★ 70 71' 75' 76 78' 79' 80 81' 82' 83 84 85
  86' Splendid 182-acre third-growth s. of CANTENAC. Dynamically run
  and making excellent vigorous wine for long maturing.

**du Glana** St-Jul. r. ★★ 70' 75' 78 79 81 82' 83 85 86
  Big Cru Bourgeois in centre of St-Julien. Undemanding quality.

**Gloria** St-Jul. r. ★★★ 66 70' 71 73 75' 76 78' 79' 80 81 82' 83 84 85
  86 Outstanding Cru Bourgeois making wine of vigour and finesse,
  among good classed-growths in quality. 110 acres. The owner, Henri
  Martin, bought Ch ST-PIERRE in 1982.

**Grand-Barrail-Lamarzelle-Figeac** St-Em. r. ★★ 70 75 78 79 81 82'
  83 85 86 48-acre property near FIGEAC, incl. Ch La Marzelle. Well-
  reputed and popular, if scarcely exciting.

**Grand-Corbin-Despagne** St-Em. r. ★★ 70 75 78 79 81 82' 83 85 86
  One of the biggest and best Grands Crus on the CORBIN plateau.

**Grand-Pontet** St-Em. r. ★★ 75 78 79 81 82' 83 85 86'
  Widely distributed 35-acre neighbour of Ch BEAU SÉJOUR-BÉCOT, in the
  same hands since 1980. "Supple", smooth wine.

**Grand-Puy-Ducasse** Pauillac r. ★★★ 75 76 78 79 80 81 82' 83 84 85
  86 Well-known little fifth-growth bought in '71, renovated and
  enlarged to 90 acres under expert management. A best buy. 2nd
  label: Ch Artigues Arnaud.

**Grand-Puy-Lacoste** Pauillac r. ★★★ 70′ 71 75 76 78′ 79′ 80 81′ 82′ 83 84 85 Leading fifth-growth famous for excellent full-bodied vigorous Pauillac. 110 acres among the "Bages" ch'x s. of the town, owned by the Borie family of DUCRU-BEAUCAILLOU.

**Gravas** Sauternes w. sw. ★★ 83′ 85 86 Small Barsac property; impressive firm wine.

**La Grave-Figeac** St-Em r. ★★ V. small neighbour of CHEVAL BL becoming known for sumptuous wine.

**La Grave Trigant de Boisset** Pom. r. ★★★ 75′ 76′ 78 79 80 81′ 82′ 83 84 85 86′ Verdant ch with small but first-class v'yd owned by Christian MOUEIX. Firm, beautifully structured Pomerol.

**Gressier Grand Poujeaux** Moulis. r. ★★★ 70 75′ 76 78 79′ 80 81 82 83′ 84 85 86 Good Cru Bourgeois, neighbour of CHASSE-SPLEEN. Fine firm wine with a good track record.

**Greysac** Médoc r. ★★ 78 79′ 81′ 82 83 85 86 Elegant 140-acre property. Easy, early-maturing wines.

**Gruaud-Larose** St-Jul. r. ★★★ 70′ 71 73 75′ 76 78′ 79 80 81 82′ 83 84 85 86 One of the biggest and best-known second-growths. 189 acres making smooth, rich, stylish, claret. Owned by CORDIER. The excellent second wine is called Sarget de Gruaud-Larose.

**Guiraud** Sauternes (r.) w. sw. (dr.) ★★★ 70′ 76 78′ 79′ 81 82 83′ 84 85 86′ Newly restored classed-growth of top quality. 250+ acres. At best excellent sweet wine of great finesse and a small amount of red and dry white. The '83 will be superb in time.

**Guiteronde-du-Hayot** Sauternes w. sw. ★★ One of the larger Barsac ch'x. Good wines well distributed.

**La Gurgue** Margaux r. ★★★ 79 81 82 83′ 84 85′ 86 Small (30-acre) well-placed property with fine typical Margaux, recently bought by owners of Ch CHASSE-SPLEEN. To watch.

**Hanteillan** Cissac r. ★★ 75 76 79′ 80 81 82′ 83 84 85 86′ Large (200+ acres) v'yd renovated and enlarged since 1973. Admirable bourgeois wine. Ch Larrivaux-Hanteillan is second quality. 50,000 cases.

**Haut-Bages-Averous** Pauillac r. ★★ 81 82 83 84 85 86 The second wine of Ch LYNCH BAGES. Delicious easy drinking.

**Haut-Bages-Libéral** Pauillac r. ★★ 75 76 78 80 81 82′ 83 84 85 86′ Lesser-known fifth-growth of 64 acres in same stable as CHASSE-SPLEEN since '83. The auguries are excellent.

**Haut-Bages-Monpelou** Pauillac r. ★★ 75′ 76 78 79 80 81 82′ 83 84 85 86 25-acre Cru Bourgeois stable-mate of Ch BATAILLEY on former DUHART-MILON land. Good minor Pauillac.

**Haut-Bailly** Graves r. ★★★ 70′ 75 78 79′ 80 81′ 82 83 84 85 86 60+ acre est. at Léognan famous for ripe, round, intelligently made, sometimes "feminine" wine since '79. 2nd label: La Parde de H-B.

**Haut-Batailley** Pauillac r. ★★★ 70′ 75′ 78′ 79 80 81 82 83 84 85 86 The smaller section of the fifth-growth Batailley estate: 49 acres. Often in a gentler vein than its sister ch, GRAND-PUY-LACOSTE. 2nd label La Tour-d'Aspic.

**Haut-Brignon** lères Côtes r. & w. dr. ★ Big producer of standard wines at Cénac, owned by a major Champagne coop. Do not confuse with the next!

**Haut-Brion** Pessac, Graves r. (w.) ★★★★ 61 62 64 66 70′ 71′ 75′ 76 78′ 79 80 81′ 82′ 83 84 85′ 86 The oldest great ch of Bordeaux and the only non-Médoc first-growth of 1855. 108 acres. Reds of singular balance, particularly good since 1975. A little full dry white in 76 78 79 81 83 84 85 86. See also Bahans-Haut-Brion.

**Haut-Marbuzet** St-Estèphe r. ★★ 75′ 76 78′ 79 80 81 82′ 83 84 85 86 One of the best of many good St-Estèphe Crus Bourgeois. 100 acres. Ch'x Tour de Marbuzet, CHAMBERT-MARBUZET, MacCarthy-Moula in same hands. New oak gives them all classic style.

**Haut-Pontet**  St-Em. r. ★★ **70 71 75 78 79** 81 82' 83 85 86
12-acre v'yd of the Côtes well deserving its Grand Cru status.

**Haut-Quercus**  St-Em. r. ★★
Oak-aged cooperative wine to a very high standard.

**Haut-Sarpe**  St-Em. r. ▮▮ ★★▮ **78 79** 81 82 83' 85 86
Small Grand Cru Classé with a very fine château. Same owner as Ch LA CROIX. To follow.

**Haut-Ségottes**  St-Em. r. ★★ 85' 86
22-acre Grand Cru resolutely run. To watch.

**Hortevie**  St-Jul. r. ▮▮★★▮ 81 82 83 84 85' 86
One of the few St. Julien Crus Bourgeois. This tiny v'yd and its bigger sister, TERREY-GROS-CAILLOU, are shining examples.

**Houissant**  St-Estèphe r. ★★ 78 79 80 81 82 83 84 85 86
Typical, robust, well-balanced St-Estèphe Cru Bourgeois Exceptionnel, also called Ch Leyssac; well known in Denmark.

**d'Issan**  Cant-Mar. r. ▮★★★▮ 70 73' 75' 76' 78 79' 80 81 82' 83' 84 85 86'  Beautifully restored moated ch with 75-acre third-growth v'yd well known for fragrant, virile but delicate wine.

**Kirwan**  Cant-Mar. r. ▮★★★▮ 75' 76 78 79' 81 82' 83' 84 85 86
Well-run 86-acre third-growth owned by SCHRÖDER & SCHYLER. New planting of '60s now mature and results tasting v. good.

**Labégorce**  Margaux r. ★★ 75' 76 78 79 80 81' 82' 83' 84 85 86
Substantial 69-acre property north of Margaux with long-lived wines of true Margaux quality.

**Labégorce-Zédé**  Margaux r. ▮★★▮ 75' 76 78 79 80 81' 82' 83' 84 85 86
Outstanding Cru Bourgeois on the road n. from Margaux. 62 acres. Typical delicate, fragrant Margaux, truly classic since '81. The same family as VIEUX-CHÂTEAU-CERTAN.

**Lacoste-Borie**  The second wine of Ch GRAND-PUY-LACOSTE.

**Lafaurie-Peyraguey**  Sauternes w. sw. ★★★ 75' 76' 78' 80 81 82 83' 85 86  Fine classed-growth of only 49 acres at Bommes, belonging to CORDIER. After a lean patch, good, rich and racy wines.

---

## Arguments for and against Decanting

*Fierce arguments take place between wine-lovers over whether it is a good or a bad thing to decant wine from its bottle into a carafe. The argument in favour is that it allows the wine to "breathe" and its bouquet to expand: against, that its precious breath is dissipated – or at the least that it makes no difference.*

*Two additional practical reasons in favour concern old wine which has deposited dregs, which can be left in the bottle by careful decanting, and young wine being consumed before it is fully developed: thorough aeration helps to create the illusion of maturity. An aesthetic one is that decanters are handsome on the table.*

*Decanting is done by pouring the wine into another container very steadily until any sediment reaches the shoulder of the bottle. To see the sediment clearly hold the bottle's neck over a light-bulb or a candle.*

---

**Lafite-Rothschild**  Pauillac r. ▮★★★★▮ 61 70' 75' 76' 78 79 80 81' 82' 83 84 85 86  First-growth of fabulous style and perfume in its great vintages, which keep for decades. Off-form for several years but resplendent since '76. Amazing circular cellars opened '87. 2nd wine: MOULIN DES CARRUADES. 225 acres.

**Lafleur**  Pomerol r. ★★★ 70' 71' 73 75' 76 78 79 80 81 82' 83' 85 86
Property of 12 acres just n. of PÉTRUS. Excellent wine of the finer, less "fleshy" kind. Same owner as LE GAY. MOUEIX oenology.

**Lafleur-Gazin**  Pomerol r. ▮★★▮ 70 71' 75' 76' 78 79 81 82' 83 85
Distinguished small MOUEIX estate on the n.e. border of Pomerol.

**Lafon-Rochet**  St-Est. r. ★★ 70' 75' 78 79 81 82 83' 85 86
Fourth-growth neighbour of Ch COS D'ESTOURNEL, restored in the '60s. 110 acres. Rather hard, dark, full-bodied St-Estèphe. Same owner as Ch PONTET-CANET.

**Lagrange** Pomerol r. ★★★ 70′ 71′ 75′ 76 78 79 80 81 82′ 83 85′ 86
20-acre v'yd in the centre of Pomerol run by the ubiquitous house of MOUEIX. Maturing vines give ever deeper flavour.

**Lagrange** St-Jul. r. ★★★ 70′ 75′ 78 79′ 81 82 83′ 84 85 86′
Formerly run-down third-growth inland from St-Julien, bought by Suntory in 1982. 123+ acres, being extensively restored. To watch. Second label: Les Fiefs de Lagrange 83′ 85 86

**La Lagune** Ludon r. ★★★ 70′ 73′ 75′ 76′ 78′ 79 80 81 82′ 83 84 85 86
Well-run ultra-modern 160-acre third-growth in the extreme s. of the Médoc. Attractively rich and fleshy wines; usually brilliant quality.

**Lalande-Borie** St-Jul. r. ★★ 78 79 81 82 83 84 85 86
A baby brother of the great DUCRU-BEAUCAILLOU created from part of the former v'yd of Ch LAGRANGE.

**Lamarque** Lamarque (Haut-Médoc) r. ★★ 75′ 78 79 80 81′ 82 83′ 84 85′ 86′ Splendid medieval fortress of the central Médoc with 113 acres giving admirable and improving wine of high "Bourgeois" standard.

**Lanessan** Cussac (Haut-Médoc) r. ★★ 75′ 76 78′ 79 80 81 82′ 83 84 85 86′ Distinguished 108-acre Cru Bourgeois Exceptionnel just s. of St-Julien. Lots of flavour. Same owner as PICHON-LONGUEVILLE.

**Langoa-Barton** St-Jul. r. ★★★ 70′ 75′ 76 78′ 79 80 81 82′ 83 84 85 86 Fine 18th-century ch housing the wine of third-growth Langoa (49 acres) as well as second-growth LÉOVILLE-BARTON. The wines are similar: Langoa slightly less potent.

**Larcis-Ducasse** St-Em. r. ★★★ 70′ 71′ 75′ 76 78 79 81 82′ 83 84 85′ 86 The top property of St-Laurent, eastern neighbour of St-Emilion, on the Côtes next to Ch PAVIE. 30 acres. Coasting?

**Larmande** St-Em. r. ★★ 75′ 78 79 80 81 82 83 84 85 86
Substantial 54-acre property related to CAP-DE-MOURLIN. Replanted and now making rich, strikingly scented wine.

**Laroque** St-Em. r. ★★ 70′ 75′ 76′ 78 79 80 81 82′ 83 84 85 86
Important 108-acre v'yd with an impressive mansion on the St-Emilion côtes in St. Christophe.

**Larose-Trintaudon** St-Lau. (Haut-Médoc) r. ★★ 75′ 78 79 80 81 82 83 84 85 86′ The biggest v'yd in the Médoc: 388 acres. Modern methods make reliable fruity and charming Cru Bourgeois wine.

**Laroze** St-Em. r. ★★ 75′ 76 78′ 79 80 81 82 83 85 86
Big v'yd (74 acres) on the w. Côtes. Relatively light wines from sandy soil; soon enjoyable. Sometimes excellent.

**Larrivet-Haut-Brion** Graves r. (w.) ★★ 75′ 76 79′ 80 81 82′ 83 84 85 86 Little property at Léognan with perfectionist standards. 500 cases of white to age up to 5 years.

**Lascombes** Margaux r. (p.) ★★★ 61 70′ 75′ 78 79 81 82 83 84 85 86
240-acre second-growth owned by the British brewers Bass-Charrington and lavishly restored. After a poor patch, new vigour and skill since '82. Second wine: Ch Segonnes.

**Latour** Pauillac r. ★★★★ 61 62 64 66 67 70′ 71 73 75′ 76′ 77 78′ 79′ 80 81′ 82′ 83 84 85 86 First-growth. The most consistent great wine in Bordeaux, in France and probably the world: rich, intense and almost immortal in great years, almost always classic and pleasing even in bad ones. British-owned. 150 acres. Second wine: LES FORTS DE LATOUR.

**Latour à Pomerol** Pomerol r. ★★★★ 70′ 71′ 75′ 76′ 78 79′ 80′ 81 82′ 83 84 85 86 Top growth of 19 acres under MOUEIX management. Pomerol of great power and perfume, yet also ravishing finesse.

**Laujac** Médoc r. ★★ 75′ 78 81 82 83 85 86
Cru Bourgeois in the n. Médoc owned by the CRUSE family. Well known but scarcely outstanding. 62 acres.

**des Laurets** St-Em. r. ★★ 75′ 76 78 79 81 82 83 85 86
Major property of Puisseguin and Montagne-St-Emilion (to the e.) with 160 acres on the Côtes. Sterling wine.

**Laville-Haut-Brion** Graves w. dr. **** 71 75 78 79 81 82 83' 84 85 86 87 A tiny production of one of the very best white Graves for long maturing, made at Ch LA MISSION-HAUT-BRION.

**Léoville-Barton** St-Jul. r. *** 61 66 70' 75' 76 78' 79 80 81 82' 83 84 85 86 90-acre portion of the great second-growth Léoville v'yd in the Anglo-Irish hands of the Barton family for over 150 years. Powerful and classic claret, made by traditional methods at the Bartons' third-growth Ch LANGOA. Always moderately priced.

**Léoville-Las Cases** St-Jul. r. **** 61 66 70' 75' 76 78' 79 80 81 82' 83 84 85' 86' The largest portion of the old Léoville estate, 210 acres, with one of the highest reputations in Bordeaux. Elegant, complex, powerful but never heavy wines. Second label: Clos du Marquis.

**Léoville-Poyferré** St-Jul. r. *** 70' 75' 78' 79 80 81 82' 83 84 85 86' For years the least outstanding of the Léovilles; since 1980 again living up to the great name. '82 is a triumph and '86 even better. 156 acres. Second label: Ch Moulin-Riche.

**Lestage** Listrac r. ** 75' 76 78' 79 80 81 82' 83 84 85 86' 130-acre Cru Bourgeois in same hands as Ch FONRÉAUD. Light, quite stylish wine, aged in oak since '85.

**Liot** Barsac w. sw. ** 70' 71 75' 76 78 79' 80 81 83 85 86 Consistent fairly light golden wines from 94 acres.

**Liversan** St-Sau. (Haut-Médoc) r. ** 75' 78 79 80 81 82' 83 84 85 86' 116-acre Grand Cru Bourgeois inland from Pauillac. Change of regime in 1984 is greatly improving standards. Ch Fonpiqueyre is a second wine in certain markets.

**Livran** Médoc r. ** 75 76' 78' 79 81 82' 83 85 Big Cru Bourgeois at St-Germain in the n. Médoc. Consistent round wines (half Merlot).

**Loudenne** St-Yzans (Médoc) r. *** (r.) 75' 78' 79 81 82' 83 84 85 86' Beautiful riverside ch owned by Gilbeys since 1875. Well-made Cru Bourgeois red and a very agreeable dry white from 120 acres. The white is best at 2-3 years.

**Loupiac-Gaudiet** Loupiac w sw. ** Reliable source of good-value almost-Sauternes, just across the river Garonne.

**La Louvière** Graves r. and w. dr. ** (r.) 75 78 79 80 81 82' 83 84 85 86 Noble 135-acre estate at Léognan. Excellent white for drinking fresh or maturing, and red recently of classed-growth standard.

**de Lussac** St-Em. r. ** 75' 78' 79 81 82 83 85 86 One of the best estates in Lussac-St-Emilion (to the n.e.).

**Lynch-Bages** Pauillac r. *** 61 66 70 75' 76 78' 79 80 81 82' 83' 84 85 86 Always popular, but now one of Pauillac's regular stars. 200 acres making rich robust wine: deliciously brambly; occasionally great, with recent vintages esp. notable.

**Lynch-Moussas** Pauillac r. ** 75' 78 79 80 81 82' 83 84 85 86 Fifth-growth restored by the director of Ch BATAILLEY since 1969. Now 60+ acres and new equipment are making serious wine, gaining depth as the young vines age.

**du Lyonnat** Lussac-St-Em. r. ** 81 82 83 85 86' 120-acre estate with well-distributed reliable wine.

**Magdelaine** St-Em. r. *** 70' 71' 73 75' 76 78 79 80 81 82 83' 85' 86 Leading first-growth of the Côtes, 28 acres next to AUSONE owned by J-P MOUEIX. Beautifully balanced wine. On top form.

**Magence** Graves r. w. dr. ** (r.) w. dr. Go-ahead 45-acre property at St Pierre de Mons, in the s. of the Graves, well known for distinctly SAUVIGNON-flavoured very dry white that ages well, and fruity red for drinking in 4-6 yrs.

**Malartic-Lagravière**  Graves r. and (w. dr.) ★★★ (r.) 70′ 75′ 76′ 78 79
80 81 82′ 83 84 85 86′ (w.) 75 76 79 81′ 82 83 84 85 86 87
Well-known Léognan classed-growth of 34 acres making well-
structured red and a very little excellent fruity SAUVIGNON white, hard
to resist young, but worth cellaring.

**Malescasse**  Lamarque (Haut-Médoc) r. ★★ 75 78 79′ 80 81 82 83 85 86
Renovated Cru Bourgeois with 100 acres in a good situation, owned
by M. Tesseron of Ch LAFON-ROCHET.

**Malescot-St-Exupéry**  Margaux r. ★★★ 70′ 71 75′ 76 78′ 79′ 80 81
82′ 83′ 84 85 86  Third-growth of 84 acres. Long-lived, eventually
fragrant and stylish Margaux.

**de Malle**  Sauternes r. w. sw./dr. ★★★ (w. sw.). 75 76 78 79 80 81′ 82 83
85 86′  Famous and beautiful ch with Italian gdns. at Preignac. 124
acres. Good sweet and dry w. and r. (Graves) Ch de Cardaillan.

**de Malleret**  Haut-Médoc r. ★★ 82 83 84 85 86
Big well-run Cru Bourgeois with beautiful château and park at Le
Pian near Bordeaux. Reliable quality.

**Maquin-St-Georges**  St-Em. r. ★★ 79 81 82 83 85 86
Steady producer of delicious "satellite" St-Em. at St-Georges.

**de Marbuzet**  St-Est. r. ★★ 75 76 78 79 81 82 83 84 85 86
Effectively the second label of Ch COS D'ESTOURNEL, and correspondingly well made.

**Margaux**  Margaux r. (w. dr.) ★★★★ 61 66 70 78′ 79 80 81′ 82′ 83′
84 85′ 86′  First-growth (with 209 acres of vines), the most
resounding and fabulously perfumed of all in its best vintages.
"Pavillon Rouge" (79′ 80 81 82′ 83′ 84 85 86) is the second wine.
"Pavillon Blanc" is the best white (SAUVIGNON) wine of the Médoc, for 3-
4 years' ageing.

**Marquis-d'Alesme**  Margaux r. ★★ 70′ 75′ 78 79 80 81 82 83 84 85 86
Tiny (17-acre) third-growth, formerly made with Ch MALESCOT;
independent since '79. Finer than its reputation.

**Marquis-de-Terme**  Margaux r. ★★★ 70′ 75′ 76 79 80 81′ 82 83 85
Renovated fourth-growth of 84 acres. Fragrant, fairly lean wines.
Sells principally in France.

**Martinens**  Margaux r. ★★ 75 76 78′ 79′ 80 81 82 83 84 85 86
75-acre Cru Bourgeois at Cantenac, recently much improved.

**Maucaillou**  Moulis r. ★★ 70′ 75′ 76′ 78 79 80 81 82 83′ 84 85′ 86′
130-acre Cru Bourgeois with cru classé standards, property of
DOURTHE family. Full, richly fruity, "Cap de Haut-M." is second wine.

**Meyney**  St-Est. r. ★★→★★★ 75′ 78′ 79 80 81 82′ 83 84 85 86
Big (125-acre) riverside property next door to Ch MONTROSE, one of
many steady Crus Bourgeois in St-Estèphe. Owned by CORDIER. Second
label: Prieur de Meyney.

**Millet**  Graves r. w. dr. ★★ 78 79 81 82 83 85 86
160-acre estate at Portets; useful Graves.

**La Mission-Haut-Brion**  Graves r. ★★★★ 61 64 66 71′ 75′ 76 78′ 79 80
81 82′ 83 84 85′ 86  Neighbour and long-time rival to Ch HAUT-BRION,
since 1984 in the same hands. Serious and grand old-style claret for
long maturing. 30 acres. Ch Latour-H-B is its second-quality wine.

**Monbousquet**  St-Em. r. ★★ 75 76 78′ 79′ 80 81 82 83 84 85 86
Fine 75-acre estate in the Dordogne valley below St-Emilion. Attractive early-maturing wine from deep gravel soil lasts well.

**Montrose**  St-Est. r. ★★★ 61 66 70′ 75′ 76 78 79′ 80 81 82′ 83 84 85
86′  158-acre family-run second-growth well known for deeply
coloured, forceful, old-style claret. But recent vintages are lighter.
2nd wine: La Dame de Montrose.

**Moulin-à-Vent**  Moulis r. ★★ 70′ 75′ 78′ 79 80 81 82′ 83 84 85 86
60-acre property now in the forefront of this up-and-coming appellation. Lively, forceful wine. La Tour Blanche (Médoc) has same owners.

**Moulin des Carruades**   The second-quality wine of Ch LAFITE.

**Moulin du Cadet**   St-Em.   ★★ 71' 75' 76 78' 79 80 81 82' 83 85 86
First-class little v'yd on the Côtes managed by MOUEIX.

**Moulinet**   Pomerol r.   ★★★ 75 76 78 79 81 82 83 85 86
One of Pomerol's bigger ch'x, 43 acres on lightish soil; wine ditto.

**Mouton-Baronne-Philippe**   Pauillac r.   ★★★ 70' 75' 76 78' 79 81 82' 83
84 85 86   Substantial fifth-growth nurtured by the late Baron
Philippe de Rothschild. 125 acres making fine but much gentler, less
rich and tannic wine than MOUTON.

**Mouton-Rothschild**   Pauillac r.   ★★★★ 61 66 67 70' 71 73 75' 76 78'
79 80 81 82' 83 84 85 86'   Officially a first-growth since 1973, though
for 20 years worthy of the title. 175 acres (87% CABERNET SAUVIGNON)
making wine of majestic richness (82 and 86 are Imperial). Also the
world's greatest museum of works of art relating to wine. Baron
Philippe, the greatest champion of the Médoc, died in 1988.

**Nairac**   Sauternes w. sw.   ★★ 73 75 76' 78 79 80 81 82 83' 85 86'
Barsac classed-growth with perfectionist owner. Fascinating wines to
lay down.

**Nenin**   Pomerol r.   ★★★ 70' 75' 78 81 83 85 86
Well-known 66-acre estate; currently below par.

**Olivier**   Graves r. and w. dr.   ★★★ (r.) 79' 81 82 83 84 85 86
90-acre classed-growth, surrounding a moated castle at Léognan.
9,000 cases r., 12,000 w., both in need of a promised upgrade. Recent
wines are intended for longer maturing.

**Les Ormes-de-Pez**   St-Est. r.   ★★ 75' 76 78' 79 80 81' 82' 83' 84 85 86'
Outstanding 72-acre Cru Bourgeois managed by Ch LYNCH BAGES.
Increasingly notable full-flavoured St-Estèphe.

**Les Ormes Sorbet**   Medoc r.   ★★ 78 79 81 82 83 85 86'
Emerging smaller producer of good solid red aged in new oak at
Couquèques. 2nd label: Ch de Conques.

**Palmer**   Cant-Mar. r.   ★★★★ 61' 66' 70 71' 75' 76 78' 79' 80 81 82 83'
84 85 86   The star ch of CANTENAC; a third-growth often on a level just
below the first-growths. Wine of power, flesh and delicacy. 110 acres
with Dutch, British and French owners. 2nd wine: Réserve du
Général.

**Pape-Clément**   Graves r. and (w. dr.)   ★★★ 70 75' 78' 79' 80 81 82' 83 84
85' 86   Ancient v'yd at Pessac, with record of seductive, scented reds,
but recent vintages less even. New resolve since '85.

**Patache d'Aux**   Bégadan (Médoc) r.   ★★ 75' 78 79' 80 81 82' 83' 85 86'
90-acre Cru Bourgeois of the n. Médoc. Fragrant, lightish wine.

**Paveil-de Luze**   Margaux r.   ★★ 75' 76' 78 79 81 82' 83 84 85 86'
Old family estate at Soussans. Small but highly regarded.

**Pavie**   St-Em. r.   ★★★ 70 71' 75' 76 78 79' 80 81 82' 83' 84 85' 86
Splendidly sited first-growth of 100 acres on the slope of the Côtes.
Typically rich and tasty St-Em., particularly since '82. The family
owns the smaller Ch'x Pavie-Decesse and La Clusière.

**Pavie-Decesse**   St-Em. r.   ★★

**Pavie-Macquin**   St-Em. r.   ★★ 75 76 78 79 82 83 85' 86
Reliable 25-acre Côtes v'yd e. of St-Emilion. Replanting and enlarg-
ing.

**Pedesclaux**   Pauillac r.   ★★ 70' 71 75' 76 78 79 80 81 82' 83 84 85 86
50-acre fifth-growth on the level of a good Cru Bourgeois. Solid strong
wines loved by Belgians. Grand-Duroc-Milon and Bellerose are
second labels.

**Petit-Village**   Pomerol r.   ★★★ 70 71' 75' 76' 78 79 80 81 82' 83 84 85 86
One of the best-known little properties: 26 acres next to VIEUX-CH-
CERTAN, same owner as Ch COS D'ESTOURNEL. Powerful plummy wine.

**Pétrus**   Pomerol r.   ★★★★ 61 64 66 67 70' 71' 73 75' 76' 78 79' 80 81 82'
83 84 85' 86   The great name of Pomerol. 28 acres of gravelly clay
giving the world's most massively rich and concentrated wine. 95%
Merlot vines. Each vintage adds lustre. The price, too, is legendary.

**Peyrabon**  St. Sauveur r. ▓ ★★  75 78 79 80 81 82 83 84 85 86
Serious 82-acre Cru Bourgeois popular in the Low Countries.

**Peyreau**  St-Em. r. ★★
Sister-ch of CLOS L'ORATOIRE.

**de Pez**  St-Est. r. ▓ ★★★  66 70′ 71′ 73 75′ 76 78′ 79 80 81 82′ 83 84 85
86  Outstanding Cru Bourgeois of 60 acres. As reliable as any of the
classed growths of the village, and nearly as fine. Needs v. long
storage. (e.g. '66 was ideal in '88.)

**Phélan-Ségur**  St-Est. r. ▓ ★★  70′ 75′ 76′ 78 79 80 81 82′ 85 86
Big and important Cru Bourgeois (125 acres) with some fine old
vintages. New owners in 1985 have put their foot down hard.

**Pichon-Longueville (Baron)**  Pauillac r. ▓ ★★★  70′ 75 76 78′ 79′ 80 81
82′ 83 84 85 86′  77-acre second-growth whose wines have varied
widely. Under new management since '87.                                    ⑧ₓ

**Pichon-Longueville, Comtesse de Lalande**  Pauillac r. ▓ ★★★★  61 66
70′ 75′ 76 78′ 79′ 80 81′ 82′ 83′ 84 85 86  Second-growth neighbour
to Ch LATOUR. 148 acres. Consistently among the very top performers;
classic long-lived wine of fabulous breed, even in lesser years. 2nd
wine: Réserve de la Comtesse.

**Pique-Caillou**  Graves r. ★★
Little-known 40-acre neighbour of HAUT-BRION in the Bordeaux
suburbs. Worth watching.

**Pindefleurs**  St-Em. r. ★★ 75 76 78 79 81 82′ 83 85 86
Up and coming 25-acre v'yd on the St-Emilion plateau.

**Piron**  Graves (r) w. dr. ▓
Producer of seductively fruity modern white Graves at St. Morillon.

**de Pitray**  Castillon r. ★★ 78 79 80 81 82 83 85 86
Substantial (62-acre) v'yd on the Côtes de Castillon e. of St-Emilion.
Good light wines

**Plagnac**  Médoc r. ★★
Cru bourgeois at Bégadan restored by Cordier, owners of GRUAUD-
LAROSE, etc.

**Plince**  Pomerol r. ★★ 75 76 78 79 80 81 82 83 85 86
Reputable 20-acre property near Libourne. Attractive, perhaps
rather simple wine from sandy soil.

**La Pointe**  Pomerol r. ★★★ 70′ 75′ 78 79 81 82 83′ 85 86
Prominent 63-acre estate, well made, but relatively spare of flesh. Ch
LA SERRE is in the same hands.

**Pontac-Monplaisir**  Graves r. (w. dr.) ★★
Another Graves property suddenly offering delicious white.

**Pontet-Canet**  Pauillac r. ★★★ 70 75′ 76 78′ 79′ 80 81′ 82′ 83′ 85 86
One of the biggest classed-growths. 182 acres, neighbour to MOUTON,
potentially better than its official rank of fifth-growth, but dragged its
feet for years. Current owners (same as LAFON-ROCHET) are trying
hard. 2nd label: Les Hauts de Pontet.

**Potensac**  Potensac (Médoc) r. ▓ ★★  75′ 76 78′ 79 80 81′ 82′ 83 84 85′
86  The best-known Cru Bourgeois of the n. Médoc. The neighbouring Ch'x Lassalle and Gallais-Bellevue belong to the same family, the
Delons, owners of LÉOVILLE-LASCASES. Class shows.

**Pouget**  Margaux ★★ 70′ 75 76 78 79 80 81 82′ 83 85 86
19-acre v'yd attached to Ch BOYD-CANTENAC. In 1983 separate chais
were built. Similar, rather lighter, wines.

**Poujeaux (Theil)**  Moulis r. ▓ ★★  70′ 75′ 76 78 79′ 80 81 82′ 83′ 84 85
86  Family-run Cru Exceptionnel of 120 acres selling its powerful,
concentrated wine largely direct to an appreciative French public.
2nd label: La Salle de Poujeaux. Also Ch Arnauld (83′).

**Prieuré-Lichine**  Cant-Mar. r. ▓ ★★★  70 75 76 78′ 79′ 80 81 82′ 83′ 84
85 86′  143-acre fourth-growth brought to the fore by Alexis Lichine
since 1952. Excellent full-bodied and fragrant Margaux.

**Puy-Blanquet**  St-Em. r. ✶✶ **75' 76 78 79 81 82' 83 85**

    The major property of St-Etienne-de-Lisse, e. of St-Emilion, with over 50 acres. Typical full St-Em., if below the top class.

**Puy-Razac**  St-Em. r. ✶✶ **75 76 78 79 80 81' 82' 83 85 86**

    Tiny brother to MONBOUSQUET at the foot of the Côtes near Ch PAVIE.

**Puygueraud**  Côte de Francs r. ✶✶ **82 83 85**

    Leading ch of this rising district. Wood-aged wines of surprising class.

**Rabaud-Promis**  Sauternes w. sw. ✶✶ **71 75 76 78 79 81 83 85**

    74-acre classed-growth at Bommes. Little seen outside France.

**Rahoul**  Graves r. and w. dr. ✶✶ (r.) **78' 79 81 82 83 84 85 86** (w.) **84 85 86' 87**  37-acre v'yd at Portets making particularly good wine from maturing vines; 80% red. White is aged in oak, too. Same Danish winemaker as DOMAINE LA GRAVE.

**Ramage-la-Batisse**  Haut-Médoc r. ✶✶ **75' 76 78 79 80 81 82 83' 85**

    Outstanding Cru Bourgeois of 130 acres at St-Sauveur, west of Pauillac. Increasingly attractive since '80.

**Rausan-Ségla**  Margaux r. ✶✶✶ **61 70' 78 79 81 82 83' 84 85 86'**

    106-acre second-growth; famous for its fragrance; a great Médoc name trying hard to regain its rank. Owned by ESCHENAUER.

**Rauzan-Gassies**  Margaux r. ✶✶ **61 75' 76 78' 79' 80 81 82 83 85 86**

    75-acre second-growth neighbour of the last with little excitement to report for two decades, now seemingly perking up.

**Raymond-Lafon**  Sauternes w. sw. ✶✶✶ **75 76 78 79 80' 81' 82 83' 85 86'**  Serious Sauternes estate run by the manager of Ch D'YQUEM. Splendid wines for long ageing. Among the top Sauternes today.

**de Rayne-Vigneau**  Sauternes w. sw. ✶✶✶ **67 71' 76' 78 81 83 85 86**

    164-acre classed-growth at Bommes. Standard sweet wine and a little dry "Raynesec". New equipment in 1985.

**Respide-Médeville**  Graves (r.) w. dr. ✶✶ (w.) **81 82 83 84' 85 86 87**

    One of the best white-wine ch'x. Full-flavoured wines for ageing.

**Reynon**  lères Côtes de Bordeaux r. and w. dr. ✶✶

    100 acres producing extraordinary dry white from very old Sauvignon vines ("Vieilles Vignes": **83' 84 85 86 87**). Also "Clos Floridène" barrel-fermented white (**84 85 86 87'**) and red since '85, D.Y.A. white and serious red (**79 81 82 83 85 86**).

**Reysson**  Vertheuil Haut-Médoc r. ✶✶ **81 82' 83 84 85 86**

    Recently replanted, up-and-coming 120-acre Cru Bourgeois with the same owners as Ch CHASSE-SPLEEN.

**Ricaud**  Loupiac w. sw. (or dr.) or r. ✶✶ **81 82 83' 85 86'**

    Substantial grower of Sauternes-like dessert wine, just across the river. New owners are working hard.

**Rieussec**  Sauternes w. sw. ✶✶✶ **70 71' 75' 76' 78 79 80 81' 82 83' 85 86**  Worthy neighbour of Ch D'YQUEM with 136 acres in Fargues, bought in 1984 by the (Lafite) Rothschilds. Not the sweetest; can be exquisitely fine. Also a dry wine: "R"; and super-wine: "Crême de Tête".

**Ripeau**  St-Em. r. ✶✶ **75 78 79 81 82 83 85 86**

    Increasingly high-performance Grand Cru in the centre of the plateau. 49 acres.

**La Rivière**  Fronsac r. ✶✶

    The biggest and most impressive Fronsac property. Tannic wines repay long ageing.

**de Rochemorin**  Graves r. (w. dr.) ✶✶ **81 82 83 84 85 86**

    An important restoration at Martillac by the owner of Ch LA LOUVIÈRE. 135 acres of new vines promise great things.

**Romer du Hayot**  Sauternes w. sw. ✶✶ **79 80 81 82 83 85 86'**

    A minor classed-growth with a growing reputation.

**Roquetaillade-la-Grange**  Graves r. w. dr. ✶✶

    Substantial estate establishing a name for fine red (s.) Graves.

**Roudier** Montagne-St-Em. r. **★★**
75-acre "satellite" St-Em. with the flavour of the real thing. Sister-ch of BALESTARD. To follow.

**Rouget** Pomerol r. **★★ 70 71 75′ 76′ 78 79 81 82′ 83 85′ 86**
Attractive old estate with rising standards on the n. edge of Pomerol. Good vintages need 10 years +.

**Royal St-Emilion** Brand name of the important and dynamic growers' cooperative. See also Haut Quercus, Berliquet.

**Ruat-Petit-Poujeaux** Moulis r. **★★ 79 80 81 82 83 84 85 86**
45-acre v'yd gaining in reputation for sound wine.

**St-André Corbin** St-Emilion r. **★★ 75′ 76′ 78 79′ 81 82′ 83 85 86**
Considerable 54-acre property in Montagne-St-Emilion with a long record of above-average wines.

**St. Bonnet** Médoc r. **★★**
Big n. Médoc estate at St. Christoly. V. flavoury wine.

**St-Estèphe, Marquis de** St-Est. r. **★ 81 82 83 84 85 86**
The growers' co-operative; over 200 members. Good value.

**St-Georges** St-Geo., St-Em. r. **★★ 70 75 76 78 79 80 81 82 83 85 86**
Noble 18th-century ch overlooking the St-Emilion plateau from the hill to the n. 125 acres; v. good wine sold direct to the public.

**St-Georges-Côte-Pavie** St. Em. r. **★★ 79 81 82 83′ 85′ 86**
Perfectly placed little v'yd on the Côtes. To watch.

**Saint-Pierre** St-Jul. r. **★★★ 70′ 71 75′ 76 78′ 79 80 81′ 82′ 83′ 84 85 86**
Small (50-acre) fourth-growth many years in Belgian ownership; bought in 1982 by Henri Martin of Ch GLORIA. A name to watch.

**St-Pierre** Graves (r.) w. dr. **★★ 81 84 85 86 87**
Estate at St Pierre de Mons making classic Graves of notable character and flavour.

**de Sales** Pomerol r. **★★★ 70′ 75′ 76′ 78′ 79 80 81 82′ 83 85 86**
The biggest v'yd of Pomerol (116 acres), attached to the grandest château. Not poetry but certainly excellent prose. Second labels: Ch Chantalouette and Ch du Delias.

**Sénéjac** Haut-Médoc r. (w. dr.) **★★ 75 76′ 78 79 80 81 82′ 83′ 84 85 86′**
43-acre Cru Bourgeois in s. Médoc run with increasing skill.

**La Serre** St-Em. r. **★★ 70 75′ 78 79 80 81 82 83 85 86**
Well-run small Grand Cru with same owner as LA POINTE.

**Sigalas-Rabaud** Sauternes w. sw. **★★★ 76′ 78 79 81 82 83′ 85 86**
The lesser part of the former Rabaud estate: 34 acres in Bommes, making first-class sweet wine in a fresh, grapey style.

**Siran** Lab-Mar. r. **★★★ 61 66 70 71′ 75′ 78′ 79 80 81′ 82′ 83 84 85 86**
74-acre property of Cru Classé quality. Elegant, long-lived wines, consistently well made.

**Smith-Haut-Lafitte** Graves r. and (w. dr.) **★★→★★★ (r.) 78 79 81 82′ 83 84 85 86 (w: age 2-3 years.)** Run-down old classed-growth at Martillac restored by ESCHENAUER in the '60s and '70s. 122 acres (14 of white). The white wine is light and fruity; the red light. Recent efforts should improve it.

**Sociando-Mallet** Haut-Médoc r. **★★ 70 75 76 78 79 81 82 83 84 85 86**
Splendid Cru Grand Bourgeois at St-Seurin in the n. 65 acres. Dark dense wine for the patient.

**Soutard** St-Em. r. **★★ 70′ 71 75′ 76 78′ 79 80 81 82′ 83 85′ 86**
Reliable 48-acre classed-growth n. of the town. Some vintages have been a bit "butch". A long-term keeper.

**Suduiraut** Sauternes w. sw. **★★★ 67 70 76′ 78 79′ 80 81 82′ 83 84 85 86** One of the best Sauternes – though rarely super-rich. Over 173 acres of the top class, under capable new management. Selection: Cuvée Madame (82, 85).

**Taillefer** Pomerol r. **★★ 70 75 76 78 79 81 82′ 83 85 86**
24-acre property on the edge of Pomerol owned by another branch of the MOUEIX family. Give it time.

**Talbot**  St-Jul. r. (w.)  ★★★  70' 71 75' 76 78' 79 80 81 82' 83 84 85 86
Important 240-acre fourth-growth, sister-ch to GRUAUD-LAROSE, wine similarly attractive: rich, satisfying, reliable and good value. (V.g.) second label: Connétable Talbot. A little white is called "Caillou Blanc".

**Tayac**  Sou-Mar. r.  ★★  81 82 83 85 86
Margaux's biggest Cru Bourgeois. Reliable if not noteworthy.

**Terrefort-Quancard**  Bordeaux r. w. dr.  ★  78 79 80 81 82 83 84 85 86
Huge producer of good value wines at St-André-de-Cubzac. Rocky sub-soil contributes to surprising quality. 33,000 cases.

**du Tertre**  Ar-Mar. r.  ★★★  70' 75 76 78 79' 80 81 82' 83' 84 85 86
Fifth-growth, isolated s. of Margaux; restored to excellence by the owner of CALON-SÉGUR. Fragrant and long-lived.

**Tertre-Daugay**  St-Em. r.  ★★★  78 79 81 82' 83' 85 86
Small, spectacularly sited, Grand Cru. Restored to its proper place since purchase in '78 by the owner of LA GAFFELIÈRE.

**Thieuley**  E-deux-M r. p. w. dr.  ★★
Substantial competent supplier, esp. of "clairet" (rosé) and grapey SAUVIGNON.

**Timberlay**  Bordeaux r. (w. dr.)  ★  81 82 83 84 85 86
The biggest property of Cubzac; 185 acres. Pleasant light wines.

**Toumilon**  Graves r. w. dr  ★★
Notable ch in St. Pierre de-Mons. Fresh and charming r. and w.

**La Tour-Blanche**  Sauternes w. sw. (r.)  ★★★  75' 76 78 79 81' 83' 85 86
Top-rank 57-acre estate at Bommes with a state wine-growing school. Not among the leaders for a long time. But '83 is v.g.

**La Tour-Carnet**  St-Lau. r.  ★★  75' 78 79 80 81 82' 83 84 85 86
Fourth-growth reborn from total neglect in the '60s. Medieval tower with 79 acres just w. of St-Julien. Lightish, pretty wine.

**La Tour de By**  Bégadan (Médoc) r.  ★★  75' 76 78' 79' 80 81 82' 83 84 85 86  Very well-run 144-acre Cru Bourgeois in the n. Médoc steadily increasing its reputation for sturdy, impressive yet appealing wine.

**La Tour-de-Mons**  Sou-Mar r.  ★★  70' 71' 78 79 80 81 82' 83 85 86
Distinguished Cru Bourgeois of 75 acres, three centuries in the same family. Sometimes excellent claret with a long life.

**La Tour-du-Pin-Figeac**  St-Em. r.  ★★
26-acre Grand Cru worthy of restoration.

**La Tour-du-Pin-Figeac-Moueix**  St-Em. r.  ★★★  78 79 81 82 83 85 86
Another 26-acre section of the same old property, owned by a branch of the famous MOUEIX family. Looking very good.

**La Tour-Figeac**  St-Em. r.  ★★  70 75 78 79 80 81 82' 83 85 86
34-acre Grand Cru between Ch FIGEAC and Pomerol, not quite showing the form that such a site suggests.

**La Tour-Haut-Brion**  Graves r.  ★★★  70 75 76 78 79 80 81 82' 83 85 86
The second label of Ch LA MISSION-HAUT-BRION. Up to '83 a plainer, very tannic wine for long life. Now more accessible.

**La Tour-Martillac**  Graves r. and w. dr.  ★★  (r.) 75' 78 79 81 82' 83 84 85 86  Small but serious property at Martillac. 10 acres of white grapes; 37 of black. The white can age admirably. The owner, Jean Kressmann, is resurrecting the neighbouring Ch Lespault.

**La Tour St-Bonnet**  Médoc r.  ★★  75' 78' 79 80 81 82' 83 85 86
Consistently well-made and typical n. Médoc from St-Christoly. 100 acres.

**La Tour du Haut Moulin**  Cussac (Haut-Médoc) r.  ★★  78 79 80 81 82 83 84 85 86  Little-known 70-acre property; concentrated wines to age.

**Tournefeuille**  Lalande de Pomerol r.  ★★  75' 76' 78 79 81' 82' 83' 85 86  The star of Néac, overlooking Pomerol from the n. A small property (43 acres), but excellent long-lived wine.

**des Tours** Montagne-St-Em. r. ★★ 75′ 78 79 81 82 83 85 86
Spectacular ch with modern 170-acre v'yd. Sound, easy wine.

**Toutigeac, Domaine de** Entre-Deux-Mers r. (w. dr) ★
Enormous producer of useful Bordeaux at Targon.

**Tronquoy-Lalande** St-Est. r. ★★ 70 71 75 76 78 79 80 81 82′ 83 85
40-acre Cru Bourgeois making typical high-coloured St-Estèphe
needing long ageing. Distributed by DOURTHE.

**Troplong-Mondot** St-Em. r. ██ 70′ 71′ 75′ 78 79 81 82′ 83 85 86
One of the bigger Grand Crus of St-Emilion. 70 acres well sited on the
Côtes above Ch PAVIE. To watch.

**Trotanoy** Pomerol r. ████ 61 70′ 71′ 73 75′ 76′ 78 79 80 81 82′ 83
84 85 86′ Perhaps the 2nd Pomerol after PÉTRUS, from the same
stable. Only 27 acres but a glorious, fleshy, perfumed wine.

**Trottevieille** St-Em. r. ★★★ 70 75′ 79′ 81 82′ 83 85 86
Grand Cru of 27 acres on the Côtes e. of the town. Dragged its feet for
years. '83 '85 '86 look better. Same owners as BATAILLEY.

**Le Tuquet** Graves r. and w. dr. ★★ 78 79 81 82 83 85 86
Big estate at Beautiran. Light fruity wines; the white better.

**Verdignan** Médoc r. ██ 75 78 79 80 81 82 83 85 86
Substantial Grand Bourgeois sister property to Ch COUFRAN. More
Cabernet than Coufran; Jack Sprat and his wife.

**Vieux-Château-Certan** Pomerol r. ███ 75 78 79 80 81 82 83 84 85
86 Traditionally rated close to PÉTRUS in quality, but totally different
in style; almost Médoc build. 34 acres. Same (Belgian) family owns
LABEGORCE-ZÉDÉ and another tiny Pomerol, Le Pin.

**Vieux-Château-Landon** Médoc r. ★★ 81 82 83 85 86
Up-to-date grower of vigorous wine worth keeping 3-4 years.

**Vieux-Château-St-André** St-Emilion r. ██ 75′ 76′ 78 79′ 81 82′ 83
85′ 86 Small v'yd in Montagne-St-Emilion owned by the leading
wine-maker of Libourne. To follow. 2,500 cases.

**Villegeorge** Avensan r. ██ 75′ 78′ 79 81 82 83′ 85 86
24-acre Cru Exceptionnel to the n. of Margaux with the same owner
as Ch BRANE-CANTENAC. Enjoyable full-bodied wine.

**Villemaurine** St-Em. r. ██ 70′ 75′ 76 78 79′ 80 81 82′ 83 84 85′ 86
Small Grand Cru with splendid cellars well sited on the Côtes by the
town. Firm wine with a high proportion of Cabernet. Recently v.g.

**Vraye-Croix-de-Gay** Pomerol ★★★ 70′ 71′ 75′ 76 78 79 81 82′ 83 85 86
Very small ideally situated v'yd in the best part of Pomerol.

**Yon-Figeac** St-Em. r. ██ 79 81 82 83 85 86
59-acre Grand Cru to follow for savoury and scented wine.

**d'Yquem** Sauternes w. sw. (dr.) ★★★★ 67′ 71′ 73 75′ 76′ 77 78 79 80 81
82 83′ 84 The world's most famous sweet-wine estate. 250 acres
making only 500 bottles per acre of very strong, intense, luscious
wine kept 4 years in barrel. Most vintages improve for at least 15 yrs.
Also dry "Ygrec" in 78 79 80 84 85

---

More Bordeaux châteaux worth noting are listed under Canon-Fronsac,
Côtes de Bourg, Cubzac, Fronsac, Côtes-de-Castillon, Lalande de Pomerol,
Loupiac, Ste-Croix-du-Mont, Premières Côtes de Blaye, Premières Côtes de
Bordeaux in the A-Z of France, pages 26-55.

# Italy

Italian wine on the threshold of the 1990s is in a revolutionary state. The 30-year-old DOC system, the basis of the country's wine-laws, is more or less discredited. Its original purpose, of defining Italy's myriad wine-making traditions, is increasingly seen more as hindrance than help when most of the best wine-makers are experimenting with untraditional ideas, grape varieties and techniques.

A Denominazione di Origine Controllata (DOC) was granted by the government in Rome to any grower or growers who could plead convincingly for a distinctive regional style and claim that it was "traditional". Once in place, a DOC stultifies progress – and has very little bearing on quality. Most regions can make more attractive (and saleable) wine by adopting the international top-selling grape varieties than by persisting with Italy's indigenous but often degenerate types. Sangiovese and the rest can be very good; but it takes time and trouble to select and propagate the best vines. So to plant Cabernet is a short-cut.

Ironically the only appellation available to non-DOC wines, however good, is the most basic of all: vino da tavola, or plain table wine. The confidence of good growers in their new products is such that they wear this apparent stigma as a talisman. In these circumstances it is the maker's name that matters most.

Meanwhile the DOC system remains, for all its faults, the only general key to the Italian wine maze. It is the approximate equivalent of France's Appellations Contrôlées. Most of Italy's traditional wines have defined areas and standards under the system. A few, like Chianti Classico, it must be said, had them long before. An increasing number, however, have not – and DOCs have been granted to many areas of only local interest: so the mere existence of a DOC proves little. The entries in this book ignore a number of unimportant DOCs and include considerably more non-DOCs. They also include a larger number of grape-name entries.

Italian wines are named in a variety of ways: some geographical like French wines, some historical, some folklorical, and many of the best from their grapes. These include old "native" grapes such as Barbera and Sangiovese and more and more imported "international" grapes from France and Germany. Many of the DOCs, particularly in the north-east, are area names applying to widely different wines from more than a dozen different varieties. No overall comment on the quality of such a diversity is really possible, except to say that general standards are rising steadily and a growing number of producers are emerging as outstanding by international standards.

The single most important fact for buyers of Italian wine in 1989 is the quality of the two vintages that are now generally in circulation. 1985 and 1986 were years to please almost everyone.

The map is the key to the province names used for locating each entry. The following abbreviations are used in the text.

| | | | |
|---|---|---|---|
| **Abr.** | Abruzzi | **Camp.** | Campania |
| **Apu.** | Apulia | **Em-Ro.** | Emilia-Romagna |
| **Bas.** | Basilicata | | |
| **Cal.** | Calabria | **Fr-VG.** | Fruili-Venezia-Giulia |

| | |
|---|---|
| **Lat.** | Latium |
| **Lig.** | Liguria |
| **Lom.** | Lombardy |
| **Mar.** | Marches |
| **M.** | Molise |
| **Piem.** | Piemonte |
| **Sard.** | Sardinia |
| **Sic.** | Sicily |
| **Tr-Aad.** | Trentino-Alto-Adige |
| **Tusc.** | Tuscany |
| **Umbr.** | Umbria |
| **V d'A.** | Valle d'Aosta |
| **Ven.** | Veneto |

**Abbazia di Rosazzo** Leading estate of COLLI ORIENTALI. White Ronco delle Acacie and red Ronco dei Roseti are v.g. single v'yd wines.

**Abboccato** Semi-sweet.

**Adanti** Maker of v.g. Sagrantino di MONTEFALCO; also v.d.t. Rosso d'Arquata, outstanding BARBERA/Canaiolo/MERLOT blend.

**Aglianico del Vulture** Bas. DOC r. (s/sw. sp.) ■ ★★★ 75 77 78 79 81 82 85 86 87 Among the best wines of s. Italy. Ages well to rich aromas. Called Vecchio after 3 yrs, Riserva after 5. Top grower: Fratelli D'Angelo.

**Alba** Major wine-centre of PIEMONTE.

**Albana di Romagna** Em-Ro. DOCG w. dr. s/sw. (sp.) ★★★ 86 87 Produced for several centuries in Romagna from Albana grapes. Absurdly Italy's first DOCG for white wine. Cold fermentation now robs it of much character. Fattoria PARADISO makes some of the best.

**Alcamo** Sic. DOC w. dr. ★ Soft neutral whites from w. Sicily. Rapitalà is the best brand.

**Aleatico** Red, slightly muscat-flavoured grape, chiefly of the south.

**Aleatico di Gradoli** Lat. DOC r. sw. or f. ★★ Aromatic, fruity; alcohol 17.5%. Made near Viterbo.

**Aleatico di Puglia** Apu. DOC r. sw. or f. ★★ Aleatico grapes make good dessert wine over a large area. Two distinct types have 15% or 18.5% alcohol.

**Alezio** Apu. DOC (r.) p. dr. ★★ 83 85 86 87 Recent Salento DOC, esp. for powerful Negroamaro rosé.

**Allegrini** High-quality producer of Veronese wines, incl. VALPOLICELLA.

**Alto Adige** Tr-Aad. DOC r. p. w. dr. sw. sp. ★★→★★★ A DOC covering some 19 different wines, usually named after their grape varieties, in 33 villages around Bolzano.

**Ama, Castello di** Modern CHIANTI CLASSICO estate nr. Gaiole. San Lorenzo is excellent top wine.

**Amabile** Semi-sweet, but usually sweeter than ABBOCCATO.

**Amaro** Bitter. When prominent on a label the contents is a "bitters", not a wine.

**Amarone** See Recioto.

**Anselmi, Roberto** A leader in SOAVE with his single v'yd Capitel Foscarino and exceptional sweet dessert RECIOTO dei Capitelli.

**Antinori** A long-established Tuscan house of the highest repute producing first-rate CHIANTI and ORVIETO, now also distinguished for pioneering new v.d.t. styles: e.g. TIGNANELLO, SOLAIA, CASTELLO DELLA SALA, PEPPOLI. See also Sassicaia.

**Arneis** Piem. w. dr. ★★ D.Y.A. Revival of this ancient wine is much in vogue. DOC under Roero, a zone n. of Alba, is imminent. Good producers incl. Bruno GIACOSA, Castello di Neive, Blangé (Ceretto), Montebertotto.

**Artimino** Ancient hill-town w. of Florence, known for its DOC CARMIGNANO.

**Assisi** Umbr. r. (w. dr.) ■ ★★ D.Y.A. Rosso di Assisi is a very attractive new red v.d.t. Drink young and cool. BIANCO is also good.

**Asti** Major wine-centre of PIEMONTE.

**Asti Spumante** Piem. DOC w. sp. ★★★ NV Sweet and very fruity muscat sparkling wine. Low in alcohol.

**Avignonesi** MONTEPULCIANO estate with range of good wines incl. VINO NOBILE, blended red Grifi, and superlative VIN SANTO.

**Azienda agricola (or agraria)** A farm producing crops, often incl. wine.

**Azienda vinicola or casa vinicola** Wine firm using primarily bought-in grapes.

**Azienda vitivinicola** A (specialized) wine estate.

**Badia a Coltibuono** 71 75 78 79 80 81 82 83 85 86 87 Fine Chianti-maker at Gaiole with a restaurant and remarkable collection of old vintages. Also fine v.d.t. "Sangioveto" 80 81 82 83 85 86 87

**Banfi**  See Villa Banfi.

**Barbacarlo (Oltrepò Pavese)**  Lomb. DOC r. dr. or sw. sp. ★★→★★★ 82 83 85 86  Delicate wines with slightly bitter after-taste from Broni.

**Barbaresco**  Piem. DOCG r. dr. ★★★→★★★★ 71 74 78 79 80 82 83 85 86 87  Neighbour of BAROLO from the same grapes but lighter, ageing sooner. At best subtle and fine. At 4 yrs becomes Riserva. Best producers incl. GAJA, Bruno GIACOSA, Marchesi di Gresy, Produttori del B, Castello di Neive.

**Barbera**  Dark acidic red grape, a speciality of Piemonte also used in Lombardy, Emilia-Romagna and other northern provinces. Its best wines are:

**Barbera d'Alba**  Piem. DOC r. dr. ▨▨ 79 82 83 85 86 87  Tasty, tannic, fragrant red. Superiore can age 7 years. Round ALBA, NEBBIOLO is sometimes added to make a VINO DA TAVOLA.

**Barbera d'Asti**  Piem. DOC r. dr. ▨▨ 79 80 82 83 84 85 86 87  To many the best of the Barberas; all Barbera grapes; grapey and appetizing, drunk young or aged up to 7 years.

**Barbera del Monferrato**  Piem. DOC r. dr. ★ 82 83 85 86 87  From a large area in the Pr of Alessandria and ASTI. Pleasant, slightly fizzy, sometimes sweetish.

**Barberani**  Leading ORVIETO producer.

**Bardolino**  Ven. DOC r. dr. (p.) ★★ D.Y.A.  Pale, light, slightly bitter red from e. shore of La Garda. Bardolino Chiaretto is even paler and lighter.

**Berlucchi, Guido**  Italy's biggest producer of sparkling METODO CLASSICO, at FRANCIACORTA. Steady quality.

**Barolo**  Piem. DOCG r. dr. ★★★→★★★★ 71 74 78 79 80 82 83 85' 86 87  Small area s. of Turin with one of the highest-rated Italian red wines, dark, rich, alcoholic (minimum 13°), dry but deep in flavour. From NEBBIOLO grapes. Ages for up to 15 yrs, Riserva after 5. Best producers incl. VIETTI, GIACOSA, CONTERNO, Pio Cesare, Marcarini, MASCARELLO, CERETTO, PRUNOTTO, CORDERO, RATTI, Rinaldi, ROCCHE DEI MANZONI, FONTANA FREDDA. The coop "Terre de Barolo" is also good.

**Bell 'Agio**  Brand of sweet white MOSCATO from BANFI.

**Bertani**  Well-known producers of quality Veronese wines (VALPOLICELLA, VALPANTENA, SOAVE, etc.), including aged AMARONE.

**Bianco**  White.

**Bianco d'Arquata**  Umbr. w. dr. ▨▨ 83 84 85 86 87  A limpid and inspiring light and fruity white from near Perugia.

**Bianco di Custoza**  Ven. DOC w. dr. (sp.) ▨▨ D.Y.A.  Virtual twin of SOAVE from w. of Verona often rivals or surpasses it in quality.

**Bianco di Pitigliano**  Tusc. DOC w. dr. ▨ D.Y.A.  A soft, fruity, lively wine made near Grosseto.

**Bianco Vergine della Valdichiana**  Tusc. DOC w. dr. ★ D.Y.A.  Pale dry light wine from Arezzo. But what music in the name.

**Bigi, Luigi & Figlio**  Famous producers of ORVIETO and other wines of Umbria and Tuscany. Their Torricella v'yd produces v.g. dry Orvieto.

**Biondi-Santi**  The original producer of BRUNELLO with cellars in MONTALCINO (Siena). His prices are v. high but ancient vintages unique. His Il Greppo v'yd is only 45 acres.

**Boca**  Piem. DOC r. dr. ▨▨ 79 82 83 85 86 87  From same grape as BAROLO in n. of Piemonte. A coming name.

**Bolla**  Famous Veronese firm producing VALPOLICELLA, SOAVE, etc. Top wines: Jago, Castellaro (84').

**Bonarda**  Minor red grape widely grown in PIEMONTE and Lombardy.

**Bonarda (Oltrepò Pavese)**  Lomb. DOC r. dr. ★★ 85 86 87  Soft, fresh, pleasant red from south of Pavia.

**Bosca**  Wine-producers from PIEMONTE known for their ASTI SPUMANTE and Vermouths; also popular fizzy Caneï.

**Boscarelli, Poderi**  Small estate with v.g. VINO NOBILE DI MONTEPULCIANO.

**Botticino**  Lomb. DOC r. dr. ★★ 85 86 87
Strong, full-bodied rather sweet red from Brescia.

**Brachetto d'Acqui**  Piem. DOC r. sw. (sp.) ★★ D.Y.A.
Sweet sparkling red with enticing muscat aroma.

**Bramaterra**  Piem. DOC. r. dr. ▇▇ 78 79 82 85 86 87
A substantial and stylish recent addition to Piemonte's reds. Nebbiolo grapes predominate.

**Breganze**  Ven. DOC ★→★★★ 79 80 82 83 85 86 87
A catch-all for many varieties around Vicenza. CABERNET and PINOT BIANCO are best. Top producer: MACULAN.

**Bricco dell'Uccellone**  Piem. r. dr. ★★★ 82 83 84 85 86 87
Barrique-aged BARBERA from firm of Giacomo Bologna.

**Bricco Manzoni**  Piem. r. ▇▇▇ 79 80 82 83 85 86 87
Excellent blend of NEBBIOLO and BARBERA from Monforte d'Alba.

**Brolio**  One of the oldest (c. 1200) and most famous CHIANTI CLASSICO estates, now owned by a British group. Good whites as well as red.

**Brunello di Montalcino**  Tusc. DOCG r. dr. ★★★★ 70 71 75 77 79 80 81 82 83 85 86 87  Italy's most celebrated red wine. Strong, full-bodied, high-flavoured and long-lived. After 5 yrs is called Riserva. Produced for over a century 25 miles s. of Siena. Top producers incl. BIONDI-SANTI, CAPARZO, Case Base, Altesino, Constanti, Il Poggione, VILLA BANFI. ROSSO DI MONTALCINO is a less expensive alternative.

**Brusco dei Barbi**  Piem. r. dr. ★★ 83 85 86 87
Lively variant on BRUNELLO, using old Chianti *governo* method.

**Buttafuoco**  Lomb. ★★ 82 83 85 86
A potent foaming red of BARBERA and other grapes. Avoid.

**Ca' del Bosco**  FRANCIACORTA estate making some of Italy's v. best sparkling wine, CHARDONNAY, and excellent reds (Pinot Noir, MAURIZIO ZANELLA and FRANCIACORTA).

**Cabernet**  Bordeaux grape much used in n.e. Italy and increasingly in Tuscany and the south.

**Cacchiano, Castello di**  First-rate CHIANTI CLASSICO estate at Gaiole, owned by RICASOLI.

**Cafaggio, Villa**  A solid CHIANTI CLASSICO estate with a good red v.d.t. called Solatio Basilica.

**Caldaro or Lago di Caldaro**  Tr-Aad. DOC r. dr. ★→★★ D.Y.A.
Alias KALTERERSEE. Light, soft, slightly bitter-almond red. Classico from a smaller area is better. From south of Bolzano.

**Caluso Passito**  Piem. DOC w. sw. (f.) ★★ 74 76 78 79 80 82 85 86
Made from selected Erbaluce grapes left to partly dry; delicate scent, velvety taste. Tiny production from a large area.

**Cannonau di Sardegna**  Sard. DOC r. (p.) dr. or s/sw. ★★ 83 84 85 86 87
Cannonau is Sardinia's basic red grape; its wine often formidably strong (min. 13.5% alc.). Less potent Cannonaus without the DOC can be easier to like.

**Cantina**  1. Cellar or winery. 2. Cantina Sociale = growers' coop.

**Capanelle**  Good producer of Tuscan v.d.t. (formerly CHIANTI CLASSICO), though overrated and overpriced.

**Caparzo, Tenuta**  MONTALCINO estate with excellent BRUNELLO La Casa; also CHARDONNAY and red blend Ca'del Pazzo.

**Capezzana, Tenuta di (or Villa)**  The Tuscan estate of the ancient Contini Bonacossi family, producers of excellent CHIANTI MONTALBANO and CARMIGNANO. Also a Bordeaux-style red, GHIAIE DELLA FURBA.

**Carpenè Malvolti**  Leading producer of classic PROSECCO and other sp. wines at Conegliano, Veneto.

**Capri**  Camp. DOC r. w. p. ★★
Widely abused name of the famous island in the Bay of Naples. Better to drink e.g. RAVELLO.

**Carema**   Piem. DOC r. dr. ★★ 71 74 78 79 80 82 83 85 86 87
Old speciality of northern PIEMONTE, NEBBIOLO grapes traditionally fermented Beaujolais-style before crushing. (See France: macération carbonique.) More conventional today.

**Carmignano**   Tusc. DOC r. dr. (p. br.)   ★★★ 79 80 81 82 83 85 86 87
Section of CHIANTI using 10% of CABERNET to make increasingly good, and some very fine, wine. See Capezzana.

**Carso**   Fr-VG. DOC r. w. dr. ★★ 86 87
New DOC near Trieste includes good MALVASIA. Terrano del C. is a soft REFOSCO-like red.

**Casa fondata nel . . .**   Firm founded in . . .

**Castel del Monte**   Apu. DOC r. p. w. dr. ★★ 79 81 83 84 85 86 87
Dry, fresh, well-balanced southern wines. The red becomes Riserva after 3 yrs. Rosé most widely known.

**Castel San Michele**   Tr-Aad. r. dr.   ★★ 82 83 85 86 87
A good red made of CABERNET and MERLOT grapes by the Trentino Agricultural College near Trento.

**Castello della Sala**   ANTINORI'S estate at ORVIETO and its fresh white. Cervaro della Sala is top wine: CHARDONNAY and GRECHETTO aged in French oak.

**CAVIT**   CAntina VITicultori, a group of cooperatives near Trento, producing large quantities of table and sp. wines.

**Cellatica**   Lomb. DOC r. dr. ★★ 85 86 87
Light red with slightly bitter after-taste of Schiava grapes, from Brescia.

**Cerasuolo**   Abr. DOC p. dr. ★★
The rosato version of MONTEPULCIANO D'ABRUZZO.

**Ceretto**   High-quality grower of v. expensive BARBARESCO, BAROLO, etc. Barb is called Bricco Asili, Barolo Bricco Rocche.

**Cerveteri**   Lat. DOC w. dr. s/sw. ★ 85 86 87
Sound wines produced n.w. of Rome between Lake Bracciano and the Tyrrhenian Sea.

**Chardonnay**   Has recently joined permitted varieties for several n. Italian DOCs. Some of the best (e.g. GAJA) are still only VINI DA TAVOLA.

**Chianti**   Tusc. DOC r. dr.   ★→★★★ 79 80 81 82 83 85 86 87
The lively local wine of Florence. Fresh but warmly fruity when young, still occasionally sold in straw-covered flasks. Variously ageworthy. Montalbano, RUFINA and Colli Fiorentini, Senesi, Aretini, Colline Pisane are sub-districts.

**Chianti Classico**   Tusc. DOCG r. dr.   ★→★★★ 78 79 80 81 82 83 85 86 87 Senior Chianti from the central area. Many estates make fine, powerful, slightly astringent wine. Riservas (after 3 yrs) often have the bouquet of age in oak. Members of the Consorzio use the badge of a black rooster, but several top firms do not belong.

**Chianti Putto**   Tusc. DOCG r. dr.   ★→★★★
Often high-quality Chianti from a league of producers outside the Classico zone. Neck-label is a pink and white cherub.

**Chiaretto**   Very light reds, almost rosé (the word means "claret") produced around Lake Garda. See Bardolino, Riviera del Garda.

**Cinqueterre**   Lig. DOC w. dr. or sw. or pa. ★★
Fragrant fruity white made for centuries near La Spezia. The PASSITO is known as Sciacchetrà.

**Cinzano**   Major Vermouth company also known for its ASTI SPUMANTE from PIEMONTE.

**Cirò**   Cal. DOC r. (p.w.) dr. ★★ 79 81 82 83 84 85 86 87
The wine of the ancient Olympic games. Very strong red, fruity white (to drink young).

**Classico**   Term for wines from a restricted, usually central, area within the limits of a DOC. By implication, and often in practice, the best of the region.

**Clastidium**  Lomb. w. dr. ✦✦✦ 78 82 83 85
　　Unique full-bodied oak-aged white of PINOTS NERO and GRIGIO. Ages splendidly.

**Collavini, Cantina**  High-quality producers of COLLIO, COLLI ORIENTALI and GRAVE DEL FRIULI wines: PINOT GRIGIO, RIESLING, MERLOT, PINOT NERO and sparkling.

**Colle Picchioni**  Estate s. of Rome making the best MARINO white; also red (CAB/MERLOT) v.d.t., Vigna del Vassallo, perhaps Latium's best.

**Colli**  Means "hills" in many wine-names.

**Colli Albani**  Lat. DOC w. dr. or s/sw. (sp.) ✦→✦✦ D.Y.A.
　　Soft fruity wine of the Roman hills.

**Colli Berici**  Ven. DOC r. w. p. dr. ✦✦ 82 83 85 86 87
　　CABERNET is the best of several promising products of these hills south of Vicenza.

**Colli Bolognesi**  Em-Ro. DOC r. p. w. dr. ✦✦ (w.) D.Y.A. 82 83 85 86 87
　　From the hills s.w. of Bologna. Six possible grape varieties.

**Colli della Toscana Centrale**  Several of the best Chianti makers are starting to use this name for table wines. (A future DOC? See Predicato.)

**Colli del Trasimeno**  Umb. DOC r. w. dr. ✦✦ 85 86 87
　　Lively wines from the province of Perugia.

**Colli di Catone**  Reliable producer of FRASCATI.

**Colli Euganei**  Ven. DOC r. w. dr. or s/sw. (sp.) ✦ 85 86 87
　　A DOC applicable to 7 wines produced s.w. of Padua. Red is adequate; white soft and pleasant. The table wine of Venice.

**Colli Orientali del Friuli**  Fr-VG. DOC r. w. dr. or sw. ✦✦→✦✦✦ 82 83 84 85 86 87  18 different wines are produced under this DOC on the hills east of Udine and named after their grapes, esp v.g. whites.

**Colli Piacentini**  Tusc. DOC r. p. w. dr. ✦→✦✦
　　DOC incl. traditional GUTTURNIO and Monterosso Val d'Arda among 11 types grown round Piacenza.

**Collio (Goriziano)**  Fr-VG. DOC r. w. dr. ✦✦→✦✦✦ 82 83 84 85 86 87  12 different wines named after their grapes from a small area between Udine and Gorizia nr. the Yugoslav border. V.g. whites.

**Colli Perugini**  Umbr. DOC r. p. w. ✦ 85 86 87
　　New DOC for light wines in the hills of Perugia.

**Coltassala**  Tusc. r. dr. ✦✦✦ 80 81 82 83 85 86 87
　　Notable new red of SANGIOVESE from the ancient CHIANTI CLASSICO estate of CASTELLO DI VOLPAIA at Radda.

**Coltiva – Gruppo Italiano Vini**  Complex of coops and wineries, now apparently the world's third largest producer.

**Conterno, Aldo and Giacomo**  Highly regarded growers of BAROLO, etc, with separate estates at Monforte d'Alba.

**Contratto**  Piemonte firm known for ASTI SPUMANTE, BAROLO, etc.

**Copertino**  Apu. DOC r. dr. ✦✦ 82 83 84 85 86 87
　　Age-worthy dark red of NEGROAMARO from the heel of Italy.

**Cordero, Paolo, di Montezemolo**  Tiny producer of top-class Barolo.

**Cori**  Lat. DOC w. r. dr./sw. ✦ 86 87
　　Soft and well-balanced wines made 30 miles south of Rome.

**Cortese di Gavi**  See Gavi.

**Cortese (Oltrepò Pavese)**  Lomb. DOC w. dr. ✦→✦✦ D.Y.A.
　　Delicate fresh white from western Lombardy.

**Corvo**  Sic. r. w. dr. ✦✦ 81 83 84 85 86 87
　　Popular Sicilian wines. Sound dry red, pleasant soft whites.

**Costanti, Emilio**  Tiny estate producing top-quality BRUNELLO DI MONTALCINO.

**d'Albola, Castello**  Formerly Pian d'Albola. Famous CHIANTI CLASSICO estate owned by ZONIN.

**D'Ambra**  Well-known producer of ISCHIA and other wines of that island.

**Darmagi** Piem. r. dr. ★★★ 82 83 85 86 87
CABERNET SAUVIGNON grown in a choice plot in BARBARESCO by GAJA has become Piemonte's most discussed and admired "foreign" red.

**Decugnano dei Barbi** Top ORVIETO estate with a unique ABBOCCATO version known as "Pourriture Noble" and a good red v.d.t.

**Dolce** Sweet.

**Dolceacqua** See Rossese di Dolceacqua.

**Dolcetto** Common low-acid red grape of PIEMONTE, the everyday wine of BAROLO and BARBARESCO-producing areas, giving its name to:

**Dolcetto d'Acqui** Piem. DOC r. dr. ★ 86 87
Good standard table wine from s. of ASTI.

**Dolcetto d'Alba** Piem. DOC r. dr. ★★ 85 86 87
Among the best Dolcetti, with a trace of bitter-almond. Superiore after 1 yr.

**Dolcetto di Diano d'Alba** Piem. DOC ★★ 85 86 87
A rival to Dolcetto d'Alba; often more potent.

**Dolcetto di Ovada** Piem. DOC r. dr. ★★ 79 80 82 83 85 86 87
Reputedly the sturdiest and longest-lived of Dolcetti.

**Donnafugata** Sic. r. w. ▓▓ ★★ 85 86 87
Sound red and zesty white from the Belici hills near Agrigento.

**Donnaz** Vd'A. DOC dr. ★★ 82 83 85 86 87
A mountain NEBBIOLO, fragrant, pale and faintly bitter. Aged for a statutory 3 yrs. Now part of the VALLE D'AOSTA regional DOC.

**Elba** Tusc. r. w. dr. (sp.) ▓▓ ★★ 83 85 86 87
The island's white is admirable with fish. Good dry red.

**Enfer d'Arvier** Vd'A. DOC r. dr. ★★ 82 83 85 86 87
Alpine speciality (cf. DONNAZ); pale, pleasantly bitter, light red.

**Enoteca** Italian for "wine library", of which there are many in the country, the impressive original being the Enoteca Italica Permanente of Siena.

**Erbaluce di Caluso** See Caluso Passito.

**Est! Est!! Est!!!** Lat. DOC w. dr. or s/sw. ★ D.Y.A.
Famous soft fruity white from Montefiascone, n. of Rome. The name is much more remarkable than the wine.

**Etna** Sic. DOC r. p. w. dr. ▓★→★★ 82 83 84 85 86 87
Wine from the volcanic slopes. The red is warm, full, balanced and ages well; the white is distinctly grapey. See Villagrande.

**Falerio dei Colli Ascolani** Mar. DOC w. dr. ▓★ D.Y.A.
Made in the province of Ascoli Piceno. Pleasant, fresh, fruity; a wine for the summer.

**Falerno** Camp. r. w. dr. ★★ 82 83 84 85 86 87
As Falernum, one of the best-known wines of ancient times. Strong red, fruity white, improving in quality.

**Fara** Piem. DOC r. dr. ▓▓ ★★ 79 82 83 85 86 87
Good NEBBIOLO wine from Novara, n. PIEMONTE. Fragrant; worth ageing. Small production.

**Faro** Sic. DOC r. dr. ★★ 83 84 85 86 87
Rare strong Sicilian red, made in sight of the Straits of Messina.

**Favonio** Apu. r. w. dr. ▓▓ ★★ 82 83 84 85 86 87
Estate east of Foggia using CABERNET, CHARDONNAY and PINOT BIANCO.

**Fazi-Battaglia** Well-known producer of VERDICCHIO, etc.

**Felluga** Brothers Livio and Marco have separate companies in the COLLIO and COLLI ORIENTALI zones. Both are highly esteemed.

**Ferrari** Firm making one of Italy's best dry sparkling wines by the champagne method near Trento, Trentino-Alto Adige.

**Fiano di Avellino** Cam. w. dr. ★★→★★★ 83 84 85 86 87
Considered the best white of Campania, smooth, pale, dry but not otherwise remarkable.

**Fiorano** Lat. r. w. dr. s/sw. ★★ 79 80 81 82 83 85 86 87
Interesting Roman reds of CABERNET and MERLOT.

**Flaccionello della Pieve**  See Fontodi.

**Florio**  The major producer of Marsala, owning several brands, controlled by CINZANO.

**Foianeghe**  Tr-Aad. r. ★★

Trentino CABERNET/MERLOT red to age 7-10 years.

**Folonari**  Large run-of-the-mill merchant at Brescia.

**Fontana Candida**  One of the biggest producers of FRASCATI. Single v'yd Santa Teresa stands out.

**Fontanafredda**  One of the biggest producers of Piemontese wines, incl. BAROLO from single v'yds and a range of ALBA DOCs. Also v.g. sparkling wines.

**Fonterutoli**  High-quality CHIANTI CLASSICO estate at Castellina.

**Fontodi**  Rising CHIANTI CLASSICO estate producing one of Italy's most highly regarded v.d.t. in Flaccionello della Pieve.

**Franciacorta Pinot**  Lomb. DOC w. (p.) dr. (sp.)  ★★→★★★

Agreeable soft white and good sparkling wines made of PINOT BIANCO, NERO or GRIGIO. CA'DEL BOSCO is outstanding.

**Franciacorta Rosso**  Lomb. DOC r. dr.  ★★  82 83 85 86

Lightish red of mixed CABERNET and BARBERA from Brescia.

**Frascati**  Lat. DOC w. dr. s/sw. sw. (sp.) ★→★★★ D.Y.A.

Best-known wine of the Roman hills: should be soft, ripe, golden, tasting of whole grapes. Most is disappointingly neutral today: look for dated wines from small producers (e.g. Conte Zandotti, Villa Simone, or single v'yd Santa Teresa from FONTANA CANDIDA). The sweet version is known as Cannellino.

**Frecciarossa**  Lomb. DOC r. w. dr. ★→★★ 83 85 86

Sound wines from an estate nr. Casteggio in the OLTREPÒ PAVESE.

**Freisa d'Asti**  Piem. DOC r. dr. s/sw. or sw. (sp.) ★★ D.Y.A.

Sometimes sweet, often FRIZZANTE red, said to taste of raspberries and roses. With enough acidity it can be highly appetizing.

**Frescobaldi**  Ancient noble family, leading pioneers of CHIANTI PUTTO at NIPOZZANO, e. of Florence. Also white POMINO and PREDICATO SAUV BLANC (Vergena) and CHARD (Mormoreto). See Montesodi.

**Friuli-Venezia Giulia**  The n.e. province on the Yugoslav border. Many wines, of which the DOCs COLLIO and COLLI ORIENTALI include most of the best.

**Frizzante**  Semi-sparkling or "pétillant", a word used to describe wines such as LAMBRUSCO.

**Gaja**  Old family firm at BARBARESCO. Top-quality Piemonte wines, esp. BARBARESCO. Pioneer with carbonic maceration to make VINÓT. Now setting trends with excellent CHARDONNAY (Gaia & Rey 84 85 86 87), CABERNET (Darmagi) and SAUV BLANC.

**Galestro**  Tusc. w. dr. ★★

Name for superior light grapey white from Chianti country.

**Gambellara**  Ven. DOC w. dr. or s/sw. (sp.) ★ D.Y.A.

Neighbour of SOAVE. Dry wine similar. Sweet (known as RECIOTO DI GAMBELLARA), agreeably fruity. Also VIN SANTO.

**Gancia**  Famous ASTI SPUMANTE house from Piemonte, also produces vermouth and dry sparkling wines.

**Garganega**  The principal white grape of SOAVE.

**Gattinara**  Piem. DOC r. dr. ★★→★★★ 70 74 78 79 82 83 85 86 87

Very tasty excellent big-scale BAROLO-type red from northern PIEMONTE. Made from NEBBIOLO, locally known as Spanna.

**Gavi (or Cortese di Gavi)**  Piem. w. dr. ★★→★★★ 85 86 87 (usually D.Y.A.)  At best almost burgundian dry white of Cortese grapes. La Scolca is best known, Castello di Tassarolo top quality, La Giustiniana and Tenuta San Pietro admirable. But v. high prices are rarely justified.

**Ghemme**  Piem. DOC r. dr.  ★★→★★★  78 79 82 83 85 86 87

Neighbour of GATTINARA, capable of Bordeaux-style finesse.

**Ghiaie della Furba** Tusc. r. dr. ★★★ 79 80 81 82 83 85 86 87
Bordeaux-style CABERNET blend from the admirable Tenuta di CAPEZ-
ZANA, CARMIGNANO.

**Giacobazzi** Well-known producers of LAMBRUSCO near Modena.

**Giacosa, Bruno** Inspired loner making excellent BARBARESCO, BAROLO and
other Piemonte wines at Neive (Cuneo).

**Girò di Cagliari** Sard. DOC r. dr. or sw. ★ 85 86 87
A formidably alcoholic red, most sympathetic when some of its sugar
content is left unfermented.

**Goldmuskateller** Aromatic grape made into wonderful dry white, esp. by
TIEFENBRUNNER.

**Gradi** Degrees (of alcohol), i.e. percent by volume.

**Grave del Friuli** Fr-VG. DOC r. w. dr. ★★ 82 83 85 86 87
A DOC covering 15 different wines named after their grapes, from
near the Yugoslav border. Good MERLOT and CABERNET.

**Grai, Giorgio** Merchant and consultant to top ALTO-ADIGE and other
estates. Own labels incl. Bellendorf.

**Grechetto (or Greco)** A traditional white grape with far more flavour
than the ubiquitous Trebbiano, increasingly used and referred to by
name in the centre and south of Italy. The name means Greek.

**Greco di Bianco (or Greco di Gerace)** Cal. DOC w. sw. ★★ 79 81 83 85 86
87 An original smooth and fragrant dessert wine from Italy's toe.
See also Mantonico.

**Greco di Tufo** Camp. DOC w. dr. (sp.) ★★★ 83 84 85 86 87
One of the best whites of the south, fruity and slightly "wild" in
flavour. A character.

---

## SOAVE CLASSICO

VINO A DENOMINAZIONE DI
ORIGINE CONTROLLATA

IMBOTTIGLIATO DAL
PRODUTTORE ALL 'ORIGINE

CANTINA SOCIALE DI SOAVE

Most Italian wines have a single name, in
contrast to the combination village and vineyard
names of France and Germany.

Soave is the name of this wine. It is qualified
only by the word Classico, a legal term for the
central (normally the best) part of many long-
established wine regions.

"Denominazione di Origine Controllata" is the
official guarantee of authenticity.

Imbottigliato . . . all'origine means bottled by
the producer. Cantina Sociale di Soave means
the growers' cooperative of Soave.

---

**Grignolino d'Asti** Piem. DOC r. dr. ★ D.Y.A.
Pleasant lively standard wine of PIEMONTE.

**Grumello** Lomb. DOC r. dr. ★★ 78 79 80 82 83 85 86
NEBBIOLO wine from VALTELLINA, can be delicate and fine.

**Guerrieri-Rizzardi** Top producer of BARDOLINO and other Veronese wines
from various family estates (esp. Villa Rizzardi, 86').

**Gutturnio dei Colli Piacentini** Em-Ro. DOC r. dr. (s/sw.) ★★ 83 85 86 87
Full-bodied BARBERA/BONARDA blend from the hills of Piacenza. Ages
admirably. (DOC is Colli Piacentini.)

**Inferno** Lomb. DOC r. dr. ★★ 78 79 82 83 85 86
Similar to GRUMELLO and like it classified as VALTELLINA Superiore.

**Ischia** Camp. DOC (r.) w. dr. ★ 86 87
The wine of the island off Naples. The slightly sharp white Superiore
is best; ideal with fish.

**Isole e Olena** Up and coming CHIANTI CLASSICO estate with fine red v.d.t.
called Cepparello.

**Isonzo** Fr-VG. DOC r. w. dr. ★ 83 85 86 87
DOC covering 10 varietal wines in the extreme north-east.

**Jermann** Estate producing top-ranked COLLIO DOCs and the singular VINTAGE TUNINA white v.d.t.

**Kalterersee** German name for Lago di CALDARO.

**Lacryma Christi del Vesuvio** Camp. r. p. w. (f.) dr. (sw.) ★—→★★ 85 86 87
Famous but usually ordinary wines in great variety from the slopes of Mount Vesuvius. (DOC is Vesuvio.) MASTROBERARDINO makes the only good example.

**Lageder, Alois** The senior producer of the Bolzano DOCs: STA. MADDALENA, etc. Exciting wines, incl. barrel-aged CHARD Portico dei Leoni (alias Löwengang), and v.g. reds.

**Lago di Caldaro** See Caldaro.

**Lagrein** Tr-Aad. DOC r. p. dr. ★★ 78 79 80 82 83 85 86 87
A Tyrolean grape with a bitter twist. Good fruity wine – at best v. satisfying. The rosé is called Kretzer, the dark Dunkel.

**Lamberti** Producers of SOAVE, VALPOLICELLA and BARDOLINO at Lazise on the east shore of Lake Garda.

**Lambrusco** DOC (or not) r. p. (w.) s/sw ▩ D.Y.A.
Bizarre but popular fizzy red, generally drunk secco (dry) in Italy but a smash hit in its sweet version in the USA.

**Lambrusco di Sorbara** Em-Ro. DOC r. (w.) dr. or s/sw. sp. ★★ D.Y.A.
The best of the Lambruscos. From near Modena.

**Lambrusco Grasparossa di Castelvetro** Em-Ro. DOC r. dr. or s/sw. sp. ★★ D.Y.A. Similar to above. Highly scented, pleasantly acidic; often drunk with rich food.

**Lambrusco Salamino di Santa Croce** Em-Ro. DOC r. dr. or s/sw. sp. ★ D.Y.A. Similar to above. Fruity smell, high acidity and a thick "head".

**Langhe** The hills of central PIEMONTE. The name is seen on many varietal v.d.t.

**Latisana** Fr-VG. DOC r. w. dr. ★★ 85 86 87
DOC for 7 varietal wines from some 50 miles n.e. of Venice. Particularly good TOCAI FRIULANO.

**Leone de Castris** Leading producer of Apulian wines with an estate at SALICE SALENTINO, near Lecce.

**Lessona** Piem. DOC r. d. ★★ 79 82 83 85 86 87
Soft, dry, claret-like wine produced in the province of Vercelli from NEBBIOLO, Vespolina and BONARDA grapes.

**Liquoroso** Strong and usually sweet (whether fortified with alcohol or not), e.g. Tuscan VIN SANTO.

**Lisini** Small estate producing some of the finest recent vintages of BRUNELLO DI MONTALCINO.

**Locorotondo** Apu. DOC w. dr. (sp.) ★ D.Y.A.
A pleasantly fresh southern white.

**Lugana** Lomb. DOC w. dr. (sp.) ★★★ D.Y.A.
One of the best white wines of s. Lake Garda: fragrant, smooth, full of body and flavour. Visconti is the best producer.

**Lungarotti** Leading producer of TORGIANO wine, with cellars and a wine museum near Perugia. Recently also fine CHARDONNAY.

**Maculan** The top producer of DOC BREGANZE. Also Torcolato, dessert VINO DA TAVOLA (★★★).

**Malfatti** Recent go-ahead estate with modern methods, near Lecce, Apulia, producing Bianco, Rosso and SALICE SALENTINO.

**Malvasia** Important white or red grape for luscious wines, incl. Madeira's Malmsey. Used all over Italy for dry and sweet, still and sparkling wines.

**Malvasia di Bosa** Sard. DOC w. dr. sw. ★★ 83 85 86 87
A wine of character. Strong, aromatic finish.

**Malvasia di Cagliari** Sard. DOC w. dr. s/sw. or sw. (f. dr. s.) ★★ 85 86 87
Interesting strong Sardinian wine, fragrant and slightly bitter.

**Malvasia di Casorzo d'Asti** Piem. DOC r. sw. sp. ★★ D.Y.A.
Fragrant grapey sweet red, sometimes sparkling.

**Malvasia di Castelnuovo Don Bosco** Piem. DOC r. sw. (sp.) ★★
  Peculiar method of interrupted fermentation gives very sweet aromatic red.

**Malvasia delle Lipari** Sic. DOC w. sw. (pa. f.) ★★★ 82 83 84 85 86 87
  Among the very best Malvasias, aromatic and rich, from the Lipari or Aeolian Islands n. of Sicily. Top producer: Carlo Hauner.

**Malvoisie de Nus** Vd'A. w. dr. s/sw. ★★★
  Rare Alpine white, with a deep bouquet of honey. Small production and high reputation. Can age remarkably well.

**Mandrolisai** Sard. DOC r. p. dr.  ★  85 86 87
  CANNONAU at a lower strength and more approachable than the traditional style.

**Manduria (Primitivo di)** Apu. DOC r. s/sw. (f. dr. or sw.) ★★ 84 85 86 87
  Heady red, naturally strong but often fortified. From nr. Taranto. Primitivo is a southern grape related to ZINFANDEL.

**Mantonico** Cal. w. dr. or sw. f. ★★ 78 79 81 83 85 86 87
  Fruity deep amber dessert wine from Reggio Calabria. Can age remarkably well. See also Greco di Bianco.

**Marino** Lat. DOC w. dr. or s/sw. (sp.)  ★★  D.Y.A.
  A neighbour of FRASCATI with similar wine, often a better buy. Look for COLLE PICCHIONI brand.

**Marsala** Sic. DOC br. dr. s/sw. or sw. f. ★★★ NV
  Dark sherry-type wine invented by the Woodhouse Brothers of Liverpool in 1773; excellent apéritif or for dessert. The dry ("virgin"), sometimes made by the solera system, must be 5 years old. Top producers: VECCHIO SAMPERI, Pellegrino, Diego RALLO.

**Marsala Speciali** These are Marsalas with added flavours of egg, almond, strawberry, etc.

**Martina Franca** Apu. DOC w. dr. (sp.) ★ D.Y.A.
  Agreeable but rather neutral southern white, first cousin to LOCOROTONDO.

**Martini & Rossi** Well-known vermouth and sparkling wine house, also famous for its splendid wine museum in Pessione, near Turin.

**Marzemino (del Trentino)** Tr-Aad. DOC r. dr. ★ 86 87
  Pleasant local red of Trento. Fruity fragrance; slightly bitter taste. Mozart's Don Giovanni liked it.

**Mascarello** The name of two top producers of BAROLO, etc: Bartolo M. and Giuseppe M. & Figli.

**Masi, Agricola** Well-known specialist producers of VALPOLICELLA, RECIOTO, SOAVE, etc, including fine red Campo Fiorin.

**Mastroberardino** The leading wine-producer of Campania, incl. TAURASI, LACRYMA CHRISTI DEL VESUVIO and GRECO DI TUFO.

**Melini** Long-established important producers of CHIANTI CLASSICO at Pontassieve. Inventors of the standard *fiasco*, or flask.

**Melissa** Cal. DOC r. w. dr. ★★ 82 83 84 85 86 87
  Mostly made from Gaglioppo grapes in the province of Catanzaro. Delicate, balanced, ages rather well.

**Meranese di Collina** Tr-Aad. DOC r. dr. ★ D.Y.A.
  Light red of Merano, known in German as Meraner Hügel.

**Merlot** Adaptable red Bordeaux grape widely grown in n.e. Italy and elsewhere. For example:

**Merlot di Aprilia** Lat. DOC r. dr. ★ 85 86 87
  Harsh at first, softer after 2-3 yrs.

**Merlot Colli Berici** Ven. DOC r. dr. ★ 82 83 85 86 87
  Pleasantly light and soft. Campo del Lago from Villa dal Ferro is one of Italy's best Merlots.

**Merlot Colli Orientali del Friuli** Fr-VG. DOC r. dr. ★★ 82 83 85 86 87
  Pleasant herby character, best at 2-3 yrs (Riserva). Some ages well; notably Vigne dal Leon.

**Merlot Collio Goriziano**  Fr-VG. DOC r. dr. ★★ 85 86 87
Grassy scent, slightly bitter taste. Best at 2-3 yrs.

**Merlot Grave del Friuli**  Fr-VG. DOC r. dr. ★★ 82 83 85 86 87
Pleasant light wine, usually best at 1-2 yrs, but potentially a keeper.

**Merlot Isonzo**  Fr-VG. DOC r. dr. ★★ 83 84 85 86 87
A DOC in Gorizia. Dry, herby, agreeable wine.

**Merlot del Piave**  Ven. DOC r. dr. ★★ 82 83 85 86 87
Sound tasty red, best at 2-4 yrs.

**Merlot di Pramaggiore**  Ven. DOC r. dr.  ★★ 82 83 84 85 86 87
A cut above most other Merlots; improves in bottle. Riserva after
2 yrs.

**Merlot (del Trentino)**  Tr-Aad. DOC r. dr.  ★ 83 85 86 87
Full flavour, slightly grassy scent, Riserva after 2 yrs. (ALTO ADIGE has
better; esp. from Margreid and Siebeneich v'yds.)

**Metodo classico or tradizionale**  Terms increasingly in use to identify
champagne method sparkling wines.

**Monica di Cagliari**  Sard. DOC r. dr. or sw. (f. dr. or sw.) ★★ 85 86 87
Strong spicy red, often fortified and comparable with Spanish Malaga.
Monica is a Sardinian grape.

**Monica di Sardegna**  Sard. DOC r. dr. ★ 83 85 86 87
Dry version of above, not fortified.

**Monsanto**  Esteemed CHIANTI CLASSICO estate, esp. for IL POGGIO v'yd.

**Montalcino**  Village in the province of Siena, Tuscany, famous for its deep
red BRUNELLO and lighter ROSSO DI MONTALCINO.

**Monte Vertine**  Top estate at Radda in Chianti. ★★★ v.d.t. Le Pergole
Torte and Sodaccio.

**Montecarlo**  Tusc. DOC w. dr. r. ★★ 85 86 87
One of Tuscany's best whites, smooth and delicate. Now applies to a
CHIANTI-style red too.

**Montecompatri Colonna**  Lat. DOC w. dr. or s/sw. ★ D.Y.A.
A neighbour of FRASCATI. Similar wine.

**Montefalco**  Umb. DOC r. dr. or sw.  ★★ 83 85 86 87
M. Rosso is standard red, Sagrantino (named for the grape) has
sweetness and bite. Top producer ADANTI.

**Montepulciano, Vino Nobile di**  See Vino Nobile di Montepulciano.

**Montepulciano d'Abruzzo (or Molise)**  Abr. & M. DOC r. p. dr.
★★★ 82 83 85 86 87  One of Italy's best reds, full of flavour and
warmth, from the Adriatic coast round Pescara. See also Cerasuolo,
Valentini.

**Monterosso (Val d'Arda)**  Em-Ro. DOC w. dr. or sw. (sp.) ★ D.Y.A.
Agreeable minor white from Piacenza. (DOC Colli Piacentini.)

**Montesodi**  Tusc. r. ★★★ 78 79 80 82 83 85 86
Tip-top CHIANTI Rufina Riserva from FRESCOBALDI.

**Moscadello di Montalcino**  Tusc. DOC w. sw./sp. ★★ D.Y.A.
Light, fizzy, not oversweet muscat. A refreshing speciality of MONT-
ALCINO, esp. VILLA BANFI.

**Moscato**  Fruitily fragrant grape grown all over Italy.

**Moscato d'Asti**  Piem. DOC w. sw. sp.  ★★ NV
Low-strength sweet fruity sparkler normally made in bulk. ASTI
SPUMANTE is the (theoretically) superior version.

**Moscato dei Colli Euganei**  Ven. DOC w. sw. (sp.) ★★ D.Y.A.
Golden wine, fruity and smooth, from near Padua.

**Moscato (Oltrepò Pavese)**  Lomb. DOC w. sw. (sp.) ★ D.Y.A.
The Lombardy equivalent of Moscato d'Asti. Rarely as good.

**Moscato di Pantelleria**  Sic. DOC w. sw. (sp.) (f. pa.) ★★★
Italy's best muscat, from the island of Pantelleria off the Tunisian
coast; rich, fruity and aromatic. Ages well. Top wine: Bukkuram from
De Bartoli.

**Moscato di Sorso Sennori**  Sard. DOC w. sw. (f.)  ★ D.Y.A.
Strong golden dessert wine from Sassari, n. Sardinia.

**Moscato di Trani**  Apu. DOC w. sw. or f. ★ 83 84 85 86 87
Another strong golden dessert wine, sometimes fortified, with "bouquet of faded roses".

**Müller-Thurgau**  Makes wine to be reckoned with in TRENTINO-ALTO ADIGE and FRIULI, esp. TIEFENBRUNNER's "Feldmarschall".

**Nasco di Cagliari**  Sard. DOC w. dr. or sw. (f. dr. or sw.) ★ 86 87
Sardinian speciality, light bitter taste, high alcoholic content.

**Nebbiolo**  The best red grape of PIEMONTE and Lombardy.

**Nebbiolo d'Alba**  Piem. DOC r. dr. s/sw. (sp.) ▮★★ 79 82 83 85 86 87
Like lightweight BAROLO; often easier to appreciate than the more powerful classic wine. Roero is a new DOC for such wine from n. of ALBA.

**Negroamaro**  Literally "black bitter"; Apulian red grape with potential for quality. See Copertino.

**Neive, Castello di**  Leading producer of BARBARESCO, in castle where Louis Oudart pioneered cask-ageing of NEBBIOLO in 1850s.

**Nipozzano, Castello di**  The FRESCOBALDI estate nr. Florence producing Montesodi. The most important outside the CLASSICO zone.

**Nozzole**  Famous estate in the heart of CHIANTI CLASSICO n. of Greve.

**Nuragus di Cagliari**  Sard. DOC w. dr. ▮★ D.Y.A.
Lively Sardinian white, not too strong.

**Oliena**  Sard. r. dr. ★★
Interesting strong, fragrant CANNONAU red; a touch bitter.

**Oltrepò Pavese**  Lomb. DOC r. w. dr. sw. sp. ★→★★
DOC applicable to 15 wines produced in the province of Pavia, mostly named after their grapes.

**Ornellaia**  New estate of Lodovico Antinori nr. Bolgheri on Tuscan coast. To watch for CAB/MERLOT and SAUV BLANC.

**Orvieto**  Umb. DOC w. dr. or s/sw. ★★→★★★ D.Y.A.
The classical Umbrian golden-white, smooth and substantial, though the dry version is sometimes flat and rather dull. O. Classico is superior. Only the finest examples, e.g. BIGI, DECUGNANO DEI BARBI, BARBERANI, age well. But see Castello della sala.

**Ostuni**  Apu. DOC r. or w. dr. ★ D.Y.A.
From the Pr of Brindisi. Nothing to write home about.

**Pagadebit**  Em-Ro. w. dr./s.sw. D.Y.A.
Pleasant traditional "payer of debts" from round Bertinoro.

**Paradiso, Fattoria**  Century-old family estate near Bertinoro (EM-RO). Excellent ALBANA, fine PAGADEBIT and unique red BARBAROSSA.

**Parrina**  Tusc. r. or w. dr. ★★ 85 86 87
Light red and fresh appetizing white from s. Tuscany.

**Pasolini Dall'Onda**  Noble family with estates in CHIANTI Colli Fiorentini and ROMAGNA producing fine traditional-style wines.

**Passito**  Strong sweet wine from grapes dried on the vine or indoors.

**Peppoli**  Estate owned by ANTINORI producing excellent CHIANTI CLASSICO in a full, round, youthful style – first vintage 85.

**Per'e Palummo**  Camp. r. dr. ★★ 83 84 85 86 87
Appetizing red produced on the island of Ischia; delicate, slightly grassy, a bit tannic, balanced.

**Petit Rouge**  Vd'A. ▮★★ 82 83 85 86 87
Good, dark, lively REFOSCO-like red. Part of VALLE D'AOSTA DOC.

**Piave**  Ven. DOC r. or w. dr. ▮★★ 82 83 85 86 87 (w. D.Y.A.)
Flourishing DOC covering 8 wines, 4 red and 4 white, named after their grapes. CAB, MERLOT and RABOSO reds all need ageing.

**Picolit (Colli Orientali del Friuli)**  Fr-VG. DOC w. s/sw. or sw. ★★★ 83 85 86 87  Delicate, well-balanced, very sweet dessert wine. Ages up to 6 years, but wildly overpriced.

**Piemonte**  The most important Italian region for quality wine. Turin is the capital, Asti and ALBA the wine-centres. See Barolo, Barbera, Grignolino, Moscato, etc.

**Pieropan** Outstanding producers of SOAVE that deserves its fame.

**Pigato** New DOC under Riviera Ligure di Ponente. Often outclasses VERMENTINO as Liguria's finest white, with unusually rich texture and structure.

**Pighin, Fratelli** Solid producers of COLLIO, GRAVE DEL FRIULI, etc.

**Pinot Bianco** Popular grape in n.e., esp. good for sparkling wine.

**Pinot Bianco (Alto Adige)** Tr-Aad. DOC. w. dr. ▓▓ 85 86 87
Italy's best and longest-lived wine of this variety.

**Pinot Bianco (dei Colli Berici)** Ven. DOC w. dr. ** D.Y.A.
Straight, satisfying dry white.

**Pinot Bianco (Colli Orientali del Friuli)** Fr-VG. DOC w. dr. ** 86 87
Good white; smooth rather than showy.

**Pinot Bianco (Collio Goriziano)** Fr-VG. DOC w. dr. ** 86 87
Similar to the above.

**Pinot Bianco (Grave del Friuli)** Fr-VG. DOC w. dr. ** 86 87
Same again.

**Pinot Grigio** Tasty, low-acid white grape increasingly popular in n.e. Italy. Best from A. ADIGE, COLLIO.

**Pinot Grigio (Collio Goriziano)** Fr-VG. DOC w. dr. ** 86 87
Fruity, soft, agreeable dry white. The best age well.

**Pinot Grigio (Grave del Friuli)** Fr-VG. DOC w. dr. ** 86 87
Hardly distinguishable from the above.

**Pinot Grigio (Oltrepò Pavese)** Lomb. DOC w. dr. (sp.) ** 86 87
Lombardy's P.G. is usually at least adequate.

**Pinot Nero** Tr-Aad. DOC r. dr. ▓▓ 82 83 85 86 87
Pinot Nero (Noir) gives lively burgundy-scented light wine in much of n.e. Italy, incl. Trentino. Riserva after 2 yrs.

**Pio Cesare** A producer of top-quality red wines of PIEMONTE, incl. BAROLO.

**Podere Il Palazzino** Small estate with admirable CHIANTI CLASSICO and v.d.t. Grosso Senese.

**Poggio al Sole** CHIANTI CLASSICO estate. Less distinguished than formerly.

**Poggione, Tenuta Il** Perhaps the most consistent top estate for BRUNELLO and ROSSO DI MONTALCINO.

**Pojer & Sandri** Top producers of TRENTINO non-DOC MÜLLER-THURGAU, CHARDONNAY.

**Pomino** Tusc. DOC (r.) w. dr. (br.) ***
Fine white, partly CHARDONNAY ("Il Benefizio" is 100%) and a SANGIOVESE/CABERNET blend. Also Vin Santo. From FRESCOBALDI.

**Polyphemo** Monster monocular Sicilian overfond of Greek red.

---

**Predicato** Name for four new kinds of VINI DA TAVOLA from central Tuscany. They illustrate the headlong rush from tradition. P. del Muschio is CHARD, P BIANCO, P. del Selvante is SAUV BLANC, P. di Biturica is CAB SAUV with SANGIOVESE, P. di Cardisco is SANGIOVESE straight. RUFFINO's Cabreo brand are examples.

---

**Primitivo di Apulia** See Manduria.

**Prosecco di Conegliano** Ven. DOC w. dr. or s/sw. (sp.) *** D.Y.A.
Popular sparkling wine of the n.e. Slight fruity bouquet, the dry pleasantly bitter, the sweet fruity; the best are known as Superiore di Cartizze. Carpené-Malvolti is famous old maker, now surpassed in quality by Pino Zardetto, Nino Franco, Canevel, Cardinal.

**Prunotto, Alfredo** Very serious ALBA company with v.g. BAROLO, BARBARESCO, NEBBIOLO, etc.

**Quintarelli, Giuseppe** True artisan producer of VALPOLICELLA, RECIOTO and AMARONE, at the top in both quality and price.

**Raboso del Piave** (now DOC) Ven. r. dr. ** 79 82 83 85 86 87
Powerful, sharp, interesting country red; needs age.

**Rallo, Diego & Figli** A leader in MARSALA with 1st class Vergine and other wines. (Giacomo Rallo is director. His wife Gabriella owns DONNAFUGATA.)

**Ramandolo**  See Verduzzo Colli Orientali del Friuli.

**Rampolla, Castello dei**  Top CHIANTI CLASSICO estate at Panzano; also excellent Cabernet-based v.d.t. Sammarco.

**Rapitalà**  See Alcamo.

**Ratti, Renato**  Maker of v.g. BAROLO and other ALBA wines; also author and industry leader.

**Ravello**  Camp. r. p. w. dr. ★★ 85 86 87
Among the best wines of Campania: full dry red, fresh clean white. Caruso is the best-known brand.

**Recioto**  Wine made partly of half-dried grapes. Speciality of Veneto. R. Amandorlato is ½ sweet, ½ dry.

**Recioto di Gambellara**  Ven. DOC w. s/sw. sp. ★ 85 86 87
Sweetish golden wine, often half-sparkling.

**Recioto di Soave**  Ven. DOC w. s/sw. (sp.) ★★ 85 86 87
Soave made from selected half-dried grapes; sweet, fruity, fresh, slightly almondy: high alcohol. Top maker: ANSELMI.

**Recioto della Valpolicella**  Ven. DOC r. s/sw. sp. ★★ 78 80 81 83 85 86
Strong late-harvested red, sometimes sparkling. "Amabile" is fully sweet.

**Recioto Amarone della Valpolicella**  Ven. DOC r. dr. ★★★★ 77 78 79 80 81 83 85 86  Dry version of the above; strong concentrated flavour, rather bitter. Impressive and expensive.

**Refosco (Colli Orientali del Friuli)**  Fr-VG. DOC r. dr. ★★ 82 83 85 86 87
Full-bodied dry red; Riserva after 2 yrs. Refosco is said to be the same grape as the MONDEUSE of Savoie (France).

**Refosco (Grave del Friuli)**  Fr-VG. DOC r. dr. ★★ 82 83 85 86 87
Similar to above but slightly lighter.

**Regaleali**  Sic. w. r. p.  ▨▧★★▨ 79 80 81 83 84 85 86 87
Perhaps the best Sicilian table wines, produced between Caltanissetta and Palermo.

**Ribolla (Colli Orientali del Friuli)**  Fr-VG. DOC w. dr. ★ D.Y.A.
Clean and fruity north-eastern white.

**Ricasoli**  Famous Tuscan family, "inventors" of CHIANTI, whose Chianti Classico is named after their BROLIO estate and castle.

**Riecine**  Tusc.  ▨★★★▨
First-class CHIANTI CLASSICO estate at Gaiole started by an Englishman, John Dunkley. First wine 1973.

**Riesling**  Formerly referred to Italian Riesling (R. Italico or "Welschriesling"). German Riesling, now ascendant, is R. Renano.

**Riesling Alto Adige**  DOC w. dr. ★★ 85 86 87
Can often be Italy's best Riesling.

**Riesling (Oltrepò Pavese)**  Lomb. DOC w. dr. (sp.) ★★
The Lombardy version, quite light and fresh. Occasionally sparkling. Keeps well. Made of both types of Riesling.

**Riesling (Trentino)**  Tr-Aad. DOC w. dr. ★★ D.Y.A.
Delicate, slightly acid, very fruity.

**Riserva**  Wine aged for a statutory period, usually in barrels.

**Riunite**  One of the world's largest coop cellars near Reggio Emilia producing huge quantities of LAMBRUSCO and other wines.

**Rivera**  Important and reliable winemakers at Andria, near Bari, with good red Il Falcone and CASTEL DEL MONTE rosé.

**Riviera del Garda Chiaretto**  Ven. and Lom. DOC p. dr. ★★ D.Y.A.
Charming cherry-pink, fresh and slightly bitter, from s.w. Garda, especially round Moniga del Garda.

**Riviera del Garda Rosso**  Ven. DOC r. dr. ★★ 82 83 85 86 87
Red version of the above; ages surprisingly well.

**Rocche dei Manzoni, Podere**  Go-ahead estate at MONFORTE D'ALBA. Excellent BAROLO, BRICCO MANZONI, other ALBA wines and Valentino Brut sparkling.

**Roero**  See Nebbiolo d'Alba.

**Rosa del Golfo**  Apu. p. dr.  ▩▩ D.Y.A.
  An outstanding example of ALEZIO rosato.

**Rosato**  Rosé.

**Rosato del Salento**  Apu. p. dr. ★→★★ D.Y.A.
  Strong but refreshing southern rosé from round Brindisi.

**Rossese di Dolceacqua**  Lig. DOC r. dr. ★★ 85 86 87
  Well-known fragrant light red of the Riviera, as clean as claret.
  Superiore is stronger.

**Rosso**  Red.

**Rosso Cònero**  Mar. DOC r. dr. ★★ 82 83 85 86 87
  Substantial CHIANTI-style wine from the Adriatic coast.

**Rosso d'Arquata**  See Adanti.

**Rosso delle Colline Lucchesi**  Tusc. DOC r. dr. ★★ 83 85 86 87
  Produced round Lucca but not greatly different from CHIANTI.

**Rosso di Montalcino**  Tusc. DOC r. dr. ▩▩→★★★★
  Recent DOC for younger wines from BRUNELLO grapes. Still variable
  but potentially a winner.

**Rosso Piceno**  Mar. DOC r. dr. ★→ ▩▩ 81 82 83 85 86 87
  Adriatic red with a touch of style. Can be Superiore.

**Rubesco**  The excellent popular red of TORGIANO.

**Rubino di Cantavenna**  Piem. DOC r. dr. ★★ 85 86 87
  Lively red, principally BARBERA, from a well-known cooperative s.e. of
  Turin.

**Rufina**  A sub-region of CHIANTI in the hills east of Florence.

**Ruffino**  The biggest and best known of all CHIANTI merchants. Riserva
  Ducale is the top wine. N.B. New PREDICATO wines.

**Sagrantino**  See Montefalco.

**Salice Salentino**  Apu. DOC r. ★★ 79 80 81 83 85 86 87
  Strong red from Negroamaro grapes, Riserva after 2 yrs, ages to
  smooth full wine. Top makers: Taurino, De Castris.

**San Felice**  Rising star in CHIANTI with fine Classico Poggio Rosso and
  prize-winning red v.d.t. Vigorello and PREDICATO di Biturica.

**Sangiovese or Sangiovete**  Principal red grape of CHIANTI, used alone for:

**Sangiovese d'Aprilia**  Lat. DOC r. or p. dr. ★ D.Y.A.
  Strong dry rosé from south of Rome.

**Sangiovese di Romagna**  Em-Ro. DOC r. dr. ★★ 82 83 85 86 87
  Pleasant standard red; gains character with a little age.

**San Giusto a Rentennano**  One of the best CHIANTI CLASSICO producers;
  stunning '85 at very reasonable prices.

**San Polo in Rosso, Castello di**  CHIANTI CLASSICO estate with 1st-rate red
  v.d.t. Cetinaia (aged in standard casks, not barriques).

**San Severo**  Apu. DOC r. p. w. dr. ★ 85 86 87
  Sound neutral southern wine; not particularly strong.

**Santa Maddalena**  Tr-Aad. DOC r. dr. ▩▩ 85 86 87
  Perhaps the best Tyrolean red. Round and warm, slightly almondy.
  From Bolzano.

**Santa Margherita**  The Veneto winery that popularized PINOT GRIGIO, now
  on a broad base with many good wines.

**Sassella (Valtellina)**  Lomb. DOC r. dr. ★★★ 78 79 80 82 83 85 86
  Considerable NEBBIOLO wine, tough when young. Known since Roman
  times, mentioned by Leonardo da Vinci.

**Sassicaia**  Tusc. r. dr. ▩▩▩▩ 72 75 76 77 78 79 80 81 82 83 85 86 87
  Outstanding pioneer CABERNET from the Tenuta San Guido of the
  Incisa family, at Bolgheri near Livorno, since 1968. Distributed by
  ANTINORI. Limited production.

**Sauvignon**  The Sauvignon Blanc: excellent white grape used in n.e.,
  perhaps best at TERLANO, ALTO ADIGE. Very good in COLLIO and COLLI
  ORIENTALI.

**Sauvignon (Colli Berici)**  Ven. DOC w. dr. ★★ D.Y.A.
  Delicate, slightly aromatic, fresh white from near Vicenza.

**Sauvignon (Colli Orientali del Friuli)** Fr-VG. DOC w. dr. ** 85 86 87
Full, smooth, freshly aromatic n.e. white.

**Sauvignon (Collio Goriziano)** Fr-VG. DOC w. dr. ** 85 86 87
Very similar to the last; slightly higher alcohol.

**Savuto** Cal. DOC r. p. dr. ** 83 85 86 87
The ancient Savuto produced in the provinces of Cosenza and Catanzaro. Fragrant juicy wine.

**Schiava** Good red grape of TRENTINO-ALTO ADIGE with characteristic bitter after-taste, used for SANTA MADDALENA, etc.

**Sciacchetrà** See Cinqueterre.

**Sebaste** Young Barolo-maker to watch.

**Secco** Dry.

**Secentenario** Tusc. r. ****
Perhaps ANTINORI's best-ever red, bottled (in magnums) for the firm's 600th anniversary in 1985.

**Sella & Mosca** Major Sardinian growers and merchants at Alghero. Their port-like Anghelu Ruju is good.

**Selvapiana** RUFINA estate owned by the Giuntini family. One of the finest Chiantis of all, rivalled by few Classicos.

**Settesoli** Sicilian growers' coop with range of adequate table wines.

**Sforzato (Valtellina)** Lomb. DOC r. dr. *** 78 79 80 82 83 85 86
Valtellina equivalent of RECIOTO AMARONE made with partly dried grapes. Velvety, strong, ages remarkably well. Also called Sfursat.

**Sfursat** See Sforzato.

**Sizzano** Piem. DOC r. dr. ** 78 79 80 82 83 85 86 87
Attractive full-bodied red produced at Sizzano in the Pr of Novara, mostly from NEBBIOLO. Ages up to 10 years.

**Soave** Ven. DOC w. dr. *** D.Y.A.
Famous, if not very characterful, Veronese white. Fresh with attractive texture. S. Classico is more restricted and better.

**Solaia** Tusc. r. *** 79 82 83
Very fine Bordeaux-style wine of CAB SAUV and now 25% SANGIOVESE from ANTINORI, first made in 1979.

---

*A top category, DOCG, Denominazione Controllata e Garantita, is gradually being added to the Italian wine classification. It is awarded only to certain wines from top-quality zones which have been bottled and sealed with a government seal by the producer. The first five areas to be "guaranteed" were Barolo, Barbaresco, Brunello di Montalcino, Chianti and Vino Nobile di Montepulciano. The sixth (and first white) was Albana di Romagna, for no discernible reason. But it should be remembered that many of Italy's best wines are not covered by the DOC system and are officially only vini da tavola – v.d.t. in this book. Examples are Sassicaia, Tignanello, Venegazzù, Bricco Manzoni.*

---

**Solopaca** Camp. DOC r. w. dr. ** 83 85 86 87
Up-and-coming from near Benevento; rather sharp when young, the white soft and fruity.

**Sorni** Tr-Aad. r. w. dr. ** 85 86 87
Made in the Pr of Trento. Light, fresh and soft. Drink young.

**Spanna** See Gattinara.

**Spumante** Sparkling, as in sweet Asti or many good dry wines, incl. both METODO CLASSICO and tank-made cheapos.

**Squinzano** Apu. DOC r. p. dr. * 80 81 82 83 84 85 86 87
Strong southern red from Lecce. Riserva after 2 yrs.

**Stravecchio** Very old.

**Sylvaner** German white grape successful in ALTO ADIGE.

**Taurasi** Camp. DOC r. dr. *** 75 77 79 80 81 82 83 85 86 87
The best Campanian red, from Avellino, has a cult following in the USA. Harsh when young. Riserva after 4 yrs.

**Tedeschi, Fratelli** Leading small producer of VALPOLICELLA, RECIOTO and AMARONE. V.g. Capitel San Rocco red and white v.d.t.

**Terlano** Tr-Aad. DOC w. dr. **★★** 86 87
A DOC for 7 white wines from the Pr of Bolzano, named by their grapes, esp. outstanding SAUVIGNON. Terlaner in German.

**Teroldego Rotaliano** Tr-Aad. DOC r. p. dr. ★★→★★★ 83 85 86 87
The attractive local red of Trento. Blackberry-scented, slight bitter after-taste, can age v. well. Top maker: Foradori.

**Terre Rosse** Distinguished small estate near Bologna. CABERNET, CHARD, SAUV BL, PINOT GRIGIO, etc, are the best of the region.

**Tiefenbrunner** Distinguished grower of some of the very best ALTO ADIGE white and red wines at Schloss Turmhof, Kurtatsch (Cortaccio).

**Tignanello** Tusc. r. dr. **★★★** 75 78 79 80 81 82 83 85 86 87
One of the leaders of the new style of Bordeaux-inspired Tuscan reds, made by ANTINORI.

**Tocai Friulano** (Collio). ★★ 86 87
North-east Italian white grape; no relation of Hungarian or Alsace Tokay. Light dry wine. The Tocais of the COLLI ORIENTALE DEL FRIULI and COLLIO GORIZIANO are best.

**Tocai di Lison** Ven. DOC w. dr. ★★ D.Y.A.
From e. Veneto, delicate smoky/fruity scent, fruity taste. Classico is better.

**Tocai (Colli Berici)** Ven. DOC w. dr. ★
Less character than the last.

**Tocai (Grave del Friuli)** Fr-VG. DOC w. dr. ★★ D.Y.A.
Similar to TOCAI DI LISON, generally rather milder.

**Tocai di S. Martino della Battaglia** Lomb. DOC w. dr. ★★ D.Y.A.
Small production s. of Lake Garda. Light, slightly bitter.

**Torbato di Alghero** Sard. w. dr. (pa.) **★★** D.Y.A.
Good n. Sardinian table wine. Top maker: SELLA & MOSCA.

**Torgiano (Rubesco di)** Umb. DOC r. w. dr. **★★★** 75 77 78 79 80 81 82 83 85 86 87 The creation of the LUNGAROTTI family. Excellent red from near Perugia comparable with top CHIANTI CLASSICO. RUBESCO is the standard quality. Riserva Monticchio is superb. Keep 10 years. White Torre di Giano is good, but not as outstanding as reds.

**Torricella** Tusc. w. dr. ★★★ 81
Remarkable aged, soft, buttery MALVASIA dry white from BROLIO.

**Traminer Aromatico** Tr-Aad. DOC w. dr. ★★ D.Y.A.
Delicate, aromatic, rather soft Gewürztraminer.

**Trebbiano** The principal white grape of Tuscany, found all over Italy. Ugni Blanc in French. Rarely remarkable unless blended.

**Trebbiano d'Abruzzo** Abr. & M. DOC w. dr. ★→★★ D.Y.A.
Gentle, rather neutral, slightly tannic. From round Pescara. Valentini is much the best producer (also of MONTEPULCIANO D'ABRUZZO).

**Trebbiano d'Aprilia** Lat. DOC w. dr. ★ D.Y.A.
Heady, mild-flavoured, rather yellow. From south of Rome.

**Trebbiano di Romagna** Em-Ro. DOC w. dr. or s/sw. (sp.) ★ D.Y.A.
Clean, pleasant white from near Bologna.

**Trentino** Tr-Aad. DOC r. w. dr. or sw. ★→★★★
DOC for as many as 20 different wines, mostly named after their grapes. Best are CHARD, P BIANCO, MARZEMINO and esp. VIN SANTO.

**Umani Ronchi** A leading producer of quality wines of the Marches; notably VERDICCHIO and ROSSO CÒNERO.

**Uzzano, Castello di** Fine old CHIANTI CLASSICO estate at Greve.

**Valcalepio** Lomb. DOC r. w. dr. ★ 85 86 87
From nr. Bergamo. Pleasant red; lightly scented, fresh white.

**Valdadige** Tr-Aad. DOC r. w. dr. or s/sw. ★
Name for the ordinary table wines of the Adige valley – in German Etschtal.

**Valle d'Aosta/Vallée d'Aosta** V'dA. DOC
Regional DOC for 15 Alpine wines including DONNAZ, etc. A very mixed bag.

**Val d'Arbia** Tusc. DOC w. dr. ★ D.Y.A.
　　Another DOC for a pleasant white from CHIANTI country.

**Valentini, Edoardo** Outstanding traditionalist maker of TREBBIANO and MONTEPULCIANO D'ABRUZZO.

**Valgella (Valtellina)** Lomb. DOC r. dr. ★★ 78 79 80 82 83 85 86
　　One of the VALTELLINA NEBBIOLOS: good dry red, growing nutty with age. Riserva at 4 yrs.

**Vallana, Antonio & Figlio** The protagonist of the "SPANNA" (Nebbiolo) near Novara, Piem. Uses the DOC name BOCA. Rich-flavoured reds.

**Valle Isarco** Tr-Aad. DOC w. dr. ★→★★ 86 87
　　A DOC applicable to 5 varietal wines made n.e. of Bolzano.

**Valpantena** Valley in the VALPOLICELLA zone. Rival to CLASSICO in quality. See Bertani.

**Valpolicella** Ven. DOC r. dr. ★→ ★★★ 85 86 87
　　Attractive light red from nr. Verona; most attractive when young. Delicate nutty scent, slightly bitter taste. (None of this is true of Valpolicella sold in litre and bigger bottles.) Classico more restricted; Superiore has 12% alcohol and 1 yr of age.

**Valtellina** Lomb. DOC r. dr. ★★→★★★ 78 79 80 82 83 85 86
　　A DOC applicable to wines made principally from Chiavennasca (NEBBIOLO) grapes in the province of Sondrio, n. Lombardy. V. Superiore is GRUMELLO, INFERNO, SASSELLA or VALGELLA.

**Vecchio Samperi** Sic. des. ★★★
　　The outstanding wine of MARSALA today, although not DOC. A dry apéritif not unlike Amontillado sherry.

**Velletri** Lat. DOC r. w. dr. or s/sw. ★★ (r.) 85 86 87
　　Agreeable Roman dry red and smooth white. Drink young.

**Vendemmia** Harvest or vintage.

**Venegazzù** Ven. r. w. dr. sp. ★★★ 78 79 82 83 85 86 87
　　Remarkable rustic Bordeaux-style red produced from CABERNET grapes nr. Treviso. Rich bouquet, soft, warm taste, "della Casa" is best quality. Also sparkling white.

**Verdicchio dei Castelli di Jesi** Mar. DOC w. dr. (sp.) ★→★★★ D.Y.A.
　　Ancient, famous and very pleasant fresh pale white from nr. Ancona. Goes back to the Etruscans. Classico is more restricted. Comes in amphora-shaped bottles.

**Verdicchio di Matelica** Mar. DOC w. dr. (sp.) ★★ D.Y.A.
　　Similar to the last, though less well known.

**Verdiso** Native white grape of n.e. Italy, used with PROSECCO.

**Verduzzo (Colli Orientali del Friuli)** Fr-VG. DOC w. dr. s/sw. or sw. ★★ 85 86 87 Full-bodied white from a native grape. The best sweet is called Ramandolo. (Top maker: Giovanni Dri.)

**Verduzzo (Del Piave)** Ven. DOC w. dr. ★★ D.Y.A.
　　Similar to the last but fresh and dry.

**Vermentino** Lig. w. dr. DOC ★★ D.Y.A.
　　The best seafood white of the Riviera: from Pietra Ligure and San Remo. DOC is Rivera Ligure del Ponente. See Pigato.

**Vermentino di Gallura** Sard. DOC w. dr. ★★ D.Y.A.
　　Soft, dry, rather strong white from northern Sardinia.

**Vernaccia di Oristano** Sard. DOC w. dr. (sw.) (f.) ★★★ 77 79 81 82 83 84 85 86 Sardinian speciality, like light sherry, a touch bitter, full-bodied and interesting. Superiore with 15.5% alcohol and 3 yrs of age.

**Vernaccia di San Gimignano** Tusc. DOC w. dr. (f.) ★★ 86 87
　　Should be a distinctive strong high-flavoured wine from near Siena. Michelangelo's favourite. Much today is light and bland. Try Teruzzi & Puthod, Falchini or (old-style) Pietrafitta. Riserva after 1 yr.

**Vernaccia di Serrapetrona** Mar. DOC r. s/sw. sp. ★★ D.Y.A.
　　Comes from the province of Macerata; aromatic, with pleasantly bitter after-taste.

**Vernatsch** German for SCHIAVA.

**Vicchiomaggio**  Important CHIANTI CLASSICO estate near Greve.

**Vietti**  Excellent small producer of some of Piemonte's most characterful wines, incl. BAROLO. At Castiglione Falletto, Prov. Cuneo.

**VIDE**  An association of better-class Italian producers for marketing their estate wines.

**Vignamaggio**  Historic and beautiful CHIANTI CLASSICO estate near Greve.

**Villa Banfi**  The production department of the biggest US importer of Italian wine. Huge new plantings at MONTALCINO, incl. MOSCADELLO, CABERNET, CHARDONNAY, are part of a drive for quality plus quantity. BRUNELLO is proving excellent. Santa Costanza is v. fruity VINO NOVELLO. In PIEMONTE Banfi produces sp. Banfi Brut, Principessa GAVI, BRACCHETO D'ACQUI, Pinot Grigio.

**Villagrande**  Imposing old estate on the slopes of Mt. Etna, Sicily, DOC ETNA.

**Vino da arrosto**  "Wine for roast meat", i.e. good robust dry red.

**Vino da pasto**  "Mealtime" wine, i.e. nothing special.

---

**Vino da tavola**  "Table wine": intended to be the humblest class of Italian wine, with no specific geographical or other claim to fame, but increasingly the category to watch (with reasonable circumspection) for top-class wines not conforming to DOC regulations. They are referred to in the A-Z as v.d.t. As always it is the maker's name that counts for most.

---

**Vino Nobile di Montepulciano**  Tusc. DOCG r. dr.  **\*\*\***  79 81 82 83 85 86 87  Impressive Chianti-like red with bouquet and style, rapidly making its name and fortune. Aged for 3 yrs Riserva; for 4 yrs Riserva Speciale. Best estates incl. BOSCARELLI, AVIGNONESI, Fognano, Poliziano.

**Vino novello**  Italy's equivalent of France's "primeurs" (as in BEAUJOLAIS).

**Vinòt**  Italy's first "VINO NOVELLO", inspired by Beaujolais Nouveau. From GAJA.

**Vinsanto or Vin Santo**  Term for certain strong sweet wines esp. in Tuscany: usually PASSITI. TRENTINO now makes Italy's best.

**Vin Santo di Gambellara**  Ven. DOC w. sw. **\*\***
Powerful velvety, golden; made near Vicenza and Verona.

**Vin Santo Toscano**  Tusc. w. s/sw. **\*\*→\*\*\***
Aromatic bouquet, rich and smooth. Aged in very small barrels known as Carratelli. Can be astonishing.

**Vintage Tunina**  Fr-VG. w. dr. **\*\*\*** 83 84 85 86 87
The trade name of a notable blended COLLIO white from the JERMANN estate.

**Voerzio, Roberto**  Young pace-maker in Barolo with admirably refreshing wines.

**Volpaia, Castello di**  First-class CHIANTI CLASSICO estate at Radda. See Coltassala.

**VQPRD**  Often found on the labels of DOC wines to signify "Vini di Qualita Prodotti in Regioni Delimitate", or quality wines from restricted areas in accordance with EEC regulations.

**Zagarolo**  Lat. DOC w. dr. or s/sw. **\*\*** D.Y.A.
Neighbour of FRASCATI, similar wine.

**Zanella, Maurizio**  Owner of CA'DEL BOSCO. His name is on top CAB/MERLOT blend, one of Italy's best (82 83 84 85 86 87).

**Zonin**  One of Italy's biggest privately owned estates and wineries, based at GAMBELLARA, with DOC VALPOLICELLA, etc. Other large estates are at ASTI and in CHIANTI, San Gimignano and FRIULI. Also at Barboursville, Virginia, USA.

# Switzerland

Switzerland has no great wines, but almost all (especially whites) are enjoyable and satisfying – and very expensive. Switzerland has some of the world's most efficient and productive vineyards. Costs are high and nothing less is viable. All the most important are lined along the south-facing slopes of the upper Rhône valley and Lake Geneva, respectively the Valais and the Vaud. For other areas see the map. Wines are known by place-names, grape-names, and legally controlled type-names. All three, with those of leading growers and merchants, appear in the following list. On the whole, D.Y.A.

**Aigle** Vaud w. dr. ★★
  Principal town of CHABLAIS, between L. Geneva and the VALAIS. Dry whites of appropriately transitional style: at best strong and well balanced.

**Amigne** Traditional white grape of the VALAIS. Heavy but tasty wine, usually made dry.

**Arvine** Another old VALAIS white grape, similar to the last; perhaps better. Makes good dessert wine. Petite Arvine is similar.

**Auvernier** Neuchâtel r. p. w. dr. (sp.) ★★
  Village s. of NEUCHÂTEL known for PINOT NOIR, CHASSELAS and OEIL DE PERDRIX.

**Blauburgunder** One of the names given to the form of PINOT NOIR grown in German-speaking Switzerland.

**Bonvin** Old-established growers and merchants at SION.

**Chablais** Vaud (r.) w. dr. ★★
  The district between Montreux on L. Geneva and Martigny where the Rhône leaves the VALAIS. Good DORIN wines. Best villages: AIGLE, YVORNE, Bex, VILLENEUVE.

**Chasselas** The principal white grape of Switzerland, neutral in flavour but taking local character. Known as FENDANT in VALAIS, DORIN in VAUD and PERLAN round Geneva.

**Clevner (or Klevner)** Another name for BLAUBURGUNDER.

**Completer** Rare Grisons (see map) grape giving liquorous wine.

**Cortaillod** Neuchâtel r. (p. w.) ★★
  Village near NEUCHÂTEL specializing in light PINOT NOIR reds.

**Côte, La** The n. shore of L. Geneva from Geneva to Lausanne. Pleasant DORIN and SALVAGNIN. Best villages incl. Féchy and Rolle.

**Dézaley**  Vaud w. dr. ★★★
Best-known village of LAVAUX, between Lausanne and Montreux. Steep s. slopes to the lake make fine, strong, fruity DORIN. Dézaley-Marsens is equally good.

**Dôle**  Valais r. ★★
Term for red VALAIS wine of PINOT NOIR or GAMAY or both grapes, reaching a statutory level of strength and quality.

**Dorin**  Vaud w. dr. ★→★★
Obsolescent name for CHASSELAS wine in the VAUD, the equivalent of FENDANT from the VALAIS. Most wines are known by village names.

**Epesses**  Vaud w. dr. and r. ★★
Well-known lakeside village of LAVAUX. Good dry DORIN.

**Ermitage**  VALAIS name for white wine from MARSANNE grapes. Rich, concentrated and heavy; usually dry.

**Fendant**  Valais w. dr. ★→★★★
The name for CHASSELAS wine in the VALAIS, where it reaches its ripest, strongest and smoothest. SION is the centre.

**Flétri**  Withered grapes for making sweet wine, often MALVOISIE.

**Gamay**  The Beaujolais grape; grown in French-speaking Switzerland.

**Glacier, Vin du**  Almost legendary long-matured white stored at high altitudes. Virtually extinct today.

**Goron**  Red VALAIS wine that fails to reach the DÔLE standard.

**Grand Cru**  Vaudois term for estate wines from top areas.

**Hammel**  Major merchant and grower of LA CÔTE at Rolle with wide range of good-value wines. One of the few exporters.

**Herrschaft**  Grisons r. (w. sw.) ★→★★★
District near the border of Austria and Liechtenstein. Small amount of light PINOT NOIR reds and a few sweet whites.

**Humagne**  Old VALAIS grape. Some red Humagne is sold: decent country wine. The strong white is a rare speciality.

**Johannisberg**  The Valais name for SYLVANER, which can make excellent stiff, dense and high-flavoured dry wine here, comparable to Frankenwein (see Germany).

**Lausanne, Ville de**  Producer of fine wines in surrounding villages for centuries, now incl. even late-harvest CHARDONNAY.

**Lavaux**  Vaud r. w. dr. ★→★★★
The n. shore of L. Geneva between Lausanne and Montreux. The e. half of the VAUD. Best villages for CHASSELAS, lively and generous, incl. DÉZALEY, EPESSES, Villette, Lutry, ST-SAPHORIN.

**Légèrement doux**  Most Swiss wines are dry. Any with measurable sugar must be labelled thus or as "avec sucre résiduel".

**Malvoisie**  VALAIS name for PINOT GRIS. Makes some wonderful late-picked sweet wines.

**Mandement**  Geneva r. (p.) w. dr. ★
Wine district just w. of Geneva (see Vin-Union-Genève). Very light reds, chiefly GAMAY, and whites (PERLAN).

**Marsanne**  The white grape of Hermitage on the French Rhône, used in the VALAIS to make ERMITAGE.

**Merlot**  Bordeaux red grape (see Grapes for red wine) used to make the better wine of Italian Switzerland (TICINO). See also Viti.

**Mont d'Or, Domaine du**  Valais w. dr. sw. ★★★★
Often considered the best wine estate of Switzerland: 60 acres of steep hillside near SION. Good FENDANT, JOHANNISBERG, AMIGNE, etc., and real Riesling. Very rich concentrated wines.

**Montreux**  The town's v'yds make some of the best CHASSELAS of the Vaud, ripe and resonant.

**Neuchâtel**  Neuchâtel r. p. w. dr. sp. ★→★★★
City and the wine from the n. shore of its lake. Pleasant light PINOT NOIR and attractive sometimes sparkling CHASSELAS.

**Nostrano**  Word meaning "ours" applied to the lesser red wine of the TICINO, made from a mixture of native and Italian grapes, in contrast to MERLOT from Bordeaux.

**Oeil de Perdrix**  Pale rosé of PINOT NOIR.

**Orsat**  Long-established wine firm at Martigny, VALAIS, recently changed hands. See next entry.

**Orsat, J. A. & P. L.**  Members of the original Orsat family have started this firm to maintain very high standards and good value in FENDANT, etc.

**Perlan**  Geneva w. dr. ★
The MANDEMENT name for the ubiquitous CHASSELAS, here at its palest, driest and least impressive.

**Provins**  The excellent central cooperative of the VALAIS.

**Rèze**  The grape, now very rare, used for VIN DU GLACIER.

**Riesling-Sylvaner**  Swiss name for MÜLLER-THURGAU, common in e. Switzerland (Thurgau), where it was bred by Dr. Müller. "A prophet is not without honour . . ."

**Rivaz**  Vaud r. w. dr. ★★
One of the better known villages of LAVAUX.

**St-Saphorin**  Vaud w. dr. ★★
One of the principal villages of LAVAUX: wines drier and more austere than DÉZALEY or EPESSES.

**Salvagnin**  Vaud r. ★→★★
Red VAUD wine of tested quality: the equivalent of DÔLE.

**Savagnin**  Swiss name for the TRAMINER, called Païen in the VALAIS.

**Schafiser**  Bern (r.) w. dr. ★→★★
The n. shore of L. Bienne (Bielersee) is well known for very dry and light CHASSELAS sold as either Schafiser or Twanner.

**Schenk, S.A.**  The biggest Swiss wine firm, based at Rolle in the VAUD, with 570 acres as well as other world-wide interests.

**Sion**  Valais w. dr. ★→★★★
Centre of the VALAIS wine region, famous for its FENDANT.

**Sierre**  Important centre for some of the best VALAIS wines.

**Spätburgunder**  PINOT NOIR: by far the commonest grape of German-speaking Switzerland, making very light wines.

**Testuz, V. & P.**  Well-known growers and merchants at Dézaley, LAVAUX.

**Thun**  Source of some of Switzerland's best RIESLING.

**Ticino**  Italian-speaking s. Switzerland. See Merlot, Viti, Nostrano.

**Twanner**  See Schafiser.

**Valais**  The Rhône valley between Brig and Martigny. Its n. side is an admirable dry sunny and sheltered v'yd, planted mainly to the CHASSELAS grape, which here makes its most potent wine.

**Vaud**  The region of L. Geneva. Its n. shore is Switzerland's biggest vineyard and in places as good as any. DORIN and SALVAGNIN are the main wines.

**Vétroz**  Valais (r.) w. dr. ★★
Village near SION in the best part of the VALAIS.

**Villeneuve**  Top-rate village for CHASSELAS between Montreux and the CHABLAIS slopes of YVORNE.

**Vevey**  Town near Montreux with a famous wine festival once every 30-odd years. The last was in 1977.

**Vin-Union-Genève**  Big growers' cooperative at Satigny in the MANDEMENT. Light reds and white PERLAN are Geneva's local wine.

**Viti**  Ticino r. ★★
Legal designation of better-quality TICINO red, made of MERLOT and with at least 12% alcohol.

**Yvorne**  Village near AIGLE with some of the best CHABLAIS v'yds.

# Germany

Since the mid-1980s German wine has suffered a crisis of confidence. To the regret of those who admire and respect the many fine examples of her unique style of wine that truly reflect her traditions, her climate and her soil, Germany is considered to have betrayed herself by offering the world a mass of low-grade watery wine at bucket-shop prices.

Some of it is imported wine dressed up to look German. Alas, much of it is genuinely German, but made to the minimum standards allowed by a too-liberal wine law. The minimum requirements for the status of Qualitätswein b.A. (see below) are such as to allow the most dreary commodity to benefit from this apparently elevated denomination.

Active debate has started about overhauling the wine law of 1971, which is largely to blame for this and other problems in the German wine industry. It is probable that restrictions on quantities of wine per hectare, plus upgrading minimum standards of ripeness, will be the Government's contribution. But meanwhile many of the best producers in certain areas have formed themselves into associations (such as "Charta" in the Rheingau) pledged to uphold high standards of their own definition, and to ignore as irrelevant the minimum standards set by the Government.

Meanwhile young wine-drinkers very reasonably call for a revision of the labelling system which they find over-complicated: long on logic but short on practical help for the consumer. "Like a Greek telex" is one newcomer's view of the stately nomenclature in Gothic script typical not just of classic wines of high quality, but suspiciously also of some very basic blends.

This is not the place to debate a reform of national legislation: only to point out that German labels need very close scrutiny, and that the differences between the fine long-lived Riesling wines of conscientious growers and the bulk of Liebfraumilch and the like are far greater than their labels, and even their official denominations, suggest. Major moves are being made to simplify labels (see p.102), and the lead is coming from the top.

Meanwhile German taste is changing dramatically. The role of wine in Germany up to very recent times has been as refreshment between meals, as an apéritif before or a succulent throatful after. To the grower delicacy and balance have been ends in themselves, with sweetness and fruity acidity counter-poised; the wine a drink to be enjoyed and contemplated alone.

The new trend is for dry wines made for drinking with meals. More than half the production of most good growers is now in the "trocken" (dry) category. This change is beneficial; drinkers rapidly realize that a poor-quality wine without even a veil of sugar to hide its nakedness is a miserable drink. The move to dry wines is therefore already raising wine-making standards.

Consumers familiar with the old pattern, in which, for example, a Spätlese was expected to be a moderately sweet wine, now need to understand the concept of a *dry* Spätlese, in which all the sugar is converted to alcohol with an effect closer to (though still not quite as strong as) a wine from Alsace.

The following
abbreviations of
regional names
are used in the text.

| | |
|---|---|
| **Bad.** | Baden |
| **Frank.** | Franken |
| **M-M** | Mittel-Mosel |
| **M-S-R** | Moselle Saar Ruwer |
| **Na.** | Nahe |
| **Rhg.** | Rheingau |
| **Rhh.** | Rheinhessen |
| **Rhpf.** | Rheinpfalz |
| **Wurtt.** | Württemberg |

# The labels and the law

German wine law is based on the ripeness of the grapes at harvest time. Vintages vary, but most German wine needs sugar added before fermentation to increase its strength, and make up for the missing sunshine in their northerly vineyards.

The exceptional wine, from grapes ripe enough not to need sugar, is kept apart as Qualitätswein mit Prädikat or QmP. Within this top category its natural sugar content is expressed by traditional terms – in ascending order of ripeness: Kabinett, Spätlese, Auslese, Beerenauslese, Trockenbeerenauslese.

But reasonably good wine is also made in good vineyards from grapes that fail to reach the natural sugar content required for a QmP label. This category is called Qualitätswein as well, but with the different qualification of bestimmter Anbaugebiete (i.e. QbA) instead of mit Prädikat. "Prädikat" is therefore (theoretically) the key word to look for. Matters are complicated, though, by growers who add sugar even to Prädikat standard juice, believing, as the French do, that slightly more alcohol gives better balance. Do not assume that *all* QbA wines are inferior.

The third level, Tafelwein, has no pretensions to quality and is not allowed to give itself airs beyond the name of the general region or sub-region it comes from. (But see Landwein.)

Though there is very much more detail in the laws this is the gist of the quality grading. Where it differs completely from the French system is in ignoring geographical differences. There are no Grands Crus, no VDQS. In theory all any German vineyard has to do to make the best wine is to grow the ripest grapes.

The law distinguishes only between degrees of geographical exactness. In labelling quality wine the grower or merchant is given a choice. He can (and almost always will) label the relatively small quantities of his best wine with the name of the precise vineyard or Einzellage where it was grown. Germany has about 3,000 Einzellage names. Obviously only particularly good ones are famous enough to help sell the wine. Therefore the law has created a second class of vineyard name: the Grosslage. A Grosslage is a group of neighbouring Einzellages of supposedly similar character and standing. Because there are fewer Grosslage names, and far more wine from each, Grosslagen have a better chance of building reputations.*

Thirdly the grower or merchant (more likely the latter) may choose to sell his wine under a regional name: the word is Bereich. To cope with the vast demand for "Bernkasteler" or "Niersteiner" or "Johannisberger" these world-famous names have been made legal for considerable districts. "Bereich Johannisberg" is the whole of the Rheingau; "Bereich Bernkastel" the whole of the Mittelmosel. By the same logic the whole of the Médoc could be called Margaux. Beware the Bereich.

A fourth alternative, now becoming fashionable, is to use the community (or village) name only, not mentioning the vineyard. This is only allowed for QbA or QmP wines. With simplification of nomenclature very much on merchants' minds, we will see more and more of this style of labelling, and also of labels stressing the style of wine, rather than its origin. "Riesling Dry" is a new concept which is already making an impact. One golden rule remains true: the name of the producer is the key.

---

| | |
|---|---|
| **MOSEL-SAAR-RUWER**<br>**BERKASTELER**<br>**SCHLOSSBERG**<br>**RIESLING AUSLESE**<br>1987<br>Qualitätswein mit Prädikat<br>A.P. NR. 12345678<br>ERZEUGERABFÜLLUNG<br>MOZARTHOF TRIER | **The traditional German label**<br>The order of wording on traditional German quality wine labels follows a standard pattern. The first mention is the Anbaugebiet or wine region. The second is the town or parish, with the suffix -er. The third is the vineyard (either Einzellage or Grosslage – see introduction and footnote). The fourth (optional) is the grape variety, the fifth the quality in terms of ripeness. For Qualitätswein mit Prädikat see page 113. For A.P. Nr. see page 104. Erzeugerabfüllung means bottled by the grower. |

---

*Where the law is less than candid, however, is in pretending to believe that the general public will know a Grosslage name from an Einzellage name, when the two are indistinguishably similar (see any entry on the following pages). It is actually against the law to indicate on the label whether the name in question is that of a particular plot or a wider grouping. The names of all relevant Grosslagen are given in this book. Note that Grosslage wines are only rarely of the quality of Einzellage wines.

# Recent vintages

## Mosel-Saar-Ruwer

Mosels (including Saar and Ruwer wines) are so attractive young that their keeping qualities are not often enough explored, and wines older than seven years or so are unusual. But well-made wines of Kabinett class gain from three or more in bottle, Spätleses by longer, and Ausleses and Beerenausleses by anything from 10 to 20 years.

As a rule, in poor years the Saar and Ruwer make sharp, thin wines, but in the best years they can surpass the whole of Germany for elegance and "breed".

1987    Rainy summer but warm Sept/Oct. 90% QbA wines, crisp and lively, to drink in 1990-93. The few QmPs will improve longer.

1986    Fair Riesling year despite autumn rain: 13% QmP wines, mostly Kabinett. Keeping well.

1985    A modest summer but beautiful autumn. 40% of the harvest is QmP. Very good Riesling vintage from best v'yds, incl. Eiswein. Drinking well.

1984    A late and rainy year. Two-thirds QbA, one-third Tafel- or Landwein. Almost no QmP. But good acidity means some wines (esp. Ruwers) have kept well.

1983    The best since 1976; much good QbA, a little Kabinett, 31% Spätlese, Ausleses few but some fine, others have sulphur problems. Drinking well.

1982    A huge ripe vintage marred by rain which considerably diluted the wines. Most is plain QbA but good sites made Kabinett, Spätlese and Auslese. Drink up.

1981    A wet vintage but some good middle Mosels up to Spätlese. Also Eiswein. Drink up.

1980    A terrible summer. Some pleasant wines but little more. Avoid.

1979    A patchy vintage after bad winter damage. But several excellent Kabinetts and better. Light but well-balanced wines should be drunk up.

1978    A similar vintage to '77, though very late and rather small. Very few sweet wines but many with good balance. Drink up.

1977    Big vintage of serviceable quality, mostly QbA. Drink up.

1976    Very good small vintage, with some superlative sweet wines and almost no dry. Most wines now ready; the best will keep 2-3 years.

1975    Very good; many Spätleses and Ausleses. Almost all now ready.

1971    Superb, with perfect balance. At its peak.

Older fine vintages: '69, '67, '64, '59, '53, '49, '45.

## Rheinhessen, Nahe, Rheinpfalz, Rheingau

Even the best wines can be drunk with pleasure after two or three years, but Kabinett, Spätlese and Auslese wines gain enormously in character by keeping for longer. Rheingau wines tend to be longest-lived, improving for 10 years or more, but wines from the Nahe and Palatinate can last nearly as long. Rheinhessen wines usually mature sooner, and dry Franconian wines are best at 2-5 years.

1987    Good average quality: lively, round and fresh. 80% QbA (keep 3-5 years), 15% QmP (keep 4-7 years).

1986    Well-balanced Rieslings, mostly QbA but some Kabinett and Spätlese, esp. in Rheinhessen and Nahe. No hurry to drink.

1985    Frost, hail and drought led to sadly small crops, but good quality, esp. Riesling. Average 65% QmP. Comparable quality to 1983. Keeping well.

1984    Poor flowering and ripening. Three-quarters QbA, with QmP only in Rheinhessen, Rheinpfalz, Baden and Nahe. But flavour can be good. Drink soon.

1983    Very good Rieslings, esp. in the Rheingau and central Nahe. Generally about half QbA, but plenty of Spätleses. No hurry to drink.

1982    A colossal vintage gathered in torrential rain. Spätleses and even Kabinett are rare, but all '82s should be drunk up.

1981    Poor conditions in the Rheingau but better in Nahe and Rheinhessen and good in Palatinate. Generally ready.

1980    Bad weather from spring to autumn. Only passable wines. Avoid.

1979    Uneven and reduced in size. Few great wines but many typical and good, esp. in Palatinate. Drink up.

1978    Satisfactory vintage saved by late autumn. 25% QmP, but very few Spätleses. Some excellent wines in the south. Drink up.

1977    Big and useful; few Kabinett wines or better. Drink up.

1976    The richest vintage since 1921 in places. Very few dry wines. Balance less consistent than 1975. Generally mature.

1975    A splendid Riesling year, a high percentage of Kabinetts and Spätleses. Should be drunk fairly soon.

1971    A superlative vintage, now at its peak.

Older fine vintages: '69, '67, '66, '64, '59, '57, '53, '49, '45.

### N.B. On the German Vintage Notation

Vintage notes after entries in the German section are given in a different form from those elsewhere, to show the style of the vintage as well as its quality. Three styles are indicated: The classic, super-ripe vintage with a high proportion of natural (QmP) wines, including Spätleses and Ausleses. Example: **83**

The "normal" successful vintage with plenty of good wine but no great preponderance of sweeter wines. Example: 79

The cool vintage with generally poor ripeness but a fair proportion of reasonably successful wines, tending to be over-acid. Few or no QmP wines, but correspondingly more selection in the QbA category. Such wines sometimes mature better than expected. Example: *84*

Where no mention is made the vintage is generally not recommended, or most of its wines have passed maturity.

---

**Achkarren** Bad. (r.) w.  ★★
    Well-known wine village of the KAISERSTUHL, esp. for SILVANER, RULÄNDER. Best site: Schlossberg.

**Adelmann, Graf** Famous grower with 37 acres at Kleinbottwar, WÜRTTEMBERG. Uses the name Brussele. Light reds; good RIESLINGS.

**Affental** An area, not a village, just s. of Baden-Baden, producing a popular red Affentaler SPÄTBURGUNDER in a bottle moulded with a monkey ("Affe") climbing it.

**Ahr** Ahr r. ★→★★ 76 83 *84* 85 86 87
    Germany's best-known red-wine area, s. of Bonn. Very light pale SPÄTBURGUNDERS.

**Amtliche Prüfungsnummer** See Prüfungsnummer.

**Anheuser** Name of two distinguished growers of the NAHE.

**Annaberg** Rhpf. w. ★★★ 75 76 79 83 *84* 85 86 87
    18-acre estate at DÜRKHEIM famous for sweet and pungent wines, esp. SCHEUREBE, with prodigious keeping qualities.

**A.P.Nr.** Abbreviation of AMTLICHE PRÜFUNGSNUMMER.

**Assmannshausen** Rhg. r. ★→★★★ 71 75 76 83 85 86 87
    RHEINGAU village known for its pale, sometimes sweet, reds. Top v'yd: Höllenberg. Grosslagen: Steil and Burgweg. Growers incl. the State Domain at ELTVILLE.

---

*The German Wine Academy runs regular courses of wine-instruction at all levels for both amateurs and professionals, in German and English. The Academy is based at the glorious 12th-century Cistercian monastery of Kloster Eberbach in the Rheingau. The course normally includes tasting-tours of Germany's wine regions. Particulars can be obtained from the Academy, P. O. Box 1705, D-6500 Mainz, West Germany.*

---

**Auslese** Specially selected wine with high natural sugar content, all the best affected by "noble rot" and correspondingly unctuous in flavour.

**Avelsbach** M-S-R (Ruwer) w. ★★★ 71 75 76 79 83 *84* 85 86 87
    Village near TRIER. Supremely delicate wines. Growers: Staatliche Weinbaudomäne (see STAATSWEINGUT), BISCHÖFLICHE WEINGÜTER. Grosslage: Römerlay.

**Ayl** M-S-R (Saar) w. ★★★ 71 75 76 79 82 83 *84* 85 86 87
    One of the best villages of the SAAR. Top v'yds.: Kupp, Herrenberger. Grosslage: Scharzberg. Growers incl. BISCHÖFLICHE WEINGÜTER.

**Bacchus** Modern highly perfumed grape variety successful for sweet wines.

**Bacharach** Romantic old town, the tourist centre of the MITTELRHEIN.

**Bacharach (Bereich)** ★→★★
    District name for the s. Mittelrhein v'yds downstream from the RHEINGAU. Steely, racy wines, some v. pleasant.

**Baden** Huge area of scattered wine-growing. The style is substantial, relatively low in acid, well adapted for mealtimes. Best areas are KAISERSTUHL and ORTENAU.

**Badische Bergstrasse/Kraichgau (Bereich)** Widespread district of n. BADEN. RIESLING and RÜLANDER are best.

**Bad Dürkheim** See Dürkheim, Bad.

**Badisches Frankenland (Bereich)** Minor district name of n. BADEN; Franconian-style wines.

**Bad Kreuznach** Na. w. ★★→★★★ 75 76 79 83 *84* 85 86 87
Main town of the NAHE with some of its best wines. Many fine v'yds, incl. Brückes, Kahlenberg, Steinweg, Krötenpfuhl. Grosslage: Kronenberg.

**Balbach Erben, Bürgermeister** One of the best NIERSTEIN growers. 44 acres, 80% Riesling. Best v'yds: Pettenthal, Ölberg.

**Basserman-Jordan** 117-acre MITTELHAARDT family estate with many of the best v'yds in DEIDESHEIM, FORST, RUPPERTSBERG, etc.

**Becker, J.B.** Excellent family estate and brokerage house at WALLUF, Rheingau.

**Beerenauslese** Extremely sweet and luscious wine from exceptionally ripe selected individual bunches, their sugar and flavour concentrated by "noble rot".

**Bereich** District within an Anbaugebiet (region). See under Bereich names, e.g. Bernkastel (Bereich).

**Bergweiler-Prüm Erben (Dr Pauly-Bergweiler), Zach., Weingut** Fine 24-acre estate based at BERNKASTEL. V'yds there and in WEHLEN etc. Also Nicolay wines from ÜRZIG and ERDEN.

**Bergzabern, Bad** Rhpf. (r.) w. ★→★★ 76 79 83 *84* 85 86 87
Town of SÜDLICHE-WEINSTRASSE. Pleasant sweetish wines. Grosslage: Liebfrauenberg.

**Bernkastel** M-M w. ★★→★★★★ 71 75 76 79 83 *84* 85 86 87
Top wine-town of the Mosel; the epitome of RIESLING. Best v'yds: Doctor (8 acres), Graben, Bratenhöfchen, etc. Grosslagen: Badstube (★★★) and Kurfürstlay (★★). Top growers incl. FRIEDRICH WILHELM GYMNASIUM, VEREINIGTE HOSPITIEN, THANISCH, PRÜM, WEGELER-DEINHARD, BERGWEILER, Pauly, etc.

**Bernkastel (Bereich)** Wide area of mixed quality but decided flowery character. Includes all the Mittelmosel.

**Bingen** Rhh. w. ★★→★★★ 71 75 76 79 83 *84* 85 86 87
Town on Rhine and Nahe with fine v'yds, incl. Scharlachberg. Grosslage: Sankt Rochuskapelle.

**Bingen (Bereich)** District name for w. Rheinhessen.

**Bischöfliche Weinguter Verwaltung** Outstanding M-S-R estate at TRIER, a union of the Cathedral properties with two other famous charities, the Bischöfliches Priesterseminar and the Bischöfliches Konvikt. 230 acres of top v'yds in AVELSBACH, WILTINGEN, SCHARZHOFBERG, AYL, KASEL, EITELSBACH, PIESPORT, TRITTENHEIM, ÜRZIG, etc.

**Blankenhornsberg** Outstanding KAISERSTUHL estate; 62 acres based at IHRINGEN.

**Blue Nun** The best-selling brand of LIEBFRAUMILCH, from SICHEL.

**Bodenheim** Rhh. w. ★★
Village nr. NIERSTEIN with delicate wines, esp. from Silberberg.

**Bodensee (Bereich)** Minor district of s. BADEN, on Lake Constance.

**Bocksbeutel** Flask-shaped bottle used for FRANKEN wines.

**Brauneberg** M-M w. ★★★ 71 75 76 79 83 *84* 85 86 87
Village near BERNKASTEL with 750 acres. Excellent full-flavoured Rieslings. Best v'yd: Juffer. Grosslage: Kurfürstlay. Growers incl, BERGWEILER, Pauly, Paulinshof, RICHTER, HAAG.

**Breisach** Baden
Frontier town on Rhine nr. KAISERSTUHL. Seat of the largest German cooperative, the ZBW.

**Breisgau (Bereich)** Minor district of BADEN, just n. of KAISERSTUHL. Best known for very pale pink WEISSHERBST.

**Brentano, von** 25-acre old family estate in WINKEL, Rheingau.

**Breuer, G. Weingut** Family estate of 20 acres in RÜDESHEIM, esp. for v.g Schlossberg.

**Buhl, von, Geheimrat** Great RHEINPFALZ family estate. 250+ acres in DEIDESHEIM, FORST, RUPPERTSBERG, etc. In the very top class.

**Bullay** M-S-R ★→ **★★** 76 83 *84* 85 86 87
Lower Mosel village. Good light wines. Growers incl. Drathen.

**Bundesweinprämierung** The German State Wine Award, organized by the DLG (see below): a gold, silver or bronze medallion on bottles of wines of a sufficiently high standard.

**Bürgerspital zum Heiligen Geist** Ancient charitable estate at WÜRZBURG. 333 acres in WÜRZBURG, RANDERSACKER, etc., make rich dry wines.

**Bürklin-Wolf, Dr** Great RHEINPFALZ family estate. 247 acres in WACHENHEIM. FORST, DEIDESHEIM and RUPPERTSBERG, with rarely a dull, let alone poor, wine.

**Castell'sches, Fürstlich Domänenamt** 142-acre princely estate in STEIGERWALD. Good typical FRANKEN wines: SILVANER, RIESLANER. Also SEKT.

**Charta** Organization of top RHEINGAU estates concentrating on TROCKEN and HALBTROCKEN RIESLINGS. Members must observe higher standards then the legal minima.

**Crown of Crowns** Popular brand of LIEBFRAUMILCH from LANGENBACH & CO.

**Crusius** 30-acre family estate at TRAISEN, Na. Excellently made, fresh RIESLINGS from Bastei and Rotenfels v'yds age v. well. Also SEKT of high quality and recently wonderful SPÄTBURGUNDER dry rosé.

**Deidesheim** Rhpf. w. (r.) **★★→★★★★** 71 75 76 79 83 *84* 85 86 87
Biggest top-quality wine-village of RHEINPFALZ with 1,000 acres. Rich, high-flavoured, lively wines. V'yds incl. Grainhübel, Herrgottsacker, Leinhöhle, Hohenmorgen, Kieselberg, Paradiesgarten, etc. Grosslagen: Hofstück (★★), Mariengarten (★★★).

**Deinhard** Famous old Koblenz merchants and growers of top-quality wines in RHEINGAU, MITTELMOSEL, RUWER and RHEINPFALZ (see Wegeler-Deinhard), also makers of v.g SEKT (brand name: Lila).

**Deinhard, Dr** 62-acre family estate in DEIDESHEIM with many of best v'yds.

**Deutscher Tafelwein** TAFELWEIN from Germany (only). See also Tafelwein.

**Deutsches Weinsiegel** A quality "seal" (i.e. neck label) for wines that have passed a statutory tasting test. Seals are yellow = dry, green = medium dry, red = sweet.

**Deutsche Weinstrasse** Popular tourist road of the southern Palatinate, Bockenheim to Schweigen.

**DLG (Deutsche Landwirtschaft Gesellschaft)** The German Agricultural Society at Frankfurt. Awards national medals for quality.

**Dhron** See Neumagen-Dhron.

**Diabetiker Wein** Wine with minimal residual sugar (less than 4gms/litre); thus suitable for diabetics – or those who like *very* dry wine.

**Dienheim** Rhh. w. ★★ 76 83 85 86 87
Southern neighbour of OPPENHEIM. Mainly run-of-the-mill wines. Best v'yds: Kreuz, Herrenberg, Schloss. Grosslagen: Güldenmorgen, Krötenbrunnen.

**Dom** German for Cathedral. Wines from the famous TRIER Cathedral properties have "Dom" before the v'yd name.

**Domäne** German for "domain" or "estate". Sometimes used alone to mean the "State domain" (Staatliche Weinbaudomäne).

**Durbach** Baden w. (r.) ★★→ **★★★** 76 83 *84* 85 86 87
775 acres of the best v'yds of BADEN. Top growers: Schloss Staufenberg, Wolf-Metternich, von Neveu. Choose their KLINGELBERGERS and KLEVNERS. Grosslage: Fürsteneck.

**Dürkheim, Bad** Rhpf. w. or (r.) ★★→★★★ 76 79 83 *84* 85 86 87
Main town of the MITTELHAARD with the world's biggest barrel (converted into a tavern). Top v'yds.: Hochbenn, Michelsberg. Grosslagen: Feuerberg, Schenkenböhl.

**Edel** Means "noble". Edelfäule means "noble rot": the condition which gives the greatest sweet wines (see p. 48).

**Edenkoben** Rhpf. w. (r.) ✷→ ░░ ★★ 76 79 83 *84* 85 86 87
Important village of n. SÜDLICHE WEINSTRASSE. Grosslage: Ludwigshöhe. The best wines have plenty of flavour.

**Egon Müller zu Scharzhof** Top Saar estate of 32 acres at WILTINGEN. His delicate, racy SCHARZHOFBERGER Rieslings are supreme in vintages that produce AUSLESES.

**Eiswein** Wine made from frozen grapes with the ice (e.g. water content) rejected, thus very concentrated in flavour and sugar, of Beerenauslese ripeness or more. Rare and expensive. Sometimes produced as late as the January or February following the vintage. Alcohol content can be as low as 5.5%.

**Eitelsbach** Ruwer w. ★★→★★★ 71 75 76 83 *84* 85 86 87
RUWER village now part of TRIER, incl. superb Karthäuserhofberg estate. Grosslage: Römerlay.

**Elbling** Traditional but generally inferior grape widely grown on upper Mosel but capable of great freshness and vitality in the best conditions (e.g. at MENNIG or in the Mittel Mosel).

**Eltville** Rhg. w. ░░**★★** →★★★ 71 75 76 79 83 *84* 85 86 87
Major wine-town with cellars of the Rheingau State domain, FISCHER and von SIMMERN estates. Excellent wines. Top v'yds: Sonnenberg, Taubenberg. Grosslage: Steinmächer.

**Enkirch** M-M w. ★★→ ░░**★★★** 71 76 83 *84* 85 86 87
Minor middle-Mosel village, often overlooked but with lovely light tasty wine. Grosslage: Schwarzlay. Best v'yds: Steffensberg, Herrenberg.

**Erbach** Rhg. w. ★★★→★★★★ 71 76 79 83 *84* 85 86 87
One of the best parts of the Rheingau with powerful, perfumed wines, incl. the great MARCOBRUNN; other top v'yds: Schlossberg, Siegelsberg, Honigberg, Michelmark. Grosslage: Deutelsberg. Major estates: SCHLOSS REINHARTSHAUSEN, VON SCHONBÖRN.

**Erden** M-M w. ★★→★★★ 71 75 76 83 *84* 85 86 87
Village between Urzig and Kröv with full-flavoured vigorous wine. Top v'yds: Prälat, Treppchen. Leading growers: BISCHÖFLICHE WEINGÜTER, BERGWEILER-PRÜM, Nicolay. Grosslage: Schwarzlay.

**Erzeugerabfüllung** Estate-bottled; bottled by the grower.

**Escherndorf** Franc. w. ★★→★★★ 76 83 86 87
Important wine-town near WÜRZBURG. Similar tasty dry wine. Top v'yds: Lump, Berg. Grosslage: Kirchberg.

---

*Remember that vintage information about German wines is given in a different form from the ready/not ready distinction applying to other countries. Read the explanation on page 104.*

---

**Fischer, Dr., Weingut** 60-acre estate of top quality at OCKFEN, incl. whole of WAWERNER Herrenberg.

**Forst** Rhpf. w. ★★→★★★★ 71 75 76 79 83 *84* 85 86 87
MITTELHAARDT village with 500 acres of Germany's best v'yds. Ripe, richly fragrant, full-bodied but subtle wines. Top v'yds: Kirchenstück, Jesuitengarten, Ungeheuer, etc. Grosslagen: Mariengarten, Schnepfenflug.

**Franken** Franconia: region of excellent distinctive dry wines, esp. SILVANER. The centre is WÜRZBURG. BEREICH names: MAINVIERECK, MAINDREIECK, STEIGERWALD.

**Freiburg** Baden w. (r.) ✷→★★ D.Y.A.
Centre of MARKGRÄFLERLAND. Good GUTEDEL.

**Freinsheim** Rhpf. ░░**★★**
Well-known village of Lower Haardt with high proportion of Riesling. Earthy, spicy wines.

**Friedrich Wilhelm Gymnasium**  Superb 111-acre charitable estate based in TRIER with v'yds in BERNKASTEL, ZELTINGEN, GRAACH, TRITTENHEIM, OCKFEN, etc., all M-S-R.

**Geheimrat 'J'**  Brand-name of trendsetting dry Riesling Spätlese from WEGELER-DEINHARD, Oestrich. Epitomizes new thinking in German wine.

**Geisenheim**  Rhg. w. ★★→★★★ 71 76 83 *84* 85 86 87
Village famous for Germany's leading wine-school and fine aromatic wines. Best v'yds incl. Rothenberg, Kläuserweg. Grosslagen: Burgweg and Erntebringer.

**Gemeinde**  A commune or parish.

**Gewürztraminer**  Spicy grape, speciality of Alsace, used a little in s. Germany, esp. RHEINPFALZ and BADEN. See Traminer.

**Gimmeldingen**  Rhpf. w. ★→★★ 76 83 *84* 85 86 87
Village just s. of MITTELHAARDT. At their best, similar wines. Grosslage: Meerspinne.

**Goldener Oktober**  Popular brand of Rhine and Mosel blends from ST. URSULA.

**Graach**  M-M w. ★★→ |★★★| 71 75 76 83 *84* 85 86 87
Small village between BERNKASTEL and WEHLEN. Top v'yds: Himmelreich, Domprobst, Abstberg, Josephshöfer. Grosslage: Münzlay.

**Green Label**  Germany's best-selling MOSEL (BEREICH BERNKASTEL). Brand-name of DEINHARD.

**Grosslage**  See Introduction, p.100.

**Guntersblum**  Rhh. w. ★→★★ 76 83 *84* 85 86 87
Big wine-town s. of OPPENHEIM. Grosslagen: Krötenbrunnen, Vogelsgarten.

**Guntrum, Louis**  Fine 164-acre family estate in NIERSTEIN, OPPENHEIM, etc., and merchant house with high and reliable standards.

**Gutedel**  German for the Chasselas grape, used in s. BADEN.

**Gutsverwaltung**  Estate administration.

**Haag, Fritz**  Top-quality little (12 acres) estate at BRAUNEBERG.

**Halbtrocken**  Medium-dry. Containing less than 18 but more than 9 grams per litre unfermented sugar. An increasingly popular category of wine intended for meal-times, often better balanced than TROCKEN.

**Hallgarten**  Rhg. w. ★★→★★★ 71 76 83 *84* 85 86 87
Important little wine-town behind HATTENHEIM. Robust, full-bodied wines. Top v'yds incl. Schönhell, Jungfer. Grosslage: Mehrhölzchen.

**Hallgarten, House of**  Well-known London-based wine-merchant.

**Hanns Christof**  Estimable Rhine-wine brand from DEINHARD.

**Hattenheim**  Rhg. w. ★★→★★★★ 71 75 76 83 *84* 85 86 87
Superlative 500-acre wine-town. V'yds incl. STEINBERG, NUSSBRUNNEN, MANNBERG, HASSEL, etc. Grosslage: Deutelsberg. MARCOBRUNN lies on the ERBACH boundary.

**Heilbronn**  Württ. w. r. ★→★★ 76 83 85 86 87
Wine-town with many small growers and a big coop. Seat of DLG competition.

**Hessische Bergstrasse**  w. ★★→★★★ 76 83 84 85 86 87
Germany's smallest wine-region (1,000 acres) n. of Heidelberg. Pleasant Riesling from State domain v'yds in Heppenheim and Bensheim.

**Hessische Forschungsanstalt für Wein-Obst-& Gartenbau ...**
Germany's top wine-school and research establishment, at GEISENHEIM, Rheingau.

**Heyl zu Herrnsheim**  Fine 72-acre estate at NIERSTEIN, 55% Riesling.

**Hochheim**  Rhg. w. ★★→★★★ 71 75 76 79 83 *84* 85 86 87
600-acre wine-town 15 miles e. of RHEINGAU. Similar fine wines. Top v'yds: Domdechaney, Kirchenstück, Hölle, Königin Viktoria Berg. Grosslage: Daubhaus. Growers incl.: Aschrott, RESS, SCHÖNBORN, WERNER.

**Hock**  English term for Rhine-wine, derived from HOCHHEIM.

**Huesgen, Adolph**  Important merchant house at TRABEN-TRARBACH.

**Huxelrebe**  Modern very aromatic grape variety used mainly for sweet wines.

**Ihringen**  Bad. r. w. ★→★★★ 81 83 *84* 85 86 87
  One of the best villages of the KAISERSTUHL, BADEN. Proud of its SPÄTBURGUNDER red, WEISSHERBST and v.g. SILVANER.

**Ilbesheim**  Rhpf. w. ★→★★ 83 85 86 87
  Base of important growers' cooperative of SÜDLICHE WEINSTRASSE. See also Schweigen.

**Ingelheim**  Rhh. r. or w. ★ 76 83 *84* 85 86 87
  Town opposite the Rheingau historically known for red (SPÄTBURGUN-DER) wine.

**Iphofen**  Franc. w. ★★→★★★ 75 76 *83* 85 87
  Village e. of WÜRZBURG. Superb top v'yd: Julius-Echter-Berg. Grosslage: Burgweg.

**Jahrgang**  Year – as in "vintage".

**Jesuitengarten**  15-acre vineyard in FORST. One of Germany's best.

**Johannisberg**  Rhg. w. ★★→★★★★ 71 75 76 79 83 *84* 85 86 87
  260-acre village with superlative subtle RIESLINGS. Top v'yds incl. SCHLOSS JOHANNISBERG, Hölle, Klaus, etc. Grosslage: Erntebringer.

**Johannisberg (Bereich)**  District name of the entire RHEINGAU.

**Josephshöfer**  Fine v'yd at GRAACH, the property of von KESSELSTATT.

**Juliusspital**  Ancient charity at WÜRZBURG with 374 acres of top FRANKEN v'yds. Look for SILVANERS.

**Kabinett**  The term for the lightest category of natural unsugared (QmP) wines. Low in alcohol (average 7–9%).

**Kaiserstuhl-Tuniberg (Bereich)**  Best v'yd area of BADEN. Villages incl. ACHKARREN, IHRINGEN.

**Kallstadt**  Rhpf. w. (r.) ★★→★★★ 75 76 83 *84* 85 86 87
  Village of n. MITTELHAARDT. Fine rich wines. Top v'yd: ANNABERG. Grosslagen: Saumagen (★★★), Kobnert (★★).

**Kammerpreismünze**  See Landespreismünze.

**Kanzem**  M-S-R (Saar) w. ▮▮▮ 71 75 76 83 *84* 85 86 87
  Small but excellent neighbour of WILTINGEN. Top v'yds: Sonnenberg, Altenberg, Grosslage: Scharzberg.

**Kasel**  M-S-R (Ruwer) w. ★★→★★★ 71 75 76 83 *84* 85 86 87
  Village with wonderfully attractive light wines. Best v'yd: Nies'chen. Grosslage: Römerlay.

**Keller**  Wine-cellar.

**Kellerei**  Winery.

**Kerner**  Modern grape variety, earlier-ripening than Riesling, of good quality but without the lingering flavour of Riesling.

**Kesselstatt, von**  The biggest private Mosel estate, 600 years old. Over 200 acres in GRAACH (Josephshöfer), PIESPORT, KASEL, MENNIG, WILTINGEN, etc., plus substantial rented or managed estates, making light and fruity typical Mosels. Now belongs to Gunther Reh of Leiwen.

**Kesten**  M-M-W w. ★→★★★ 71 75 76 79 83 *84* 85 86 87
  Neighbour of BRAUNEBERG. Best wines (from Paulinshofberg v'yd) similar. Grosslage: Kurfürstlay.

**Kiedrich**  Rhg. w. ★★→★★★★ 71 76 79 83 *84* 85 86 87
  Neighbour of RAUENTHAL; almost as splendid and high-flavoured. Top v'yds: Gräfenberg, Wasseros, Sandgrub. Grosslage: Heiligenstock.

**Klevner (or Clevner)**  Red Klevner (synonym, Blauer Frühburgunder), grown in WÜRTTEMBERG, is supposedly either a mutation of Pinot Noir or Italian Chiavenna, an early-ripening black Pinot. Also an ORTENAU (BADEN) synonym for TRAMINER.

**Klingelberger**  BADEN term for the RIESLING, esp. at DURBACH.

**Kloster Eberbach**  Glorious 12th-century Abbey at HATTENHEIM, Rheingau, now State domain property and H.Q. of the German Wine Academy. See panel, p. 104.

**Klüsserath** M-M w. ★★→ ▭▭▭ 71 76 83 *84* 85 86
Minor Mosel village worth trying in good vintages. Best v'yds: Bruderschaft, Königsberg. Grosslage: St. Michael.

**Kraichgau** Small BADEN region s. of Heidelberg. Best-known wines are from Neckarzimmern and Wiesloch.

**Kreuznach (Bereich)** District name for the entire northern NAHE. See also Bad Kreuznach.

**Kröv** M-M w. ★→★★★ 76 83 85 86 87
Popular tourist resort famous for its Grosslage name: Nacktarsch, meaning "bare bottom".

**Landespreismünze** Prizes for quality at state, rather than national, level. Considered by some more discriminating than DLG medals.

**Landgräflich Hessisches Weingut** Wide-ranging 75-acre estate in JOHANNISBERG, WINKEL, KIEDRICH and ELTVILLE.

**Landwein** A category of better quality TAFELWEIN (the grapes must be slightly riper) from 15 designated regions. It must be TROCKEN or HALBTROCKEN. Similar in intention to France's *vins de pays*.

**Lauerburg** One of the four owners of the famous Doctor v'yd in BERNKASTEL, with THANISCH, DEINHARD and Heilig-Geist-Armenspende.

**Liebfrauenstift** 26-acre v'yd in the city of WORMS, said to be the origin of the name LIEBFRAUMILCH.

**Liebfraumilch** A much-abused name, accounting for 50% of all German wine exports – much to the detriment of Germany's better products. Legally defined as a QbA "of pleasant character" from RHEINHESSEN, RHEINPFALZ, NAHE or RHEINGAU, of a blend with at least 51% of RIESLING, SILVANER, KERNER *or* MÜLLER-THURGAU. Most is mild semi-sweet wine from Rheinhessen and Rheinpfalz. The rules now say it must have more than 18 gms. per litre unfermented sugar. Sometimes very cheap and of inferior quality, depending on brand/ shipper. It makes a mockery of the term "Quality wine".

**Lieser** M-M w. ★→ ▭▭ 71 76 83 *84* 85 86 87
Little-known neighbour of BERNKASTEL. Best v'yd: Schlossberg. Grosslage: Kurfürstlay.

**Lorch** Rhg. w. (r.) ★→★★ 71 76 83 85 86 87
At extreme w. end of Rheingau. Some fine light RIESLINGS more like MITTELRHEIN wines. Best grower: von Kanitz.

**Löwenstein, Fürst** 66-acre FRANKEN estate: classic dry, powerful wines. HALLGARTEN property rented by MATUSCHKA-GREIFFENCLAU.

**Maikammer** Rhpf. w. (r.) ★→ ▭▭ 83 85 86 87
Village of n. SÜDLICHE WEINSTRASSE. Very pleasant wines incl. those from coop at Rietburg. Grosslage: Mandelhöhe.

**Maindreieck (Bereich)** District name for central part of FRANKEN, incl. WÜRZBURG.

**Marcobrunn** Historic RHEINGAU; vineyard; one of Germany's best. See Erbach.

**Markgräflerland (Bereich)** Minor district s. of Freiburg (BADEN). GUTEDEL wine is delicious refreshment when drunk very young.

**Martinsthal** Rhg. w. ★★→ ▭▭▭ 71 75 76 82 83 *84* 85 86
Little-known neighbour of RAUENTHAL. Top v'yds: Langenberg, Wildsau. Grosslage: Steinmächer.

**Matuschka-Greiffenclau, Graf Erwein** Owner of the ancient SCHLOSS VOLLRADS estate and tenant of the Fürst Löwenstein Weingut at Hallgarten. President of the VDP association.

**Maximin Grünhaus** M-S-R (Ruwer) w. ★★★★ 71 75 76 79 83 *84* 85 86 87 Supreme RUWER estate of 80 acres at Mertesdorf. Wines to mature 20 years+.

**Maximinhof** Top-quality 12-acre estate in WEHLEN, GRAACH, BERNKASTEL. Owner: Stephan Studert-Prüm.

**Mennig**  M-S-R (Saar) w.  ★★  71 75 76 79 82 83 *84* 85 86 87
 Village between TRIER and the SAAR. Its Falkensteiner v'yd is more famous than the village (Nieder-Obermennig).

**Mertesdorf**  See Maximin Grünhaus.

**Mittelheim**  Rhg. w. ★★→  ★★★  71 75 76 79 *82* 83 *84* 85 86 87
 Minor village between WINKEL and OESTRICH. Top grower: WEGELER-DEINHARD. Grosslage: Honigberg.

**Mittelhaardt**  The north-central and best part of RHEINPFALZ, incl. FORST, DEIDESHEIM, RUPPERTSBERG, WACHENHEIM, etc., largely planted with RIESLING.

**Mittelhaardt-Deutsche Weinstrasse (Bereich)**  District name for the northern and central part of RHEINPFALZ.

**Mittelmosel**  The central and best part of the Mosel, incl. BERNKASTEL, WEHLEN, PIESPORT, etc. Its best sites are entirely RIESLING.

**Mittelrhein**  Northern Rhine area of domestic importance, incl. BACHARACH. Some attractive steely RIESLINGS, esp. in 1983, 1985, 1986.

**Mönchhof, Weingut**  Top-quality 12-acre estate in ÜRZIG, Erden, ZELTINGEN and WEHLEN.

**Morio-Muskat**  Stridently aromatic grape variety popular in RHEINPFALZ. D.Y.A.

**Mosel**  The TAFELWEIN name of the area. All quality wines from the area must be labelled MOSEL-SAAR-RUWER. (Moselle is the French − and English − spelling for this beautiful river.)

**Moseltaler**  New registered name for MOSEL-SAAR-RUWER QbA, intended to simplify selection (*cf.* LIEBFRAUMILCH) but maintain a higher standard than the latter.

**Mosel-Saar-Ruwer**  31,000-acre QUALITÄTSWEIN region between TRIER and KOBLENZ. Includes MITTELMOSEL, SAAR, RUWER and lesser areas. Grows more RIESLING than any region on earth.

**Müller, Felix**  Fine small SAAR estate with delicate SCHARZHOFBERGER, now run by VON KESSELSTATT.

**Müller zu Scharzhof, Egon**  See Egon Müller.

**Müller-Thurgau**  Fruity, early-ripening, usually low-acid grape variety; the commonest in RHEINPFALZ and RHEINHESSEN, the NAHE, BADEN and FRANKEN, and increasingly planted in all areas, including the Mosel; there generally to the detriment of quality.

**Mumm, von**  173-acre estate in JOHANNISBERG, RÜDESHEIM, etc. Under the same control as SCHLOSS JOHANNISBERG.

**Munster**  Nahe w.  ★→★★★  71 75 76 83 *84* 85 86 87
 Best village of northern NAHE, with fine delicate wines. Top grower: State Domain. Grosslage: Schlosskapelle.

**Nackenheim**  Rhh. w. ★→  ★★★  75 76 79 83 85 86 87
 Neighbour of NIERSTEIN; best wines (Engelsberg, Rothenberg) similar. Grosslagen: Spiegelberg (★★★), Gutes Domtal (★).

**Nahe**  Tributary of the Rhine and high-quality wine region. Balanced, fresh and clean but full-flavoured wines, the best are RIESLING. Two Bereiche: KREUZNACH and SCHLOSS BÖCKELHEIM.

**Nahesteiner**  Brand name of new NAHE HALBTROCKEN blend of RIESLING, SILVANER and MÜLLER THURGAU. French-shape bottle and modern label.

**Neef**  M-S-R w. ★→  ★★  71 76 83 85 86 87
 Village of lower Mosel with one fine v'yd: Frauenberg.

**Neipperg, Graf**  71-acre top WÜRTTEMBERG estate at Schwaigern, esp. known for red wines and TRAMINER.

**Nell, von (Weingut Thiergarten)**  40-acre family estate at TRIER and AYL.

**Neumagen-Dhron**  M-M w. ★★→★★★  71 75 76 83 *84* 85 86 87
 Neighbours of PIESPORT. Top v'yd: Hofberger. Grosslage: Michelsberg.

**Neustadt**  Central city of RHEINPFALZ, with a famous wine school.

**Niederhausen**  Na. w. ★★→★★★★  71 75 76 79 83 *84* 85 86 87
 Neighbour of SCHLOSS BÖCKELHEIM and H.Q. of the Nahe State Domain. Wines of grace and power. Top v'yds incl. Hermannshöhle, Steinberg. Grosslage: Burgweg.

**Niedermennig** See Mennig.

**Niederwalluf** See Walluf.

**Nierstein (Bereich)** Large e. RHEINHESSEN district of very mixed quality.

**Nierstein** Rhh. w. ★→★★★ 71 75 76 83 *84* 85 86 87
    Famous but treacherous name. 1,300 acres incl. superb v'yds:
    Hipping, Ölberg, Pettenthal, etc., and their Grosslagen Rehbach,
    Spiegelberg, Auflangen: ripe aromatic wines with great "elegance".
    But beware Grosslage Gutes Domtal: no guarantee of anything
    (except boredom).

---

*Germany's Quality Levels*
*The range of qualities in ascending order is*
*1) Deutscher Tafelwein; sweetish light wine of no special character.*
*2) Landwein: dryish Tafelwein with some regional style.*
*3) Qualitätswein: dry or sweetish wine with sugar added before fermen-
    tation to increase the strength, but tested for quality and with distinct
    local and grape character.*
*4) Kabinettwein: dry or dryish natural (unsugared) wine of distinct
    personality and distinguishing lightness. Can be very fine.*
*5) Spätlese: stronger, often sweeter than Kabinett. Full bodied. The trend
    today is towards drier or even completely dry Spätleses.*
*6) Auslese: sweeter, sometimes stronger than Spätlese, often with honey-
    like flavours, intense and long.*
*7) Beerenauslese: very sweet and usually strong, intense, can be superb.*
*8) Trockenbeerenauslese: intensely sweet and aromatic.*
*9) Eiswein: (Beeren- or Trockenbeerenauslese) concentrated, sharpish
    and very sweet. Extraordinary and everlasting.*

---

**Nobling** New white grape variety giving light fresh wine in BADEN, esp.
    Markgräflerland.

**Norheim** Nahe w. ★→★★★ 71 76 79 83 *84* 85 86 87
    Neighbour of NIEDERHAUSEN. Top v'yds: Klosterberg, Kafels, Kirsch-
    heck. Grosslage: Burgweg.

**Oberemmel** M-S-R (Saar) w. ★★→★★★ 71 75 76 83 85 86 87
    Next village to WILTINGEN. Very fine wines from Rosenberg, Hütte, etc.
    Grosslage: Scharzberg.

**Obermosel (Bereich)** District name for the upper Mosel above TRIER.
    Generally uninspiring wines from the Elbling grape unless they are
    enjoyed *very* young.

**Ockfen** M-S-R (Saar) w. ★★→★★★ 71 75 76 83 *84* 85 86 87
    200-acre village with superb fragrant, austere wines. Top v'yds:
    Bockstein, Herrenberg. Grosslage: Scharzberg.

**Oechsle** Scale for sugar-content of grape-juice (see p.20).

**Oestrich** Rhg. w. ★★→★★★ 71 75 76 83 *84* 85 86 87
    Big village; variable but capable of splendid Riesling Ausleses. V'yds
    incl. Doosberg, Lenchen, Klosterberg. Grosslage: Gottesthal. Major
    grower: WEGELER-DEINHARD.

**Oppenheim** Rhh. w. ★→★★★ 71 75 76 79 83 *84* 85 86 87
    Town s. of NIERSTEIN with a 13th-century cathedral. Best wines (Kreuz,
    Sackträger) similar. Grosslagen: Guldenmorgen (★★★) Kröten-
    brunnen (★).

**Ortenau (Bereich)** District just s. of Baden-Baden. Good KLINGELBERGER
    and RÜLANDER. SPÄTBURGUNDER (not so good) is a speciality. Best village
    DURBACH.

**Palatinate** English for RHEINPFALZ.

**Perlwein** Semi-sparkling wine.

**Pfalz** See Rheinpfalz.

**Piesport** M-M w. ★★→★★★★ 71 75 76 83 *84* 85 86 87
    Tiny village with famous amphitheatre of vines giving (at best)
    glorious, gentle, fruity RIESLINGS. Top v'yds: Goldtröpfchen, Falken-
    berg. Treppchen is on flatter land and inferior. Grosslage: Michels-
    berg (much planted with MÜLLER-THURGAU).

**Plettenberg, von** Fine 100-acre Nahe estate at BAD KREUZNACH.

**Pokalwein** Wine by the glass. A pokal is a big glass.

**Portugieser** Second-rate red-wine grape now often used for WEISSHERBST.

**Prädikat** Special attributes or qualities. See QmP.

**Prüfungsnummer** The official identifying test-number of a quality wine.

**Prüm, J. J.** Superlative 34-acre Mosel estate in WEHLEN, GRAACH, BERN-KASTEL. Delicate, long-lived wines, esp. in Wehlener Sonnenuhr.

**Prüm, S. A., Erben** Small separate part of the Prüm family estate making fine Wehleners, etc.

**Qualitätswein bestimmter Anbaugebiete (QbA)** The middle quality of German wine, with sugar added before fermentation (as in French "chaptalization"), but strictly controlled as to areas, grapes, etc.

**Qualitätswein mit Prädikat (QmP)** Top category, incl. all wines ripe enough to be unsugared, from KABINETT to TROCKENBEERENAUSLESE.

**Rappenhof, Weingut** 90-acre Rheinhessen estate at Alsheim. Esp. for dry Spätlese "Rheinblick".

**Randersacker** Franc. w. ★★→★★★  76 79 *83* 86 87
 Leading village for distinctive dry wine. Top v'yds incl. Teufelskeller. Grosslage: Ewig Leben.

**Rauenthal** Rhg. w. ★★★ ▒▒▒ →★★★★  71 75 76 79 83 *84* 85 86 87
 Supreme village for spicy complex wine. Top v'yds incl. Baiken, Gehrn, Wulfen. Grosslage: Steinmächer. The State Domain is an important grower.

**Rautenstrauch Erben** Owners of the Karthäuserhof, EITELSBACH.

**Reh, Franz & Sohn** Thriving wine-merchant at Leiwen (Mosel) with two small estates.

**Ress, Balthasar** RHEINGAU grower with 50 acres of good land, cellars in HATTENHEIM. Also runs SCHLOSS REICHARTSHAUSEN. Fine fresh wines; highly original artists' labels.

**Restsüsse** Unfermented sugar remaining in wine to give it sweetness. New-style TROCKEN wines have very little, if any.

**Reverchon, Eddie** Substantial SAAR estate in Filzen, WITTINGEN, etc.

**Rheinart Erben** 26-acre SAAR estate known for its OCKFENER BOCKSTEIN.

**Rheinburgengau (Bereich)** District name for the v'yds of the MITTELRHEIN round the famous Rhine gorge. Wines with "steely" acidity needing time to mature.

**Rheingau** The best v'yd region of the Rhine, near Wiesbaden. 7,000 acres. Classic, substantial but subtle RIESLING. Bereich name, for the whole region, JOHANNISBERG.

**Rheinhess** New name for blended HALBTROCKEN Rheinhessen wines.

**Rheinhessen** Vast region (62,000 acres of v'yds) between Mainz and Worms, bordered by the river NAHE, most second-rate, but incl. top wines from NIERSTEIN, OPPENHEIM, etc.

**Rheinhessen Silvaner (RS)** New uniform label for dry wines from Silvaner designed to give a modern quality image to the region.

**Rheinpfalz** 56,000-acre v'yd region s. of Rheinhessen. (See Mittelhaardt and Südliche Weinstrasse.) This and RHEINHESSEN are the chief sources of LIEBFRAUMILCH. Grapes ripen to relatively high degrees. The great classics are rich wines, but TROCKEN and HALBTROCKEN are increasingly fashionable.

**Rhodt** Village of SÜDLICHE WEINSTRASSE with well-known cooperative. Agreeable fruity wines. Grosslage: Ordensgut.

**Richter, Max Ferd, Weingut** 37-acre MITTELMOSEL family estate based at Mülheim. Fine barrel-aged RIESLINGS from WEHLEN, GRAACH, BRAUNE-BERG (Juffer), Mülheim (Helenenkloster).

**Rieslaner** Cross between SILVANER and RIESLING; has made fine Auslesen in FRANKEN, where most is grown.

**Riesling** The best German grape: fine, fragrant, fruity, long-lived. Only Chardonnay can compete as the world's best white grape.

**Roseewein** Rosé wine made of red grapes fermented without their skins.

**Rotwein**   Red wine.

**Rüdesheim**   Rhg. w. **★★→★★★★**   71 75 76 79 *81* 82 83 *84* 85 86 87
Rhine resort with 650 acres of excellent v'yds; the three best called Rüdesheimer Berg...... Full-bodied wines, fine-flavoured, often remarkable in "off" vintages. Grosslage: Burgweg.

**Rüdesheimer Rosengarten**   Rüdesheim is also the name of a NAHE village near BAD KREUZNACH. Do not be misled by the ubiquitous blend going by this name. It has nothing to do with Rheingau RÜDESHEIM.

**Ruländer**   The PINOT GRIS: grape giving soft, full-bodied wine, alias Grauburgunder. Best in BADEN.

**Ruppertsberg**   Rhpf. w. **★★→★★★**   75 76 79 83 *84* 85 86 87
Southern village of MITTELHAARDT. Top v'yds incl. Hoheburg, Reiterpfad, Linsenbusch. Grosslage: Hofstück.

**Ruwer**   Tributary of Mosel near TRIER. Very fine delicate wines. Villages incl. EITELSBACH, MERTESDORF, KASEL.

**Saar**   Tributary of Mosel s. of RUWER. Brilliant, austere, "steely" RIESLINGS. Villages incl. WILTINGEN (SCHARZHOFBERG), AYL, OCKFEN, SERRIG. Grosslage: Scharzberg.

**Saar-Ruwer (Bereich)**   District incl. the two above.

**Salem, Schloss**   190-acre estate of Margrave of Baden on L. Constance in s. Germany. MÜLLER-THURGAU and WEISSHERBST.

**St. Ursula**   Well-known merchants at BINGEN; owners of VILLA SACHSEN.

**Scharzberg**   Grosslage name of WILTINGEN and neighbours.

**Scharzhofberg**   Saar w. **★★★★**   71 75 76 79 83 *84* 85 86 87
Superlative 30-acre SAAR v'yd: austerely beautiful wines, the perfection of RIESLING. Do not confuse with the last entry. Top estate: EGON MÜLLER.

**Schaumwein**   Sparkling wine.

**Scheurebe**   Fruity aromatic grape of good quality used in RHEINHESSEN and RHEINPFALZ.

**Schillerwein**   Light red or rosé QbA, speciality of WÜRTTEMBERG (only).

**Scholl & Hillebrand**   RÜDESHEIM merchants with fine BREUER estate wines and highly successful "Riesling Dry".

**Schlossböckelheim**   Nahe w. **★★→★★★★**   71 75 76 79 82 83 *84* 85 86 87
Village with the best NAHE v'yds, incl. Kupfergrube, Felsenberg. Firm yet delicate wine. Grosslage: Burgweg.

**Schloss Böckelheim (Bereich)**   District name for the whole southern NAHE.

**Schloss Groenesteyn**   Fine Rheingau estate (80 acres) in KIEDRICH and RÜDESHEIM, owned by Baron von Ritter zu Groenesteyn. Top-grade wines.

**Schloss Johannisberg**   Rhg. w. **★★★**   76 79 83 *84* 85 86 87
Famous RHEINGAU estate of 86 acres owned by Prince Metternich and the Oetker family, and now run in conjunction with von MUMM. Wines incl. fine SPÄTLESE and KABINETT TROCKEN. Formerly one of Germany's undoubted "first growths".

**Schloss Reichartshausen**   10-acre formerly Cistercian HATTENHEIM v'yd run by RESS.

**Schloss Reinhartshausen**   Fine 165-acre estate in ERBACH, HATTENHEIM, etc. Changed hands in 1987.

**Schloss Vollrads**   Rhg. w. **★★★→★★★★**   71 76 83 85 86 87
Great estate at WINKEL, since 1300. 116 acres producing classical RHEINGAU RIESLING, esp. since 1977. TROCKEN and HALBTROCKEN wines a speciality. The owner, Graf MATUSCHKA GREIFFENCLAU, leads the "German wine with food" campaign.

**Schmitt, Gustav Adolf**   Merchant house with fine old 250-acre family estate at NIERSTEIN.

**Schmitt, Franz Karl**   Even older 74-acre ditto.

**Schönborn, Schloss**   One of the biggest and best Rheingau estates, based at HATTENHEIM. Full-flavoured wines, at best excellent. Also very good SEKT.

**Schoppenwein**  Café wine: i.e. wine by the glass.

**Schorlemer, Freiherr von**  Historically important MOSEL estate of 116 acres in 5 parts. Current financial and other problems have clouded its reputation.

**Schubert, von**  Owner of MAXIMIN GRÜNHAUS.

**Schweigen**  Rhpf. w. ★→  ★★  83 *84* 85 86 87
Southernmost Rheinpfalz village with important cooperative, Deutsches WEINTOR. Grosslage: Guttenberg.

**Sekt**  German (QbA) sparkling wine, best when RIESLING is on the label. SEKT B.A. is the same thing, but from a specified area.

**Senfter, Reinhold**  One of the best growers in NIERSTEIN, with 32 acres. Best v'yds: Niersteiner Hipping and Oppenheimer Sackträger.

**Serrig**  M-S-R (Saar) w. ★★→★★★ 71 75 76 79 83 *84* 85 86 87
Village known for "steely" wine, excellent in hot years. Top growers: VEREINIGTE HOSPITIEN and State Domain. Grosslage: Scharzberg.

**Sichel H., Söhne**  Famous wine-merchants of London and Mainz with new KELLEREI in Alzey, Rhh. Owners of "Blue Nun" LIEBFRAUMILCH.

**Silvaner**  The third most-planted German white grape, best in FRANKEN and the KAISERSTUHL. But look for good Silvaners from RHEINHESSEN.

**Simmern, Langwerth von**  Top 120-acre family estate at ELTVILLE. Famous v'yds: Mannberg, MARCOBRUNN, Baiken, etc. Some of the very best, most typical RHEINGAU RIESLINGS.

**Sonnenuhr**  "Sun-dial." Name of several v'yds, esp. the famous one at WEHLEN.

**Spätburgunder**  PINOT NOIR: the best red-wine grape in Germany esp. in BADEN and WÜRTTEMBERG – though its wines are not appreciated outside Germany.

**Spätlese**  "Late gathered." One better (stronger/sweeter) than KABINETT. Wines to age *at least* three years. Dry Spätleses can be v. fine.

**Spindler, Wilhelm**  Fine 33-acre family estate at FORST, Rheinpfalz.

**Staatlicher Hofkeller**  The Bavarian State Domain. 287 acres of finest FRANKEN v'yds with spectacular cellars under the great baroque Residenz at WÜRZBURG.

**Staatsweingut (or Staatliche Weinbaudomäne)**  The State wine estate or domain.

**Staufenberg, Schloss**  69-acre DURBACH estate of the Margrave of Baden. Fine "Klingelberger" (RIESLING).

**Steigerwald (Bereich)**  District name for eastern part of FRANKEN.

**Steinberg**  Rhg. w. ★★★→★★★★ 71 75 76 79 83 *84* 85 86 87
Famous 79-acre v'yd at HATTENHEIM walled by Cistercians 700 yrs. ago. Now property of the State Domain, ELTVILLE.

**Steinwein**  Wine from WÜRZBURG'S best v'yd, Stein. In the past the term was loosely used for all Franconian wine.

**Stuttgart**  Chief city of WÜRTTEMBERG, producer of some pleasant wines (esp. Riesling), recently beginning to be exported.

**Südliche Weinstrasse (Bereich)**  District name for the S. RHEINPFALZ. Quality has improved tremendously in the last 25 years.

**Tafelwein**  "Table wine." The vin ordinaire of Germany. Mostly blended with other EEC wines. But DEUTSCHER TAFELWEIN must come from Germany alone. See also Landwein.

**Thanisch, Weingut Wwe. Dr. H.**  16-acre BERNKASTEL family estate of top quality, incl. part of Doctor v'yd. Another 16 acres changed hands in 1987; the new name is Erben Müller-Burggref.

**Traben-Trarbach**  M-M w. ★★ 76 83 85 86 87
Secondary wine-town, some good light wines. Top v'yds incl. Würzgarten, Schlossberg. Grosslage: Schwarzlay.

**Traisen**  Na. w. ★★★ 71 75 76 79 83 *84* 85 86 87
Small village incl. superlative Bastei and Rotenfels v'yds, making RIESLINGS of great concentration and class.

**Traminer**  See Gewürztraminer.

**Trier** M-S-R w. ★★→★★★
Important wine city of Roman origin, on the Mosel, adjacent to RUWER, now incl. AVELSBACH and EITELSBACH. Grosslage: Römerlay.

**Trittenheim** M-M w. ★★ 71 75 76 83 *84* 85 86
Attractive light wines from the s. end of the Mittel-Mosel. Top v'yds Apotheke, Altärchen, Grosslage: Michelsberg.

**Trocken** Dry. On labels Trocken *alone* means with a statutory maximum of unfermented sugar (9 grams per litre). But see next entry. See also Halbtrocken.

**Trockenbeerenauslese** The sweetest and most expensive category of wine, extremely rare and with concentrated honey flavour, made from selected withered grapes (esp. Riesling). See also Edel.

**Trollinger** Common red grape of WÜRTTEMBERG: locally very popular.

**Ungstein** Rhpf.w. ★★→ ★★★ 71 75 76 79 83 *84* 85 86 87
MITTELHAARDT village with fine harmonious wines. Top v'yd: Herrenberg. Top growers: Fuhrmann (Weingut Pfeffingen), Fitz-Ritter, BASSERMANN-JORDAN. Grosslage: Honigsäckel.

**Ürzig** M-M w. ★★★ 71 75 76 79 87 83 *84* 85 86 87
Village famous for lively spicy wine. Top v'yd: Würzgarten. Grosslage: Schwarzlay. Growers incl. MÖNCHHOF.

**VdP** Verband Deutscher Prädikats und Qualitätsweinguter, an association of premium growers.

**Vereinigte Hospitien** "United Hospitals." Ancient charity at Trier with large holdings in SERRIG, WILTINGEN, TRIER, PIESPORT, etc.

**Verwaltung** Administration (of property/estate etc).

**Villa Sachsen** 67-acre BINGEN estate belonging to ST. URSULA Weingut.

**Wachenheim** Rhpf. w. ★★★ →★★★★ 71 75 76 79 83 *84* 85 86 87
840 acres, incl. exceptionally fine Rieslings. V'yds incl. Gerümpel, Böhlig, Rechbächel. Top grower: BÜRKLIN-WOLF. Grosslagen: Schenkenböhl, Schnepfenflug, Mariengarten.

**Waldrach** M-S-R (Ruwer) w. ★★ 75 76 79 83 *84* 85 87
Some charming light wines. Grosslage: Römerlay.

**Wallhausen, Schloss** The 25-acre estate of the Prince Zu Salm at Dalberg, Nahe. 50% Riesling. Good TROCKEN wines.

**Walluf** Rhg. w. ★★ 75 76 79 83 *84* 85 87
Neighbour of ELTVILLE; formerly Nieder-and Ober-Walluf. Underrated wines. Grosslage: Steinmächer.

**Walporzheim Ahrtal (Bereich)** District name for the whole AHR valley.

**Walthari-Hof** Much-discussed estate at Edenkoben, Rheinpfalz, making wine without recourse to sulphur dioxide.

**Wawern** M-S-R (Saar) w. ★★→★★★ 71 75 76 83 *84* 85 86 87
Small village with fine RIESLINGS. Grosslage: Scharzberg.

**Wegeler-Deinhard** 136-acre RHEINGAU estate. V'yds in OESTRICH, MITTELHEIM, WINKEL, GEISENnEIM, RÜDESHEIM, etc. Consistent quality; dry SPÄTLESES, classic AUSLESES, finest EISWEIN. Also 67 acres in MITTELMOSEL, incl. major part of BERNKASTELER DOCTOR (WEHLENER, SONNENUHR etc.) and 46 acres in MITTELHAARDT (FORST, DEIDESHEIM, RUPPERTSBERG).

**Wehlen** M-M w. ★★★ →★★★★ 71 75 76 79 83 *84* 85 86 87
Neighbour of BERNKASTEL with equally fine, somewhat richer, wine. Best v'yd: Sonnenuhr. Top growers: PRÜM family. Grosslage: Münzlay.

**Weil, Dr.** Fine 46-acre estate at KIEDRICH.

**Weinbaugebiet** Viticultural region for TAFELWEIN (e.g. Mosel, Rhein, Saar).

**Weingut** Wine estate. Can only be used on the label by estates that grow all their own grapes, make their wines from these grapes and bottle these same wines.

**Weinkellerei** Wine cellars or winery. See Keller.

**Weinstrasse** "Wine road." Scenic route through v'yds. Germany has several, the most famous the Duetsche Weinstrasse in RHEINPFALZ.

**Weintor, Deutsches** See Schweigen.

**Weissherbst**  Very pale pink or "blush" wine of QbA standard or above, even occasionally BEERENAUSLESE, the speciality of BADEN, WÜRTTEMBERG and RHEINPFALZ. Currently v. popular in Germany.

**Werner, Domdechant**  Fine 33-acre family estate on the best slopes of HOCHHEIM.

**Werner Klein (Mosbacher Hof)**  25-acre estate, 90% Riesling, in FORST and DEÏDESHEIM. Good TROCKEN wines.

---

*Remember that vintage information about German wines is given in a different form from the ready/not ready distinction applying to other countries. Read the explanation on page 104.*

---

**Wiltingen**  Saar w. ★★→★★★★ 71 75 76 79 83 85 86 87
The centre of the Saar. 790 acres. Beautiful subtle, austere wine. Top v'yds incl. SCHARZHOFBERG, Braune Kupp, Braunfels, Klosterberg. Grosslage (for the whole Saar): Scharzberg.

**Winkel**  Rhg. w. ★★★→★★★★ 71 75 76 79 83 *84* 85 86 87
Village famous for fragrant wine, incl. SCHLOSS VOLLRADS. V'yds incl. Hasensprung, Jesuitengarten. Grosslagen: Honigberg and Erntebringer.

**Winningen**  M-S-R. w.  ★★
Village of lower Mosel near Koblenz with some fine delicate RIESLING. Best v'yds: Uhlen, Röttgen.

**Wintrich**  M-M w. ★★→★★★ 71 75 76 83 *84* 85 86 87
Neighbour of PIESPORT; similar wines. Top v'yds: Grosser Herrgott, Ohligsberg, Sonnenseite. Grosslage: Kurfürstlay.

**Winzergenossenschaft**  Wine-growers' cooperative, usually making good and reasonably priced wine.

**Winzerverein**  The same as the last.

**Wirsching, Hans**  Well-known estate in IPHOFEN, FRANKEN. Robust, full-bodied wines. 100 acres in top v'yds: Julius-Echter-Berg, Kalb, etc.

**Wonnegau (Bereich)**  District name for s. RHEINHESSEN.

**Württemberg**  Vast s. area little known for wine outside Germany. Some good RIESLINGS, esp. from Neckar valley. Also TROLLINGER.

**Würzburg**  Franc. ★★→★★★★ 71 76 81 *83* 85 86 87
Great baroque city on the Main, centre of Franconian (FRANKEN) wine: fine, full-bodied and dry. Top v'yds: Stein, Leiste, Schlossberg. No Grosslage. See also Maindreieck.

**ZBW (Zentralkellerei Badischer Winzergenossenschaften)**  Germany's (and Europe's) biggest ultra-modern cooperative, at Breisach, BADEN, with 25,000 grower-members with 12,000 acres, producing 80% of Baden's wine at all quality levels.

**Zell**  M-S-R w. ★→★★ 76 83 85 86 87
The best-known lower Mosel village, esp. for its Grosslage name Schwarze Katz ("Black Cat"). RIESLING on steep slate gives aromatic light wines.

**Zell (Bereich)**  District name for the whole lower Mosel from Zell to Koblenz.

**Zeltingen-Rachtig**  M-M w.  ★★ →★★★★ 71 75 76 79 83 *84* 85 86 87
Important Mosel village next to WEHLEN. Typically lively crisp RIESLING. Top v'yds: Sonnenuhr, Schlossberg. Grosslage: Münzlay.

**Zentralkellerei Mosel-Saar-Ruwer**  The biggest coop of the MOSEL, incl. Saar-Winzer-Verein at Wiltingen. Its 5,200 members produce 25% of all M-S-R wines.

**Zilliken, Forstmeister Geltz**  Former estate of the Prussian royal forester at Saarburg, Saar. 21 acres of Riesling make old-style wines for maturing.

**Zwierlein, Freiherr von**  55-acre family estate in Geisenheim. 100% Riesling. Best v'yds: Rothenberg, Kläuserweg.

# Spain & Portugal

The following abbreviations of regional names are used in the text.

| | | | |
|---|---|---|---|
| **Alen.** | Alton Alentejo | **Est'a.** | Estremadura | **N.Cas.** | New Castile |
| **Alg.** | Algarve | **Ext.** | Extremadura | **O.Cas.** | Old Castile |
| **And.** | Andalucia | **Gal.** | Galicia | **R'a.A.** | Rioja Alta |
| **Ara.** | Aragon | **g.** | see Vino generoso | **R'a.Al.** | Rioja Alavesa |
| **B'a.al.** | Beira Alta | **Gui.** | Guipuzcoa | **R'a.B.** | Rioja Baja |
| **Bei. Lit.** | | **Lev.** | Levante | **Res.** | Reserva |
| Beira Littoral | | **M'o.** | Minho | **Trás-os-m.** | |
| **Cat.** | Catalonia | **Nav.** | Navarra | Trás-os-Montes |

In 1986 Spain and Portugal joined the European Common Market, a move which symbolized (and greatly added to) a new wave of interest in the rapidly growing scope and quality of their wine industries. Modern ideas have arrived to enrich (or replace) their traditions. The state of ferment is highly productive, and splendid new wines are appearing, both in their few traditional quality areas, and in former bulk-wine regions.

Currently in Spain (apart from the sherry country), Catalonia, Rioja, Navarra, Rueda and Ribera del Duero hold most interest; in Portugal (apart from port and Maderia) Bairrada, the Douro, the Ribatejo, Alentejo and Estremadura, and the Minho. New delimited ("VQPRD") areas are tending to overshadow the old-fashioned appellations.

The listing here includes the best and most interesting types and regions of each country, whether legally delimited or not. Geographical references (see map) are to the traditional divisions of Spain into kingdoms and Portugal into provinces.

Sherry, port and Madeira are listed separately on pages 132 to 137.

# Spain

**A.G.E., Bodegas Unidas** R'a.A. r. (p.) w. dr. or sw. res. ✶→✶✶ 73 74 75 78 80 81 82 83 84 Large bodega making a wide range of wines, of which the best are the red Siglo Saco and Marqués de Romeral.

**Alavesas, Bodegas** R'a.Al. r. (w. dr.) res ✶✶→✶✶✶ 73 74 75 76 78 80 81 83 Pale orange-red SOLAR DE SAMANIEGO is one of the most delicate of the soft, fast-maturing Alavesa wines. Quality since 1983 has been seriously variable.

**Albariño del Palacio** Gal. w. dr. ✶✶
Flowery and pétillant young wine from FEFIÑANES near Cambados, made with the Albariño grape, the best of the region.

**Alella** Cat. r. (p.) w. dr. or sw. ✶✶
Small demarcated region just n. of Barcelona. Makes pleasantly fresh and fruity wines. (See Marfil and Marqués de Alella.)

**Alicante** Lev. r. (w.) ✶
Demarcated region: wines tend to be "earthy" and overstrong.

**Almansa** Lev. r. ✶
Demarcated region w. of ALICANTE, with similar wines.

**Aloque** N. Cas. r. ✴ D.Y.A.
A light (though not in alcohol) variety of VALDEPEÑAS, made by fermenting together red and white grapes.

**Almendralejo** Ext. r. w. ✶
Commercial wine centre of the Extremadura. Much of its produce is distilled to make the spirit for fortifying sherry.

**Alvear, S.A.** And. g. ✶✶✶
The largest producer of excellent sherry-like apéritif and dessert wines from MONTILLA-MORILES.

**Ampurdán** See Perelada.

**Año** 4° Año (or Años) means 4 years old when bottled.

**Bach, Masia** Cat. r. p. w. dr. or sw. res. ✴✴ →✶✶✶ 70 74 78 80 81 82 83 85 Excellent villa-winery nr. SAN SADURNÍ DE NOYA, now owned by CODORNÍU. Best known for luscious oaky white Extrisimo Bach. Now also good red reserva.

**Banda Azul** R'a.A. r. ✶✶ 75 76 80 81 84
Big-selling wine, very variable in quality, from BODEGAS PATERNINA.

**Berberana, Bodegas** R'a.A. r. (w. dr.) res. ✶→✶✶✶ 64 66 70 73 74 75 76 78 79 80 82 83 84 The fruity, full-bodied reds are best: the 3° año Carta de Plata, the 5° año Carta de Oro and the velvety reservas.

**Beronia, Bodegas** R'a.A. r. w. dr. res. ✶✶→✶✶✶ 73 75 77 78 80 81 82 83 A small modern bodega making excellent reds in the traditional oaky style. Their light CRIANZA "Beron" is also very attractive.

**Bilbainas, Bodegas** R'a.A. r. (p.) w. dr. sw. or sp. res. ✴✴ →✶✶✶ 66 69 70 72 73 75 76 78 79 81 82 Large bodega in HARO, with a wide reliable range including dark Viña Pomal, Pomal Junior, lighter Viña Zaco, Vendimia Especial Reservas and "Royal Carlton" CAVA.

**Blanco** White.

**Bodega** Spanish for 1. a wineshop; 2. a concern occupied in the making, blending and/or shipping of wine and 3. a cellar.

**Campanas, Las** See Vinicola Navarra.

**Campo Nuevo** Nav. r. p. w. dr. ✴
Good value everyday red and white Navarra from the Coop Vinícola Murchantina.

**Campo Viejo, Bodegas** R'a.A. r. (w. dr.) res. ✴ →✶✶✶ 64 66 70 71 73 75 76 78 79 80 81 82 83 84 Branch of Savin S.A., one of Spain's largest wine companies. Makes the popular and tasty 2° año San Asensio and some big, fruity red reservas, esp. Marqués de Villa-magna.

**Can Rafols de Caus** Cat. r. w. dr. ✶✶ 85 86
New small PENEDÈS bodega, growing its own fruity CAB SAUV and pleasant CHARD.

SP

**Cañamero** Ext. w. ★
    Remote village near Guadalupe whose wines grow FLOR and acquire a sherry-like taste.

**Caralt, Cavas Conde de** Cat. sp. r. w. res. ★★· 78 80 81 82 83 84
    "CAVA" sparkling wines from SAN SADURNÍ DE NOYA; also pleasant still wines.

**Carbonell** And. br. ★★
    Producer of good Montilla ("Sombra") and olive oil, at Cordoba.

**Cariñena** Ara. r. (p. w.) ★
    Demarcated region and large-scale supplier of strong wine for everyday drinking, dominated by cooperatives but now being invigorated (and its wines lightened) by modern technology.

**Casar de Valdaiga** O.Cas. r. w. dr. ★★
    Producer in El Bierzo, n. of LÉON, with a light, very dry CLARETE of fair quality.

**Castellblanch** Cat. sp. ★★
    PENEDÈS CAVA firm, owned by FREIXENET. Recently much praised for Brut Zero and slightly sweeter Cristal Seco.

**Castillo Ygay** See Marqués de Murrieta.

**Cava** Any Spanish sparkling wine made by the champagne method. Also the bodega making it.

**Cenalsa** Nav. r. w. dr. ★★
    A marketing organization shipping a range of Navarra wines, incl. a flowery new-style and a fruity red "Agramont".

**Cenicero** Wine township in the RIOJA ALTA with ancient Roman origins.

**Cepa** Wine or grape variety.

**Chacolí** Gui. (r.) w. ★ D.Y.A.
    Alarmingly sharp pétillant wine from the Basque coast. It contains only 9% to 11% alcohol.

**Chaves, Bodegas** Gal. w. dr. ★★→★★★ 81 82 84 (D.Y.A.)
    Small family firm making a good and fragrant, though slightly acidic, ALBARIÑO; arguably the best Galician wine exported.

**Chivite, Bodegas Julián** Nav. r. (p.) w. dr. or sw. res. ★★ 81 82 83 84 86 Biggest bodega in NAVARRA, producing full-bodied, fruity red wines and a flowery, well-balanced white.

**Clarete** Term frowned upon by the EEC describing light red wine (occasionally dark rosé).

**Codorníu, S.A.** Cat. sp ★★→★★★
    One of the two largest and best known of the firms in SAN SADURNÍ DE NOYA making good CAVA by the champagne method. Non Plus Ultra is matured, Ana de Codorníu a fresher style.

**Compañía Vinícola del Norte de España (CVNE)** R'a.A. r. (p.) w. dr. or sw. res. ★★→★★★ 66 70 73 74 75 76 78 80 81 82 83 84
    The 3° año is among the best young red Riojas and Monopole one of the best slightly oaky whites. Excellent red Imperial and Viña Real reservas. CVNE is pronounced "Coonay".

**Conca de Barberá** Cat. (r. p.) w. dr.
    Demarcated region supplying Parellada grapes for making CAVA. Its best wine is the TORRES Milmanda Chardonnay.

**Consejo Regulador** Official organization for the defence, control and promotion of a DENOMINACIÓN DE ORIGEN.

**Contino** R'a.Al. r. res. ★★★ 74 75 76 78 80 81 82
    Superior single-vineyard red wine made by a subsidiary of COMPAÑIA VINICOLA DEL NORTE DE ESPAÑA.

**Corral S.A., Bodegas** R'a.A. r. (p. w. dr.) res. ★★ 71 73 75 78
    Long-established bodega now operating from new premises at Navarrete. Best known for red Don Jacobo.

**Cosecha** Crop or vintage.

**Criado y embotellado por . . .** Grown and bottled by . . .

**Crianza** Literally, "nursing", the ageing of wine. New or unaged wine is "sin crianza". Wines labelled crianza are at least 2 years old, with one year in oak.

**Cumbrero** See Montecillo, Bodegas.

**De Muller** Cat. (r. w. dr.) br. ★★→★★★
Old TARRAGONA firm famous for altar wines, making a good PRIORATO and superb v. old solera-aged dessert wines, incl. PRIORATO DULCE and Paxarete. Also fragrant Moscatel Seco.

**Denominación de origen** Officially regulated wine region. (See introduction, p. 118).

**Domecq, S.A.** R'a.Al. r. (w. dr.) res. ★★→★★★ 73 74 76 78 80 82
Riojan outpost of Pedro Domecq (see Sherry). Best wines are the fruity red Domecq Domain, exceptional in '76, and Marqués de Arienzo RESERVAS.

**Dulce** Sweet.

**Elaborado y añejado por . . .** Made and aged by . . .

**El Coto, Bodegas** R'a.Al. r. (w. dr.) res. ★★→★★★ 73 76 78 80 81 82
Bodega in which Alexis Lichine has recently taken an interest, best-known for light, soft red El Coto and Coto de Imaz.

**Espumoso** Sparkling (but see Cava).

**Faustino Martinez, S.A.** R'a.Al. r. w. dr. (p.) res. ★★ →★★★ 64 70 72 73 74 75 76 78 80 81 82 Good red wines and light, fruity white Faustino V. Gran Reserva is Faustino I. Do not be put off by the repellent bottles.

**Ferrer, José L.** Majorca r. res. ★★
His bodega in Binisalem is still the only one of any distinction in Majorca.

**Flor** A wine yeast peculiar to Fino sherry and certain other wines that oxidize slowly and tastily under its influence.

**Franco-Españolas, Bodegas** R'a.A. r. w. dr. or sw. res. ★→★★ 64 68 70 73 74 75 76 78 79 82 83 Reliable wines from LOGROÑO. Bordón is a fruity red. The semi-sweet white Diamante is a favourite in Spain.

**Freixenet, S.A., Cavas** Cat. sp. ★★→★★★
CAVA, rivalling CODORNÍU in size through recent acquisitions, making a range of good sparkling wines. Also owns GLORIA FERRER in California and the Champagne house of Henri Abelé in Reims. Paul Cheneau is a low-price brand.

**Gonzalez y Dubosc, S.A., Cavas** Cat. sp. ★★
A branch of the sherry giant GONZALES BYASS. Pleasant sparkling wines exported as "Jean Perico".

**Gran Vas** Pressurized tanks (*cuves closes*) for making inexpensive sparkling wines; also used to describe this type of wine.

**Green Wines** There are objections from the EEC and the Portuguese to the use of this harmless English translation of VINHOS VERDES.

**Gurpegui, Bodegas** R'a.B. r. (p. w. dr.) res. ★→★★ 70 73 75 78 81 82
Large family firm making some of the best wines from the RIOJA BAJA, labelled as Berceo. They incl. a fresh rosé.

**Haro** The wine centre of the RIOJA ALTA, a stylish old town.

**Huelva** And. r. w. br. ★→★★
Demarcated region w. of Cadiz. White table wines and sherry-like *generosos*, formerly sent to JEREZ for blending.

**Irache, S.L.** Nav. r. p. (w. dr) res. ★★ 64 70 73 78 81 82
Well-known bodega with substantial exports.

**Jean Perico** See Gonzalez Dubosc.

**Jerez de la Frontera** The capital city of sherry. (See p. 134).

**Jumilla** Lev. r. ★ (w. dr. p.) ★→★★
Demarcated region in the mountains n. of MURCIA. Its overstrong wines (up to 18% alcohol) are being lightened by earlier picking and better wine-making. Rosés are best.

**Juvé y Camps** Cat. sp. ★★→★★★
Family CAVA firm aiming for top quality.

**Labastida, Cooperativa Vinícola de**  R'a.Al. r. res.  ★★ →★★★ 66
70 75 78 82  Makers of very drinkable Manuel Quintano, fruity, well-
balanced Montebuena, Gastrijo and Castillo Labastida reservas and
gran reservas, and a fresh dry white with masses of flavour.

**La Granja Remélluri**  R'a.Al. r. res. ★★★ 74 76 79 80 81 83
Small firm (founded 1970), making good red Riojas by traditional
methods.

**Laguardia**  Picturesque walled town at the centre of LA RIOJA ALAVESA.

**Lagunilla, Bodegas**  R'a.A. r. ★★ 73 75 78 81
Modern firm owned by the British Grand Met. Co. Easy oaky light reds
incl. Viña Herminia and Gran Reserva.

**Lan, Bodegas**  R'a.A. r. (p. w.) res. ★★→★★★ 73 75 78 82
Huge modern bodega, lavishly equipped and making aromatic red
Riojas, incl. the good Lancorta and fresh white Lan Blanco.

**La Rioja Alta, Bodegas**  R'a.A. r. (p.) w. dr. (or sw.) res.
★★→★★★ 64 68 70 73 76 78 80 81 83  Excellent wines, esp.
the red 3° año Viña Alberdi, the velvety 5° año Ardanza, the lighter 6°
año Araña, the splendid Reserva 904 and marvellous Reserva 890. In
future this bodega will be making only reservas and gran reservas.

**León**  O.Cas. r. p. w. ★→★★ 78 81
Northern region on the move. Its wines, esp. those from the
unfortunately named V.I.L.E. (e.g. the young Coyanza and full-
blooded Don Suero reserva), are fruity, dry and refreshing.

**León, S.A., Jean**  Cat. r. w. dr. res ★★★ 74 75 77 78 79 80 81 82
Small firm owned by a Los Angeles restaurateur. Good oaky
CHARDONNAY and deep, full-bodied CABERNET that repays long bottle-
ageing, though less so since 1980.

**Logroño**  Principal town of the RIOJA region. (I prefer HARO.)

**López de Heredia, S.A.**  R'a.A. r. (p.) w. dr. or sw. res.
★★→ ★★★★ 64 68 70 73 75 76 77 78 79 80 81 82 83
Superb old-established bodega in HARO with typical and good dry red
Viña Tondonia of 6° año or more. Its wines are exceptionally long-
lasting, and the Tondonia whites are also impressive.

**Lopez Hermanos**  Malaga ★★
Large bodega making commercial Malaga wines, incl. popular
Malaga Virgen and Moscatel Flor de Malaga.

---

### Rioja Vintages

*Thanks to a more consistent climate and the blending of a proportion of
wine from better vintages in poor years, Riojas do not vary to the same
extent as the red wines from Bordeaux and Burgundy. With few
exceptions the '72 and '77 vintages were a disaster, owing to high
rainfall and the onset of rot and oidium. Of other recent years, the best
were: 52 55 58 64 66 68 70 73 76 78 80 81 82 83 and 85. (Those in bold
type were outstanding.)*

*Riojas are put on the market when they are ready to drink. The best
reservas of the best vintages, however, have very long lives and improve
with more bottle age. The best '64s are now at their peak.*

---

**Los Llanos**  N.Cas. r. (p. w. dr.) res.  ★★ 75 78 81
One of the few VALDEPEÑAS bodegas to age wine in oak. Señorío de Los
Llanos Gran Reserva is remarkably scented and silky. Also a clean
and fruity white "Armonioso".

**Magaña, Bodegas**  Nav. r. res. 80 81 82 ★★
Small new bodega making vigorous red with MERLOT (vines bought
from Pétrus) and CABERNET SAUVIGNON.

**Majorca**  No wine of interest except from José FERRER.

**Málaga**  And. br. sw. ★★→★★★
Demarcated region around the city of Málaga. At their best, its
dessert wines yield nothing to tawny port.

**Mancha** N.Cas. r. w. ★

Large demarcated region n. and n.e. of VALDEPEÑAS. Mainly white wines, lacking the lively freshness of the best Valdepeñas, but showing marked signs of improvement. To watch.

**Marfil** Cat. r. (p.) w. ★★

Brand name of Alella Vinicola (Bodegas Cooperativas), best known of the producers in ALELLA. Means "ivory".

**Marqués de Alella** Cat. w. dr. (sp.) ★★→★★★ 83 84 85 86 (D.Y.A.)

Small bodega making light and fragrant white ALELLA wines by modern methods. Also a little CAVA.

**Marqués de Cáceres, Bodegas** R'a.A. r. p. w. dr. res. ★★→★★★ 70 71 73 75 76 78 80 81 82 83 84 Good red Riojas of various ages made by French methods from CENICERO (R'a.A.) grapes and also a surprisingly light and fragrant white (D.Y.A.).

**Marqués de Griñon** O.Cas. (r.) w. dr. ★★★ (r.) 82 83 84

Enterprising nobleman making very fine CABERNET nr. Toledo, not a recognized wine region. Also refreshing white from Verdejo grapes in RUEDA.

**Marqués de Monistrol, Bodegas** Cat. w. r. (dr. or sw.) sp. res. ★★→★★★ 75 77 78 80 Old bodega now owned by Martini & Rossi. Refreshing whites, esp. the Vin Nature, a good red reserva and an odd sweet red wine.

**Marqués de Murrieta, S.A.** R'a.A. r. p. w. dr. res. ★★→ ★★★★ 34 42 60 62 64 68 70 73 74 75 76 78 79 80 81 82 83 Highly reputed bodega near LOGROÑO making some of the best of all Riojas. Makes 4° año Etiqueta Blanca, superb red Castillo Ygay, an "old-style" oaky white, dry, fruity, and worth bottle-ageing, and a wonderful old-style ROSADO.

**Marqués de Riscal, S.A.** R'a.Al. r. (p. and w. dr.) res. ★★→★★★ 64 65 68 71 73 75 76 78 80 81 82 83 84 The best-known bodega of the RIOJA ALAVESA. Its red wines are relatively light and dry. Old vintages are very fine; recent ones disappointing. Its white wines from RUEDA, incl. a v.g. SAUVIGNON BLANC, are some of the best from this region.

**Marqués de Romeral** R'a.A. r. w. dr. ★★ 76 78

Everyday Romeral and Gran Reserva are both v.g. value.

**Marqués del Puerto** R'a.A. r. (p. w. dr.) res. ★★→★★★ 73 76

Small concern, founded as Bodegas Lopez Agos, making a red reserva Señorio de Agos highly praised in Spain.

**Martinez-Bujanda** R'a.Al. r. w. dr. res ★★★ 73 75 80 82 83

Refounded (1985) family-run RIOJA bodega, remarkably equipped. Excellent wines, incl. fruity SIN CRIANZA as well as reservas.

**Mascaró, Cavas** Cat. sp. (w. dr. r.) ★★→ ★★★

Maker of some of the best Spanish brandy, good sparkling wine and a refreshing dry white Viña Franca.

**Mauro, Bodegas** O.Cas. r. ★★★ 81 83

New bodega in Tudela del Duero nr. Valladolid with v.g. round, fruity Tinta Fina red.

**Méntrida** N.Cas. r. w. ★

Demarcated region w. of Madrid, source of everday red wine.

**Milmanda** See Conca de Barberá, Torres.

**Monopole** See Compania Vinicola del Norte de España.

**Montánchez** Ext. r. g. ★

Village near Mérida, interesting because its red wines grow FLOR yeast like FINO sherry.

**Montecillo, Bodegas** R'a.A. r. w. (p.) res. ★★ 75 76 78 80 81 82 84

"State of the art" Rioja bodega owned by Osborne (see Sherry). Red and fresh dry white Cumbrero are currently among the best of the 3° año wines. Viña Monty is the worthy Reserva.

**Montecristo, Bodegas** ★★

Well-known brand of MONTILLA-MORILES wines.

**Monterrey**  Gal. r. ★

Region near the n. border of Portugal, making strong wines like those of VERIN.

**Montilla-Moriles**  And. g.  ███ ★★★

Demarcated region near Cordoba. Its crisp, sherry-like FINO and AMONTILLADO contain 14% to 17.5% natural alcohol and remain unfortified and singularly toothsome.

**Morenito, Bodegas**  N.Cas. r. (p. w. dr.) res. ★★ 78 79

Old Valdepeñas bodega which has suffered from changes in ownership. It ages its best reds in oak. Whites are poor.

**Muga, Bodegas**  R'a.A. r. (w.) res. (sp.)  ★★★  70 73 75 76 78 80 81 82

Small family firm in HARO, making some of the best red Rioja by traditional methods. Wines are light but intensely aromatic, with long complex finish. The best is Prado Enea. Whites not so good.

**Navarra**  Nav. r. p. (w.) ★→  ★★

Demarcated region; mainly fresh and fruity rosés and sturdy red wines, but some reservas up to Rioja standards. See Cenalsa, Chivite, Magaña, etc.

**Nuestro Padre Jésus del Perdón, Coop de**  N.Cas. r. w. dr.  ★  D.Y.A.

Bargain Yuntero, Casa la Teja and fresh white Lazarillo.

**Olarra, Bodegas**  R'a.A. r. (w. p.) res. ★★→★★★ 70 73 75 76 78 80 81

82  Vast modern bodega near LOGROÑO, one of the show-pieces of RIOJA, making good red and white wines and excellent Cerro Añon reservas. Since '81, Añares is the top reserva.

**Palacio de Arganza**  O.Cas. r. p. w. dr. res. ★★→★★★ 65 70 74 76 79

Best-known bodega in El Bierzo, between LEON and GALICIA. White Vega Burbia; red Almeña del Bierzo.

**Palacio de Fefiñanes**  Gal. w. res. ★★★

Best of all the ALBARIÑO wines, though without appreciable pétillance, since it is aged in oak for 3-5 yrs.

---

### Rioja's Characteristic Style

*To the Spanish palate the taste of luxury in wine is essentially the taste of oak. Oak contains vanillin, the taste of vanilla. Hence the characteristic vanilla flavour of all mature Spanish table wines of high quality – exemplified by the reservas of Rioja (red and white).*

*Historically the reason for long oak-ageing was to stabilize the best wines while their simple fruity flavours developed into something more complex and characteristically winey. Fashion has swung (perhaps too far) against the oaky flavour of old Rioja whites. But the marriage of ripe fruit and oak in red Rioja is still highly appreciated.*

---

**Paternina, S.A., Bodegas**  R'a.A. r. (p.) w. dr. or sw. res. ★→★★★ 28 59

67 68 71 73 75 76 78 79 80 81 82 83  A household name, esp. for Banda Azul red and Banda Dorada white. Fine older wines, but recent vintages disappointing. Most consistent red is Viña Vial.

**Pazo**  Gal. r. p. w. dr. ★ D.Y.A.

Brand name of the cooperative at RIBEIRO, making wines akin to Portuguese VINHOS VERDES. The rasping red is the local favourite. The pleasant slightly fizzy Pazo and Xeiro whites are safer, and the Viña Costeira is a wine of real quality.

**Peñafiel**  O.Cas. r. and w. dr. res. ★★ 64 74 76 79 80 83 85 86

Village on the R. Duero near Valladolid. Best wines are fruity reds from the Coop de RIBERO DEL DUERO, incl. tasty 5° año PROTOS.

**Penedès**  Cat. r. w. dr. sp. ★→★★★

Demarcated region including Vilafranca del Penedès, SAN SADURNÍ DE NOYA and SITGES. See also Torres.

**Perelada**  Cat. (r. p.) w. sp. ★★

In the demarcated region of Ampurdán on the Costa Brava. Best known for sparkling wines made both by the champagne and tank or CUVE CLOSE systems.

**Pérez Pascua Hnos.** O.Cas. r. (p.) res. ★★★ 81 83

Tiny, scrupulously kept family bodega in Ribera del Duero. In Spain, its fruity and complex red Viña Pedrosa is rated one of the country's best.

**Pesquera** O.Cas. r. ★★★ 80 82 85

RIBERA DEL DUERO red made in small quantity by Alejandro Fernandez. Robert Parker rates it a match for Bordeaux GRANDS CRUS.

**Piqueras, Bodegas** N.Cas. r. ▪

Makers of inexpensive and drinkable red Castillo de Almansa with more style than most of the region's wines.

**Priorato** Cat. br. dr. r. ★★

Demarcated region, an enclave in that of TARRAGONA, known for its alcoholic "rancio" wines and also for almost black full-bodied reds, often used for blending. Lighter blended Priorato is a good carafe wine in Barcelona. See De Muller, Scala Dei.

**Protos** See Peñafiel.

**Raimat** Cat. r. w. p. sp, ★→★★ (Cab) 76 81 82 83

Intriguing, well-made wines from old v'yds near Lérida, recently replanted by CODORNÍU with CABERNET, CHARDONNAY and other foreign vines. Also a good 100% CHARD CAVA.

**René Barbier** Cat. r. w. dr. res. ★★ 73 80

Part of the FREIXENET group known for fresh white Kraliner and red R.B. Reservas.

**Reserva** Good-quality wine matured for long periods. Red reservas must spend at least 1 year in cask and 2 in bottle; Gran Reservas 2 in cask and 3 in bottle.

**Ribeiro** Gal. r. (p.) w. dr. ★→★★

Demarcated region on the n. border of Portugal making wines similar to Portuguese VINHO VERDE – and others.

**Ribera del Duero** Demarcated region e. of Valladolid, potentially excellent for Tinto Fino (TEMPRANILLO) reds. See Vega Sicilia, Peñafiel, Mauro, Torremilanos, Pesquera, Pérez Pascua.

---

**Rioja** O.Cas. r. p. w. sp. esp. 64 66 68 70 73 75 76 78 80 81 82 83 85 86 87

This upland region along the R. Ebro in the n. of Spain produces most of the country's best table wines in some 50 BODEGAS DE EXPORTACIÓN. It is sub-divided into:

**Rioja Alavesa** North of the R. Ebro and the R'a.Al. produces fine red wines, mostly light in body and colour.

**Rioja Alta** South of the R. Ebro and w. of LOGROÑO, the R'a.A. grows most of the finest red and white wines; also some rosé.

**Rioja Baja** Stretching e. from LOGROÑO, the Rioja Baja makes coarser red wines, high in alcohol and often used for blending.

---

**Riojanas, Bodegas** R'a.A. r. (w. p.) res. ★★→★★★ 34 42 56 64 66 68 70 73 74 75 76 78 80 81 82 One of the older bodegas, making a good traditional Viña Albina. Monte Real reservas are big, mellow, above average.

**Rioja Santiago, S.A.** R'a.A. r. (w. dr. or sw. p.) res. ★→★★★ 78 82

Bodega at HARO with well-known wines. The flavour sometimes suffers from pasteurization, and appropriately, as it now belongs to Pepsi-Cola, it makes the biggest-selling bottled SANGRÍA. Top reds: Condal and Gran Enologica.

**Rosada** Rosé.

**Rovellats, S.A.** Cat. sp. ★★→★★★

Small family firm producing limited amounts of exclusive and expensive CAVA, stocked in some of Spain's leading restaurants.

**Rovira, S.A., Pedro** Cat. r. p. w. dr. or sw. br. res. ★→★★

Large firm with branches in the DOs TARRAGONA, TERRA ALTA and PENEDÈS, making beverage, apéritif and dessert wines.

**Rueda**  O.Cas. br. w. dr. ★—→★★
  Small demarcated area w. of Valladolid. Traditional producer of flor-growing sherry-like wines up to 17° alcohol, now making fresh whites incl. those of the MARQUÉS DE RISCAL and MARQUÉS DE GRIÑON.

**Salceda, S.A., Bodegas Viña**  R'a.Al. r. res. ★★—→★★★ 73 75 78 80 81 82  Makes fruity, well-balanced red wines.

**Sangre de Toro**  Brand name for a rich-flavoured red wine from TORRES.

**Sangría**  Cold red wine cup with citrus fruit, fizzy lemonade, ice and brandy.

**Sanlúcar de Barrameda**  Centre of the Manzanilla district. (See Sherry p. 132).

**San Sadurní de Noya**  Cat. sp.  ★★—→★★★
  Town s. of Barcelona, hollow with cellars where dozens of firms produce sparkling wine ("CAVA") by the champagne method. Standards are high, even if the taste of champagne is lacking.

**San Valero, Bodega Cooperative**  Ara. r. p. (w.) res.  ★—→★★
  Large CARIÑENA coop with some modern wines. Good red CRIANZA Villalta; fresh Perceval rosado with slight spritz; and good value young, unoaked Don Mendo red.

**Sarría, Señorio de**  Nav. r. (p. w. dr.) res.  ★★—→★★★ 64 73 74 75 76 78 81 82 84  The vineyards and model winery near Pamplona produce wines up to (high) RIOJA standards.

**Scala Dei, Cellers de**  Cat. r. res. ★★
  One of the few bodegas in the tiny DO PRIORATO. Wines are massive reds with a superplus of fruit, body and alcohol.

**Scholtz, Hermanos, S.A.**  And. br. ★★—→ ★★★
  Makers of the best MÁLAGA, including a good, dry 10-year-old amontillado, excellent Moscatel and traditional Dulce y Negro. Best is the dessert Solera Scholtz 1885.

**Seco**  Dry.

**Segura Viudas, Cavas**  Cat. Sp. ★★—→★★★
  CAVA of PENEDÈS. Buy the N.V.

**Siglo**  Popular sack-wrapped RIOJA brand of Bodegas A.G.E.

**Sin Crianza**  See Crianza.

**Sitges**  Cat. w. sw. ★★
  Coastal resort s. of Barcelona formerly noted for sweet dessert wine made from Moscatel and MALVASIA grapes.

**Tarragona**  Cat. r. w. dr. or sw. br. ★—→★★★
  1. Table wines from the demarcated region; of little note. 2. Dessert wines from the firm of DE MULLER.

**Tierra de Medina**  O.Cas. w. ★—→★★
  Area w. of Valladolid. Includes La Nava and RUEDA.

**Tinto**  Red.

**Toro**  O.Cas. r. ★—→★★
  Newly demarcated region 150 miles n.w. of Madrid, making powerful (to 16°) red wines. Leading producer Bodegas Mateos. His 3° año is good.

**Torremilanos**  O.Cas. r. res.  ★★ 76 79 81 82 83
  Label of Bodegas López Peñalba, a small family firm near Aranda de Duero. Their red wines from the Tinto Fino (TEMPRANILLO) grape are lighter and more Rioja-like than most. Also labelled "Peñalba".

**Torres, Bodegas**  Cat. r. w. dr. or semi-sw. p. res.  ★★—→★★★★ 64 70 71 73 74 75 76 77 78 79 80 81 82 83 84  Distinguished family firm making the best wines of PENEDÈS, esp. flowery white Viña Sol and Gran Viña Sol, MILMANDA oak-fermented CHARD., semi-dry aromatic Esmeralda, Waltraud RIESLING, red Tres Torres and Gran Sangredetoro, superlative Gran Coronas (Cabernet) reservas, and Santa Digna Pinot Noir. The family now also has vineyards in Chile and California.

**Utiel-Requeña**  Lev. r. (w.) p.

Demarcated region w. of Valencia. Apart from sturdy reds and chewy vino de doble pasta for blending, it makes some really light and fragrant rosé.

**Valbuena**  O.Cas. r.  ★★★  75 76 77 78 79 80 82 83

Made with the same grapes as VEGA SICILIA but sold as 3° año or 5° año. Best at about 10 years. Some prefer it to its elder brother.

**Valdeorras**  Gal. r. w. dr.  ★→★★

Demarcated region e. of Orense. Dry and refreshing wines.

**Valdepeñas**  N.Cas. r. (w.)  ★→  ★★

Demarcated region near the border of Andalucia. Its mainly red wines, though high in alcohol, are sometimes surprisingly light in flavour. Some superior wine is now being matured in oak.

**Valencia**  Lev. r. w.  ★

Demarcated region producing earthy high-strength wine.

**Vega Sicilia**  O.Cas. r. res.  ★★★★  41 48 53 59 61 64 66 67 69 72 73 76

One of the very best Spanish wines, full-bodied, fruity, piquant and fascinating. Contains up to 16% alcohol. VALBUENA is the same wine with less time in oak (78 79 80 82).

**Vendimia**  Vintage.

**Verín**  Gal. r.  ★

Town near n. border of Portugal. Its wines are the strongest from Galicia, without a bubble, and up to 14% alcohol.

**Vicente, Suso y Pérez, S.A.**  Ara. r.  ★★

A bodega s. of Saragossa producing superior CARIÑENA.

**Viña**  Literally, a vineyard. But wines such as Tondonia (LOPEZ DE HEREDIA) or Zaco (BILBAINAS) are not necessarily made with grapes exclusively from the vineyard named.

**Vinícola de Castilla**  N.Cas. r. p. w. dr.  ★

One of the largest firms in La MANCHA, marketing its wines under the labels of "Castillo de Manza" and Gran Verdad.

**VINIVAL**  Lev. r. w.  ★

Huge Valencian consortium marketing the most widely drunk wine in the region, Torres de Serrano.

**Vino Blanco**  White wine.

**Vino comun/corriente**  Ordinary wine.

    **clarete**  Light red wine.

    **dulce**  Sweet wine.

    **espumoso**  Sparkling wine.

    **generoso**  Apéritif or dessert wine rich in alcohol.

    **rancio**  Maderized (brown) white wine.

    **rosado**  Rosé wine.

    **seco**  Dry wine.

    **tinto**  Red wine.

    **verde**  Wine akin to Portuguese VINHO VERDE.

**Yecla**  Lev. r. w.  ★

Demarcated region n. of Murcia. Its cooperative, "La Purisima", is said to be Spain's biggest. Its wines, formerly all heavy-weight bruisers, have been lightened for export.

**Ygay**  See Marqués de Murrieta.

# Portugal

For port and Madeira see pp. 132-137.

**Adega** A cellar or winery.

**Alentejo** Alen. r. (w.)   ★→★★★
> Vast tract of southern Portugal with only sparse vineyards near the Spanish border. The great bulk of its wine is cooperative-made. Estate wines from ROSADO FERNANDES, Quinta de Mouchão and Esporão show remarkable potential. Best coops are at Redondo, BORBA and Reguengos de Monsarraz.

**Algarve** Alg. r. w. ★
> Newly demarcated region in the holiday area. Its wines are nothing to write home about.

**Aliança, Caves** r. w. dr. sp. res.   ★★→★★★
> Large BAIRRADA-based firm, making champagne-method sparkling wines. Reds and whites include good Bairrada wines and mature DÃOs. Tinta Velha is the best-selling red in Portugal.

**Amarante** Sub-region in the VINHOS VERDES area. Rather heavier and stronger wines than those from farther north.

**Arruda, Adega Cooperative de** B'a.al. r. res.   ★
> Vinho Tinto Arruda is a best buy. Avoid the Reserva.

**Aveleda** Douro w. dr. ★★ D.Y.A.
> A first-class VINHO VERDE made on the Aveleda estate of the Guedes family. Sold dry in Portugal but sweetened for export.

**Bacalhoa, Quinta de** Est'a. r. res. ★★★ 81 82 83 84 85
> American-owned estate near Setúbal, whose excellent CABERNET SAUVIGNON wine is vinified by João PIRES.

**Bairrada** Bei. Lit. r. w. dr. and sp. ★→   ★★ 66 70 75 76 77 82
> Recently demarcated region supplying much of Oporto's carafe wine and some excellent red GARRAFEIRAS. Also good-quality sparkling wines by the champagne method. A potential star.

**Barca Velha** ("Ferreirinha") Trás-os-m. r. res. ★★★★ 57 64 65 66 78
> Perhaps Portugal's best red, made in very limited quantity by the port firm of FERREIRA. Powerful and fine with deep bouquet.

**Barrocão, Cavas do** Bei. Lit. r. w. dr. res. ★→   ★★★
> Based in the BAIRRADA, the firm blends good red DÃOs and makes first-rate old BAIRRADA garrafeiras, such as 60 and 64.

**Basto** A sub-region of the VINHOS VERDES area on the R. Tamego, producing more astringent red wine than white.

**Borba** Alen. r. ★
> Small VQPRD area nr. Evora, making some of best wine from ALENTEJO.

**Borges & Irmão** Merchants of port and table wines at Vila Nova de Gaia. Brands incl. Gatão and (better) Gamba VINHOS VERDES. Also Fita Azul sparkling.

**Braga** Sub-region of the VINHOS VERDES area, good red and white.

**Buçaco** B'a.al. r. (p.) w. res.   ★★★★ r. 51 53 57 58 60 63 67 70 72 75 77; w. 56 65 66 70 72 75   The legendary speciality of the luxury Palace hotel at Buçaco nr. Coimbra, not seen elsewhere. Incredible quality.

**Bucelas** Est'a. w. dr. ★★★ 79
> Tiny demarcated region just n. of Lisbon. CAVES VELHAS make delicate, perfumed wines with 11% to 12% alcohol.

**Camarate, Quinta de** Est'a. r.   ★★ 74 78 80 82
> Notable CLARETE from FONSECA at Azeitão, s. of Lisbon, incl. detectable CABERNET SAUVIGNON.

**Carcavelos** Est'a. br. sw. ★★★
> Minute demarcated region w. of Lisbon. Its excellent sweet apéritif or dessert wines average 19% alcohol and are drunk cold.

**Cartaxo** Ribatejo r. w. ★
> A district in the Ribatejo n. of Lisbon, now a VQPRD area making everyday wines popular in the capital.

**Carvalho, Ribeiro & Ferreira** B'a. al. r. w. des. ★★→★★★
Large merchants bottling and blending SERRADAYRES and excellent RIBATEJO GARRAFEIRAS.

**Casa de Sezim** M'o. w. dr. ★★→★★★ D.Y.A.
One of the best estate-bottled VINHO VERDES from a member of the new association of private producers, APEVV.

**Casal García** Douro w. dr. ★★ D.Y.A.
One of the biggest-selling VINHOS VERDES in Portugal, made by SOGRAPE.

**Casal Mendes** M'o. w. dr. ★★ D.Y.A.
The VINHOS VERDES from CAVES ALIANÇA.

**Casaleiro** Trademark of Caves Dom Teodosio-João T. Barbosa, who make a variety of reliable wines: DÃO, VINHOS VERDES, etc.

**Caves Velhas** Bei. Lit. r. w. dr. res ★★→★★★
Only maker of BUCELAS; also good DÃO and Romeira GARRAFEIRAS.

**Cepa Velha** M'o. (r.) w. dr. ★★★
Brand name of Vinhos de Monção, Lda. Their Alvarinho, from the grape of that name, is one of the best VINHOS VERDES.

**Clarete** Light red wine.

**Colares** Est'a. r. ★★★
Small demarcated region on the coast w. of Lisbon. Its classical dark red wines, rich in tannin, are from vines which survived the phylloxera epidemic. Drink the oldest available.

**Conde de Santar** B'a.al. r. (w. dr.) res. ★★→★★★ 70 73 78
The only estate-grown DÃO, later matured and sold by the port firm of CÁLEM. The reservas are fruity, full-bodied and exceptionally smooth.

**Dão** B'a.al. r. w. res. ★→ ★★★ 66 67 69 70 71 74 75 80 83
Demarcated region round Viseu on the R. Mondego. Produces some of Portugal's best table wines: solid reds of some subtlety with age: substantial dry whites. All are sold under brand names.

**Douro** The northern river whose valley produces port and more than adequate demarcated table wines.

**Evelita** Trás-os-m. r. ★→★★★ 75
Reliable middle-weight red made near VILA REAL by Real Companhia Vinícola do Norte de Portugal. Ages well.

**Fonseca, J.M. da** Est'a. r. w. dr. br. res. ★→★★★★
Large, old-established family firm in Azeitão making a wide range of good wines, incl. the red PERIQUITA, PASMADOS and QUINTA DE CAMARATE (formerly known as Palmela) and Terras Altas DÃO, as well as the famous MOSCATEL DE SETÚBAL.

**Fonseca Internacional J.M. da** Est'a. p. ★
Formerly part of the last, now owned by Grand Met. Produces LANCERS rosé and sparkling LANCERS Brut, made by a continuous process for the mass market.

**Gaeiras** Est'a. r. ★★
Dry, full-bodied and well-balanced red made near Obidos.

**Garrafeira** The "private reserve" aged wine of a merchant aged for a minimum of 2 years in cask and 1 in bottle, but often much longer; usually his best, though often of indeterminate origin.

**Gatão** M'o. w. dr. ★★ D.Y.A.
Reliable "GREEN WINE" from the firm of Borges & Irmão, fragrant but sometimes a little sweetened.

**Gazala** M'o. w. dr. ★★ D.Y.A.
A new VINHO VERDE made at Barcelos by SOGRAPE since the AVELEDA estate went to a different branch of the Guedes family.

**Grão Vasco** B'a.al. r. w. res. ★★→★★★ 70 73 75 78 80 81
One of the best brands of DÃO, blended and matured at Viseu by SOGRAPE. Fine red reservas; fresh young white (D.Y.A.)

**Lagoa** See Algarve.

**Lagosta** M'o. w. dr. ★★ D.Y.A.
Well-known VINHO VERDE from the Real Companhia Vinícola do Norte de Portugal.

**Lancers**  Est'a. p. ★

Sweet carbonated rosé and sparkling white extensively shipped to the USA by FONSECA INTERNACIONAL.

**Lima**  Sub-region in the n. of the VINHOS VERDES area making mainly astringent red wines.

**Madeira**  Island br. dr./sw. ★★→★★★★

Source of famous apéritif and dessert wines. See pp. 132-137.

**Magrico**  M'o. w. dr.  ██ D.Y.A.

Many VINHOS VERDES are slightly sweetened for export. This is a genuinely dry one.

**Mateus Rosé**  Trás-os-m. p. (w.) ★

World's biggest-selling medium-sweet carbonated rosé, made by SOGRAPE at VILA REAL and Anadia in the BAIRRADA.

**Monção**  Sub-region of the VINHOS VERDES area on R. Minho, producing the best of them from the ALVARINHO grape.

**Palacio de Brejoeira**  M'o. (r.) w. dr. ★★★

Outstanding estate-made VINHOS VERDE from MONÇÃO, with astonishing fragrance and full, fruity flavour.

**Penafiel**  Sub-region in the s. of the VINHOS VERDES area.

**Periquita**  Est'a. r.  ██ 71 74 77 78 80 84

One of Portugal's most enjoyable robust reds, made by J. M. da FONSECA at Azeitão s. of Lisbon from a grape of that name much used in the ALENTEJO.

**Pinhel**  B'a.al. (r.) w. sp. ★

VQPRD region e. of the DÃO, making similar white wine, mostly processed into sparkling.

**Planalto**  Douro w. dr. ★★

Good white wine from SOGRAPE.

**Pires, João**  Est'a. r. w. dr./sw. res.  ██→★★★

Producers of red TINTO DE ANFORA, white dry Moscato, Catarina CHARDONNAY and CAB SAUV. (See Bacalhoa, Quinta de.)

**Ponte de Lima, cooperativa de**  M'o. r. ★★

Maker of one of the best bone dry red VINHOS VERDES.

**Quinta da Insua**  Ba.al. r. w. ★★

One of the very few single estate DÃOs, made with a proportion of CAB SAUVIGNON in an old cellar currently being re-equipped and modernized.

**Quinta da Pacheca**  Trás-os-m. r. w. ★★ 82

Superior Douro table wines, estate-grown, made and bottled.

**Quinta de Ribeirinho**  Bei. Lit. r. sp. ★★→★★★

Luis Pato makes some of the best estate-grown BAIRRADA wines: fruity red and fresh méthode champenoise sparkling.

**Quinta de S. Claudio**  M'o. w. dr. ★★★ D.Y.A.

Estate at Esposende and maker of some of the best VINHO VERDE outside MONÇÃO.

**Quinta do Côtto**  Trás-os-m. r. w. dr. res. ★★→★★★ 82

Red Grande Escolha and Q. do Côtto are dense, fruity, tannic wines that will repay long keeping. Also port.

**Quinta do Corval**  Trás-os-m. r. ★★

Estate near Pinhão making good light CLARETES.

**Raposeira**  B'a.al. sp. ★★

One of the best-known Portuguese sparkling wines, made by the champagne method at Lamego. Ask for the Bruto.

**Redondo**  See Alentejo.

**Reguengos de Monsarraz**  See Alentejo.

**Ribalonga, Vinícola**  B'a.al. r. res.  ██ 71 74 76 78 80 82

Makers of a sound and very reasonably priced red DÃO.

**Ribatejo**  Region on the R. Tagus n. of Lisbon. Source of several good GARRAFEIRAS, etc.

**Rosado Fernandes, Jose de Sousa**  Alen. r. res. ★★ 71 75 79 83 86
Small private firm, recently acquired by J. M. da FONSECA, producing the most sophisticated of the full-bodied wines from the Alentejo, fermenting them in *Tinajas* and ageing them in oak.

**Santola**  B'a.al. w. dr. ★★ D.Y.A.
A refreshing dry VINHO VERDE from Vinhos Messias.

**São João, Caves**  Bei. Lit. r. w. dr. sp. res. ★★→□ ★★★ 70 75 76 78 80
One of the best firms in the BAIRRADA, known for its fruity and full-bodied reds and Porto dos Cavaleiros DÃOs. Also fizz.

**Serradayres**  Est'a. r. (w.) res. ★★ 78
Blended RIBATEJO table wines from CARVALHO, RIBEIRO & FERRERIRA. Usually sound and very drinkable, but recently very tart.

**Setúbal**  Est'a. br. ★★★
Small demarcated region s. of the R. Tagus, where J. M. da FONSECA make an aromatic dessert muscat, 6 and 25 yrs old.

**Sogrape**  Sociedad Comercial dos Vinhos de Mesa de Portugal. Largest wine concern in the country, making VINHOS VERDES, DÃO, MATEUS ROSÉ, VILA REAL red, etc., and now owners of FERREIRA port.

**Terras Altas**  B'a.al. r. w. res. ★★ 75 76 78 79 80 82 83 84
Good DÃO wines made by J. M. da FONSECA.

**Tinto de Anfora**  Est'a. r. ★★ 78 80 81 82 84 85 86
Deservedly popular juicy and fruity red from JOÃO PIRES.

**Torres Vedras**  Est'a. r. w. dr. ★
Area n. of Lisbon famous for Wellington's "lines". Major supplier of bulk wine with one of the biggest coops in Portugal.

**Vila Real**  Trás-os-m. r. ★→□ ★★
Town in the newly demarcated DOURO region, now making some good red table wine.

**Vinho branco**  White wine.
  **consumo**  Ordinary wine.
  **doce**  Sweet wine.
  **espumante**  Sparkling wine.
  **garrafeira**  A reserve with min. 2 years in cask and 1 in bottle.
  **generoso**  Apéritif or dessert wine rich in alcohol.
  **maduro**  A mature table wine – as opposed to a VINHO VERDE.
  **rosado**  Rosé wine.
  **seco**  Dry wine.
  **tinto**  Red wine.
  **verde**  See under Vinhos Verdes.

**Vinhos Verdes**  M'o. and Douro. r. ★ w. dr. ★→★★★
Demarcated region between R. Douro and n. frontier with Spain, producing "green wines": wine made from barely ripe grapes and undergoing a special secondary fermentation which leaves it with a slight sparkle. Ready for drinking in the spring after the harvest. It may be white or red. "Green wine" is not an official term.

---

*Remember that vintage years generally ready for drinking in 1989 are printed in* **bold type.** *Those in light type will benefit from being kept.*

# Sherry,
# Port & Madeira

The original, classical sherries of Spain, ports of Portugal and madeiras of Madeira are listed below. References to their many imitators in South Africa, California, Australia, Cyprus, Argentina will be found under their respective countries. (N.B. "British Sherry" is an outrageous theft of the name to describe a drink made of dehydrated must and water – not legally wine at all.)

The map on page 118 locates the port and sherry districts. Madeira is an island 400 miles out in the Atlantic from the coast of Morocco, a port of call for west-bound ships: hence its historical market in North America.

In this section most of the entries are shippers' names followed by a brief account of their wines. The names of wine-types are included in the alphabetical listing.

**Almacenista**
> Individual old unblended sherry; high-quality, usually dark dry wines for connoisseurs. Often superb quality and value.

**Amontillado**
> In general use means medium sherry; technically means a FINO which has been aged to become more powerful and pungent.

**Amoroso**
> Type of sweet sherry, not much different from a sweet OLOROSO.

**Barbadillo, Antonio**
> The largest SANLUCAR firm, with a range of 50-odd MANZANILLAS and sherries, incl. Sanlucar Fino, Solera Manzanilla Pasada, Eva Cream, etc. Also fresh young Castillo de San Diego table wines.

**Barbeito**
> Shippers of good-quality Madeira, the last independent family firm in the business. Wines include one of the driest and best apéritif Madeiras: "Island Dry". Also Crown Malmsey.

**Bertola**
> Sherry shippers, best known for their Bertola Cream Sherry.

**Blandy** Historic family firm of Madeira shippers. Duke of Clarence Malmsey is their most famous wine. 10-year-old Malmsey is v. popular.

**Blazquez**
> Sherry bodega at JEREZ with outstanding FINO, "Carta Blanca", and "Carta Oro" amontillado "al natural" (unsweetened).

**Brown sherry**
> British term for a style of dark sweet sherry.

**Bual** One of the best grapes of Madeira, making a soft smoky sweet wine, not usually as sweet as Malmsey.

**Caballero**
> Sherry shippers best known for Pavon Fino, Oloroso Mayoral Cream, excellent Ponche and "Burdon" sherries.

**Cálem** Old Portuguese house with a good reputation. esp. for vintage wines. Owning the excellent Quinta da Foz. Vintages: 50 58 **60** 63 **70 75** 77 78 83 85. Adequate light tawny.

**Churchill**
> The only recently founded port shipper, already respected for excellent vintages '82 and '85.

**Cockburn**
> British-owned port shippers with a range of good wines incl. 20-year-old "Directors' Reserve". Fine vintage port from very high v'yds can look deceptively light when young, but has great lasting power. Vintages: **55 60** 63 67 **70 75** 83 85.

**Cossart Gordon**
Leading firm of Madeira shippers founded 1745, best known for their "Good Company" range of wines but also producing old vintages (latest, 1952) and soleras (esp. superb Sercial Duo Centenary).

**Cream Sherry**
A style of amber sweet sherry made by sweetening a blend of well-aged OLOROSOS.

**Crofts**
One of the oldest firms shipping vintage port: 300 years old in 1978. Bought early this century by Gilbey's. Well-balanced vintage wines last as long as any. Vintages: 55 60 63 66 70 75 77 82 85, and lighter vintage wines under the name of their Quinta da Roeda in several other years ('80). Also now in the sherry business with Croft Original (PALE CREAM), Delicado (FINO), and good PALO CORTADO.

**Crusted**
Term for a vintage-style port, but blended from several vintages not one, bottled young and aged in bottle, so forming a "crust" in the bottle. Needs decanting.

**Delaforce**
Port shippers owned by I.D.V., particularly well known in Germany. "His Eminence" is an excellent tawny. "Vintage Character" is also good. Vintage wines are very fine, among the lighter kind: 55 58 60 63 66 70 75 77 82. "Quinta da Corte" in 1980.

**Diez-Merito, S.A.**
Fast-growing JEREZ firm owned by BODEGAS INTERNACIONALES, specializing in "own-brand" sherries. Latest acquisition is Zoilo Ruiz Mateos, formerly part of the ill-fated Rumasa empire. Its own Fino Imperial and Oloroso Victoria Regina are excellent. DON ZOILO wines are outstanding.

**Domecq**
Giant family-owned sherry bodegas at JEREZ. Double Century Original Oloroso is their biggest brand, La Ina their excellent FINO. Other famous wines incl. Celebration Cream, Botaina (old amontillado) and the magnificent Rio Viejo (dry oloroso). Now also in Rioja (p. 138).

**Don Zoilo**
Luxury sherries, incl. deep velvety FINO, sold by DIEZ-MERITO.

**Dow**
Old name used on the British market by the port shippers Silva & Cosens, well known for their relatively dry but none the less splendid vintage wines, said to have a faint "cedarwood" character. Also v.g. "Vintage Character" and Boardroom Tawny. Vintages: 55 58 60 63 66 70 75 77 80 83 85. Dow, WARRE, GRAHAM, GOULD CAMPBELL, QUARLES HARRIS and SMITH WOODHOUSE all belong to the Symington family.

**Dry Sack**
See Williams & Humbert.

**Duff Gordon**
Sherry shippers best known for their El Cid AMONTILLADO. Owned by the big Spanish firm Bodegas Osborne.

**Duke of Wellington**
Luxury range of sherries from BODEGAS INTERNACIONALES.

**Eira Velha, Quinta da**
Small port estate with old-style vintage wines shipped by HARVEY's of Bristol. Vintages: 72 78 80 82 85.

**Ferreira**
The biggest Portuguese-owned port growers and shippers (since 1751) recently bought by Sogrape; well known for old tawnies and good, relatively light, vintages: 60 63 66 70 75 77 80 83. Also Special Reserve, Donna Antonia and sublime tawny Duque de Braganza.

**Findlater's**
Old established London wine merchant shipping his own very successful brand of medium sherry: Dry Fly amontillado.

**Fino**
Term for the lightest and finest of sherries, completely dry, very pale and with great delicacy. Fino should always be drunk cool and fresh: it deteriorates rapidly once opened. TIO PEPE is a classic example.

**Flor**   The characteristic natural yeast which gives FINO sherry its unique flavour.

**Fonseca**
British-owned port shipper of stellar reputation, connected with TAYLOR. Robust, deeply coloured vintage wine, sometimes said to have a slight "burnt" flavour. Vintages: 55 60 63 66 70 75 77 83 85. Also popular Vintage Character "Bin 27".

**Garvey's**
Famous old sherry shippers at JEREZ. Their finest wines are Fino San Patricio, Tio Guillermo Dry Amontillado and Ochavico Dry Oloroso. San Angelo Medium Amontillado is the most popular. Also Bicentenary Pale Cream.

**Gonzalez Byass**
Enormous concern shipping the world's most famous and one of the best sherries: Tio Pepe. Other brands incl. La Concha Medium Amontillado, Elegante Dry Fino, San Domingo Pale Cream, Nectar Cream and Alfonso Dry Oloroso. Matusalem and Apostoles are respectively medium and sweet old olorosos of rare quality.

**Gould Campbell**   See Smith Woodhouse.

**Graham**   Port shippers famous for one of the richest and sweetest of vintage ports, largely from their own Quinta Malvedos, also excellent brands, incl. Ruby, Late Bottled 10- and 20-year-old Emperor Tawny. Vintages: 55 58 60 63 66 70 75 77 80 85.

**Harvey's**
Probably the largest sherry firm, having recently bought PALOMINO and DE TERRY. World-famous Bristol shippers of Bristol Cream and Bristol Milk sweet sherries, Club Amontillado and Bristol Dry, which are medium, Luncheon Dry and Bristol Fino, which are dry, and excellent PALO CORTADO. Also a very good new range: "1796". Harvey's also control COCKBURN.

---

### Sherry & Food

*By a quirk of fashion the wines of sherry, Madeira and to some extent port are currently being left on the sidelines by a world increasingly hypnotized by a limited range of "varietal" wines. Yet all three include wines with every quality of "greatness", and far more gastronomic possibilities than the world seems to realize. It is notorious that for the price of e.g. a bottle of top-class white burgundy you can buy three of the very finest fino sherry, which with many dishes (see Wine & Food) will make an equally exciting accompaniment. Mature Madeiras give the most lingering farewell of any wine to a splendid dinner. Tawny port is a wine of many uses. Perhaps it is because the New World cannot rival these Old World classics that they are left out of the headlines.*

---

**Henriques & Henriques**
Well-known Madeira shippers of Funchal. Their wide range includes a good dry apéritif wine: Ribeiro Seco.

**Internacionales, Bodegas**
Once the pride of RUMASA and incorporating such famous houses as BERTOLA, Varela and DIEZ-MERITO, Internacionales is now the cornerstone of a new empire embracing PATERNINA and FRANCO ESPAÑOLES in Rioja. Its own best-known sherries are the Duke of Wellington range.

**Jerez de la Frontera**
Centre of the sherry industry, between Cadiz and Seville in s. Spain. The word sherry is a corruption of the name, pronounced in Spanish "Hereth". In French, Xérés.

**Late-bottled vintage**
Port of a single vintage kept in wood for twice as long as vintage port (about 5 years). Therefore lighter when bottled and ageing quicker. A real "L.B.V." will "throw a crust" like vintage port.

**Leacock**
>One of the oldest Madeira shippers. Most famous wine is "Penny Black" Malmsey. 10-year-old Malmsey and 13-year-old Bual are excellent.

**Lustau** The largest independent family-owned sherry bodega in JEREZ, making many wines for other shippers, but with a very good "Dry Lustau" range (particularly the OLOROSO) and "Jerez Lustau" PALO CORTADO. Also shippers of excellent ALMACENISTA wines.

**Macharnudo**
>One of the best parts of the sherry v'yds, n. of Jerez, famous for wines of the highest quality, both FINO and OLOROSO.

**Malmsey**
>The sweetest form of Madeira; dark amber, rich and honeyed yet with Madeira's unique sharp tang.

**Manzanilla**
>Sherry, normally FINO, which has acquired a peculiar bracing salty character from being kept in bodegas at Sanlucar de Barrameda, on the Guadalquivir estuary near JEREZ.

**Morgan** A subsidiary of CROFT port, best known in France.

**Offley Forester**   SPM
>Port shippers and owners of the famous Quinta Boa Vista. Their vintage wines tend to be round, "fat" and sweet, good for relatively early drinking. Vintages: **60 62 63 66 67 70 72 75** 77 83 85.

**Oloroso**
>Style of sherry, heavier and less brilliant than FINO when young, but maturing to greater richness and roundness. Naturally dry, but generally sweetened for sale, as CREAM.

**Osborne**
>Well known brandy, but also good sherries include Fino Quinta, Coquinero, dry AMONTILLADO, 10 R.F. Oloroso.

**Pale Cream**
>Increasingly popular style of sherry made by sweetening FINO, pioneered by CROFTS "Original".

**Palo Cortado**
>A style of sherry close to OLOROSO but with some of the character of an AMONTILLADO. Dry but rich and soft. Not often seen.

**Palomino & Vergara**
>Sherry shippers of JEREZ bought in 1986 by HARVEY's, best known for Palomino Cream, Medium and Dry. Best FINO: Tio Mateo.

**Puerto de Santa Maria**
>Second city of the sherry area, with important bodegas.

**P.X.** Short for Pedro Ximénez, the grape part-dried in the sun used in JEREZ for sweetening blends.

**Quarles Harris**
>One of the oldest port houses, since 1680, now owned by the Symingtons (see Dow). Vintages: **60 63** 66 **70 75** 77 80 83.

**Quinta** Portuguese for "estate".

**Quinta do Côtto**
>Single-vineyard port from Miguel Champalimaud, best known of a new association of grower-bottlers. V.g. vintage '82.

**Quinta do Noval**
>Great Portuguese port house making intensely fruity, structured and elegant vintage port; a few pre-phylloxera vines still at the Quinta make a small quantity of "Nacional" – very dark, full and slow-maturing wine. Also v.g. 20-year-old Tawny. Vintages: **55 58 60 63 66 70 75** 78 82 85.

**Rainwater**
>A fairly light, not very sweet blend of Madeira – in fact of VERDELHO wine – traditionally popular in eastern N. America.

**Real Tesoro, Marqués de**

One of the smaller family firms of JEREZ, with excellent MANZANILLA La Bailadora and a range of good sherries, esp. their AMONTILLADO.

**Rebello Valente**

Name used for the vintage port of ROBERTSON. Their vintage wines are light but elegant and well-balanced, maturing rather early. Vintages: 55 60 63 66 67 70 75 77 80 83 85.

**La Riva**

Distinguished firm of sherry shippers making one of the best FINOS, Tres Palmas, among many good wines.

**Rivero, J.M.**

The famous "C.Z." brand of the oldest sherry house now belongs to A. Parra Guerrero, who make and market Rivero sherries as well as their own.

---

*Passing the Port*

*Vintage port is almost as much a ritual as a drink. It always needs to be decanted with great care (since the method of making it leaves a heavy deposit in the bottle). The simplest and surest way of doing this is by filtering it through clean muslin or a coffee filter-paper into either a decanter or a well-rinsed bottle. All except very old ports can safely be decanted the day before drinking. At table the decanter is traditionally passed from guest to guest clockwise. Vintage port can be immensely long-lived. Particularly good vintages older than those mentioned in the text include 1950, '48, '45, '35, '34, '27, '20, '11, '08, '04.*

---

**Robertson**

Subsidiary of SANDEMAN, shipping REBELLO VALENTE vintage and L.B.V. and Robertson's Privateer Reserve, 10-year-old Pyramid and 20-year-old Imperial.

**Rozes** Port shippers controlled by Moët-Hennessy. Tawny very popular in France; also Ruby and 77.

**Ruby** The youngest (and cheapest) style of port: very sweet and red. The best are vigorous and full of flavour. Others can be merely strong and rather thin.

**Rutherford & Miles**

Madeira shippers with one of the best known of all Bual wines: Old Trinity House. Also Old Custom House Sercial and Old Artillery House Malmsey.

**Sanchez Romate**

Family firm since 1781. Best known in Spanish-speaking world esp. for their brandy, Cardinal Mendoza. Makes good sherry – Fino Cristal, Oloroso Don Antonio, Amontillado N.P.U.

**Sandeman**

Giant of the port trade and a major figure in the sherry one, owned by Seagrams. Founder's Reserve is their well-known vintage character; their vintage wines are robust – some of the old vintages were superlative (55 58 60 63 66 67 70 75 77 80 82 85). Of the sherries, Medium Dry Amontillado is best-seller, Don Fino is v.g. and a new range of wonderful luxury sherries incl. Royal Ambrosante, Imperial Corregidor, Character Oloroso, etc. Not to be missed.

**Sanlucar**

Seaside sherry-town (see Manzanilla).

**Sercial**

Grape (reputedly a RIESLING) grown in Madeira to make the driest of the island's wines – a good apéritif.

**Smith Woodhouse**

Port firm founded in 1784, now owned by the Symington family (see Dow). GOULD CAMPBELL is a subsidiary. Wines incl. Old Priory Vintage Character, Old Lodge Tawny, 70 75 77 80 83 85

**Solera**   System used in making both sherry and (in modified form) Madeira; also some port. It consists of topping up progressively more mature barrels with slightly younger wine of the same sort: the object being to attain continuity in the final wine. Most commercial sherries are blends of several solera wines.

**Tarquinio Lomelino**
Madeira shippers famous for their collection of antique wines. Standard range is Don Henriques; top range, "Lomelino".

**Tawny**   A style of port aged for many years in wood (in contrast to vintage port, which is aged in bottle) until tawny in colour. Low-price tawnies are blends of red and white ports. Taste the difference.

**Taylor**   Perhaps the best port shippers, particularly for their full, rich, long-lived vintage wine and tawnies of stated age (40-year-old, 20-year-old, etc.). Their Quinta de Vargellas is said to give Taylor's its distinctive scent of violets. Vintages: **55 60** 63 **66** 70 75 77 80 83. Vargellas is shipped unblended in certain (lesser) vintages (**67 72 74**). Their L.B.V. is also better than most.

**Terry, Fernando A. de**
Bodega at PUERTO DE SANTA MARIA with a good range of sherries, bought in 1986 by HARVEY's.

**Tio Pepe**
The most famous of FINO sherries (see Gonzalez Byass).

**Valdespino**
Famous family-owned bodega at JEREZ, owner of the Inocente v'yd, making the excellent FINO of the same name. Tio Diego is their splendid dry AMONTILLADO, Solera 1842 a ditto oloroso, Matador the name of their popular range.

**Varela**   Sherry shippers best known for their Medium and Cream.

**Verdelho**
Madeira grape making fairly dry wine without the distinction of SERCIAL. A pleasant apéritif. Some fine old vintage wines.

**Vintage Port**
The best port of exceptional vintages is bottled after only 2 years in wood and matures very slowly, for up to 20 years or even more, in its bottle. It always leaves a heavy deposit and therefore needs decanting.

**Vintage Character**
Somewhat misleading term used for a good-quality full and meaty port like a first-class RUBY made by the solera system. Lacks the splendid "nose" of vintage port.

**Warre**   Probably the oldest of all port shippers (since 1670), now owned by the Symington family (see Dow). Fine long-maturing vintage wines, a good TAWNY, Nimrod, and Vintage Character Warrior. Vintages: **55 58 60** 63 **66** 70 75 77 80 83 85

**White Port**
Port made of white grapes, golden in colour. Formerly made sweet, now more often dry: a good apéritif but a rather heavy one.

**Williams & Humbert**
Famous and first-class sherry bodega. Dry Sack (medium AMONTILLADO) is their best-selling wine. Pando is an excellent FINO. Canasta Cream and Walnut Brown are good in their class. Dos Cortados is their famous PALO CORTADO.

# Central & South-east Europe

LANGENLOIS  WEINVIERTEL
WACHAU  Vienna
MÁTRAAL
Austria
SOMLÓ
SOPRON  Budapest
BURGENLAND
Graz  Hungary
STYRIA  BALATON
LUTOMER
VILLANYI-PÉCS
Ljubljana
Italy
SLAVONIA
SLOVENIA
VOJVODINA
Trieste  Zagreb
CROATIA

BOSNIA-HERZEGOVINA
Yugoslavia
DALMATIA  Sarajevo
Adriatic Sea
Split
MONTENEGR

Dubrovnik

Corfu

The countries covered by this map, on both sides of the Iron Curtain, offer some very good value for money, complete with off-the-beaten-track characters which true wine-lovers will enjoy exploring. Quality is moderate to high, tending to improve, and pretty consistent, if rarely exciting.

The references are arranged country by country, with all geographical references back to the map on this page.

Labelling in all the countries except Greece and Cyprus is broadly based on the German, now international, pattern of place-name plus grape-variety. The main grape-varieties are therefore included alongside areas and other terms in the alphabetical listings. Quality ratings in this section are given where experience justifies more than a single, everyday, star.

# Austria

The Austrian wine industry, equipped with new laws and new wine regions, is starting to recover from its scandal of 1985, when diethylene glycol was found in wines claiming high natural sweetness, particularly from the Burgenland. Although nobody was poisoned enormous damage was done to many innocent and well-run businesses. New legislation should now ensure that nothing of the kind happens again. The laws include curbs on yields (Germany please copy) and impose higher levels of ripeness for each category than their German counterparts. Austria offers good value in fresh, fruity, dry wines and succulent sweet ones. Encouragingly, growers are raising their sights and aiming for quality rather than quantity.

**Recent vintages:**

**1987**  A third small harvest, but quality is good.

**1986**  An outstanding vintage in most cases, though small.

**1985**  A small but excellent-quality harvest.

**1984**  Good wines for early drinking.

**1983**  Outstandingly ripe; many sweet wines though some are low in acidity.

**Apetlon**  Burgenland w. s./sw. or sw. ★→ ▨ ★★
   Village of the SEEWINKEL making tasty whites on sandy soil, incl. very good sweet wines, esp. from LENZ MOSER.

**Ausbruch**  Term used for very sweet wines between Beerenauslese and Trockenbeerenauslese (see Germany) in richness.

**Baden**  Vienna (r.) w. dr. or sw. ★→★★★
   Town and area s. of VIENNA incl. GUMPOLDSKIRCHEN. Some good lively high-flavoured wines, whites best from ROTGIPFLER and ZIERFÄNDLER grapes.

**Blaufränkisch**  Reputedly the GAMAY grape; gives adequate reds. Kékfrankos in Hungary.

**Bouvier**  Native Austrian grape giving soft but aromatic wine esp. for Beerenauslese and Trockenbeerenauslese.

**Burgenland**  Burgenland r. w. dr. sw. ★→ ▨ ★★★
   Region on the Hungarian border with ideal conditions for sweet wines and 45,000 acres. Four wine-regions: NEUSIEDLERSEE (e. of the lake), Neusiedlersee-Hügelland (w. shore and around EISENSTADT) and Mittel- and Südburgenland. "Noble rot" occurs regularly and AUSBRUCH, Beerenausleses, etc., are abundant. (See Oggau, Rust, etc.)

**Donauland-Carnuntum**  Unwieldy new name for Danube (Donau) valley wine region incl. KLOSTERNEUBURG.

**Dürnstein**  w. dr. sw. ★★→★★★
   Wine centre of the WACHAU with a famous ruined castle and the important WINZERGENOSSENSCHAFT WACHAU. Some of Austria's best whites, esp. Rheinriesling and GRÜNER VELTLINER.

**Eisenstadt**  Burgenland (r.) w. dr. or sw. ★★→★★★
   Capital of BURGENLAND and historic seat of the ESTERHÁZY.

**Esterházy**  Noble and historic family (patrons of Haydn) whose AUSBRUCH and other BURGENLAND wines are often of superlative quality.

**Falkenstein**  See Weinviertel.

**Grinzing**  Vienna w. ★★ D.Y.A.
   Suburb of VIENNA with delicious lively HEURIGE wines.

**Grüner Veltliner**  Austria's most characteristic white grape (32% of her white v'yds) making short-lived but marvellously spicy and flowery, racy and vital wine – ideal HEURIGE, in fact.

**Gumpoldskirchen** Vienna (r.) w. dr. or sw. ★★→★★★

Pretty resort s. of VIENNA with wines of great character from ROTGIPFLER and ZIERFÄNDLER grapes. See Thermenregion.

**Heiligenkreuz, Stift** Cistercian Monastery at THALLERN making some of Austria's best wine, particularly RIESLING from a fine steep v'yd: Wiege.

**Heurige** Means both new wine and the tavern where it is drunk.

**Kahlenberg** Vienna w. ★★

Village and v'yd hill n. of VIENNA, famous for HEURIGEN.

**Kamptal-Donauland** (r.) w. dr. or sw. ★→★★

Wine region around KREMS and the Kamp valley, a tributary of the Danube (Donau), with pleasant Veltliner (see Grüner Veltliner) and RIESLING.

**Klöch** Steiermark (r.) p. w. ★→★★

The chief wine town of Styria, the s.e. province. No famous wines, but several agreeable ones, esp. Traminer.

**Klosterneuberg** Danube r. w. ★→★★★

District just n. of VIENNA, with a famous monastery, which is a major producer, a wine college and a research station.

**Kloster Und** New wine college and tasting centre in restored Capuchin monastery at KREMS.

**Krems** Danube w. ★→★★★

Town and district just e. of the WACHAU with good GRÜNER VELTLINER and Rheinriesling (see Riesling) esp. from Austria's biggest WINZER-GENOSSENSCHAFT.

**Langenlois** Langenlois r. w. ★→★★

Chief town of the KAMPTAL with many modest and some good wines, esp. peppery GRÜNER VELTLINER and Rheinriesling (see Riesling) from its loess soil. Reds less interesting.

**Lenz Moser** Major wine grower, recently purchased by a big retail chain. Invented a high vine system and makes good to excellent wine at Röhrendorf near KREMS, APETLON and elsewhere. Took over SIEGENDORF in 1988.

**Mailberg** Weinviertel w. ★★

Town of the WEINVIERTEL known for lively light wine.

**Mörbisch** Burgenland r. w. dr. or sw. ★→ ███ ★★★

Leading wine-village of BURGENLAND. Good sweet wines. Reds and dry whites not inspiring.

**Müller-Thurgau** Far less interesting than GRÜNER VELTLINER, but none the less 10% of all Austria's vines.

**Muskat-Ottonel** The strain of muscat grape grown in e. Europe, incl. Austria.

**Niederösterreich** Lower Austria: i.e. all the n.e. corner of the country.

**Neuberger** Popular white grape: pleasant wine in KREMS/LANGENLOIS but soft and coarse in BURGENLAND.

**Neusiedlersee** A broad shallow lake in flat sandy country on the Hungarian border, creating autumn mists and giving character to the sweet wines of BURGENLAND. Under the new law, centre of two wine regions: see Burgenland.

**Nussdorf** Vienna w. ★★

Suburb of VIENNA with well-known HEURIGEN.

**Oggau** Burgenland (r.) w. sw. ★★→ ███ ★★★

One of the wine-centres of BURGENLAND, famous for Beerenausleses (see Germany) and AUSBRUCH.

**Portugieser** With BLAUFRÄNKISCH, one of the two main red-wine grapes of Austria, giving dark but rather characterless wine.

**Retz** Weinviertel (r.) w. ★

Leading wine-centre of the WEINVIERTEL, known for pleasant GRÜNER VELTLINER, etc.

**Ried** Single vineyard: when named on the label it is usually a good one.

**Riesling** When used alone is German Riesling. Wälschriesling, which is always inferior, is labelled as such.

**Rotgipfler** Good and high-flavoured grape peculiar to BADEN and GUMPOLDS-KIRCHEN. Used with ZIERFÄNDLER to make powerful but lively whites. Very heavy/sweet on its own.

**Rust** Burgenland (r.) w. dr. or sw. ★→★★★
    Most famous wine centre of BURGENLAND, long and justly famous for its AUSBRUCH, often made of mixed grapes.

**St. Laurent** Traditional Austrian red grape, faintly muscat-flavoured.

**Saloman, Fritz** ★★→★★★
    Top grower of oak-aged RIESLING and Gewürztraminer at Weinkelleri Undhof in the Danube valley near KREMS.

**Schilcher** Pleasant sharp rosé, a speciality of STYRIA.

**Schloss Grafenegg** w. dr./sw. ★★→★★★
    Famous castle and estate of the Metternich family near KREMS. Good standard whites and excellent Ausleses incl. a remarkable trocken (dry) '82 MÜLLER-THURGAU of formidable strength.

**Schluck** Name for the common white wine of the WACHAU, good when drunk very young. Also a good brand of GRÜNER VELTLINER from LENZ MOSER.

**Seewinkel** "Sea corner": the sandy district around the NEUSIEDLERSEE.

**Sepp Hold** Well-known BURGENLAND grower and merchant.

**Siegendorf, Klosterkeller** First-class private BURGENLAND wine estate.

**Sievering** Vienna w. ★★
    Picturesque suburb of VIENNA with notable HEURIGEN.

**Spätrot** Another name for the ZIERFÄNDLER grape.

**Spitzenwein** Top wines – as opposed to TISCHWEIN: ordinary table wines.

**Steiermark (Styria)** Province in the s.e., not remarkable for wine but well supplied with it. Three wine regions: Süd (south), Süd-Ost (south-east) and West-Steirmark. Sauvignon Blanc showing promise here. See Klöch.

**Stift** The word for a monastery. Monasteries have been, and still are, very important in Austria's wine-making, combining tradition and high standards with modern resources.

**Thallern** Vienna (r.) w. dr. or sw. ★★→★★★
    Village near GUMPOLDSKIRCHEN and trade-name of wines from Stift HEILIGENKREUZ.

**Thermenregion** New name for wine (and spa) region s. of VIENNA, incl. GUMPOLDSKIRCHEN.

**Tischwein** Everyday wine, as opposed to SPITZENWEIN.

**Traiskirchen** Vienna (r.) w. ★★
    Village near GUMPOLDSKIRCHEN with similar wine.

**Veltliner** See Grüner Veltliner.

**Vöslau** Baden r. (w.) ★
    Spa town s. of BADEN (and WIEN) known for its reds made of PORTUGIESER and BLAUFRANKISCH: refreshing but no more.

**Wachau** Wine region on the bank s. of the Danube round DÜRNSTEIN with cliff-like slopes giving some of Austria's best whites, esp. Rheinriesling (see Riesling) and GRÜNER VELTLINER.

**Weinviertel** "The wine quarter": name given to the huge and productive district between VIENNA and the Czech border. Mainly light white wines. Formerly divided into Falkenstein-Matzen (east) and Retz (west).

**Wien (Vienna)** The capital city, with 1,800 acres of v'yds in its suburbs to supply its cafés and HEURIGEN.

**Weissburgunder** Alias Pinot Blanc. Increasingly used for solid, often dry wines.

**Winzergenossenschaft** Growers' cooperative.

**Zierfändler** White grape of high flavour peculiar to the BADEN area. Used in a blend with ROTGIPFLER.

# Hungary

The traditional and characteristic firmness and strength of character which used to make Hungarian wine the most exciting of Eastern Europe have been modified by modern ideas. Average quality is still high; whites are generally lively and at least some reds made to last, but much of the drama has gone at least from the standard exported lines. Foreign buyers seem frightened of real character. Visitors to the country will find plenty of excellent wines in the old style. They are distinguished by numbered bottles (and higher prices).

**Alföld** Hungary's Great Plain, producer of much everyday wine. See also Hajós.

**Aszú** Word meaning "shrivelled" applied to very sweet wines, esp. Tokay (TOKAJI), where the "aszú" is late-picked and "nobly rotten" as in Sauternes. (See p. 48)

**Aszú Eszencia** Tokaji br. sw. ★★★★
The highest quality of Tokay commercially available: superb amber wine of Yquem-like quality.

**Badacsony** Balaton w. dr. sw. ██ ★★→★★★★
Famous 1,400 ft. hill on the n. shore of Lake BALATON, whose basalt soil can give rich high-flavoured white wines, among Hungary's best.

**Balatonfüred** Balaton (r.) w. dr. sw. ★★
Town on the n. shore of Lake BALATON centre of the Balatonfüred-Csopak district. Good but softer, less fiery wines.

**Balaton** Balaton r. w. dr. sw. ██ ★ →★★★
Hungary's inland sea and Europe's largest lake. Many wines take its name and most are good. The ending "i" (e.g. Balatoni, Egri) is the equivalent of -er in Londoner.

**Bikavér** Eger r. ★
"Bulls Blood." The historic name of the best-selling red wine of EGER: formerly full-bodied and well-balanced, but disconcertingly variable in its export version today.

**Csopak** Village next to BALATONFÜRED, with similar wines but drier.

**Debrö** Mátraalja w. sw. ★★
Important centre of the MÁTRAALJA famous for its pale, aromatic and sweet HÁRSLEVELÜ.

**Eger** Eger district r. w. dr. sw. ★→★★
Best-known red wine centre of n. Hungary; fine baroque city of cellars full of BIKAVÉR. Also delicate white LEÁNYKA (perhaps its best product today) TRAMINI and dark sweetish MÉDOC NOIR.

**Eszencia** The fabulous quintessence of Tokay (TOKAJI): intensely sweet grape-juice of very low, if any, alcoholic strength, reputed to have miraculous properties. Now almost unobtainable.

**Ezerjó** The grape grown at MÓR to make one of Hungary's best dry white wines: potentially distinguished, fragrant and fine

**Furmint** The classic grape of Tokay (TOKAJI), with great flavour and fire, also grown for table wine on Lake BALATON, sometimes with excellent results.

**Hajós** Alföld r. ██ █
Village in s. Hungary known as a centre for good lively CABERNET SAUVIGNON reds of medium body and ageing potential.

**Hárslevelü** The "lime-leaved" grape used at DEBRÖ and as the second main grape of TOKAJI. Gentle sweet wine.

**Hungarovin** Largest wine traders with huge cellars at Budafok near Budapest.

**Kadarka** The commonest red grape of Hungary, grown in vast quantities for light everyday wine on the plains in the s.; capable (e.g. at SZEKSZÁRD and VILLÁNY) of ample flavour and interesting maturity.

**Kékfrankos**  Hungarian for Blaufränkisch; reputedly related to Gamay. Makes good light reds at SOPRON on the Austrian border and goes in to "Bulls Blood" at EGER.

**Kéknyelü**  High-flavoured white grape making the best and "stiffest" wine of Mt. BADACSONY. It should be fiery and spicy stuff, like a distant cousin to Pinot Gris from Alsace.

**Különleges Minöség**  Special vintage. Wines so labelled are generally worth trying.

**Leányka**  Old Hungarian white grape also grown in Transylvania. Makes admirable pale soft dry wine at EGER.

**Mátraalja**  Wine-district in the foothills of the Mátra range in n. Hungary, incl. DEBRÖ, GYÖNGYÖS and NAGYREDE.

**Mecsekalja**  District in the foothills of the Mecsek range in s. Hungary, known for the good whites of PÉCS.

**Médoc Noir**  Grape apparently similar to MERLOT, used to make sweet red and in the blend of BIKAVÉR, at EGER.

**Monimpex**  The main Hungarian wine-export company.

**Mór**  North Hungary w. dr. ★★★
Town in n. Hungary famous for its fresh dry EZERJÓ.

**Muskotály**  Makes light though long-lived Muscat wine at Tokay (TOKAJI) and EGER. Very occasionally made ASZÚ at Tokay.

**Nagyburgundi**  Literally "great burgundy" – an indigenous grape and not P NOIR as sometimes thought. Makes sound solid wine in s. Hungary, esp. round VILLÁNY and SZEKSZÁRD.

**Olaszrizling**  The Hungarian name for the Italian, or Welschriesling.

**Pécs**  Mecsek (r.) w. dr.  ▮*▮ →★★
Town in the Mecsek hills known in the West for its agreeable well-balanced (if rather sweet) OLASZRIZLING.

**Puttonyos**  The measure of sweetness in Tokay (TOKAJI). A 7-gal. container from which ASZÚ is added to SZAMORODNI. One "putt" makes it sweetish; 6 (the maximum) very sweet indeed. Each "putt" is a 20-25 kilo hod of ASZÚ grapes added to 136 litres of base wine. The minimum now made is 3 putts, the maximum 6.

**Sauvignon Blanc**  A stranger in Hungary, but recent results at BALATON have been impressive – with plenty of Hungarian vigour.

**Siklos**  Southern district known for its white wines.

**Siller**  Pale red or rosé. Usually made from KADARKA or KÉKFRANKOS grapes.

**Somló**  North Hungary w. dr. ★★
Isolated small v'yd district n. of BALATON making white wines formerly of high repute from FURMINT.

**Sopron**  West Hungary r. ★★
Little Hungarian enclave in Burgenland s. of the Neusiedlersee (see Austria) specializing in light KÉKFRANKOS reds.

**Szamorodni**  Word meaning "as it comes"; used to describe TOKAJI without the addition of ASZÚ grapes. Can be dry or (fairly) sweet depending upon the proportion of ASZÚ grapes naturally present.

**Szürkebarát**  Literally means "grey friar": Hungarian for PINOT GRIS, which makes rich (not nec. sweet) heavy wine in the BADACSONY v'yds.

**Szekszárd**  r.  ▮**▮
District in south-central Hungary. Dark strong KADARKA red wine which needs age (say 3-4 years).

**Tokaji (Tokay)**  Tokaji w. dr. sw.  ▮**▮ →★★★★
The ASZÚ is Hungary's famous strong sweet wine, comparable to a maderized Sauternes, from hills in the n.e. close to the Soviet Union. See Aszú, Eszencia, Furmint, Puttonyos, Szamorodni.

**Tramini**  The TRAMINER grape; increasingly grown in Hungary.

**Villány**  Siklos r. p. (w.)  ▮**▮
Southernmost town of Hungary and well-known centre of red wine production. Villányi Burgundi is largely KÉKFRANKOS and rather good See also Nagyburgundi.

**Welschriesling**  Austrian name sometimes used for Olasz (Italian) Rizling.

# Romania

The wine industry is orientated towards Russia as its biggest customer, and consequently specializes in the sweet wines that Russians like. Recent Soviet moves to discourage drinking threaten this trade. The need for foreign currency makes export to the West highly desirable, so the best qualities are available at subsidized prices. They include sound and cheap reds and whites, including dry ones, but at present nothing memorable.

**Alba Iulia**
Town in the TIRNAVE area in Transylvania, known for off-dry whites blended from Italian RIESLING, FETEASCA and MUSKAT-OTTONEL.

**Aligoté**
The junior white burgundy grape makes pleasantly fresh white wine in Romania.

**Babeasca**
Traditional red grape of the FOCSANI area: agreeably sharp wine tasting slightly of cloves.

**Banat** The plain on the border with Serbia. Workaday Italian RIESLING and light red CADARCA.

**Cabernet**
Increasingly grown, particularly at DEALUL MARE, to make dark intense wines, though often too sweet for Western palates.

**Cadarca**
Romanian spelling of the Hungarian Kadarka.

**Chardonnay**
Used at MURFATLAR to make sweet dessert wine.

**Cotesti**
Part of the FOCSANI area making reds of PINOT NOIR, MERLOT, etc., and dry whites claimed to resemble Alsace wines.

**Cotnari**
Romania's most famous historical wine but rarely seen: light dessert wine from MOLDAVIA. Rather like very delicate Tokay.

**Dealul Mare**
Important up-to-date v'yd area in the s.e. Carpathian foothills. Red wines from CABERNET, MERLOT, PINOT NOIR, etc.

**Dobruja**
Black Sea region round the port of Costanta. MURFATLAR is the main vineyard area.

**Dragasani**
Region on the river Olt s. of the Carpathian Mts. Both traditional and "modern" grapes. Good MUSKAT-OTTONEL.

**Feteasca**
Romanian white grape of mild character, the same as Hungary's Leanyka (and some say Switzerland's Chasselas).

**Focsani**
Important eastern wine region including those of COTESTI, ODOBESTI and NICORESTI.

**Grasa** A form of the Hungarian Furmint grape grown in Romania and used in, among other wines, COTNARI.

**Mehana** Branded wines shipped to Britain, tending to sweetness.

**Moldavia**
The n.e. province, now largely within the USSR.

**Murfatlar**
Big modern v'yds near the Black Sea specializing in sweet wines, incl. CHARDONNAY. Now also dry reds and whites.

**Muskat-Ottonel**
The e. European muscat, a speciality of Romania.

**Nicoresti**
Eastern area of FOCSANI best known for its red BABEASCA.

**Odobesti**

> The central part of FOCSANI; mainly white wines of FETEASCA, Italian RIESLING, etc.

**Perla** The speciality of TÎRNAVE: a pleasant blended semi-sweet white of Italian RIESLING, FETEASCA and MUSKAT-OTTONEL.

**Pitesti**

> Principal town of the Arges region s. of the Carpathian Mtns. Traditionally whites from FETEASCA, TAMÎIOASA, RIESLING.

**Premiat**

> Reliable range of higher-quality wines for export.

**Riesling**

> Italian Riesling. Very widely planted. No exceptional wines.

**Sadova** Town in the SEGARCEA area exporting a sweetish rosé.

**Segarcea**

> S. wine area near the Danube. Exports rather sweet CABERNET.

**Tamîioasa**

> Traditional white-wine grape of no very distinct character.

**Tîrnave**

> Important Transylvanian wine region, known for its PERLA and MUSKAT-OTTONEL.

**Trakia** Branded wines shipped to USA. Better judged for Western palates than most other Romanian wines.

**Valea Calugareasca**

> "The Valley of the Monks," part of the DEALUL MARE v'yd with a well-known research station. CABERNET, MERLOT and PINOT NOIR are generally made into heavy sweetish wines.

# Yugoslavia

A well-established supplier of wines of international calibre if not generally exciting quality. Yugoslav "Riesling" was the pioneer, now followed by Cabernet, Pinot Blanc and Traminer, as well as such worthwhile specialities as Zilavka Plavać and Prokupać. All parts of the country except the central highlands make wine, almost entirely in giant cooperatives. Tourists on the Dalmatian coast and in Macedonia will find more original products all worth trying. 1985 was a very good vintage.

**Amselfelder**

> German marketing name for the Red Burgundac (Spätburgunder or PINOT NOIR) wine of KOSOVO. Disagreeably sweet.

**Babic** Standard red of the Dalmatian coast, ages better than ordinary PLAVAĆ.

**Banat** Sandy north-eastern area, partly in Romania, with up-to-date wineries making adequate RIESLING.

**Beli Pinot**

> The PINOT BLANC, a popular grape in SLOVENIA.

**Bijelo** White.

**Blatina**

> The red grape and wine of MOSTAR. Not in the same class as the white ZILAVKA.

**Bogdanusa**

> Local white grape of the Dalmatian islands, esp. Hvar and Brac. Pleasant refreshing faintly fragrant wine.

**Burgundac Bijeli**

> The CHARDONNAY, grown a little in SLAVONIA and VOJVODINA.

**Cabernet**
>   Now introduced in many places with usually pleasant, occasionally exciting, results. See Kosovo.

**Crno** Black.— i.e. red wine.

**Cvíćek** Traditional pale red or dark rose of the Sava valley, SLOVENIA.

**Dalmaciajavino**
>   Important co-operative based at Split and selling a full range of Dalmatian coastal and island wines.

**Dalmatia**
>   The middle coast of Yugoslavia from Rijeka to Dubrovnik. Has a remarkable variety of wines of character.

**Dingac** Heavy sweetish red from the local PLAVAĆ grape, speciality of the mid-Dalmatian coast.

**Faros** Substantial age-worthy PLAVAĆ red from the island of Hvar.

**Fruska Gora**
>   Hills in VOJVODINA, on the Danube n.w. of Belgrade, with modern v'yds and a wide range of wines, incl. rather higher strength Traminer and Sauvignon Blanc.

**Grasevina**
>   Slovenian for Italian Riesling (also called Wälschriesling, LASKI RIZLING, etc.). The normal Riesling of Yugoslavia.

**Grk** White grape, speciality of the island of Korcula, giving strong, even sherry-like wine (and also a lighter pale one).

**Istria** Peninsula in the n. Adriatic, Porec its centre, with a variety of pleasant wines, the MERLOT as good as any.

**Jerusalem**
>   Yugoslavia's most famous v'yd, at LJUTOMER. Its best wines are late-picked RAJNSKI RIZLING, LASKI RIZLING.

**Kadarka**
>   The major red grape of Hungary, widely grown in SERBIA.

**Kosovo (or Kosmet)**
>   Region in the south between SERBIA and Macedonia, with modern v'yds. The source of AMSELFELDER and some lively CABERNET.

**Kraski** Means grown on the coastal limestone "karst" of SLOVENIA.

**Laski Rizling** Yet another name for Italian Riesling.

**Ljutomer (or Lutomer)-Ormoz**
>   Yugoslavia's best-known and probably best white-wine district, in n.e. SLOVENIA, famous for its LASKI RIZLING: full-flavoured, full-strength and at its best rich and satisfying wine.

**Malvasia**
>   White grape giving luscious heavy wine, used in w. SLOVENIA.

**Marastina**
>   Strong dry white of the Dalmatian islands, best from Cara Smokviča on Hvar.

**Maribor**
>   Important wine-centre of n. SLOVENIA. White wines, mainly from VINAG, incl. LASKI RIZLING, RIESLING, SAUV BLANC, PINOT BLANC, TRAMINER.

**Merlot** Grown in SLOVENIA and ISTRIA with reasonable results.

**Mostar** Islamic-looking little city inland from DALMATIA, making admirable dry white from the ZILAVKA grape. Also BLATINA.

**Muskat-Ottonel**
>   The East European muscat, grown in VOJVODINA.

**Navip** The big growers' co-operative of SERBIA, with its headquarters at Belgrade.

**Opol** Pleasantly light pale red made of PLAVAĆ grapes round Split and Sibenik in DALMATIA.

**Plavac Mali**
>   Native red grape of SLOVENIA and DALMATIA; capable of great body and strength and ageing well. See Dingac, Postup, Opol, etc. Ordinary reds are often called "Plavać". There is also a white Plavać Beli.

**Plavina**

Light red of the DALMATIAN coast round Zadar.

**Plovdina**

Native red grape of Macedonia in the south, giving mild wine. Generally blended with tastier PROKUPAĆ.

**Portugizac**

Austria's Portugieser: plain red wine.

**Pošip** Pleasant, not-too-heavy white wine of the Dalmatian islands, notably Korcula.

**Postup** Sweet and heavy DALMATIAN red from the Peljesać peninsula near Korcula. Highly esteemed locally.

**Prokupać**

Principal native red grape of s. SERBIA and Macedonia: 85% of the production. Makes good dark rosé (RUZIĆA) and full-bodied red of character. Some of the best comes from ZUPA. PLOVDINA is often added for smoothness.

**Prošek** The dessert wine of DALMATIA, of stupefying natural strength but variable quality. The best is excellent, but hard to find.

**Radgonska Ranina**

Ranina is Austria's BOUVIER grape (see Austria). Radgona is near MARIBOR. The wine is sweet and carries the trade name TIGROVO MLJEKO (Tiger's Milk).

**Rajnski Rizling**

The Rhine Riesling, rare in Yugoslavia but grown a little in LJUTOMER-ORMOZ.

**Refosco**

Italian grape grown in e. SLOVENIA and ISTRIA under the name TERAN.

**Renski Rizling**

Alternative spelling for Rhine Riesling.

**Riesling**

Used without qualification formerly meant Italian Riesling. Now legally limited to real Rhine Riesling.

**Ruzića** Rosé, usually from PROKUPAĆ. Darker than most; and better.

**Serbia** The e. state of Yugoslavia, with nearly half the country's v'yds, stretching from VOJVODINA to Macedonia.

**Sipon** Yugoslav name for FURMINT of Hungary, grown in SLOVENIA.

**Slamnak**

A late-harvest LJUTOMER estate Riesling.

**Slavonia**

Northern Croatia, on the Hungarian border between SLOVENIA and SERBIA. A big producer of standard wines, mainly white, including most "Yugoslav Riesling".

**Slovenia**

The n.w. state, incl. Yugoslavia's most European-style v'yds and wines: LJUTOMER, etc. Slovenija-vino, the sales organization, is Yugoslavia's biggest.

**Smederevka**

Important white grape of SERBIA and KOSOVO. Fresh dry wines.

**Teran** Stout dark red of ISTRIA. See Refosco.

**Tigrovo Mljeko** See Radgonska Ranina.

**Tocai** The PINOT GRIS, making rather heavy white wine in SLOVENIA.

**Traminać**

The TRAMINER. Grown in SLOVENIA and VOJVODINA. Particularly successful in the latter.

**Vinag** Huge production cellars at MARIBOR.

**Vojvodina**

An autonomous province of n. SERBIA developing substantial v'yds. Wide range of grapes, both European and Balkan.

**Vranać** Red grape making attractive vigorous wine in Montenegro.

**Vugava** Rare white variety of Vis in DALMATIA. Linked in legend with the VIÒGNIER of the Rhône valley.

**Zilavka**
The white wine of MOSTAR in Hercegovina. Can be one of Yugoslavia's best: dry, pungent and memorably fruity, with a faint flavour of apricots. Exported samples are disappointing.

**Zupa** Central SERBIAN district giving its name to above-average red and rosé (or dark and light red) of PROKUPAĆ and PLOVDINA: respectively Zupsko Crno and Zupsko Ruzića.

# Bulgaria

A dramatic entry into the world's wine-diet in the late 1970s. State-run and state-subsidized wineries have learned a great deal from the New World and offer Cabernet and Chardonnay at bargain prices and in rapidly improving quality and variety. Controlled appellation ("Controliran") wines introduced in 1985 have marked an important new step in quality. Recent anti-drink policies in the USSR have greatly curtailed Bulgaria's export market. A new regime is aiming for higher quality (and prices) and has banned planting outside "Controliran" zones.

**Asenovgrad**
Main MAVRUD-producing cellar on the outskirts of Plovdiv, Bulgaria's second city.

**Cabernet**
The Bordeaux grape is highly successful in n. Bulgaria. Dark, vigorous, fruity and well-balanced wine drinks well young, but top qualities mature well for 5-6 years.

**Chardonnay**
The white burgundy grape is scarcely less successful. Very dry but full-flavoured wine improves with a year in bottle. Recent oak-aged examples are developing real quality.

**Controliran** See introductory note.

**Dimiat** The common native white grape, grown in the east towards the coast. Agreeable dry white without memorable character.

**Euxinograd (Château)**
Ageing cellar on the coast, part of the ex-King's palace. Wines reserved for State functions and top restaurants.

**Fetiaska**
The same grape as Romania's Feteasca and Hungary's Leanyka. Pleasant pale wine, best a trifle sweet, sold as Donau Perle.

**Gamza** Good red grape, Hungary's Kadarka. Aged examples, esp. from PAVLIKENI, can be delicious.

**Han Krum**
Bulgaria's most modern white-wine plant, near Varna in the east.

**Iskra** The national brand of sparkling wine, normally sweet but of fair quality. Red, white or rosé.

**Kadarka**
Popular brand of GAMZA red from n. Bulgaria.

**Karlovo**
Town in central Bulgaria famous for the "Valley of Roses" and its very pleasant white MISKET.

**Lozitza**
"Controliran" CABERNET from the north; perhaps Bulgaria's most elegant red wine yet.

**Mavrud**  Darkly plummy red from s. Bulgaria, esp. ASENOVGRAD. Improves with age. Traditionally considered the country's best.

**Melnik**  City of the extreme s.e. and its highly prized grape. Such concentrated red wine that locals say it can be carried in a handkerchief. Needs at least 5 years and lasts for 15.

**Merlot**  Soft red grape variety grown mainly in Haskovo in the south.

**Misket**  Muscat-flavoured local grape used for sweet whites.

**Muscat Ottonel**
    Normal muscat grape, grown in eastern Bulgaria for medium-sweet, fruity whites.

**Novi Pazar**
    Controlled appellation CHARDONNAY winery near VARNA. Finer wines than VARNA.

**Novo Selo**
    "Controliran" red MISKET from the north.

**Orjahoviza**
    Major south area for "Controliran" CABERNET/MERLOT. Rich savoury red best at 4–5 years.

**Pamid**  The light soft everyday red of the south-west and north-west.

**Pavlikeni**
    Northern wine town with a prestigious estate specializing in GAMZA and CABERNET of high quality.

**Pleven**  Northern cellar important for PAMID, GAMZA and CABERNET. Also Bulgaria's wine research station.

**Provadya**
    East of SHUMEN, near the coast, another centre for good white wines, especially dry CHARDONNAY.

**Rcatzitelli**
    One of Russia's favourite white grapes for strong, sweet wine. Grown in north-east Bulgaria to produce bulk dry or medium white wines.

**Riesling**
    Normally refers to Italian Riesling. Some Rhine Riesling is grown and is now made into Germanic-style whites.

**Sauvignon Blanc**
    Grown in eastern Bulgaria, recently released as dry white wine on export markets.

**Shumen**  Eastern Bulgaria's largest white wine-producing cellar specializing in dry wines. Also makes rather good brandy.

**Sonnenkuste**
    Brand of medium-sweet white sold in Germany.

**Suhindol**
    PAVLIKENI's neighbour, site of Bulgaria's first cooperative (1909). Good cellar for GAMZA, CABERNET and PAMID.

**Sungarlare**
    Eastern town giving its name to a dry "controliran" MISKET.

**Svishtov**
    CABERNET-producing winery by the Danube in the north. The front-runner in Bulgaria's controlled appellation wines.

**Sylvaner**
    Some pleasant dry Sylvaner is exported as "Klosterkeller".

**Tamianka**
    Sweet white; sweeter than HEMUS.

**Targovichte**
    Independent (non-VINPROM) white wine cellar near SHUMEN that concentrates on medium and sweet wines.

**Tirnovo**
    Strong sweet dessert red wine.

**Trakia**  "Thrace". Brand name of a good export range.

**Varna**  Major coastal appellation for CHARDONNAY.

**Vinimpex**

The "State Commercial Enterprise for Export and Import of Wines and Spirits".

**Vinprom**

State body controlling all 145 cooperative cellars and responsible for dramatic quality improvements over last 8 years. Owns 10% of the country's vineyards and 3 research institutes.

# Greece

Entry into the EEC gives Greece the challenge of modernizing and internationalizing a wine industry that has been up a backwater for two thousand years. A new EEC-style system of 29 appellations is now in place and much is spoken of the hopeful future for Greek wines. So far evidence is scarce. Athenian waiters try to sell over-priced brands and look snooty when you ask for Retsina (which is usually the best value). But look for local wines in the country, especially in the north.

**Achaia-Clauss**

The best-known Greek wine merchant, with cellars at Patras, n. PELOPONNESE, makers of DEMESTICA, etc.

**Agioritikos**

Mount Athos, the monastic peninsula in Chalkidiki. Source of CABERNET and other grapes for TSANTALI wines. Brand name of a good dry rosé.

**Aminteion** (Appellation)

Crisp red or rosé from the mountains of Macedonia.

**Attica** Region round Athens, the chief source of RETSINA.

**Boutari**

Merchants and makers with high standards in Macedonian and other wines, esp. NAOUSSA. Grand Réserve is the best wine.

**Calliga**

Modern winery with 800 acres on CEPHALONIA. ROBOLA white and reds from idigenous grapes are adequately made but grossly over-dressed.

**Cambas, Andrew**

Important Athenian wine-growers and merchants.

**Carras, John**

Hotelier at Sithonia, Chalkidiki, n. Greece, producing interesting red and white wines under the names Château Carras, Porto Carras and CÔTES DU MELITON. Ch Carras is a Bordeaux-style barrel-aged red, particularly good in **79 80 81 82**.

**Castel Danielis**

One of the best brands of dry red wine, from ACHAIA-CLAUSS.

**Cephalonia (Kephalonia)**

Ionian (western) island with good white ROBOLA and red Thymiatiko. Also MAVRODAPHNE. See also Gentilini, Calliga.

**Corfu** Adriatic island with wines scarcely worthy of it. Ropa is the traditional red.

**Côtes du Meliton** (Appellation)

Thracian red, white and rosé of fair quality, made by CARRAS.

**Courtakis, D.**

Athenian merchant with good dark NEMEAN red.

**Crete** Island with the name for some of Greece's better red wine. Appellations are: Archanes, Daphnes, Peza and Sitia. But Cretan white can also be very good.

**Demestica**

A reliable brand of dry red and white from ACHAIA-CLAUSS.

**Gamalafka**

Speciality of Mykonos. Alarmingly like sherry vinegar.

**Gentilini**

New ('84) up-market white from CEPHALONIA, a Robola blend, soft and appealing. To watch.

**Goumenissa** (Appellation)

Good-quality, oak-aged mid-weight red from BOUTARI.

**Hymettus**

Standard brand of red and dry white without resin.

**Kokkineli**

The rosé version of RETSINA: like the white. Drink cold.

**Lac des Roches**

Sound, blended Dodecanese white from BOUTARI.

**Lindos**  Name for the higher quality of RHODES wine, whether from Lindos itself or not. Acceptable; no more.

**Malvasia**

The famous grape is said to originate from Monemvasia in the s. PELOPONNESE.

**Mantinia** (Appellation)

A fresh white from the PELOPONNESE, offered by CAMBAS.

**Mavro**  "Black" – the word for dark (usually sweet) red wine.

**Mavrodaphne** (Appellation)

Literally "black laurel": dark, sweet, concentrated red; a speciality of the Patras region, n. PELOPONNESE.

**Mavroudi**

The red wine of Delphi and the n. shore of the Gulf of Corinth: dark and plummy.

**Metsovo** (Appellation)

CABERNET red from Epirus in the north.

**Minos**  Popular Cretan brand; the Castello red is best.

**Naoussa** (Appellation)

Above-average strong dry red from Macedonia in the north, esp. from BOUTARI and TSANTALI.

**Nemea** (Appellation)

Town in the e. PELOPONNESE famous for its lion (a victim of Hercules) and its fittingly forceful MAVRO.

**Patras** (Appellation)

Important wine town at the mouth of the Gulf of Corinth.

**Peloponnese**

The south landmass of mainland Greece, with a half of the whole country's vineyards.

**Pendeli**

Reliable brand of dry red from ATTICA, grown and bottled by Andrew CAMBAS.

**Retsina**

White wine with Aleppo pine resin added, tasting of turpentine and oddly appropriate with Greek food. The speciality of ATTICA. Drink very cold.

**Rhodes**  Easternmost Greek island. Its sweet MALVASIAS are its best wines. LINDOS is the brand name for tolerable table wines.

**Robola (or Rombola)** (Appellation)

The fashionable dry white of Cephalonia; island off the Gulf of Corinth. Can be a pleasant soft wine of some character.

**Samos** (Appellation)

Island off the Turkish coast with a reputation for its sweet pale-golden muscat. The normal quality is nothing much.

**Santorini**

Dramatic volcanic island north of Crete, making sweet Vinsanto from sun-dried grapes, and dry white Thira. Unrealized potential here.

**Tsantali**

Producers at Agios Pavlos with a wide range of table wines, including Macedonian Cabernet, wine from the monks of Mt. Athos, NAOUSSA and Muscat from PATRAS. "Cava" is a blend.

**Verdea** The dry white of Zakinthos, the island just west of the PELOPON-NESE. The red is Byzantis.

**Xynomavro**

The best Greek red grape, basis for NAOUSSA and other northern wines.

# Cyprus

A well-established exporter of strong wines of reasonable quality, best known for very passable Cyprus sherry, though old Commandaria, a treacly dessert wine, is the island's finest product. Until recently only traditional grape varieties of limited potential were available; now better kinds are beginning to improve standards, but regrettably slowly.

**Afames** Village at the foot of Mt. Olympus, giving its name to one of the better red (MAVRON) wines from SODAP.

**Aphrodite**

Full-bodied medium-dry white from KEO, named after the Greek goddess of love.

**Arsinöe**

Dry white wine from SODAP, named after an unfortunate female whom Aphrodite turned to stone.

**Bellapais**

Fizzy medium-sweet white from KEO named after the famous abbey near Kyrenia. Essential refreshment for holidaymakers.

**Commandaria**

Good-quality brown dessert wine made since ancient times in the hills north of LIMASSOL, named after a crusading order of knights. The best (sold as "100 yrs old") is superb, of incredible sweetness. Most is standard Communion wine.

**Domaine d'Ahera**

Modern-style lighter red from KEO.

**Emva Cream**

Best-selling sweet sherry from Etko, a HAGGIPAVLU subsidiary.

**Etko** See Haggipavlu.

**Haggipavlu**.

Well-known wine-merchant at LIMASSOL. Trades as Etko.

**Hirondelle**

The sweet white and some of the other wines of this popular brand are produced by Etko (see Emva).

**Keo** One of the biggest and most go-ahead firms in the wine trade at LIMASSOL.

**Khalokhorio**

Principal COMMANDARIA village, growing only XYNISTERI.

**Kokkineli**

Rosé: the name is related to "cochineal".

**Kolossi**

Red and white table wines from SODAP.

**Limassol**

"The Bordeaux of Cyprus". The wine-port in the south.

**Loel**  Major producer. Amathus and Kykko brands, Command Cyprus
    sherry and good Negro red.

**Mavron**  The black grape of Cyprus (and Greece) and its dark wine.

**Mosaic**  KEO's brand of Cyprus sherries. Includes a fine dry wine.

**Othello**
    A good standard dry red: solid, satisfying wine from KEO.

**Palomino**
    Soft dry white made of this (sherry) grape by LOEL. Very drinkable ice-
    cold.

**Pitsilia**
    Region south of Mt. Olympus producing the best white and COMMAN-
    DARIA wines.

**Rosella**
    Brand of strong medium-sweet rosé.

**St Panteleimon**
    Brand of strong sweet white from Keo.

**Semeli**  Good traditional red from HAGGIPAVLU.

**Sherry**  Cyprus makes a full range of sherry-style wines, the best
    (particularly the dry) of very good quality.

**SODAP**  Major wine cooperative at LIMASSOL.

**Xynisteri**
    The native white grape of Cyprus.

**Zoopiyi**
    Principal COMMANDARIA village, growing MAVRON grapes.

# Asia & North Africa

**Algeria** The massive v'yds of Algeria have dwindled in the last decade from 860,000 acres to under 500,000. Red, rosé and white wines of some quality are made in the coastal hills of Tlemcen, Mascara, Haut-Dahra, Zaccar and Ain-Bessem. Most goes for blending.

**China** Germans and Russians started making wine on the Shantung (now Shandong) peninsula in the early 1900s. Since 1980 a modern industry, initiated by Rémy Martin, has produced the adequate white Dynasty and Tsingtao wines, and new more sophisticated plantings of better varieties in Shandong and Tianjin, further north, promise more interest in the future.

**India** In 1985 a Franco-Indian firm launched a Chardonnay-based sparkling wine, Omar Khayyam, made at Narayangoan, s.e. of Bombay. Plans are to export up to 2m. bottles. It is remarkably good.

**Israel** Israeli wine, since the industry was re-established by a Rothschild in the 1880s, has been primarily of Kosher interest until recently, when CABERNET, SAUVIGNON BLANC, SÉMILLON, PETITE SIRAH and GRENACHE of fair quality have been introduced. Carmel is the principal brand. Since 1986 Yarden from the Golan Heights has set a higher standard.

**Japan** Japan has a small wine industry in Yamanashi Prefecture, w. of Tokyo. Wines are here blended with imports from Argentina, E. Europe, etc. Premium wines of SÉMILLON, CHARDONNAY, CABERNET and the local white grape, Koshu, are light but can be good, though expensive. Much the most interesting (and expensive) is Suntory's Sauternes-like Château Lion. The main producers are Suntory, Mercian, Mann's. In 1985 tainted Austrian wine was discovered being sold as Japanese by a major company. Regrettably, Japanese labelling laws are so lax that misrepresentation of imported wines as "Japanese" has been the rule rather than the exception. There are at last signs of more honourable conduct.

**Lebanon** The small Lebanese wine industry, based on Ksara in the Bekaa valley n.e. of Beirut, continues against all odds to make red wine of real vigour and quality. Château Musar ★★★ produces splendid matured reds, largely of CABERNET SAUVIGNON.

**Morocco** Morocco today makes North Africa's best wine from v'yds along the Atlantic coast and round Meknes. In ten years the v'yds have declined from 190,000 to 54,000 acres. Chante Bled and Tarik are the best reds, Gris de Guerrouane a very pale dry rosé.

**Tunisia** Tunisia now has 75,000 acres compared with 120,000 ten years ago. Her speciality is sweet muscat, but reasonable reds and rosés come from Carthage, Mornag and Cap Bon.

**Turkey** Most of Turkey's huge v'yds produce table grapes. But her wines, from Thrace, Anatolia and the Aegean, are remarkably good. Trakya (Thrace) white and Buzbag (Anatolian) red are the well-known standards of the State wineries. Doluca and Kavaklidere are private firms of good quality. Villa Doluca red from Thrace is very well made. Buzbag is a bargain.

**USSR** With over 3 million acres of v'yds the USSR is the world's fourth-biggest wine-producer – almost entirely for home consumption. Ukraine (incl. the Crimea) is the biggest v'yd republic, followed by Moldavia, the Russian Republic and Georgia. The Soviet consumer has a sweet tooth, for both table and dessert wines. Of the latter the best come from the Crimea (esp. Massandra). Moldavia and Ukraine use the same grapes as Romania, plus CABERNET, RIESLING, PINOT GRIS, etc. The Russian Republic makes the best Rieslings (Arbau, Beshtau, Anapa) and sweet sparkling Tsimlanskoye "Champanski". Georgia uses antique methods to make extremely tannic wines for local consumption, and modern methods to make blended products for export (e.g. Tsinandali, Mukuzani). Georgian sparkling is extremely cheap and drinkable.

# California

California has made wine for 150 years, but her modern wine industry has grown from scratch in scarcely more than 25. In the past ten it has challenged the world with good-quality cheap wines and a growing number of luxury wines of brilliant quality. Since 1975 the industry has expanded and altered at a frenzied pace. Many of the wineries listed here have a history shorter than ten years. Quality ratings must therefore be tentative. In this edition many star-ratings have been reduced to give a more accurate picture of the international standing of a winery. Some new entries have provisional ratings (in brackets).

Appellation areas are an important new fact of life in California. They are being registered thick and fast; the current total is about thirty. It is still too soon to use them as a useful guide to style. Listed below are the broad regions traditionally referred to.

Grape varieties combined with brand-names are the key to California wine. Since grapes in California play many new roles they are listed separately over.

# Principal vineyard areas

**Amador** County in the Sierra foothills e. of Sacramento. Grows very good Zinfandel, esp. in Shenandoah Valley.

**Central Coast** A long sweep of coast with increasing though scattered wine activity, from San Francisco Bay s. to Santa Barbara.

**Central Coast/Santa Barbara**
Some of the most promising vineyard land (esp. for white wines) in the state is in the Santa Ynez Valley n. of Santa Barbara, where coastal fog gives particularly cool conditions.

**Central Coast/Santa Cruz Mts.**
Wineries are scattered round the Santa Cruz Mts. s. of San Francisco Bay, from Saratoga down to the HECKER PASS.

**Central Coast/Hecker Pass**
Pass through the Santa Cruz Mts. s. of San Francisco Bay with a cluster of small old-style wineries.

**Central Coast/Salinas Valley/Monterey**
The Salinas Valley runs inland s.e. from Monterey. After frenzied expansion in the '70s, many vines were removed. What are left make wines of great character.

**Central Coast/San Luis Obispo**
Edna Valley just s. of San Luis Obispo and new more scattered v'yds nr. Paso Robles.

**Livermore** Valley e. of San Francisco Bay long famous for white wines but now largely built over.

**Lodi** Town and district at the n. end of the San Joaquin Valley, its hot climate modified by a westerly air-stream.

**Mendocino** Northernmost coastal wine country; a varied climate coolest in Anderson Valley nr. coast, warm around Ukiah inland.

**Napa** The Napa valley, n. of San Francisco Bay, long established as a top-quality wine area. Coolest at southern end (Los Carneros).

**San Joaquin Valley**
The great central valley of California, fertile and hot, the source of most of the jug wines and dessert wines in the State.

**Sonoma** County n. of San Francisco Bay, between Napa and the sea. Most v'yds are in the north (see below). A few, historically important, are in the Valley of the Moon in the south. Vineyards extend south into Los Carneros. (See also Napa.)

**Sonoma/Alexander Valley/Russian River**
Top-quality area from Alexander Valley (n. of Napa Valley) towards the sea (Russian River). Incl. Dry Creek Valley.

**Temecula (Rancho California)**
New small area in s. California, 25 miles inland, halfway between San Diego and Riverside.

---

California has adopted the world's repertoire of "classic" grapes: for notes on these see pages 6-10. Grapes specific to California include:

**Emerald Riesling** an original in the German manner. Clean, flowery/fruity and a touch tart.

**Flora** mildly flowery white, best made sweet and/or sparkling.

**Gamay Beaujolais** not true Gamay but a Pinot Noir clone.

**Gray Riesling** not Riesling, makes full-bodied standard white.

**Johannisberg Riesling** real (also called Rhine) Riesling.

**Petite Sirah** no relation to Syrah, a synonym for the obscure French Durif.

**Ruby Cabernet** California-bred cross between Carignan and Cabernet Sauvignon, with enough of the latter's character to be interesting. Good in hot conditions.

**Zinfandel** California's own red, open to many interpretations from light-weight and fruity to galumphing. The current fad is for white or "blush" Zin. The red is capable of ageing to high quality.

# Recent vintages

The Californian climate is far from being as consistent as its reputation. Although on the whole the grapes ripen regularly, they are subject to severe spring frosts in many areas, sometimes a wet harvest-time, and such occasional calamities as the two-year drought of 1976-7. 1987 was a very early, rather small crop, highly promising for white wines. The size of the harvest has the useful effect of balancing supply and demand after a run of big vintages, which generated a glut of grapes and wine.

Wines from the San Joaquin Valley tend to be most consistent year by year. The vintage date on these, where there is one, is more important for telling the age of the wine than its character.

Vineyards in the Central Coast are widely scattered; there is little pattern. The Napa and Sonoma valleys are the area where comment can usefully be made on the last dozen vintages of the top varietal wines: Cabernet Sauvignon and Chardonnay. All Chardonnays can be considered "ready" at 2 years, though the best can develop for up to 10 years.

|      | Chardonnay | Cabernet Sauvignon |
|------|------------|--------------------|
| 1987 | Ideal weather: very good wines. | Considered extremely promising. |
| 1986 | Cool season; fine wines. | Early reactions very favourable. |
| 1985 | Big crop, good acidity, excellent. | Coolish ripening season. Excellent balance; some great wines. |
| 1984 | Wonderfully perfumed when young, now fully mature. | Exceptional; very ripe and fragrant. Will improve for years. |
| 1983 | Drink soon. | Similar to '80 but maturing faster. |
| 1982 | Sound, agreeable; drink up. | Many outstanding; now mostly mature. |
| 1981 | Good if not too strong. Drink. | Should be drunk soon. |
| 1980 | Small crop; high alcohol. Drink up. | Outstanding for current drinking. |
| 1979 | Excellent; drink up. | Rain; generally light. |
| 1978 | Very good but drink up. | Excellent. Generally ready. |
| 1977 | Generally excellent. Drink up. | Attractive; fully mature. |
| 1976 | Should have been drunk. | Small crop but splendid. Mature. |
| 1975 | Very good; getting old. | Delicate: charming; drink soon. |
| 1974 | Should have been drunk. | Difficult: but many superb. Mature. |
| 1973 | Very good, but drink up. | Big and good; drink up. |
| 1970 | Should have been drunk. | One of the best ever. Mature. |

# California wineries

**Acacia** Napa. ★★★ CH 81 83 84 85 86 PN 80 81 82 83 84 85
Carneros winery, now owned by CHALONE, specializing in CHARDONNAY and P NOIR. Both are fulfilling marvellous promise.

**Adelaida Cellars** Central Coast/San Luis Obispo. (★★)
Skilful maker of soft CHARD and supple CAB at Paso Robles.

**Alderbrook** Sonoma. ■**■** CH 84 85 86
New ('82) winery using owner-grown and other grapes to make full-flavoured whites. CHARD, SAUV BLANC and SEMILLON all good.

**Alexander Valley Vineyards** Alexander Valley. ■**-★★★** CH 83 84 85 86 CS 81 82 83 84 85 Small winery best known for well-balanced CHARD, and J.R. CABERNET also v. well made.

**Almaden** Central Coast. ★→★★ CS 79 80 81 82 83
Famous pioneer name bought in '87 by Heublein to be dismantled and downgraded.

**S. Anderson Vineyard** Napa. ★★ CH 83 84 85
Young winery with extensive caves. Good CHARDONNAY and recently good sparkling wine.

**Balverne** Sonoma/Russian River. ★★ CH 81 83 84 CS 82
Small winery near Windsor, started in '80 with fine CHARD, SAUV BLANC, and blended "Healdsburger". CAB SAUV is above average.

**Beaulieu** Napa. ★★★ cs 74 76 77 78 79 80 81 82 83 84
Justly famous medium-size growers and makers of esp. CABERNET. Top wine: De Latour Private Reserve Cabernet. Crackerjack SAUV BLANC. Now owned by Grand Metropolitan.

**Bel Arbres** A second label of FETZER.

**Belvedere Wine Co.** Sonoma. ★★ cs 82 CH 85
Born-1980 winery featuring single-v'yd wines. incl. Robert Young CAB from Alex Valley, York Mtn. Napa CAB, Bacigalupi Russian River CHARD. They go down well.

**Beringer** Napa. ★★→★★★ CH 83 84 85 86 cs 80 81 82 83
Century-old winery recently restored to the front rank. Increasingly fine wines incl. esp. CHARD (excellent Private Reserve), CABERNET (ditto) and "Nightingale", the eponymous winemaker's induced-botrytis dessert wine.

**Boeger** Amador. ★★ cs 79 80 81 82 83 CH 85
Small winery in Sierra foothills. Good ZIN.

**Bonny Doon Vineyard** C. Coast/Santa Cruz Mtns. ★★ CH 86
Small winery (since '81) with original ideas about Rhône grapes, incl. Syrah, Grenache, and even Roussanne and Marsanne. (e.g. Le Cigare Volant; Grenache spiced with Mourvèdre).

**Brander** Central Coast/Santa Barbara. ★★ cs 83 85 86
Small new winery specializes in excellent SAUVIGNON BLANC of Santa Ynez Valley grapes. Now also hitting high notes with CAB FRANC and MERLOT labelled "Bouchet". (84, 85)

**Bruce, David** Central Coast. ★★ CH 83 84 85
Small luxury winery with heavy-weight wines. Improving.

**Buena Vista** Sonoma. ★★ CH 83 84 85 86 cs 83 84
Historic pioneer winery with German owners and very sound recent record esp. in whites (CHARD, RIESLING, FUMÉ BLANC).

**Burgess Cellars** Napa. ★★ CH 83 84 85 cs 80 81 82 83 z 81 82 83
Small hillside winery, in former Souverain cellars, making good CABERNET, very good ZIN, and CHARD.

**Bynum, Davis** Sonoma. ★★ CH 83 84 85 cs 82
Well-established maker of standard varieties, w. of Healdsburg Esp. GEWÜRZ, CHARD, P NOIR.

**B.V.** Abbreviation of BEAULIEU VINEYARDS used on their labels.

**Cakebread** Napa. ★★★ CH 83 84 85 86 cs 80 81 82 83 84 85
Started 1973. Increasing reputation, esp. for SAUVIGNON BLANC and CABERNET (79 N.B.); also CHARDONNAY.

**Calera** Monterey-San Benito. ★★ PN 80 81 82 83 84 85 CH 85
1975 winery ambitious with PINOT NOIR; also high-alcohol ZIN and now CHARDONNAY.

**Callaway** S. California. ★★ CH 83 84 85 86
Mid-sized winery in new territory at TEMECULA. Sound whites.

**Carmenet** Sonoma. ★★→★★★
Where CHA: ONE emulates Burgundy, the same owners have chased Bordeaux here since '82 with SAUV BL from Sonoma, and CAB/MERLOT from high above Sonoma town (83, 84). Also "Gavilan" FRENCH COLOMBARD from Napa.

**Carneros Creek** Napa. ★★★ CH 83 84 85 cs 74 77 80 81 82 83
The first winery in the cool Carneros area between Napa and San Fransisco Bay. Good P NOIR., CHARDONNAY and CABERNET. Good-value MERLOT.

**Caymus** Napa. ★★★ →★★★★ cs 74 75 76 77 78 79 80 81 82 83 84
Outwardly modest small winery at Rutherford with v. high standards, esp. for notably complex CAB and ZIN; also white P NOIR, CHARDS, SAUV BLANC. Second label: Liberty School (value.)

**Chalk Hill** Sonoma/Russian River. ★★ CH 84 85 86 cs 83 84 85
Considerable vineyards in Chalk Hill near Windsor. Encouraging early wines.

Ca

**Chalone** Central Coast/Salinas. ★★★★ CH 80 81 83 84 85 86 PN 80 81 82 83 Unique small hilltop v'yd/winery at the Pinnacles. French-style CHARDONNAY and PINOT NOIR of super quality. Also excellent PINOT BLANC. See also Acacia, Carmenet.

**Chappellet** Napa. ███ ★★★ CH 81 83 84 85 CS 74 75 76 78 79 80 81 82 83 84 Luxury winery and beautiful amphitheatrical hillside v'yd. Excellent very long-lived CABERNET, CHARDONNAY and RIESLING: very good dry CHENIN BLANC.

**Château Bouchaine** Napa/Carneros. ★★→★★★ CH 83 84 85 PN 85 New firm in old Carneros barn started with Acacia-style oaky PINOT NOIR. Now v.g. similar CHARDONNAY and SAUV BLANC.

**Château Montelena** Napa. ★★★ CH 83 84 85 86 CS 75 77 78 79 80 81 82 83 Small 1969 winery making very good distinctive CHARDONNAY and very tannic CABERNET SAUVIGNON.

**Château St Jean** Sonoma. ★★★ CH 83 84 85 86 Impressive winery specializing in whites from individual v'yds, incl. CHARD, P BLANC and esp. late-harvest RIES. Now also fine sparkling wine and bargain "Vin Blanc". Owned by Suntory.

**Château Souverain** Alexander Valley. ★★ CH 83 84 85 86 CS 78 79 80 81 82 83 84 Luxurious mid-sized winery with a record of competent wines, bought by BERINGER in 1986. '86 Carneros Reserve CHARD is first-rate.

**Christian Brothers** Napa and San Joaquin. ███★→★★★ CH 85 86 CS 84 The biggest Napa winery, run by a religious order. Sound and improving CABERNET, attractive CHARD, useful FUMÉ BLANC, sweet white Ch La Salle, very good brandy and ZIN "port".

**Clos du Bois** Sonoma. ███★★ →★★★ CH 83 84 85 86 CS 78 79 80 81 82 83 84 85 Healdsburg winery of big grower in Dry Creek and Alexander Valleys. V.g. GEWÜRZ, P NOIR, MERLOT, CHARD, SAUV BLANC. Named-v'yd wines are outstanding.

**Clos du Val** Napa. ███★★★ CH 83 84 85 86 CS 77 78 79 80 81 82 83 84 French-run. V.g. bold ZIN, fine delicate CAB, MERLOT, CHARD and SEM.

**Clos Pegase** Napa. (★★) Amazing post-modernist building near STERLING. So far wines are simply steady.

**Concannon** Livermore. Table. ★★ CH 83 84 Substantial winery first famous for whites; reds now prominent. May be changing hands. A name to follow.

**Congress Springs** Santa Clara/Santa Cruz. ★★ CH 84 85 86 Tiny winery above Saratoga with growing reputation. Well-made whites, e.g. SAUVIGNON BLANC, SEMILLON, CHARD and esp. PINOT BLANC.

**Conn Creek** Napa. ★★→★★★ CH 83 84 85 CS 78 79 80 81 82 83 Winery built on Silverado Trail in 1979 has built a solid following. Now owned by Ch Ste. Michelle of Washington. Best known for CABERNET.

**Cooks** "Cooks Champagne" – See Guild.

**Corbett Canyon** Central Coast/San Luis Obispo. ███★★ CH 84 85 86 New ('83) Edna Valley winery to make sizeable amounts of varietal and generic ("Coastal Classic") wines (value.) Also Shadow Creek sparkling.

**Cuvaison** Napa. ★★→★★★ CH 83 85 86 CS 78 79 80 81 82 83 Small winery with expert new direction. Formerly austere CABERNET and CHARDONNAY now more approachable; CHARD from own Carneros v'yd is tops.

**Culbertson** San Diego. ★★ Young sparkling-wine specialist using local grapes of an improbable region with medal-winning results.

**Dehlinger** Sonoma. ★★→ ███★★★ CH 83 84 85 86 CS 78 80 81 82 83 84 Small winery and v'yd w. of Santa Rosa. Since 1976 CHARDONNAY, CABERNET and since '81 P NOIR all extremely well made.

**DeLoach Vineyards**  Sonoma.  ★★★ CH 83 84 85 86 PN 80 81 82 83 84
Russian River winery founded 1975 for CHARDONNAY, GEWÜRZ, P NOIR.
Also good ZIN (v.g. white ZIN), and SAUV BLANC.

**De Moor**  Napa.  ★★ CH 83 84 85 CS 80 81 82 83 84
Small Yountville winery (formerly Napa Cellars) with steady record,
esp. for CAB and ZIN. New (European) owners.

**Diamond Creek**  Napa.  ★★★ CS 74 75 76 77 78 79 80 81 82 83 84 85
Small winery since the 60s with austere, long-ageing CABERNET from
hills w. of Calistoga, e.g. "Volcanic Hill", "Gravelly Meadow".

**Domaine Chandon**  Napa.  ★★★
Californian outpost of Moët & Chandon Champagne. Launched 1976.
Promise is being fulfilled. First Reserve wine (released in 1985) was a
showstopper. So is second.

**Domaine Laurier**  Sonoma.  ★★★ CH 83 84 85 CS 78 79 80 81 82 83 84
Small new winery with beautifully structured wines, esp. CABERNET
and SAUVIGNON BLANC, using the new appellation Green Valley. A
classic in the making. CHARD now equally fine.

**Domaine Mumm**  Napa. (★★)
Seagram-owned. Sparkling-wine house on STERLING property. First
wine released '86, promising, and promises kept.

**Dominus**  Napa. (★★★★) 84
First fruits (1984 vintage released '88) of partnership ("John Daniel
Society") between inheritor of ex-Inglenook v'yd n. of Yountville and
Christian Moueix of Pomerol. B'x-style Cabernets-Merlot blend shows
immense promise.

**Dry Creek**  Sonoma.  ★★★ CH 83 84 85 86 CS 79 80 81 82 83 84
Small winery with high ideals, making old-fashioned dry wines, esp.
whites, incl. CHARDONNAY, CHENIN BLANC and FUMÉ BLANC and outstanding CAB SAUV.

**Duckhorn Vineyards**  Napa.  ★★→★★★ M 79 80 81 82 83 84 85 CS 79 80
81 82 83 84  Small winery on Silverado Trail best known for reds,
esp. v.g. MERLOT. Also SAUVIGNON BLANC and now "Robert Hunter"
Sparkling Brut de Noirs from Sonoma grapes.

**Durney Vineyard**  Central Coast/Monterey. ★★ CS 79 80 81 82 83
Well-established source of rich and robust CABERNET. Also CHENIN BL,
RIESLING.

**Eberle Winery**  C. Coast/San Luis Obispo. ★★
Most stylish and consistent CAB producer in Paso Robles area since
'79. Also CHARD.

**Edna Valley Vineyard**  Cen. Coast/San Luis Obispo. ★★→★★★ CH 84 85
86  Joint venture of grape-grower with CHALONE winemakers. Fat
CHARDONNAY full of character, and fragrant PINOT NOIR.

**Estancia**  See Franciscan.

**Estrella River**  San Luis Obispo/Santa Barbara. ★★ CH 83 84 85 86
Impressive winery with 700 acres. CHARDONNAY, RIESLING, MUSCAT,
SYRAH are competent and satisfying.

**Far Niente**  Napa. ★★ CH 83 84 85 86 CS 84
Founded 1885; reactivated in 1979. Full-flavoured CHARDONNAY first;
now similar CABERNET.

**Felton-Empire Vineyards**  Cent. Coast/Santa Cruz Mts. ★★
The famous old Hallcrest property revived. Excellent RIESLING; good
GEWÜRZ. Reds still rather shaky.

**Fetzer**  Mendocino.  ★★→★★★★ CH 83 84 85 86 CS 79 80 81 82 83 84
85  Rapidly expanding winery with interesting reliable wines, esp.
CHARD and CAB. Also SAUV BLANC, RIES and strong dark ZIN. A byword for
value.

**Ficklin**  San Joaquin. ★★★
Family firm making California's best "port".

**Field Stone**  Sonoma (Alexander Valley). ★★
Small subterranean winery founded by mechanical harvester maker.
Good wines incl. delicious CABERNET rosé.

**Firestone**  Central Coast/Santa Barbara. ★★★ CH 83 84 85 CS 81 82 83 84
Ambitious 1973 winery n. of Santa Barbara. Cool conditions are producing full spectrum of unusual wines of gentle savour.

**Fisher**  Napa. (★★)
Small mountain estate nr. Calistoga for v.g CAB and CHARD.

**Flora Springs Wine Co.**  Napa. ★★ CH 83 84 85 CS 80 81 82 83 84
Old stone cellar in St. Helena reopened 1979. CHARDONNAY and SAUV BLANC are v. successful, CABERNET less certain.

**Folie à Deux**  Napa. ★★★
Tiny producer of impeccable Chardonnays, v. good CHENIN BL, CAB, from bought-in grapes.

**Foppiano**  Sonoma. ★★
Old winery at Healdsburg refurbished with estate varieties incl. CHENIN BLANC, FUMÉ BLANC, CAB, ZIN, PETITE SIRAH.

**Franciscan Vineyard**  Napa. ★★ CH 83 84 85 CS 80 81 82 83
Growing enterprise with a meet-the-folks approach. Good ZIN, CAB, CHARD and RIES; also "Harvest Nouveau". Wines from own SONOMA v'yds are labelled "Estancia".

**Franzia**  San Joaquin. ★
Large old winery with well-distributed brands. Various labels, but all say "made and bottled in Ripon".

**Freemark Abbey**  Napa. ★★★★ CH 83 84 85 CS 74 75 76 77 78 79 80 81 82 83 84  Small connoisseur's winery with high reputation for CABERNET, CHARDONNAY and RIESLING (esp. late-harvest "Edelwein"). Top Cab is "Bosché" (74 75 78 79 80' 81 82 83 84)

**Frog's Leap**  Napa. ★★
Little St Helena winery as charming as its name. Now CAB SAUV and CHARD outclass the original SAUV BL and ZIN.

**Gallo, E. & J.**  San Joaquin. ★→★★★ CS 80
The world's biggest winery, pioneer in both quantity and quality. Family owned. Hearty Burgundy and Chablis Blanc set national standards. Varietals incl. SAUV BLANC (esp.), GEWÜRZ, RIES, CABERNET. CHARD not so good. Vintage-dated Cab has won wide approval. Drink it fairly young. Also "André" fizz and many others.

**Geyser Peak**  Sonoma. ★★
Old winery revived by Schlitz Brewery then sold to local grower Henry Trione. Best wines bear his name.

**Giumarra**  San Joaquin. ★★
Modern installation in hottest part of San Joaquin Valley with broad range from valley and Central Coast grapes.

**Glen Ellen**  Sonoma. ★★→★★★ CH 84 85 CS 83 84
Father-and-son team making restrained elegant wines from own-grown and other Sonoma grapes. SAUV BLANC, CHARD and CABERNET. "Proprietor's Reserve" indicates bought-in wines.

**Gloria Ferrer**  Sonoma. ★★
Big new sparkling winery launched in '85 by FREIXENET of Spain. An impressive start.

**Grand Cru**  Sonoma. ★★ CS 78 79 80 81 82 83 84
Small 1971 winery making good GEWÜRZ and increasingly CABERNET, CHENIN and SAUVIGNON BLANC.

**Green and Red**  Napa ★★
Tiny Pope Valley winery with vigorous ZIN.

**Grgich Hills Cellars**  Napa. ★★★ CH 83 84 85 Z 77 78 79 80 81 82 83 84  Grgich (formerly of Ch Montelena) is winemaker, Hills grows the grapes – esp. CHARDONNAY and RIESLING. Lively wines include high-strength ZINFANDEL and (esp.) CABERNET.

**Guenoc Vineyards**  Lake County. ★★ CH 84 85
Ambitious new vineyard/winery venture just beyond the Napa county line. CHENIN BLANC and PETITE SIRAH are esp. appealing.

**Guild**   San Joaquin. ★

Big growers' cooperative. B. Cribari is table wine label. "Cooks Champagne" a runaway success.

**Gundlach-Bundschu**   Sonoma. ★★ CH 83 84 85 86 CS 79 80 81 82 83

Very old small family winery revived by the new generation. Excellent CABERNET, MERLOT, ZIN and good whites: CHARDONNAY, GEWÜRZ, RIESLING.

**Hacienda**   Sonoma. ★★ CH 83 84 85 CS 79 80 81 82

Small winery at Sonoma specializing in high-quality CHARDONNAY and GEWÜRZ. CABERNET has wobbled recently.

**Hanzell**   Sonoma. ★★★ CH 83 84 85 PN 80 81 82

Small winery whose (late) founder revolutionized Californian CHARDONNAYS in the '50s. Chard and P NOIR are both huge wines. CABERNET first released in 1986.

**Haywood Vineyard**   Sonoma. ★★ CH 83 84 85 CS 83 84 85

Small new estate on hills above SEBASTIANI. First wines were lovely fruity CHARDONNAY and RIESLING. NOW CABERNET.

**Heitz**   Napa. ★★★★ CH 83 84 85 CS 76 77 78 79 80 81 82 83

An inspired individual winemaker who has set standards for the whole industry. His CABERNETS (esp. "Martha's Vineyard" and "Bella Oaks") are dark, deep and emphatic, his best CHARDONNAYS potent and long-lived. But Chard and other wines can be eccentric. Added substantial new v'yds in 1984.

**Hill, William, Winery**   Napa. ★★→★★★ CH 83 84 85 86 CS 80 81 82 83 84   Huge new plantings in the Mayacamas Mts. and a new winery have yielded very emphatic (but well-received) early wines.

**Hop Kiln**   Sonoma/Russian River. ★★ CH 83 84 85

Small winery. Individual, tasty PETITE SIRAH, ZIN, GEWÜRZ.

**Husch Vineyards**   Mendocino. ★★ CH 86 CS 84 85

Reliable CHARD and P NOIR from Anderson Valley; CAB and SAUV BLANC from Ukiah.

**Inglenook**   Napa and San Joaquin. ★→★★★★ CS 76 77 78 79 80 81 82 83   One of the great old Napa wineries much changed by current owners: Heublein Corp (now Grand Metropolitan). Inglenook Napa Valley is Napa label, with two qualities: "Cask" (Reserve) and Estate, now joined ('83) by hugely tannic "Reunion". CHARD and SAUV BLANC now v. well made. PETITE SIRAH is tasty. Inglenook Navalle are good-value Central Valley wines, only nominally related.

**Iron Horse Vineyards**   Sonoma. ★★★ CH 83 84 85 86 CS 79 80 81 82 83 84   Stylish Russian River property with CHARDONNAY, CABERNET, P NOIR and SAUV BLANC of vivid flavours. Sparkling IRON HORSE is v. dry and fine. Tin Pony is second label.

**(Italian Swiss) Colony**   San Joaquin and Sonoma. ★

Honourable old name from Sonoma apparently owned by someone called The Beverage Source. Standards have been recovering.

**Jekel Vineyards**   Central Coast/Monterey. ★★→★★★ CH 83 84 CS 78 79 81 82 83   Well-made RIESLING, CHARDONNAY, and CABERNET have rich resounding flavours. Wines (esp. whites) mature fast but tastily.

**J. Lohr**   Central Coast.

Substantial winery in San José with its own v'yds in SALINAS. Reliable RIESLING, CABERNET rosé and CHENIN BLANC.

**Johnson-Turnbull**   Napa. ★★ CS 80 81 82 83 84

Very small new estate producing balanced and distinguished, not overweight, CABERNETS from next door to MONDAVI.

**Johnsons of Alexander Valley**   Sonoma. ★★ CS 79 80 81 82 83 84

Small winery with good v'yd land. CABERNET best.

**Jordan**   Sonoma. ★★★ CH 83 84 85 CS 76 77 78 79 80 81 82 83

Extravagant winery. CABERNET modelled on Bordeaux, smooth CHARDONNAY. Polished wines to please sophisticates.

**Karly**   Amador. ★★

Stylish producer of esp. ZIN from Sierra foothills.

**Keenan, Robert**  Napa. ★★ CH 83 84 85 CS 83

V'yds on Spring Mountain started with over-strong and tannic wines. More polite recent style is winning approval.

**Kendall-Jackson**  Lake County. ★★→★★★ CH 84 85 86 CS 84

Young (1980) and growing maker of good uncomplicated CHARD. RIES, SAUV BLANC, CABERNET and ZIN show real promise. A name on many lips.

**Kenwood Vineyards**  Sonoma. ★★★→★★★ CH 83 84 85 CS 78 79 80 81 82 83 84  Small producer of steadily stylish reds, esp. CABERNET and ZIN also v.g. SAUV BLANC, good CHARD and CHENIN.

**Kistler Vineyards**  Sonoma. ★★ CH 83 84 85 86 CS 80 81 82 83

Young small winery in hills. First CHARDONNAY ('79) was overwhelming; recent wines show more restraint. Now also CAB and P NOIR

**Konocti Cellars**  Lake County ★★

Mid-sized cooperative winery in remote north, half-owned by John PARDUCCI. RIESLING, Fumé Blanc, CAB SAUV are consistently attractive.

**Korbel**  Sonoma ★★

Long-established sparkling wine specialists. "Natural" and "Brut" are among California's best standard "champagnes". Also brandy.

**Kornell, Hanns**  Napa. ★★

Independent-minded sparkling wine house using RIES to make full-flavoured dry wines: Brut and Sehr Trocken.

**Krug, Charles**  Napa. ★→★★ CS 74 77 78 79 80 81 82 83 CH 86

Historic old winery with generally sound wines. Good CABERNET (incl. releases of mature vintages), sweet CHENIN BLANC and very sweet Muscat Canelli. Charles Krug is the jug-wine brand.

**La Crema**  Sonoma. ★★ CH 83 84 85 86 PN 79 80 81 82

Founded 1979 at Petaluma. CHARD has been huge; P NOIR impressive.

**Lakespring Winery**  Napa. ★★

Steady small winery for well-made MERLOT, CAB SAUV. Also powerful whites.

**Lambert Bridge**  Sonoma. ★★ CS 80 81 82 83 84

Small 1975 winery nr. Healdsburg. CHARD less oaky than formerly; CABERNET austere, needs ageing.

**Landmark**  Sonoma. ★★ CH 83 84 85 CS 78 79 80 81

Young winery nr. Windsor; sound CHARD and CAB. Signs of class.

**Laurel Glen**  Sonoma. ★★ CS 81 82 83 84 85

Splendid '81 CABERNET was first wine of tiny Glen Ellen winery. '83 and '84 look very good.

**Laurent Perrier**  Central Coast/San Jose. ★★

Almaden-linked branch of the French Champagne firm started 1981 with excellent dry still CHARDONNAY. Future uncertain.

**Leeward Winery**  Central Coast/Ventura. ★★ CH 83 84 85 86 CS 80 81 82 83 84  CHARDONNAY from Monterey and San Luis Obispo grapes started this new venture near Santa Barbara well in 1980.

**Long Vineyards**  Napa. ★★ CH 83 84 CS 79 80 81 82 83

Tiny winery in eastern hills nr. CHAPPELLET. First good CHARDONNAY and late-harvest RIESLING, now CABERNET.

**Lyeth Vineyard**  Sonoma. ★★

New winery with ambitions for Bordeaux-style red and white. Red is 78% CAB SAUV, 12% MERLOT, etc. – and promising.

**Lytton Springs**  Sonoma. ★★ Z 83 84 85 86

Small specialist in Russian River ZIN; thick, heady, tannic.

**Maison Deutz**  Sonoma. (★★)

New sparkling winery with Champagne parentage. Promising first wines.

**Mark West**  Sonoma ★★→★★★ CH 83 84 85 86 PN 79 80 81 82 83 84

Young winery in cool sub-region. Very satisfactory GEWÜRTZ, CHARDONNAY. Now P NOIR and sparkling Blanc de Noirs.

**Markham**  Napa. ★★ CS 78 79 80 81 82 83 CH 85

1979 winery with 300 acres. CAB very sound, not thrilling. Good bone dry CHENIN BLANC. CHARD gaining a reputation. Now Japanese owned.

**Martin Bros** C. Coast/San Luis Obispo. ★★
Excellently crisp SAUV BL, CHENIN BL and CHARD. The small family winery aims to justify Nebbiolo in Paso Robles.

**Martini, Louis** Napa. ★★→ ▓▓▓▓ CS 78 79 80 81 82 83 84 Z 78 79 80 81 82 83 84 Large but individual winery with very high standards at every level. CABERNET "Vineyard Selection" one of California's best. BARBERA, MERLOT, PETITE SIRAH, P NOIR, ZIN, GEWÜRZ, FOLLE BLANCHE and Moscato Amabile are all well made. Second label: "Glen Oaks".

**Masson, Paul** Central Coast. ★→★★
Famous old name sold by Seagram's in '87, moved to Monterey. Future uncertain.

**Matanzas Creek** Sonoma. ★★ CH 83 84 85 CS 79 80 81 82 83
Young winery now settled in with well-balanced CHARD, SAUV BL, and MERLOT.

**Mayacamas** Napa. ★★★ CH 81 83 84 CS 76 77 78 79 80 81 82 83
First-rate very small v'yd and winery offering CABERNET, highly eccentric monster CHARD, also SAUV BLANC and ZINFANDEL (sometimes).

**McDowell Valley Vineyards** Mendocino. ★★ CS 80 81 82 83
Big new development using old-established v'yd to make wide range. To watch, esp. for ZIN and real SYRAH.

**Milano Winery** Mendocino. ★★ CH 83 84 85 CS 79 80 81 82
Very small winery worth noting for CHARD. CAB is overweight.

**Mill Creek** Sonoma. ★★ CH 84 85
1974 winery near Healdsburg with pleasant, easy-going CHARDONNAY, MERLOT, CABERNET.

**Mirassou** Central Coast. ★★
Dynamic mid-sized growers and makers, the fifth generation of the family. Pioneers in SALINAS v'yds. Notable GAMAY BEAUJOLAIS, GEWÜRZ and very pleasant sparkling.

**Mondavi, Robert** Napa. ★★ →★★★★ CH 83 84 85 86 CS 74 75 76 77 78 79 80 81 82 83 84 Twenty-three-year-old winery with a brilliant record of innovation in styles, equipment and technique. Solid successes incl. CABERNET, SAUV BLANC (sold as Fumé Blanc), CHARDONNAY, PINOT NOIR. "Reserves" are marvellous – regularly among California's best. Also useful table wines. See also Opus One.

**Monterey Peninsula** Central Coast/Salinas. ★★ CH 83 84 85 CS 78 80 81 82 Very small winery near Carmel making chunky v. long-living ZINFANDEL and CABERNET from SALINAS and other grapes.

**Monterey Vineyard** Central Coast/Salinas. ★★
The first big modern winery of SALINAS, opened 1974. Now owned by Seagrams. Good ZIN, GEWÜRZ and SYLVANER and fruity feather-weight GAMAY BEAUJOLAIS. "Classic Red" is value.

**Monteviña** Amador. ★★ CS 79 80 81 82 83 Z 80 81 82 83 84
Pioneer small winery in revitalized area: the Shenandoah Valley, Amador County, in the Sierra foothills. ZINFANDEL, BARBERA and SAUVIGNON BLANC are achieving balance.

**Monticello Cellars** Napa. ★★★ CH 83 84 85 86 CS 80 81 82 83 84 85
Ultra-modern new winery near TREFETHEN. Outstanding GEWÜRZ and SAUVIGNON BLANC first caught the eye. Now v.g. CHARDONNAY, fine tannic CABERNET, and SEMILLON (called Chevrier Blanc).

**Morgan** Central Coast/Salinas. (★★)
Ex-JEKEL winemaker now making his own v.g. CHARD.

**J. W. Morris** Sonoma. ★★★
Small former specialist in high-quality port-types from SONOMA grapes. Now in Healdsburg, with table wines under Black Mtn. label.

**Mount Eden Vineyards** Central Coast. ★★ CH 83 84 85
Company owning a major share of what were MARTIN RAY Vineyards. Expensive wines. Mount Eden Vineyards is a second-line label.

**Mount Veeder** Napa. ★★ CS 74 75 77 78 79 80 81 82 83 84
Ambitious little 1973 winery. High prices but good CABERNET.

**Navarro Vineyards**  Mendocino.  ★★

Grower of first-rate CHARD, P NOIR, outstanding GEWÜRZ and RIESLING in cool Anderson Valley.

**Newton Vineyards**  Napa.  ★★★ CH 85 CS 84

Luxurious estate. Big oak-scented CAB SAUV, MERLOT, CHARD, SAUV BL.

**Opus One**  Napa.  ★★★★ CS 79 80 81 82 83

Not a winery but a wine; the joint venture of Robert Mondavi and the late Baron Philippe de Rothschild. So far, in effect, a Mondavi Reserve of Reserves at a far-fetched price, however good.

**Papagni, Angelo**  San Joaquin.  ★★

Long-established grower with a technically outstanding modern winery at Madera. Dry coastal-style varietals incl. ZIN, CHARD, light "Moscato d'Angelo" and enjoyable Alicante Bouschet.

**Parducci**  Mendocino.  ★★ →★★★ CH 83 84 85 86 CS 78 79 80 81 82

Well-established mid-sized winery with v'yds in several locations. Good sturdy reds: CABERNET (and an excellent Cab/Merlot blend), PETITE SIRAH, ZIN, "Burgundy". Also pleasant CHENIN BLANC and FRENCH COLOMBARD. N.B. the no-oak CHARD.

**Pat Paulsen Vineyards**  Sonoma.  ★★

Property of T.V. comedian offers thoroughly well-made range, esp. SAUV BLANC, and incl. a near-dry Muscat.

**Pecota, Robert**  Napa.  ★★ CH 83 84 85 86 CS 84

Small cellar of ex-BERINGER man with high standards. Wines are CABERNET, SAUV BLANC, CHARD, good light GAMAY.

**Pedroncelli**  Sonoma/Russian River.  ★★→★★★★ CH 83 84 85 86 CS 78 79 80 81 82 83  Long-established family business with recent reputation for well-above-average ZIN and CHARDONNAY, all growing more stylish with practice.

**Pepi, Robert**  Napa.  ★★ CH 83 84 85 CS 82 83

Young stone hilltop winery between Oakville and Yountville has launched well, esp. as a SAUVIGNON BLANC specialist.

**Phelps, Joseph**  Napa.  ★★★ →★★★★ CH 80 81 83 84 85 86 CS 74 75 76 77 78 79 80 81 82 83 84  De-luxe mid-size winery and v'yd. Late harvest RIESLING exceptional. Very good CHARDONNAY, CABERNET, SYRAH. The "Reserve" wine, "Insignia", can be monstrously tannic. Whites age v. well, too (e.g. '80 GEWÜRZ perfection in '88).

**Pine Ridge**  Napa.  ★★ CH 83 84 85 CS 79 80 81 82 83 84

Small winery near STAG'S LEAP has made constantly stylish CHARD, MERLOT and CAB. Also mild but fresh, off-dry CHENIN BLANC.

**Piper-Sonoma**  Sonoma.  ★★★

A joint venture between Piper-Heidsieck of Champagne and Sonoma Vineyards released its first (very good) sparkling cuvée in 1980. The '81 needed until '85 to round out.

**Preston**  Sonoma.  ★★ CS 83 84

Tiny winery with very high standards in Dry Creek Valley, Healdsburg, esp. for SAUV BLANC, ZIN and now SYRAH.

**Quady Winery**  Central Valley.  ★★

Imaginative dessert wines from Madera since '75. Celebrated orangey "Essencia"; "Elysium" from Black Muscat.

**Quail Ridge**  Napa.  ★★ CH 84 85 86

Small specialist in barrel-fermented CHARD. Also CAB. Good, if pricey.

**Quivira**  Sonoma.  (★★)

New ('86) winery with highly promising SAUV BL and ZIN from Dry Creek Valley.

**Rafanelli, A.**  Sonoma.  ★★

Tiny cellar specializing in outstanding ZIN; also Gamay.

**Raymond Vineyards**  Napa.  ★★★ CH 83 84 85 86 CS 77 78 79 80 81 82 83 84  Small 1974 winery near St. Helena with experienced owners. CHARD, RIESLING and CABERNET all excellent.

**Ridge**  Central Coast S. CRUZ. ★★★★ CS 77 78 79 80 81 82 83 84
> Small winery of high repute among connoisseurs for concentrated reds needing long maturing in bottle. Notable CAB and ZIN from named v'yds; esp. Montebello and York Creek, Napa.

**River Oaks**  Sonoma. ★→★★
> Sound commercial wines from same winery as CLOS DU BOIS, but different vineyards.

**Roederer USA**  Mendocino. (★★★)
> The Anderson Valley branch of the Reims Champagne house. First wine 1988.

**Rombauer Vineyards**  Napa. ★★ CH 85 CS 84
> Young ('80) small winery buying Napa grapes for impressive CHARD and CAB SAUV.

**Roudon-Smith**  Santa Clara/Santa Cruz. ★★→ ★★★ CH 83 84 CS 78 79 81 82  Small winery offering really stylish CHARDONNAY.

**Round Hill**  Napa. ★★→★★★ CH 83 84 85 86 CS 80 81 82 83 84
> Consistent good value, esp. GEWÜRZ and FUMÉ BLANC, from big new winery in St. Helena. Rutherford Ranch is label for best wines.

**Rutherford Hill**  Napa. ★★★ CH 83 84 85 86 CS 79 80 81 82 83
> Larger stable-mate of FREEMARK ABBEY. Good GEWÜRZ. Excellent CHARD, MERLOT and CABERNET.

**Rutherford Ranch**  See Round Hill.

**Rutherford Vintners, Inc.**  Napa. ★★★ CH 83 84 85 CS 77 78 79 80 81 82 83  Small winery started in 1977 by Bernard Skoda. "Chateau Rutherford" is "Reserve" label.

**St. Andrews**  Napa. ★★ CH 83 84 85 86 CS 83 84
> Small CHARDONNAY estate on Silverado Trail near Napa city. Steadily excellent wine.

· **St. Clement**  Napa. ★★→★★★ CH 83 84 85 CS 78 79 80 81 82 83
> Small production. Good CABERNET, powerful CHARD and delicious SAUVIGNON BLANC.

**St. Francis**  Sonoma. ★★→★★ CH 83 84 85 86
> New small winery is using excellent CHARD, CABERNET, GEWÜRZ grapes from older v'yd. Wines have been disappointing so far.

**Saintsbury**  Napa. ★★★ CH 83 84 85 86 PN 81 82 83 84 85 86
> Young winery using Carneros grapes to make perhaps the best P NOIR and CHARD of this region.

**Sanford**  Santa Barbara. ★★★ CH 84 85 86
> New winery started with striking 1982 SAUV BLANC and CHARDONNAY in the toast and oak school. P NOIR is beautifully made; also P Noir Blanc.

**San Martin**  Central Coast. ★★ CH 78 80 81 82 83
> Restructured old company using SALINAS and SAN LUIS OBISPO grapes to make clean, correct varietals. "Select Vintage" is top label. Also pioneers in "soft" (low-alcohol) wines. More restructuring imminent.

**Santa Cruz Mountain V'yd.**  C. Coast. ★★ CS 78 79 80 81 82 83 PN 79 80 81 82 83 84  Small winery in the hills with hopes for fine PINOT NOIR, but problems with overbearing alcohol. Now CABERNET too.

**Santa Ynez Valley Winery**  Santa Barbara. ★★ CH 83 84 85 86
> Established producer of very good SAUV BLANC and CHARD.

**Sausal**  Sonoma. ★★
> Small specialist in stylish ZIN, etc.

**Scharffenberger**  Mendocino. ★★
> The major pioneer of champagne method sparkling Mendocino. Move planned from Ukiah to Anderson Valley.

**Schramsberg**  Napa. ★★★★
> A dedicated specialist using historic old cellars to make California's best "champagne", incl. splendid "Reserves". "Blanc de Noirs" is outstanding, deserves 2-3 years' ageing.

**Schug Cellars**  Napa. ★★ CH 83 84 85 PN 80 81 82 83
> New (1982) enterprise of PHELPS' ex-winemaker. Very tough PINOT NOIR.

**Sebastiani**  Sonoma.  ★→★★  cs 78 79 80 81 82 83 84

Substantial and distinguished old family firm with robust appetizing wines, incl. BARBERA. Top wines have SONOMA appellation. Keep under observation.

**Seghesio**  Sonoma.  ★

Old Healdsburg bulk producer offers notable value in P NOIR and ZIN.

**Sequoia Grove**  Napa  ★★★  CH 83 84 85  cs 83 84 85

Small winery nr. Oakville. CHARD since '79 has been well-balanced. CAB SAUV (Napa and Alexander valleys) is tannic and meant to age.

**Shadow Creek**  See Corbett Canyon.

**Shafer Vineyards**  Napa.  ★★→★★★  CH 81 83 84  cs 80 81 82 83 84

Young winery and vineyard near STAG'S LEAP is making polished CHARDONNAY and very stylish CABERNET and MERLOT.

**Shaw, Charles F., Vineyards and Winery**  Napa.  ★★  CH 83 84 85

St. Helena specialist in GAMAY light red, has added CHARD, CABERNET, SAUVIGNON BLANC.

**Silver Oak**  Napa.  ★★→★★★  cs 78 79 80 81 82 83

Small 1972 winery succeeding with oaky CABERNETS, incl. v. expensive "Bonny's Vineyard".

**Silverado Vineyards**  Napa.  ★★★  CH 84 85 86  cs 83 84

A showy new winery east of Yountville. Early CHARD and SAUV BLANC made news. Now CAB is even better. The owner is Mrs. Walt Disney, which suggests adequate capital.

**Simi**  Alexander Valley.  ★★★  CH 83 84 85 86  cs 78 79 80 81 82 83 84 85  Restored historic winery with expert direction of Zelma Long. Some of America's best, most lively CHARDONNAY, delicate CABERNET and (since '82) splendid SAUV BLANC. Also good CHENIN BLANC, irresistible rosé.

**Smith-Madrone**  Napa.  ★★→★★★  CH 83 84 85  cs 79 80 81 82

New v'yd high on Spring Mountain made first good RIESLING in '77. CHARD is now eye-catching. Also P NOIR and CAB.

**Sonoma-Cutrer Vineyards, Inc.**  Sonoma.  ★★★★  CH 81 82 83 84 85 86

Perhaps the ultimate (so far) in specialist estates, using new techniques to display the characters individual v'yds give to CHARDS (as in Burgundy). So far Les Pierres v'yd is No. 1.

**Spring Mountain**  Napa.  ★★  CH 83 84  cs 75 77 78 79 81

Renovated small 19th-century property with winery noted for good CHARDONNAY, SAUVIGNON BLANC and CABERNET.

**Stag's Leap Wine Cellars**  Napa.  ★★★→★★★★  CH 83 84 85  cs 74 75 76 77 78 79 80 81 82 83 84  Celebrated small v'yd and cellar with the highest standards. Excellent CABERNET and MERLOT, fresh GAMAY, fine CHARD.

**Sterling**  Napa.  ★★★  CH 83 84 85 86  cs 82 83 84

Extremely proficient (also scenic) winery owned by Seagrams. Strong, tart SAUVIGNON BLANC and CHARDONNAY; oaky CABERNET and MERLOT. See also Domaine Mumm.

**Stonegate**  Napa.  ★★  CH 83 84  cs 78 79 80 81 82 83

Small privately owned winery and v'yd making CABERNET, CHARDONNAY and better and better SAUV BLANC.

**Stony Hill**  Napa.  ★★★★  CH 74 75 76 77 78 79 80 81 82 83 84 85

Many of California's very best whites have come from this minute winery over 30 years. Owner Fred McCrea died in 1977; his widow Eleanor carries on. Stony Hill CHARDONNAY, GEWÜRZ and RIESLING are all delicate and fine. Chard recently weightier.

**Stratford**  Napa.  ★★  CH 84 85 86  cs 83 84

First wine ('82) was an impressive blended CHARD. New winery nr. Rutherford to provide more; also good SAUV BL (from '85).

**Strong, Rodney, Vineyards**  Sonoma/Russian River.  ★★ →★★★  CH 85 86  cs 78 79 80  Formerly called Sonoma Vineyards. Well regarded, esp. for CHARD. Range includes single-v'yd wines, esp. Alexander's Crown CABERNET.

**Sutter Home** Napa. ⭐ z 77 78 79 80 81 82 83 84 85
Small winery revived and hugely expanded on the success of its sweet, pink "white" ZINFANDEL (1m. cases a year).

**Swan, J.** Sonoma. ⭐⭐ z 74 76 77 78 80 81 82 83 84 85 PN 85
Young one-man winery with a name for rich ZIN, CHARD, P NOIR.

**Trefethen** Napa. ⭐⭐→⭐⭐⭐ CH 80 81 83 84 85 86 CS 74 75 76 77 78 79 80 81 82 83  Growing family-owned winery in Napa's finest old wooden building. Very good dry RIESLING, CABERNET, P NOIR. Tense CHARDONNAY for ageing and a notable low-price blend, Eshcol.

**Tudel** Napa. ⭐⭐
Small estate winery since '79 just n. of St. Helena. Excellent dark age-worthy CABERNET.

**Tulocay** Napa. ⭐⭐ CS 80 81 82 83 84
Tiny young winery at Napa City. PINOT NOIR and CABERNET can be really accomplished.

**Ventana** Central Coast/Monterey. ⭐⭐ CH 83
New in '78 with flavoury PINOT BLANC and CHARDONNAY.

**Vichon Winery** Napa. ⭐⭐→⭐⭐⭐ CH 83 84 85 CS 77 78 79 80 81 82
Founded 1980; original and ambitious. Fine CHARDONNAY and blended (50/50) SAUVIGNON/SEMILLON "Chevrignon Blanc". Now promising CABS. Bought (1985) by Robert MONDAVI.

**Villa Mount Eden** Napa. ⭐⭐ CH 83 84 CS 77 78 79 80 81 82
Small Oakville estate has made excellent dry CH BLANC, good CHARD, outstanding CAB. Bought (1986) by CH STE. MICHELLE. (p. 170).

**Weibel** Central Coast and Mendocino ⭐→⭐⭐⭐  Veteran mid-sized winery giving value in its class. Specialist in own-label sparkling wines.

**Wente** Livermore and Central Coast. ⭐→⭐⭐⭐ CH 84 85
Important and historic specialists in Bordeaux-style whites. Fourth-generation Wentes are as dynamic as ever, CHARD, SAUV, BLANC and RIESLING are all successful. Arroyo Secco Chard is v.g. Now also sparkling.

**Whitehall Lane** Napa. ⭐⭐
Small St. Helena producer to follow for fresh and lively P NOIR.

**White Oak** Sonoma. (⭐⭐)
Small Healdsburg winery using Alexander Valley CHARD, SAUV BLANC, CHENIN BLANC for rich, ripe wines.

**William Wheeler Winery** Sonoma. ⭐⭐ CH 86 CS 82 83 84
Young Dry Creek Valley family firm. Big CAB, good SAUV BLANC, CHARD to watch with interest.

**Zaca Mesa** Central Coast/Santa Barbara ⭐⭐ CH 81 82 83 84 85 CS 79 80 81 82 83  Santa Ynez Valley pioneer with good CHARD and RIESLING now scaling the heights with P NOIR.

**Z D Wines** Napa. ⭐⭐ CH 83 84 85 86 CS 79 80 81 82 83
Very small winery (moved from Sonoma to Rutherford) with a name for powerful PINOT NOIR and CHARDONNAY.

# Texas
In the past six years a brand new Texan wine industry has sprung noisily to life. It already seems past the experimental stage, with some very passable wines, though such a short track record can only confirm the state potential. The biggest winery is Ste. Genevieve, at Fort Stockton. Wines include Sauv Blanc, Chenin Blanc, French Colombard. But money problems have slowed progress. Llano Estacado, near Lubbock, is a substantial enterprise with 220 acres. Nearby and much smaller is Pheasant Ridge, which has made good Chardonnay and Semillon. Cypress Valley, near Round Mountain has some 60 acres. Fall Creek is a new name to watch for v.g. Carnelian.

# The Pacific North-West

There are now over 16,000 acres of vines and over 100 wineries in the States of Washington, Oregon and Idaho.

Oregon's vines lie mainly in the cool-temperate Willamette and warmer Umpqua valleys between the Coast and Cascades ranges. Those of Washington and Idaho are mainly east of the Cascades in the semi-arid Yakima Valley and Columbia basin areas, with very hot days and cold nights. Most Oregon-grown wines are consequently more delicate, Washington's more intensive in flavour. Individual wineries, with some notable exceptions, can be hard to characterize. In Oregon most are small and have yet to establish a steady track-record. Vintages are also as uneven as in e.g. Burgundy, whose Pinot Noir is Oregon's most talked about grape. Drouhin of Burgundy has encouraged the talk by buying land. Yet whites remain in the majority, and a serious over-supply threatens the finances of the industry in the north-west. Its excellent Riesling is sadly out of fashion (and is consequently a first-rate bargain). The principal producers are:

**Adelsheim Vineyard**  Willamette, Oregon.
> Small winery: promising P NOIR, oaky CHARDONNAY, fresh PINOT GRIS.

**Alpine Vineyards**  Willamette, Oregon.
> Young small estate winery with high spots, incl. P NOIR, RIESLING.

**Amity Vineyards**  Willamette, Oregon.
> 1976 70-acre winery; variable quality; PINOT NOIR best.

**Arbor Crest**  Spokane, Washington.
> Expanding and encouraging newcomer. Early CHARD and SAUV BLANC v.g. Reds also promising, if unpredictable.

**Bethel Heights**  nr. Salem, Oregon.
> Much praised newcomer, esp. for PINOT NOIR.

**Champs de Brionne**  George, Washington.
> New winery. Fast start in whites but ? direction.

**Château Benoit**  Oregon.
> Sound producer of MÜLLER-THURGAU, CHARD, and P NOIR has acquired a winemaker from Chablis and is launching sparkling.

**Château Ste. Chapelle**  Caldwell, Idaho.
> The first Idaho winery, near Boise. Early CHARD and RIESLING had intense flavours but beautiful balance. Now well settled in.

**Château Ste. Michelle**  Seattle, Columbia and Yakima valleys, Washington. The largest north-west winery, though now operating separately from COLUMBIA CREST. Wineries at Grandview and Woodinville offer wide range incl. v.g. CABERNET, SEMILLON, CHARDONNAY, MERLOT and sparkling.

**Columbia**  (formerly Associated Vintners) Washington.
> A Washington pioneer and still a leader, at Redmond, nr. Seattle. CABERNET, RIESLING, dry spicy GEWÜRZ and esp. SEMILLON have all been successful. Good value. Now good CHARDONNAY.

**Columbia Crest**  Washington.
> The label used by CHÂTEAU STE. MICHELLE for a range of blended wines from River Run, the group's biggest and newest winery, in the Columbia Valley.

**Covey Run**  (formerly Quail Run) Yakima, Washington.
> Admirable whites incl. ALIGOTÉ; reds are over-strength in alcohol and flavour.

**Elk Cove Vineyards**  Willamette, Oregon.

Very small 1977 winery. Good CHARDONNAY and RIESLING from named v'yds. PINOT NOIR inconsistent.

**The Eyrie Vineyards**  Willamette, Oregon.

Early (1965) winery with Burgundian ideas. Oregon's most famous and consistently good P NOIR, and v. oaky CHARD. Also Pinots Gris and Meunier and dry Muscat.

**Hillcrest Vineyard**  Umpqua Valley, Oregon.

Early (1961) winery in warmer area. Inconsistent; CAB best.

**Hogue Cellars**  Yakima Valley, Washington.

Expanding young winery outstanding for off-dry whites, esp. RIESLING, CHENIN BLANC, SAUV BLANC, and bold CHARD. Since '83 really stylish CAB, MERLOT. The leader in the region.

**Kiona Vineyards**  Yakima Valley, Washington.

Small cellar and v'yd nr. Benton City attracting attention with RIESLING, and CHARD.

**Knudsen Erath**  Willamette, Oregon.

Oregon's second-biggest winery with reliable good-value PINOT NOIR, esp. Vintage Select. Austere CHARDONNAY.

**F. W. Langguth Winery**  Yakima Valley, Washington.

German Mosel-maker succeeded with German-style RIESLINGS, esp. late harvest, now sold to SNOQUALMIE.

**Latah Creek**  Spokane, Washington.

Recent source of fruity, off-dry whites, esp. CHENIN BL, RIES, SAUV BL.

**Mercer Ranch**  Columbia Valley, Washington.

New winery has made some outstanding CABERNET and (unusually) Limberger from established v'yds.

**Oak Knoll**  Willamette, Oregon.

Fruit-winemaker making fair-value red and white wines, esp. P NOIR.

**Preston Wine Cellars**  Yakima Valley, Washington.

Early winery with broad range of sound to very good wines.

**Rex Hill**  Yamhill City, Oregon.

Well-balanced assault on top levels of P NOIR from individual v'yds, incl. Reserve wines. Also RIES. Fine new winery.

**Saddle Mountain**  Label previously used for second wines by F.W. LANGGUTH, now merged with Quail Ridge, California.

**Shafer Vineyard**  Cellars Willamette, Oregon.

Small meticulous P NOIR specialist. White P NOIR may be Oregon's best; CHARD almost certainly is.

**Snoqualmie**  Yakima Valley, Washington.

Company – bought F.W. LANGGUTH winery, but apparent financial confusion makes commentary difficult.

**Sokol Blosser Vineyards**  Willamette, Oregon.

Largest Oregon winery with wide range, incl. CHARD (esp. "Yamhill County"), SAUV BLANC, MERLOT and RIESLING. P NOIR is best effort.

**Staton Hills**  Yakima Valley, Washington.

Reliable, occasionally excellent source of easy, not very dry whites.

**Stewart Vineyards**  Yakima Valley, Washington.

New estate nr. Sunnyside. Early whites v. impressive.

**Paul Thomas**  Seattle, Washington.

Former fruit winery nr. Seattle now making v.g. SAUV BLANC, RIESLING.

**Tualatin Vineyards**  Willamette, Oregon.

Third-largest Oregon winery. Mainly whites with emphasis on CHARD, P NOIR (red and white). Both Washington and home-grown grapes. Mixed reports.

**Woodward Canyon**  Walla Walla, Washington.

New district, small cellar but first SEM, CAB SAUV v. stylish.

**Yamhill Valley**  Oregon.

First wines, made at SOKOL BLOSSER, were good. Own v'yds may confirm prospects.

# The North & East

New York State and its neighbours Ohio and Ontario have traditionally made their own style of wine from grapes of native American ancestry. American grapes have a flavour known as "foxy"; a taste acquired by many easterners. Fashion is steadily moving in favour of hybrids between these and European grapes with less, or no, foxiness, and now increasingly towards true European varieties. Recent examples of European-style wines both from old vineyards and new areas such as Long Island indicate a bright future for the industry. Chardonnays and Rieslings can both be excellent. The entries below include both wineries and grape varieties.

**Andres** Canada's second-largest wine-producer, with wineries in Ontario and British Columbia.

**Aurora** One of the best white French-American hybrid grapes, the most widely planted in New York. Good for sparkling wine.

**Baco Noir** One of the better red French-American hybrid grapes. High acidity but good clean dark wine.

**Banfi** 55-acre CHARDONNAY v'yd at Old Brookville, Long Island, released its first wine in 1986. First impressions v. favourable.

**Benmarl** Highly regarded and expanding v'yd and winery at Marlboro on the Hudson River. Wines are mainly from French-American hybrids (e.g. Seyval Blanc), but CHARD can be splendid.

**Bridgehampton Wine Co.**
Tiny property on Long Island. RIESLING and CHARD

**Brights** Canada's biggest winery, in Ontario, now tending towards French-American hybrids and experiments with European vines. Their BACO NOIR is a sound red, CHARDONNAY is steely, ALIGOTÉ pleasant. Now also in British Columbia.

**Bully Hill** FINGER LAKES winery founded 1970, using both American and hybrid grapes to make varietal wines.

**Canandaigua Wine Co.** Major traditional eastern winemaker ("the nation's third largest"). Bought WIDMERS in 1986. Also in California.

**Château des Charmes** Smaller Ontario winery, doing well with CHARD, P NOIR, GAMAY, RIESLING.

**Château Gai** Big Canadian (Ontario) winery making European and hybrid wines, incl. v. light CHARD, GAMAY, MERLOT.

**Catawba** One of the first American wine-grapes, still the second most widely grown. Pale red and foxy flavoured.

**Chautauqua** The biggest grape-growing district in the east, along the s. shore of Lake Erie from New York to Ohio.

**Chelois** Popular red hybrid. Dry wine with some richness, slightly foxy.

**Delaware** Old American white-wine grape making pleasant, slightly foxy dry wines. Used in "champagne" and for still wine.

**De Chaunac** A good red French-American hybrid grape, popular in Canada as well as New York. Full-bodied dark wine.

**Finger Lakes** Century-old wine district in upper New York State, best known for its "Champagne". The centre is Hammondsport.

**Finger Lakes Wine Cellars**
Young winery making good CHARD and (esp.) RIES.

**Glenora Wine Cellars**
Recent FINGER LAKES winery. Very successful RIES and CHARD.

**Gold Seal** One of New York's biggest and best wineries, makers of Charles Fournier "champagne" and the HENRI MARCHANT range. Recent CHARDONNAY has been excellent, winning major prizes.

**Great Western** The brand name of the PLEASANT VALLEY WINE CO'S "champagne", one of New York's sound traditional wines.

**Hargrave Vineyard** Trend-setting winery planting extensively on North Fork of Long Island, N.Y. Well established with CHARDONNAY and PINOT NOIR.

**Henri Marchant** GOLD SEAL's range of mainly traditional American wines.

**Heron Hill Vineyards** Small FINGER LAKES estate with good RIES, CHARD, etc.

**Inniskillin** Leading quality Canadian winery at Niagara. European and hybrid wines, incl. good MARÉCHAL FOCH, also CHARDONNAY.

---

*Phylloxera is an insect that lives on the roots of the vine. Its arrival in Europe from North America in the 1860s was an international catastrophe. It destroyed almost every vineyard on the Continent before it was discovered that the native American vine is immune to its attacks. The remedy was (and still is) to graft European vines on to American rootstocks. Virtually all Europe's vineyards are so grafted today. Whether their produce is just as good as the wine of pre-phylloxera days is a favourite debate among old-school wine-lovers.*

---

**Maréchal Foch**
Useful red French hybrid between PINOT NOIR and GAMAY.

**Niagara** Old American white grape used for sweet wine. Very foxy.

**Pindar Vineyards** Substantial young company on North Fork, Long Island. RIESLING has been successful.

**Pleasant Valley Wine Co.** Famous old winery at Hammondsport, FINGER LAKES, owned by TAYLOR's, producing GREAT WESTERN wines.

**Seibel** Celebrated French grape hybridist. Many successful French-American crosses originally known by numbers, since christened as AURORA, DE CHAUNAC, CHELOIS.

**Seyve-Villard** Another well-known French hybridist. His best-known cross, no. 5276, known as Seyval Blanc, is the most successful variety of its kind, making clean, aromatic wine with good acidity.

**Taylor's** The biggest wine-company of the E. States, based in the FINGER LAKES. Brands incl. GREAT WESTERN and Lake Country. Most vines are American. Also in California. Changed hands in 1987.

**Vinifera Wines** Small but influential winery of Dr Konstantin Frank, pioneer in growing European vines, incl. RIESLING, CHARDONNAY and PINOT NOIR, in the FINGER LAKES area. Some excellent wines.

**Wagner Vineyards**
Excellent CHARD, also GEWÜRZ, AURORA from Finger Lakes.

**Widmers** Major FINGER LAKES winery selling native American varietal wines: DELAWARE, NIAGARA, etc. Now also good RIESLING.

**Wiemer, Herman J.** Creative and daring German FINGER LAKES winemaker. Fine RIESLINGS; ferments v.g. CHARDONNAY in oak.

# Missouri
Has a small but long-established wine industry at Augusta, where Mount Pleasant Vineyards makes some very good white, esp. from Seyval Blanc. Their high acidity gives them the capacity to age remarkably: five years is not too long.

# Virginia
Gaining self-confidence with thriving local sales of Chardonnay and Riesling, which are lean-bodied but fresh flavoured.

NE

# South America

The vineyards of Argentina (the world's fifth largest) and Chile are known to the world chiefly as a source of cheap wine of sometimes remarkable quality. Most of it is drunk within South America. Recently Chile has been gaining in international reputation with some striking advances in technology. Argentina meanwhile continues to raise her standards despite a chronic grape glut. Brazil also has an expanding wine industry in the Rio Grande do Sul area, but as yet no exports. Peru has one good winery Viña Tacama with amazing Sauv Blanc.

## Argentina

The quality vineyards are concentrated in Mendoza province in the Andean foothills at about 2,000 feet. They are all irrigated. San Rafael, 140 miles s. of Mendoza city, is centre of a slightly cooler area. Salta, to the north, and Rio Negro, to the south, also produce interesting wines. Salta won a gold medal in Bordeaux in '87 (see Etchart).

**Bianchi, Bodegas** Well-known premium wine producer at San Rafael owned by Seagram's. "Don Valentin" CABERNET and Bianchi Borgoña are best-sellers. "Particular" is their top Cabernet.

**Canale, Bodegas** Restored winery in Rio Negro: promising SÉMILLON.

**Crillon, Bodegas** 1972-built winery owned by Seagram's, only for tank-method sparkling wines.

**Esmeralda** Producers of a good CABERNET and CHARD, St Felician, at Mendoza.

**Etchart** Salta winery making typical aromatic but dry Torrontes white (gold medal Bd'x, '87) and sound range of reds in Salta and Mendoza.

**Flichman, Bodegas** Old Mendoza firm now owned by a bank. Top "Caballero de la Cepa" white and red, plus SYRAH, MERLOT and sp.

**Giol** The enormous State cooperative of Maipu province. Mainly bulk wines. Premium range called "Canciller" is good.

**Gonzales Videla, Bodegas** Old-established family firm re-equipped for modern methods. Brands include "Tromel" and "Panquehue".

**Goyenechea, Bodegas** Basque family firm in San Rafael making old-style wines, including Aberdeen Angus red.

**La Rural, Bodegas** ("San Filipe")
  Family-run winery at Coquimbito (Mendoza) making some of Argentina's best RIESLING and GEWÜRZ whites and some good reds. Also a charming wine museum.

**Lopez, Bodegas** Family firm best known for their "Château Montchenot" red and white and "Château Vieux" CABERNET.

**Norton, Bodegas** Old firm, originally English. Reds (esp. Malbec) are best. "Perdriel" is their premium brand. Also good sparkling wines.

**Orfila, José** Long-established bodega at St. Martin, Mendoza. Top wines: Cautivo CAB and white Extra Dry (P BLANC).

**Peñaflor** Argentina's biggest wine company, reputedly the world's third-largest. Bulk wines, but also some of Argentina's finest premium wines' incl. Trapiche (esp. "Medalla"), Andean Vineyards and Fond de Cave CHARDONNAY and CABERNET. A sherry, Tio Quinto, is exported.

**H. Piper** Sparkling wine made under licence from Piper-Heidsieck of Champagne. Challenges PROVIAR.

**Proviar, Bodega** Producers of "Baron B" and "M. Chandon" sparkling wine under MÖET & CHANDON supervision. Also still reds and whites including v.g. Castel Chandon, less exciting Kleinburg, Wunderwein (whites), smooth Comte de Valmont, Beltour and Clos du Moulin reds.

**Santa Ana, Bodegas**  Small, old-established family firm at Guaymallen, Mendoza. Wide range of wines include good Syrah Val Semina.

**San Telmo**  Modern winery with a Californian air and outstanding fresh, full-flavoured CHARD, MERLOT, CAB and esp. MALBEC.

**Suter, Bodegas**  Swiss-founded firm owned by Seagram's making best-selling "Etiquetta Marron" white and good "Etiquetta Blanca" red.

**Toso, Pascual**  Old Mendoza winery at San José, making one of Argentina's best reds, Cabernet Toso. Also RIES and sparkling wines.

**Trapiche**  See Peñaflor.

**Weinert, Bodegas**  Small winery. Tough old-fashioned reds led by good CAB/MERLOT/MALBEC "Cavas de Weinert" and promising SAUV BLANC.

# Chile

Natural conditions are ideal for wine-growing in central Chile, just south of Santiago. But political conditions have been difficult for decades, and the country's full potential has only really started to be explored in the past three years. Chilean Cabernets lead the way with resounding flavours that will one day lead to worldwide renown. New oak barrels are starting to revolutionize standards. The principal bodegas ("Viñas") exporting wine from Chile are:

**Canepa, José**  Chile's most modern big bodega, handling wine from several areas. Very good frank and fruity CABERNET from Lontué, Curico, 100 miles south; recently particularly good SAUV BLANC. Also SÉMILLON, sweet Moscatel.

**Concha y Toro**  The biggest and most outward-looking wine firm, with several bodegas and 2,500 acres in the Maipo valley. Remarkable dark and deep CABERNET, MERLOT, Verdot. Brands are St. Emiliana, Marques de Casa Concha, Casillero del Diablo. CHARDONNAY and SAUV BLANC are now becoming established.

**Cousiño Macul**  Distinguished and beautiful old estate near Santiago. Very dry SÉMILLON and CHARDONNAY. Don Luis light red, Don Matias dark and tannic, are good CAB. Antiguas Reservas ('81) is their top export CAB.

**Errazuriz Panquehue**  Historic firm in Aconcagua valley, n. of Santiago, making very rich full-bodied wines.

**Los Vascos**  Family estate in Colchagua Prov. 400 acres making (since '83) some of Chile's best CAB ('84, '85) influenced by Bd'x and California. Also stylish SAUV/SÉM.

**Santa Carolina**  Architecturally splendid old Santiago bodega with old-style "Reserva de Familia" and better "Ochagavia" wines.

**San Pedro**  Long established at Lontué, Cutico. The second-biggest exporter, with a range of good wines. Gatto Negro and Gatto Blanco are biggest sellers. Llave de Oro is good CAB and Castillo de Molina is top Cab. Also aromatic "blush" Amigo. Santa Helena is associated.

**Santa Rita**  Long-established bodega in the Maipo valley s. of Santiago. "120" brand CABERNET ('84) has recently made a name in Europe and USA. Standard Cab also v.g.

**Torres, Miguel**  New enterprise of Catalan family firm (see Spain) at Lontué. Good SAUV BLANC ("Bellaterra" is oak-aged) and CHARD, v.g. RIESLING. CAB is made more "elegantly" than others in Chile, ages well.

**Undurraga**  Famous family business; one of the first to export to the USA. Wines in both old and modern styles: good clean SAUVIGNON BLANC and oaky yellow "Viejo Roble".

**Viña Linderos**  Small family winery in the Maipo valley exports good full-bodied CABERNET which gains from bottle-age.

# England

The English wine industry started again in earnest in the late 1960s after a pause of some 400 years. Well over a million bottles a year are now being made from over 1,200 acres; almost all white and generally Germanic in style, many from new German and French grape varieties designed to ripen well in cool weather. Natural acidity is high, which means that good examples have a built-in ability (and need) to age. Four years is a good age for many, and up to ten for some. Mature wines can be really excellent. The annual Gore-Brown Trophy is awarded for the best English wine. N.B. Beware "British Wine", which is neither British nor wine, and has nothing to do with the following.

**Adgestone** nr. Sandown, Isle of Wight. K. C. Barlow.
Prize-winning 8½-acre v'yd on chalky hill site. Vines are MÜLLER-THURGAU, Reichensteiner, SEYVAL BLANC. First vintage 1970. Light, fragrant, dryish wines age exceedingly well.

**Barnsgate Manor** nr. Uckfield, Sussex.
A showpiece 21 acres of MÜLLER-THURGAU, Reichensteiner, Kerner, Seyval, P NOIR, CHARD.

**Barton Manor** East Cowes, Isle of Wight. Mr & Mrs A. Goddard.
10-acre v'yd producing an aromatic medium-dry blend, regular prize-winner. Consistently good.

**Beaulieu** nr. Lymington, Hampshire. The Hon. Ralph Montagu.
6-acre v'yd, principally of MÜLLER-THURGAU, established in 1960 by the Gore-Brown family on an old monastic site.

**Biddenden** nr. Tenterden, Kent. R. A. Barnes.
22-acre mixed v'yd planted in 1970, making crisp medium-dry white of MÜLLER-THURGAU and Ortega; also a rosé with PINOT NOIR. Also makes wine for other growers. Gold medal winner in 1983.

**Bosmere** nr. Chippenham, Wiltshire. G. H. Walton.
16 acres of MÜLLER-THURGAU and SEYVAL BLANC; GAMAY and PINOT NOIR.

**Breaky Bottom** nr. Lewes, Sussex. P. Hall.
Good dry wines from 4-acre vineyard.

**Bruisyard** nr. Saxmundham, Suffolk. I. H. Berwick.
10 acres of MÜLLER-THURGAU making medium-dry wines since 1976.

**Carr Taylor Vineyards** nr. Hastings, Sussex. D. Carr-Taylor.
21 acres, planted 1974. Gutenborner, Huxelrebe, KERNER and Reichensteiner. Also a KERNER/Reichensteiner *méthode champenoise*. Exports to France.

**Cavendish Manor** nr. Sudbury, Suffolk. B. T. Ambrose.
10½-acre v'yd of MÜLLER-THURGAU planted on a farm. Fruity dry wine has won several awards at home and abroad since 1974.

**Chilford Hundred** Linton, nr. Cambridge. S. Alper.
18 acres of MÜLLER-THURGAU, Schönburger, Huxelrebe, Siegerrebe and Ortega making fairly dry wines since 1974.

**Chilsdown** nr. Chichester, Sussex. Paget Brothers.
10 acres of MÜLLER-THURGAU, Reichensteiner and SEYVAL BLANC making full dry French-style white since 1974.

**Ditchling** nr. Hassocks, Sussex. D. & A. Mills.
5-acre v'yd well reputed for consistency.

**Downers Vineyard** Henfield, Sussex. E. G. Downer.
6 acres of MÜLLER-THURGAU, planted 1976.

**Elmham Park** nr. East Dereham, Norfolk. R. Don.
3-acre v'yd of a wine-merchant/fruit farmer, planted with MÜLLER-THURGAU, Madeleine-Angevine, etc. "Mosel-style" light, dry, flowery wines. First vintage 1974. Also a fine dry cider.

**Felsted** (formerly Felstar) Felsted, Essex. K. Dawson, winemaker.
  A pioneer 8-acre v'yd planted 1966. MÜLLER-THURGAU, Seyval, P NOIR, Madeleine-Angevine.

**Gamlingay** nr. Sandy, Bedfordshire. G. P. & N. Reece.
  8½ acres MÜLLER-THURGAU, Reichensteiner and SCHEUREBE since 1970.

**Hambledon** nr. Petersfield, Hampshire. Hambledon Vineyards Ltd.
  The first modern English v'yd, planted in 1951 on a chalk slope with advice from Champagne. Grapes are CHARDONNAY, PINOT NOIR and SEYVAL BLANC. Now 7½ acres. Fairly dry wines.

**Highwaymans** nr. Bury St. Edmunds, Suffolk. Macrae Farms.
  25 acres, planted 1974. MÜLLER-THURGAU and PINOT NOIR.

**Lamberhurst Priory** nr. Tunbridge Wells, Kent. K. McAlpine.
  England's biggest producing v'yd with 55 acres, planted 1972. Largely MÜLLER-THURGAU, SEYVAL BLANC, also Reichensteiner, Schönburger. Production capacity approx. half a million bottles a year including winemaking for other small v'yds. Also makes Horam Manor, 8 acres at Heathfield, Sussex. A regular prize-winner.

**Lexham Hall** nr. King's Lynn, Norfolk. W.R.B. Foster.
  8 acres, planted 1975. MÜLLER-THURGAU, SCHEUREBE, Reichensteiner and Madeleine-Angevine.

**New Hall** nr. Maldon, Essex. S. W. Greenwood.
  24 acres of a mixed farm planted with Huxelrebe, MÜLLER-THURGAU and PINOT NOIR. Makes award-winning whites. Experimental reds.

**Penshurst** nr. Tunbridge Wells, Kent. D. E. Westphal.
  12 acres of the usual varieties in production since 1976.

**Pilton Manor** nr. Shepton Mallet, Somerset. J. M. Dowling.
  22-acre hillside v'yd, chiefly of MÜLLER-THURGAU and SEYVAL BLANC, begun 1966 and recently expanded. Also *méthode champenoise* sp.

**Pulham** nr. Norwich, Norfolk. P. W. Cook.
  6-acre v'yd planted 1973; principally MÜLLER-THURGAU, Auxerrois and experimental Bacchus.

**Rock Lodge** nr. Haywards Heath, Sussex. N. D. Cowderoy.
  7-acre v'yd of MÜLLER-THURGAU and Reichensteiner making dry white since 1970.

**St. Etheldreda** nr. Ely, Cambridgeshire. N. Sneesby.
  2-acre v'yd making a MÜLLER-THURGAU and a CHARDONNAY since 1974.

**St. George's** Waldron, Heathfield, E. Sussex. P. & G. Biddlecombe.
  20 acres planted since 1979. MÜLLER-THURGAU, etc, and some GEWÜRZ. Well-publicized venture has sold wine to Japan, etc.

**Staple** nr. Canterbury, Kent. W. T. Ash.
  7 acres, mainly MÜLLER-THURGAU. Some Huxelrebe and Reichensteiner. Dry and fruity wines.

**Stocks** nr. Suckley, Worcestershire. R. M. O. Capper.
  Successful 11-acre v'yd. All MÜLLER-THURGAU.

**Tenterden** nr. Tenterden, Kent. W. Garner.
  18 acres of a 100-acre fruit farm. Planted 1977. Six wines from very dry to sweet, incl. MÜLLER-THURGAU, SEYVAL BLANC and rosé.

**Three Choirs** nr. Newent, Gloucestershire. T. W. Day.
  20 acres of MÜLLER-THURGAU and Reichensteiner.

**Wellow** nr. Romsey, Hampshire. Andrew Vining.
  Ambitious new venture which at 80 acres is England's biggest. 12 varieties, incl. CHARDONNAY, predominantly MÜLLER-THURGAU and BACCHUS. First (small) vintage 1987.

**Westbury** nr. Reading, Berkshire. B. H. Theobald
  12½ acres of a mixed farm. 11 varieties in commercial quantities since 1975, incl. England's only real PINOT NOIR red.

**Wootton** nr. Wells, Somerset. Major C. L. B. Gillespie.
  6-acre v'yd of Schönburger, MÜLLER-THURGAU, SEYVAL BLANC, etc., making award-winning fresh and fruity wines since 1973.

**Wraxall** nr. Shepton Mallet, Somerset. A. S. Holmes.
  6 acres of MÜLLER-THURGAU and SEYVAL BLANC. Planted 1974.

# Australia

Map labels: CLARE/WATERVALE, MURRAY VALLEY, MUDGEE, RIVERINA, BAROSSA, Adelaide, SOUTHERN VALES, LANGHORNE CREEK, RUTHERGLEN, PADTHAWAY KEPPOCH, CENTRAL VICTORIA, NORTH EAST VICTORIA, Goulburn River, COONAWARRA, GREAT WESTERN, YARRA VALLEY, Melbourne, GEELONG, Canberra

It is only 20 years since new technology revolutionized Australia's 150-year-old wine industry, ending the dominance of fortified wines and making table wines of top quality possible. Old-style Australian wines were thick-set and burly Shiraz reds or Semillon or Riesling whites grown in warm to hot regions. A progressive shift to cooler areas, to new wood fermentation and maturation, to noble varieties (with Cabernet, Merlot, Pinot Noir, Chardonnay and Sauvignon Blanc at the forefront) has seen a radical change in style which has by no means run its course. Nonetheless, extract and alcohol levels continue to be high and the best wines still have great character and the ability to age splendidly.

Exports have suddenly assumed great importance for Australia, increasing from 8 million to 40 million litres in four years. At last Australia's best wines are to be found in London and New York. But it is not easy to keep tabs on them. There are now almost 500 wineries in commercial production. Labels are becoming less garrulous (but less informative) as Australian consumers become more sophisticated. Such information as they give can be relied on, while prizes in shows (which are highly competitive) mean a great deal. In a country lacking any formal grades of quality the buyer needs all the help he can get.

## Wine areas

The vintages here are those rated as good or excellent for the reds of the areas in question. Excellent recent vintages are marked with an accent.

**Adelaide Hills** (Sth Aust) 84' 85' 86' 87
 Spearheaded by PETALUMA: numerous new v'yds at very cool 1,500 ft sites in Mt Lofty ranges coming into production.

**Adelaide Plains** (Sth Aust) 79 80 82 83 84' 86' 87
 Small area immediately n. of Adelaide formerly known as Angle Vale. Wineries incl. Anglesey, Normans, PRIMO ESTATE.

**Barossa**  (Sth Aust) 66 73 75 76 79 80 81 82' 84' 85 86' 87'
Australia's most important winery (though not v'yd)
area, processing grapes from diverse sources (local, to
MURRAY VALLEY, through to high-quality cool regions
from adjacent hills to far-distant COONAWARRA) to make
equally diverse styles.

**Bendigo/Ballarat**  (Vic.) 73 75 76 78 79 80' 82 84' 85 87
Widespread small v'yds some of extreme quality, re-creating the
glories of the last century. 14 wineries incl. CH LE AMON, BALGOWNIE,
Heathcote Winery and Passing Clouds.

**Canberra District (ACT)**  10 wineries now sell cellar door to local and
tourist trade. Quality is variable, as is style.

**Clare Watervale**  (Sth Aust) 70' 71' 73' 76' 79' 80' 82' 84' 85' 86' 87
Small high-quality area 90 miles n. of Adelaide best known for
RIESLING; also planted with SHIRAZ and CABERNET. 17 wineries spill over
into new adjacent sub-district of Polish Hill River.

**Coonawarra**  (Sth Aust) 66 70 71 76 77 79 80' 82' 84 85 86' 87'
Southernmost and greatest v'yd of state, long famous for well-
balanced reds, recently successful with RIESLING, CHARDONNAY. Numerous recent arrivals incl. Hollicks, Haselgrove, Koppamurra, Ladbroke
Grove, Zema Estate.

**Geelong**  (Vic.) 78 80' 82 84' 85 86 87
Once famous area destroyed by phylloxera, re-established mid-60s.
Very cool, dry climate produces firm table wines from premium
varieties. Names incl. IDYLL, HICKINBOTHAM.

**Goulburn Valley**  (Vic.) 68 71 76 79 80' 82 84' 85 86
A mixture of old (e.g. CH TAHBILK) and new (e.g. MITCHELTON) wineries in
temperate region; full-flavoured table wines.

**Great Western/Avoca**  (Vic.) 78 80' 82' 84 85 86 87
Adjacent cool to temperate regions in central w. of state; Avoca also
known as Pyrenees area. High-quality table and sparkling wines. Now
8 wineries, 6 of recent origin.

**Hunter Valley**  (N.S.W.) 66 67 70 73 75 76 79 80' 82 84 85' 86' 87
The great name in N.S.W. Broad, soft, earthy SHIRAZ reds and SEMILLON
whites with a style of their own. Now also CABERNET and CHARDONNAY.
Many changes in identity.

**Keppoch/Padthaway**  (Sth Aust) 75 76 79 80 81 82' 84 85 86' 87
Large new v'yd area (no wineries) developed by big companies as an
overspill of adjacent COONAWARRA. Cool climate; good commercial reds
and whites and CHARD/PINOT NOIR sparkling wines.

**N.E. Victoria**  66' 70' 71' 73' 75' 76' 80' 82' 86' 87
Historic area incl. Rutherglen, Corowa, Wangaratta. Heavy reds and
magnificent sweet dessert wines.

**Margaret River**  (W. Aust) 75' 76' 79' 81' 82' 83' 85 86
New cool coastal area producing superbly elegant wines, 174 miles s.
of Perth. 15 operating wineries; others planned.

**Mornington Peninsula**  (Vic.) 84' 86' 87
Five commercial wineries on dolls-house scale making exciting wines
in new cool coastal area 25 miles s. of Melbourne. 20 growers,
wineries incl. ELGEE PARK, Merricks.

**Mount Barker/Frankland River**  (W. Aust) 76 80 81' 82 83
Promising new far-flung cool area in extreme south of state.

**Mudgee**  (N.S.W.) 72 74 75 78 79 80 82' 84' 86 87'
Small isolated area 168 miles n.w. of Sydney. Big reds of colour and
flavour and full coarse whites, recently being refined.

**Murray Valley**  (Sth Aust, Vic. & N.S.W.) NV
Important irrigated v'yds near Swan Hill, Mildura (N.S.W. and Vic.),
Renmark, Berri, Loxton, Waikerie and Morgan (S.A.). Principally
"cask" table wines. 40% of total wine production.

**Pyrenees** (Vic.) **82' 84' 85' 86 87'**
Central Vic. region with seven wineries producing rich minty reds and one or two interesting whites, esp. FUMÉ BLANC.

**Riverina** (N.S.W.) NV
Large volume producer centred around Griffith; good-quality "cask" wines esp. whites.

**Southern Vales** (Sth Aust) 67' 71' 75' 76' 80' 81' 82' 84 85 **86'** 87
Covers energetic McLaren Vale/Reynella regions on s. outskirts of Adelaide. Big styles now being rapidly refined and improved; promising CHARDONNAY.

**Swan Valley** (W. Aust) 75' 78' 81' **82' 84'** 85' 86
The birthplace of wine in the west, on the n. outskirts of Perth. Hot climate makes strong low-acid table, good dessert wines. Declining in importance viticulturally.

**Tasmania** 82' 84' **85 86 87'**
13 vineyards now offer wine for commercial sale, producing over 200,000 litres in all. Has great potential, particularly for CHARDONNAY and P NOIR.

**Upper Hunter** (N.S.W.) 75' 79' 80' 81' 83' 85' 86' 87
Est. early 60s; the irrigated vines produce mainly white wines, lighter and quicker developing than Hunter whites. Often good value.

**Yarra Valley ("Lillydale")** 76' 78' **80'** 81' 82' **84'** 85 86' 87'
Historic wine area near Melbourne fallen into disuse, now being redeveloped by enthusiasts with small wineries. A superb viticultural area with noble varieties only.

# Wineries

**Allandale** Hunter Valley. Table ★→★★★
Small winery without v'yds buying selected local grapes. Quality variable; can be outstanding; esp. CHARD.

**Allanmere** Hunter Valley. Table ★★→★★★
Small winery run by expatriate English doctor making excellent SEM, CHARD and smooth reds.

**All Saints** N.E. Vic. Full range ★
Once famous old family winery with faltering quality.

**Angove's** Riverland. Table and dessert ★→★★
Family business in Adelaide and Renmark in the Murray Valley. Notable value in CAB and esp. CHARD and other whites.

**Arrowfield** Upper Hunter. Table ★★→★★
Substantial vineyard, on irrigated land. Light CABERNET, succulent "Show Reserve" CHARD; also "wooded" SEM.

**Bailey's** N.E. Vic. Table and dessert ★★→★★★★
Rich old-fashioned reds of great character, esp. Bundarra Hermitage, and magnificent dessert MUSCAT and TOKAY.

**Balgownie** Bendigo/Ballarat. Table ★★★
Specialist in fine reds, particularly straight CAB and P NOIR. Also exceptional CHARD. Now owned by MILDARA.

**Basedow** Barossa Valley. Table ★★→★★★
Small winery buying grapes for reliably good range of red and white.

**Berri-Renmano Coop** Riverland. Full range ★→★★
By far Aust's largest winery following recent merger with Renmano, selling mostly to other companies. Now developing own brands on local and export markets. (See Renmano.)

**Best's** Great Western. Full range ★★ →★★★
Conservative old family winery at Great Western with good mid-weight reds and original tasty whites, incl. sparkling.

**Blass, Wolf (Bilyara)** Barossa. Table and sp. ★★★
Wolf Blass is the ebullient German winemaker. Dazzling labels and extraordinary wine-show successes, with mastery of blending varieties, areas and lashings of new oak. Not to be missed.

**Bowen Estate** Coonawarra. Table ★★★
  Small Coonawarra winery; intense but not heavy CAB, good RIESLING. Sparkling CHARD on the way.

**Brand** Coonawarra. Table ★★→★★★
  Family estate. Fine, bold and stylish CAB and SHIRAZ under the Laira label. A few quality blemishes in late 70s/early 80s, now rectified.

**Brokenwood** Hunter Valley. Table ★★★
  Exciting quality of (partly COONAWARRA) CAB and SHIRAZ since 1973; new winery 1983 added high-quality CHARD and SEM.

**Brown Brothers** Milawa. Full range ★→★★★
  Old family firm with new ideas, wide range of rather delicate varietal wines, many from cool mountain districts. CHARD and dry white MUSCAT outstanding in a reliable range.

**Buring, Leo** Barossa. Full range ★★→ ★★★
  "Château Leonay", old white-wine specialists, now owned by LINDEMAN. Steady "Reserve Bin" Rhine Riesling.

**Campbells of Rutherglen** N.E. Vic. Full range ★★
  Impressive lively whites, smooth reds plus good dessert wines.

**Cape Clairault** Margaret River, W.A. Table ★★
  Progressive producer of SEM, SAUV BL and CAB in reasonable quantity and with promise of better things to come.

**Cape Mentelle** Margaret River. Table ★★→★★★★
  Idiosyncratic robust CAB departs from district style and can be magnificent; also ZINFANDEL and v. popular SEM.

**Capel Vale** S.W. Western Aust. ★★★
  Outstanding range of whites, incl. GEWÜRZ. New v.g. CAB.

**Chambers' Rosewood** N.E. Vic. Full range ★★→★★★
  Good cheap table and great dessert wines, esp. TOKAY.

**Château Le Amon** Bendigo. Table ★★★
  Very stylish minty CAB and peppery SHIRAZ.

**Château Hornsby** Alice Springs, N. Territory. ★→★★
  A charming aberration. Full-flavoured clean reds from the Bush.

**Château Rémy** Great Western/Avoca. Sp. and table ★★
  Owned by Rémy Martin. Trebbiano/CHARD blend surprisingly successful. Also good "Blue Pyrenees" reds.

**Château Tahbilk** Goulburn Valley. Table ★★→★★★
  Beautiful and historic family-owned estate making long-lived CAB, SHIRAZ, Rhine Riesling and Marsanne. "Private Bins" are outstanding.

**Coldstream Hills** Yarra Valley, Vic. Table ★★★
  New winery, Yarra's second largest, built 1987 by wine critic James Halliday. '86 CHARD (esp.) and P NOIR are highly promising start. All eyes on '87s, and CAB SAUV.

**Conti, Paul, Wines** Swan Valley. Table ★★
  Elegant Hermitage, also fine CHARD and other estate whites.

**Craigmoor** Mudgee. Table and port ★★→★★★
  Oldest district winery now part of MONTROSE group and making very good CHARD and SEM, the two blended, and CAB/SHIRAZ.

**Cullens Willyabrup** Margaret River. Table ★★★
  Butch but kindly CAB/MERLOT, pungent SAUV BLANC and bold "wooded" CHARD are all real characters.

**d'Arenberg** S. Vales. Table and dessert ★→★★
  Old-style family outfit with strapping rustic reds and RIESLING.

**De Bortoli** Griffith, N.S.W. ★→★★★
  Irrigation-area winery. Standard reds and whites but magnificent sweet "botrytized" Beerenausleses of SEM, GEWÜRZ, RIESLING.

**Delatite** Central Vic. Table ★★★
  Rosalind Ritchie makes appropriately willowy and feminine RIESLING, GEWÜRZ, P NOIR and CAB from this very cool mountainside v'yd.

**Diamond Valley** Yarra Valley. Vic. Table ★★→ ★★★
  Producer of outstanding P NOIR in significant quantities; other wines good rather than great.

**Domaine Chandon**  Yarra Valley. Vic. Sp.
  The showpiece of the Yarra Valley. Substantial production from
  grapes grown in all the cooler parts of Australia, with strong direction
  from owner Moët & Chandon. Early indications of exciting, perhaps
  exceptional, quality; first commercial release late 1988.

**Drayton's Bellevue**  Hunter Valley, N.S.W. Table ★★
  Traditional Hermitage and SEM; occasionally good CHARD; recent
  quality improving after lapse.

**Dromana Estate**  Mornington Peninsula. Table ★★★
  Largest and best producer in district. Great skill in making glorious
  CAB, P NOIR and CHARD.

**Elgee Park**  Mornington Pensinsula. Table ★★
  Substantial modern winery on longest-established v'yd producing
  very good CAB/MERLOT, CHARD, RIESLING and a hatful of VIOGNIER.

**Enterprise Wines**  Clare Valley. Table ★★★
  Tim Knappstein, an exceptionally gifted winemaker, produces Rhine
  Riesling. FUMÉ BLANC, GEWÜRZ and CABERNET. Now part of Wolf Blass
  group.

**Evans and Tate**  Swan Valley. Table ★★→★★★
  Fine elegant reds from the Margaret River Redbrook and Swan Valley
  Gnangara v'yds. Good SEM too.

**Evans Family**  Hunter Valley, N.S.W. ★★★
  Excellent CHARD, fermented in new oak, from small v'yd owned by
  family of Len Evans.

**Forest Hills**  Mount Barker, W.A. Table ★★→★★★
  Pioneer vineyard in region, with wines made under contract at
  PLANTAGENET. RIESLING, CHARD and CAB can all be and usually are
  excellent.

**Hardy's**  S. Vales, Barossa, Keppoch, etc. Full range ★→★★★
  Famous family-run company using and blending wines from several
  areas. St. Thomas Burgundy, Old Castle Riesling are standards. Top
  wines are "Collection" series and Australia's greatest vintage ports.
  Hardy's bought HOUGHTON and REYNELLA and, most recently, STANLEY.
  Reynella's beautifully restored buildings are now group headquarters.

**Heathcote**  Bendigo. Table ★★→★★★
  Stylish producer of eclectic range of white and red varietals, showing
  abundant flavour and technical perfection.

**Heemskerk**  Tasmania. Table ★★★
  Most successful commercial operation in Tasmania. Herby CAB;
  promising CHARD. Also P NOIR and RIESLING. Recent partnership with
  Louis Roederer plans high-class sparkling wine in years to come.

**Henschke**  Barossa. Table ★★★
  Family business known for sterling SHIRAZ and v.g. CAB. New high-
  country v'yds on Adelaide Hills add excitement.

**Hickinbotham Winemakers**  Geelong. Table ★★→★★★
  Innovative winemaking by Hickinbotham family (since 1980) has
  produced some fascinating styles incl. carbonic maceration CABERNET
  ("Cab Mac"), dry Ausleses, etc.

**Hollick**  Coonawarra. Table ★★★
  Ian and Wendy Hollick won instant stardom with trophy-winning '84
  CAB; also v.g. CHARD and RIES from small winery.

**Houghton**  Swan Valley, W.A. Full range ★→★★★
  The most famous old winery of W.A. Soft, ripe White Burgundy is top
  wine; also excellent CAB, VERDELHO etc. See Hardy's.

**Hungerford Hill**  Hunter Valley and Coonawarra. Table ★→★★★
  Medium-sized winery producing high-class varietals; esp. RIESLING
  and CABERNET from COONAWARRA.

**Huntington Estate**  Mudgee. Table ★★→★★★
  Small winery; the best in Mudgee. Fine CABERNETS and clean SEMILLON
  and CHARDONNAY. Invariably under-priced.

**Idyll** Geelong. Vic. ★★★
Small winery with CAB and GEWÜRZ of highest quality.

**Jeffrey Grosset** Clare. Table ★★→★★★
Exceedingly elegant RIESLING and CABERNET made in consistent style by fastidious young winemaker.

**Kaiser Stuhl** Barossa. Full range ★→★★★
Now part of Penfolds; a huge winery processes fruit from diverse sources. "Individual v'yd" RIESLINGS can be excellent. So can Red Ribbon reds.

**Katnook Estate** Coonawarra. Table ★★★
Excellent pricey CAB and CHARD; also SAUV BL, P NOIR, RIES.

**Lillydale Vineyards** Yarra Valley. Table ★★★
Foremost producer of CHARD using sophisticated techniques; also scented GEWÜRZTRAMINER and crisp RIESLING. CAB and P NOIR recent additions.

**Krondorf Wines** Barossa Valley. Table ★★→ ▮▮▮
Acquired by MILDARA in 1986, but quality and brand image will be preserved. "Burge and Wilson" wines are best.

**Lake's Folly** Hunter Valley. Table ★★★★
The work of an inspired surgeon from Sydney. CABERNET and new barrels make fine complex reds. Also exciting CHARD.

**Leeuwin Estate** Margaret River. Table ★★→★★★★
Lavishly equipped estate leading W. Australia with superb (and very expensive) CHARD; developing fine P NOIR, RIES, and CAB.

**Lehmann Wines, Peter** Barossa. Table ★★→ ▮▮▮
Defender of the Barossa faith, Lehmann makes vast quantities of wine, mostly sold in bulk, and v.g. special cuvées under his own label.

**Leconfield** Coonawarra. Table ★→★★★
Coonawarra CABERNET of great style. RIESLING improving.

**Lindeman** Orig. Hunter, now everywhere. Full range ▮→★★★★
One of the oldest firms, now a giant owned by Phillip Morris. Its Ben Ean "Moselle" is market leader. Owns BURINGS in Barossa and Rouge Homme in COONAWARRA, and important v'yds at Padthaway: outstanding CHARD. Many inter-state blends. Pioneered new styles, yet still makes fat old-style "Hunters".

**McWilliams** Hunter Valley and Riverina. Full range ★→★★
Famous family of Hunter winemakers at Mount Pleasant (HERMITAGE and SEMILLON). Pioneers in RIVERINA with noble varieties, incl. CABERNET and sweet white "Lexia".

**Mildara** Coonawarra. Murray Valley. Full range ★→★★★
Sherry and brandy specialists at Mildura on the Murray River also making fine CABERNET and RIESLING at COONAWARRA. Now own BALGOWNIE, KRONDORF and YELLOWGLEN.

**Mitchells** Clare Valley. Table ▮▮▮
Small family winery, excellent RIESLING and CABERNET.

**Mitchelton** Goulbourn Valley, Vic. Table ▮▮▮
Big modern winery. A wide range incl. v.g. wood-matured Marsanne, CAB and botrytized RIESLING from COONAWARRA.

**Montrose** Mudgee, N.S.W. Table ★★ →★★★
Recent winemaking and marketing initiatives have had much success; superb CHARD, interesting BARBERA and NEBBIOLO.

**Moorilla Estate** Tasmania. Table ★★★
Senior winery on outskirts of Hobart on Derwent River producing superb P NOIR, V.G. CHARD and CAB in tiny quantities.

**Morris** N.E. Vic. Table and dessert ★★ →★★★★
Old winery at Rutherglen making Australia's greatest dessert muscats and tokays; recently v.g. cheap table wines.

**Moss Wood** Margaret River. Table ★★★★
Best Margaret River winery (with only 29 acres). CABERNET SAUVIGNON, PINOT NOIR, CHARDONNAY all with rich fruit flavours not unlike the best Californians.

Aus

**Mount Langi Ghiran**  Great Western, Vic. Table ★→ ▪▪▪
  Producer of superb rich peppery Rhône-like SHIRAZ, v.g. CAB and less exhilarating RIESLING.

**Mount Mary**  Yarra Valley, Vic. Table ★★★
  Dr. John Middleton is a perfectionist with tiny amounts of CHARD, P NOIR and (best of all) CAB SAUV/CAB FRANC/MERLOT.

**Oakridge**  Yarra Valley. Red Table ▪▪▪
  Cabernet specialist making Yarra's finest examples, albeit in small quantities.

**Orlando (Gramp's)**  Barossa Valley. Full range ★★→ ▪▪▪
  Great pioneering company, bought by management 1988. Full range from good standard Jacob's Creek Claret to excellent COONAWARRA CABERNET; CHARDONNAY and great Steingarten RIESLING. William Jacob is a low-price line.

**Penfold's**  Orig. Adelaide, now everywhere. Full range ★→★★★★
  Ubiquitous and excellent company: in BAROSSA, RIVERINA, COONAWARRA, CLARE VALLEY, etc. Grange Hermitage (75', 76', 78, 80) is ★★★★, St. Henri Claret some way behind. Bin-numbered wines are usually outstanding. "Grandfather Port" is sensational. New: "Magill Estate" (84, 85) from old Grange v'yd and "Clare Estate" from Clare v'yd.

**Petaluma**  Adelaide Hills. ★★★★
  A recent rocket-like success with CAB, CHARD and RIESLING, now centred around new winery in ADELAIDE HILLS using COONAWARRA and CLARE grapes. Bollinger now part owner, with ambitious sparkling wine v'yds and facilities in ADELAIDE HILLS. Sp. wine, called "Croser" (after the boss, Brian C.), from '85.

**Petersons**  Hunter Valley. Table ★★★
  On show results, most accomplished small Hunter winery, with exceptional CHARD and v.g. SEM.

**Piper's Brook**  Tasmania. Table ★★★
  Cool-area pioneer with very good RIESLING, P NOIR, superb CHARD from Tamar Valley near Launceston. Lovely labels.

**Pirramimma**  S. Vales, S.A. Full range. ▪→★★
  Big supply of good standard; reds best.

**Plantaganet**  Mt. Barker. Full range ★★→★★★
  The region's largest producer with a wide range of varieties, esp. rich CHARD, SHIRAZ and vibrant, potent CAB.

**Quelltaler**  Clare Watervale. Full range. ★→★★
  Old winery known for good "Granfiesta" sherry. Recently good Rhine Riesling and SEMILLON. Bought by Wolf Blass 1987.

**Redman**  Coonawarra. Red Table ★→★★
  The most famous old name in COONAWARRA make two wines (Claret, CABERNET). Recent quality disappointing.

**Renmano**  Murray Valley, S.A. Full range. ★→ ▪▪
  Huge coop (see Berri-Renmano). "Chairman's Selections" v.g. value.

**Reynella**  S. Vales, S.A. Full range ★★→★★★
  Historic red wine specialists s. of Adelaide. Rich CAB (partly COONAWARRA), Claret and excellent "port". See Hardy's.

**The Robson Vineyard**  Hunter Valley. Table ★★→★★★
  Financially troubled but fastidious winery. Wide range of varietals; CHARDONNAY, CABERNET and Hermitage consistently show winners.

**Rockford**  Barossa Valley, S.A. Table ▪▪
  Small producer, but a wide range of thoroughly individual styles often made from grapes grown on very old low-yielding v'yds.

**Rosemount**  Upper Hunter and Coonawarra. Table ★→★★★
  Rich, unctuous HUNTER "Show" CHARD is an international smash. This and COONAWARRA CAB lead the wide range.

**Rothbury Estate**  Hunter Valley. Table ★★→ ▪▪▪
  Important syndicate-owned estate. Traditional HUNTER: "Hermitage" and long-lived SEMILLON: "Black Label" best. New CHARDONNAY (from Cowra) and PINOT NOIR are promising.

**S. Smith & Sons**  Barossa. Full range ★→ ▓▓▓
Big old family firm with considerable verve, using computers, juice evaluation, etc., to produce full spectrum of high-quality wines, incl. "Hill-Smith Estate". "Heggies Vineyard" is best.

**St. Huberts**  Yarra Valley. Vic. Table ★→★★★
Erratic, much sought-after CABERNET; recent change in ownership should improve consistency for this largest YARRA winery.

**St. Leonards**  N.E. Vic. Full range ▓▓
Excellent varieties sold only at cellar door and mailing list, incl. exotics. e.g. Fetyaska and Orange Muscat.

**St. Matthias**  Tamar Valley, Tas. Table ★★
Has joined the "big three" Tasmania wineries almost overnight; superbly situated v'yd and cellar-door sales on banks of Tamar estuary. Wines made under contract at HEEMSKERK.

**Saltram**  Barossa. Full range ★→★★★
Seagram-owned winery making wines of variable quality. "Pinnacle Selection" best wines; also Mamre Brook.

**Sandalford**  Swan Valley. Table ★
Fine old winery with contrasting styles of red and white varietals from Swan and Margaret rivers. Wonderful old Verdelho.

**Saxonvale**  Hunter Valley. Table ▓▓
Medium-sized operation now making good early-maturing SEMILLON and CHARDONNAY. Also good soft CABERNET, SHIRAZ. Acquired by WYNDHAM ESTATE in 1986.

**Seaview**  S. Vales, S.A. ▓▓
Brand name owned by PENFOLD'S, used for good value CAB, CHARD.

**Seppelt**  Barossa, Great Western, Keppoch, etc. Full range ★→★★★
Far-flung producers of Australia's most popular "champagne" (Gt. Western Brut), good dessert wines, the reliable Moyston claret and some very good private bin wines, incl. CHARD, from Gt. Western and Drumborg in Victoria, and Keppoch and Barossa in South Australia. Top sp. is called "Salinger".

**Seville Estate**  Yarra Valley. Table ★★→★★★
Tiny Yarra Valley winery with well-made CHARDONNAY, very late-picked RIESLING, SHIRAZ, PINOT NOIR, etc.

**Stanley**  Clare Valley. Full range ★→ ▓▓▓
Important medium-size quality winery purchased by HARDY late 1987. Good RHINE RIESLING, CHARD and CABERNET and complex Cabernet/Shiraz/Malbec blends under Leasingham label.

**Stanton & Killeen**  N.E. Vic. Table and dessert ★★
Small old family firm. Rich muscats, also strong Moodemere reds.

**Taltarni**  Great Western/Avoca. Table ★★★
Dominique Portet, brother of Bernard (Clos du Val, Napa), son of André (Ch Lafite), produces huge but balanced reds, good SAUV BLANC and fine sparkling wines.  🔴 Aus

**Tarrawarra**  Yarra Valley. Table ★★
Multi-million dollar investment making limited quantities of idiosyncratic and expensive CHARD, with P NOIR planned for the future.

**Taylors Wines**  Clare Valley. Table ★→★★
Large new red wine-producing unit (CABERNET and HERMITAGE) turning to whites (RHINE RIESLING, CHARD, generics).

**Tisdall Wines**  Goulburn Valley. Table ★★→★★★
Exciting young winery in the Echuca River area, making local ("Rosbercon") wines plus finer material from central ranges (Mount Helen CABERNET, CHARDONNAY, RHINE RIESLING).

**Tollana**  Barossa, S.A. Full Range ▓▓→★★★
Old company once famous for brandy, has latterly made some quite fine CABERNET and RHINE RIESLING. Acquired by PENFOLD'S 1987.

**Tulloch**  Hunter Valley, N.S.W. Table ▓★→★★★
An old name at Pokolbin, with good dry reds, RIESLING and VERDELHO, now part of PENFOLD'S group.

**Tyrrell**  Hunter Valley, N.S.W. Table ★★→ ███ ★★★
Some of the best traditional Hunter wines, Hermitage and SEMILLON, are "Vat 47". Also big rich CHARDONNAY, delicate PINOT NOIR and v.g. sparkling.

**Vasse Felix**  Margaret River. Table ★★→★★★
The pioneer of the Margaret River. Elegant CABERNETS notable for mid-weight balance, bought by Robert Holmes à Court 1987.

**Virgin Hills**  Bendigo/Ballarat. Table ★★★★
Tiny supplies of one blended (CAB/SHIRAZ/MALBEC) red of legendary style and balance.

**Westfield**  Swan Valley. Table ★→ ███ ★★
John Kosovich's CABERNETS, CHARDONNAYS and VERDELHOS show particular finesse in a hot climate. Also good "port".

**Wirra Wirra**  S. Vales, S.A. Table ★★→★★★
Under PETALUMA influence high-quality, beautifully packaged whites and reds have made a big impact recently.

**Woodleys**  Barossa, S.A. Table ★★
Well known for low-price Queen Adelaide label. "Reference" CAB is best wine. Acquired by SEPPELT in late 1985.

**Wyndham Estate**  Branxton, N.S.W. Full range ★ →★★
Aggressive large new Hunter group with Richmond Grove, Hunter Estate, Hollydene and Saxonvale as its brands.

**Wynn**  Coonawarra, S. Vales. Table ███ →★★★
Larger inter-state company, originators of flagon wines, with largest winery and vineyards at COONAWARRA, making good CAB (esp. "John Riddoch"). Acquired by PENFOLD's in 1985.

**Yalumba**  See S. Smith & Sons.

**Yarra Burn**  Yarra Valley. Table ★→★★★
Substantial boutique producing wines of variable quality and style, but usually excellent P NOIR and CAB.

**Yarra Yering**  Yarra Valley. Table ███ ★★★
One of the best Lillydale boutique wineries. Esp. racy powerful P NOIR and deep CABERNET.

**Yellowglen**  Bendigo/Ballarat. Sparkling ★→★★
High-flying sparkling winemaker acquired by MILDARA. Sales are more impressive than quality.

**Yeringberg**  Yarra Valley. Table ★★★
Historic estate now again producing v. high-quality CHARD, CAB, P NOIR, in minute quantities.

# New Zealand

In the past 10 years New Zealand has made an international impact with table wines of startling quality, particularly whites, well able to compete with those of Australia or California. It is now regarded as the foremost cool-climate viticultural region among the world's newer wine countries.

Progress has accelerated since new vineyard areas were planted in the early '70s in both North and South Islands. There are now well over 12,000 acres remaining after a Government subsidized removal of 3,750 acres in 1986 of lesser varieties which had created a surplus of wine on the domestic market. White grapes predominate. Müller-Thurgau is the most planted variety, but is being overtaken by varieties in demand overseas: Sauvignon Blanc and Chardonnay in whites, Cabernet Sauvignon and Merlot for reds.

New vineyard areas are opening up in Martinborough (North Island, north of the capital city, Wellington), and Canterbury and Central Otago, in South Island. NZ now boasts the world's southernmost (Otago) and easternmost (East Cape) vineyards.

The general style of wine is relatively light, with intensity of fruit and varietal character, and crisp acidity. Barrel fermentation and/or ageing are adding to the complexity and interest of its wines. The principal producers are:

**Antipodean** Matakana, n. of Auckland.

V. small new ('86) boutique with very promising CAB/MERLOT blend.

**Auckland** Largest city in NZ, location of head offices of major wineries, plus largest number of medium and small wineries in outskirts.

**Babich** Henderson, nr. Auckland.

Old Dalmatian family firm of some size, highly respected in NZ for consistent quality and value. Also using grapes from GISBORNE and HAWKES BAY. Good CHARDS (esp. "Irongate"), SAUV BL, SEMILLON/CHARD, GEWÜRZ, CAB SAUV and CAB/MERLOT.

**Brookfields** Meeanee, Hawkes Bay.

Small boutique newcomer to export. Noted for SAUV BL, CHARD and CAB.

**Cape Mentelle** Renwick, Marlborough.

Offshoot of W. Australia winery, better known by its NZ brand name, "Cloudy Bay" after nearby coastal feature. Excellent initial SAUV BL now joined by outstanding CHARD.

**Collard** Henderson, nr Auckland.

Small family winery using grapes from several areas, CHARD, SAUV BL, dry CHENIN BL and CAB/MERLOT.

**Cooks** Wineries at Te Kauwhata, s. of Auckland and in Hawkes Bay. Large company now merged with Corbans and former McWilliams, using grapes from GISBORNE and HAWKES BAY. Steadily good record with CHARD, GEWÜRZ, CHENIN BL and CAB SAUV, now producing matching sauv bl, also late picked MÜLLER-THURGAU.

**Cooper's Creek** Huapai Valley, n.w. of Auckland.

Small winery augmenting own grapes with GISBORNE and HAWKES BAY fruit. Exporting good CHARD (esp. Swamp Rd label), SAUV BL, RIES, GEWÜRZ and popular blends Coopers Dry (White) and Coopers Red.

**Corbans** Henderson, nr. Auckland.

Old-established firm with wineries at GISBORNE and HAWKES BAY. Now incorporating Cooks and McWilliams, and second largest in NZ. New premium brand, "Stoneleigh", from vineyards in Marlborough producing v.g SAUV BL, CHARD, RIES and CAB SAUV. Wide range of sound wines under Corban label. Additional premium wines under affiliate label Robard & Butler.

**De Redcliffe**  Mangatawhiri, s.e. of Auckland.
>Small progressive winery with associated resort "Hotel du Vin"; producing good CHARD, SEMILLION and CAB/MERLOT.

**Delegat's**  Henderson, nr. Auckland.
>Medium-sized family winery, using grapes from GISBORNE and HAWKES BAY for good CHARD, SAUV BL and CAB SAUV, plus impressive Auslese style now from RIESLING.

**Esk Valley**  Bayview, Hawkes Bay.
>Former large family concern, now merged with VILLA MARIA/VIDAL group, concentrating on small range of premium whites and reds.

**Giesen**  Burnham, s. of Christchurch, Canterbury, South Island.
>Small winery established by immigrant German family, using own v'yd and MARLBOROUGH grapes. Good CHARD, SAUV BL, RIES and reds.

**Gisborne**  Site of three large wineries, MONTANA, CORBANS and PENFOLDS, and centre of large viticultural area incl. MATAWHERO and TOLAGA BAY. Some 10% of vineyards were destroyed by a tropical cyclone in March 1988. Good area for MÜLLER-THURGAU, CHARD, SEMILLON and GEWÜRZ.

**Goldwater**  Waiheke Island in Hauraki Gulf, nr. Auckland.
>Small vineyard at sea edge, known best for CAB/MERLOT and SAUV BL.

**Hawkes Bay**  Large viticultural region on e. coast of North Island, s. of GISBORNE, known for high-quality grapes, esp. CHARD and CAB SAUV.

**Hunters**  Marlborough.
>Small, progressive winery using only MARLBOROUGH grapes. Highly reputed for outstanding SAUV BL (and oaky "Fumé" style), and CHARD.

**Kumeu River**  Kumeu, n.w. of Auckland.
>Premium label of small San Marino family winery, establishing reputation for SAUV FUMÉ, CHARD, CAB/MERLOT and light fruity CAB FRANC under Brajkovich family crest label.

**Marlborough**  Leading export wine region, at north end of South Island, on stony plain formed by Wairau River. Well suited to white varieties CHARD, SAUV BL and RIESLING, but also good CAB SAUV and promising PINOT NOIR. Potential here for v.g. sparkling.

**Martinborough**  New smallish viticultural area in s. Wairarapa, North Island (n. of Wellington). Stony soils, similar to MARLBOROUGH. Own appellation.

**Martinborough Vineyards**  Martinborough.
>Largest of the small operations in the area. Awards already for CHARD, "Fumé" SAUV BL and PINOT NOIR.

**Matawhero**  nr Gisborne.
>Small winery with longstanding reputation for GEWÜRZ, CHARD and SAUV BL.

**Matua Valley**  n.w. of Auckland.
>Medium-sized family winery, pioneer with new varieties. Own grapes supplemented by HAWKES BAY and GISBORNE. Well known for Judd Chard (Gisborne), unwooded SAUV BL labelled "Fumé", unique PINOT NOIR/BLANC and excellent CAB SAUV and late-harvest Muscat.

**Millton**  nr. Gisborne.
>Small new producer using organic cultivation methods. Good SAUV BL/SEMILLON blend, CHARD and RIESLING (both dry and late harvest).

**Mission**  Greenmeadows, Hawkes Bay.
>The oldest continuing winemaking establishment in NZ, founded by French missionaries and still operated by Society of Mary. Good SEMILLON/SAUV BL blend and CAB/MERLOT.

**Montana**  Auckland.
>Largest winemaking enterprise in NZ, with wineries in GISBORNE and MARLBOROUGH and now incorporating Penfold's NZ operations. Pioneered viticulture in MARLBOROUGH, but draws grapes also from GISBORNE and HAWKES BAY. Marlborough labels incl. SAUV BL, CHARD, RIESLING, CAB SAUV and PINOT NOIR. Gisborne CHARD also sound wine and big seller. Success with "Lindauer" *méthode champenoise* has led to licensing agreement with Champagne DEUTZ.

**Morton Estate**   Katikati, nr. Tauranga, e. coast North Island.

Expanding new winery with high reputation for CHARD from HAWKES BAY (esp. premium black label), SAUV BL, and CAB SAUV. Recently released its first (v.g.) *méthode champenoise.*

**Ngatarawa**   nr. Hastings, Hawkes Bay.

Boutique winery in old stables of established HAWKES BAY family. Good CHARD, SAUV BL and CAB/MERLOT under "Glazebrook" family name label.

**Nobilo**   Huapai Valley, n.w. of Auckland.

NZ's largest family-owned winery, with own grapes plus fruit from GISBORNE, HAWKES BAY, MARTINBOROUGH and MARLBOROUGH. Good CHARD (esp. from Gisborne), SAUV BL, SEMILLON, and long-established reputation for age-worthy reds, CAB SAUV and PINOT NOIR. Associate label, "Classic Hills".

**Penfolds**   See Montana.

**Robard & Butler**   See Corbans.

**St. Nesbit**   Karaka, nr. Papakura, s. of Auckland.

Expanding boutique winery, specializing in single red wine blended from CAB SAUV, CAB FRANC and MERLOT, well made and matured in barriques.

**Selak's**   Kumeu, n.w. of Auckland.

Small family firm with good export reputation for SAUV BL, SAUV BL/SEMILLON blend (in "Fumé" style), CHARD and CAB SAUV. ("Founders" label for top wines of two last named).

**Stoneleigh**   See Corbans.

**Te Mata**   Havelock North, Hawkes Bay.

Oldest winery premises in continuous operation, now restored and producing good CHARD and SAUV BL from nearby vineyards, plus excellent "Coleraine" CAB/MERLOT from proprietor's home vineyard.

**Vidal**   Hastings, Hawkes Bay.

Atmospheric old winery now merged with Villa Maria (see below). Good HAWKES BAY CHARD, SAUV BL, CAB SAUV and PINOT NOIR.

**Villa Maria**   Mangere, outskirts s. Auckland.

Large company, now incorporating VIDAL and ESK VALLEY. Uses grapes from Ihumatao (nr. Auckland airport), GISBORNE and HAWKES BAY. Full range of wines, with emphasis on barrel-fermented CHARD, SAUV BL (and wooded "Fumé" variation), GEWÜRZ, CAB SAUV and CAB/MERLOT.

**Weingut Seifried**   Upper Moutere, nr. Nelson, South Island.

Small winery started by Austrian immigrant. Good CHARD, SAUV BL, RIESLING (in dry and late-harvest styles) and PINOT NOIR.

NZ

# South Africa

Quality in S. Africa's table wines began around 1970 when vineyard owners began to plant Cabernet Sauvignon, followed by better white varieties. The success of small new cellars encouraged wineries to buy oak barrels from France. These wines date from about 1980. Cellarmasters are now showing more care in harvesting and cellar treatment and standards are rising steadily, though still not at (e.g.) New Zealand's pace.

**Allesverloren** ★★

Estate in MALMESBURY with 395 acres of v'yds, well known for "port", and now also specializing in powerful, almost roasted, reds, incl. ripe, soft CABERNET, and Tinta Barocca.

**Alphen** ★

Vineyard at Somerset West. Name is used as a brand by Gilbeys.

**Alto** ★★

STELLENBOSCH estate of 247 acres high on a hill, best known for massive-bodied CAB and a good SHIRAZ/CAB blend: Alto Rouge.

**Backsberg** ★★ →★★★

A prize-winning 395-acre estate at PAARL with notably good white wines (incl. CHARD) and medium-bodied CABERNET and SHIRAZ.

**Bellingham** ★★→★★★

Top brand name of Union Wine Co. Reliable reds and whites, esp. CABERNET. Johannisberger and GRAND CRU are top-selling blends.

**Bergkelder** Big wine concern at STELLENBOSCH, member of the UDE MEESTER group, making and distributing many brands (FLEUR DU CAP, GRÜNBERGER) and estate wines. Part of same financial group as STELLENBOSCH FARMERS' WINERY.

**Bertrams** ★★

Gilbey's brand of reds, good CAB and SHIRAZ.

**Blaauwklippen** ★★→★★★

Estate S. of STELLENBOSCH producing some of S. Africa's very best reds, CAB, P NOIR and ZIN, and good RHINE RIES and SAUV BLANC.

**Boberg** Controlled region of origin for fortified wines consisting of the districts of PAARL and TULBAGH.

**Le Bonheur** ★★★

STELLENBOSCH estate producing one of the Cape's best whites, Blanc Fumé, a non-wooded SAUV BLANC. Also Médoc-style CAB.

**Boschendal** ★★★

Vast (617-acre) estate in PAARL area on an old fruit farm. Emphasis on white wines and sparkling "Brut", but CABERNET improving. Also a charming restaurant.

**Breede River Valley** Fortified wine region east of Drakenstein Mtns.

**La Bri** ★★

Interesting whites made in coop cellar from SAUV BL, RHINE RIES and SÉMILLON. Blanc de la Bri best.

**Buitenverwachting** (★★)

Model estate with superb v'yd areas. Quality improving as young vines develop maturity. Good RHINE RIES.

**Bukettraube** White-wine grape with high acidity and muscat aroma, most popular as a blend component.

**Cabernet** The great Bordeaux grape, particularly successful in the COASTAL REGION. Sturdy, long-ageing wines. Use of new oak from about '82 has made great improvement.

**Cavendish Cape** ★★

Range of remarkably good sherries from the K.W.V.

**Chardonnay** Classic white variety, very rare in S. Africa due to official restrictions. Recent release of good vines has resulted in leap in quality of the few on the market. Great expectations.

**Chenin Blanc** Work-horse grape of the Cape; one vine in four. Adaptable and sometimes very good. Alias STEEN. K.W.V. makes a very good example at a bargain price.

**Cinsaut** The principal bulk-producing French red grape in S. Africa; formerly known as Hermitage. Very seldom seen with varietal label.

**Coastal Region** Demarcated wine region, includes PAARL, STELLENBOSCH, DURBANVILLE, SWARTLAND, TULBAGH.

**Colombard** The "French Colombard" of California. High acidity and fruity flavour add interest to blended whites.

**Constantia** Once the world's most famous Muscat wine, from the Cape. Now the southernmost district of origin.

**Delheim (★★★)** Winery at Driesprong in one of the highest areas of STELLENBOSCH, known for delicate STEEN and GEWÜRZ whites and impressive reds: CABERNET, PINOTAGE, SHIRAZ. Grande Reserve (CAB SAUV, CAB FRANC, MERLOT) is top class.

**Drostdy ★★★** Quality range of sherries from BERGKELDER.

**Edelkeur ★★★★** Excellent intensely sweet white made with nobly rotten (p. 48) grapes by NEDERBURG.

**Estate wine** Strictly controlled term applying only to registered estates making wines from grapes grown on the same property.

**Fleur du Cap ★★** Popular and well-made range of wines from the BERGKELDER. Good CAB; interesting SAUV BL.

**Gewürztraminer** The famous spicy grape of Alsace, best at SIMONSIG. Naturally low acidity makes this variety difficult to handle at the Cape. Term for a totally dry white, with no Grand Cru (or Premier Grand Cru).

**Groot Constantia (★★★)** Historic estate, now government owned, near Cape Town. Source of superlative muscat wine in the early 19th century. Now making wide range of wines, esp. good RHINE RIESLING, GEWÜRZ.

**Grünberger ★** BERGKELDER brand using STEEN to make to range of dry and semi-sweet white wines.

**Hamilton-Russell ★★★** Young estate in cool coastal valley. Among leaders with P NOIR, CHARDONNAY and SAUV BLANC.

**Hanepoot** Local name for the sweet Muscat of Alexandria grape.

**Hartenberg ★★** Previously known as Montagne. Stellenbosch estate producing fine CABERNET and SHIRAZ.

**Hazendal ★★** Family estate in W. STELLENBOSCH specializing in semi-sweet STEEN, marketed by the BERGKELDER.

**Kanonkop ★★★** Outstanding estate in n. STELLENBOSCH. Stylish full-bodied CAB and PINOTAGE. Paul Sauer Fleur is a Bordeaux-style blend.

**Klein Constantia (★★★)** Sophisticated new estate. No expense spared in vineyard or cellar. Top class SAUV BLANC and RIESLING.

**Koopmanskloof ★★** STELLENBOSCH estate making good dry Chenin Blanc-based blend "Blanc de Marbonne".

**K.W.V.** The Kooperatieve Wijnbouwers Vereniging, S. Africa's national wine cooperative created 60 years ago by the State to absorb surpluses. Vast premises in PAARL making a range of good wines, particularly sherries.

**Laborie (\*\*)**
k.w.v.-owned showpiece estate on Paarl Mtn. Blended white and red.

**Landgoed** South African for estate; a word which appears on estate-wine labels and official seals.

**Landskroon \*\***
Family estate owned by Paul and Hugo de Villiers. Good dry reds – PINOT NOIR, TINTA BAROCCA and CABERNETS SAUV and FRANC.

**Late Harvest** Term for a mildly sweet wine. "Special Late Harvest" must be naturally sweet (no added concentrate). "Noble Late Harvest" is the highest quality level of all.

**Lemberg (\*\*)**
Tiny estate in Paarl, making full-bodied, wood-aged Harsleveld and SAUV BLANC. Growing reputation.

**Leyland (\*\*←\*\*\*)**
Little-known winery with modest packaging. Beginning to develop a reputation. RHINE RIESLING placed highly at 1988 Gault et Millau Paris Olympiad.

**J.C. Le Roux \*\***
Old Cape brand revived as BERGKELDER's sparkling wine house. SAUV BLANC (Charmat) and R NOIR (Méthode Champenoise).

**Malmesbury** Centre of the SWARTLAND wine district, on the w. coast n. of Cape Town, specializing in dry whites and distilling wine.

**Meerendal \*\***
Estate near Durbanville producing traditional robust reds (esp. SHIRAZ and PINOTAGE) marketed by the BERGKELDER.

**Meerlust \*\*\***
Beautiful old family estate s. of STELLENBOSCH making outstanding CABERNET, Rubicon (Médoc-style blend), MERLOT and R NOIR.

**Monis \*\*←\*\*\***
Well-known wine concern of PAARL, with fine "Vintage Port".

**Monpellier \***
Pioneering TULBAGH estate with 370 acres of v'yds, specializing in white wine. Wines are distinctly dull today.

**Muratie \***
Ancient estate in STELLENBOSCH, best known for its port. Recently sold; bright future expected.

**Nederburg \*\*\***
The most famous wine farm in modern S. Africa, operated by the STELLENBOSCH FARMERS' WINERY. Its annual auction is a major event. Pioneer in modern cellar practice and with fine CABERNET. "Private Bin" blends, DREAKEUR and GEWÜRZ. Also good sparkling wines and Paarl Rieslings.

**Neethlingshof (\*\*)**
Being replanted. Full-bodied Colombard and cab best. To watch.

**Neil Ellis Vineyards (\*\*)**
Wines made in central cellar from grapes grown in widely differing areas. Very fine SAUV BLANC, CAB.

**Overberg** Demarcated wine district in the Caledon area, COASTAL REGION, with some of the coolest Cape vineyards. (No labels from this area yet.)

**Overgaauw \*←\*\*\***
Estate w. of STELLENBOSCH making good STEEN, very good CABERNET, and Tria Corda, a CABERNET/MERLOT blend.

**Paarl** South Africa's wine capital, 30 miles n.e. of Cape Town, and the surrounding demarcated district, among the best in the country, particularly for white wine and sherry.

**Paarlsack \***
Well-known range of sherries made at PAARL by the k.w.v.

**Pierre Jourdan (\*\*\*)**
Impressive *méthode champenoise* bubbly from CHARD and R NOIR.

**Pinot Noir** Like counterparts in California and Australia, Cape producers struggle to get complexity of flavour. Best are HAMILTON RUSSELL, BLAAUWKLIPPEN, MEERLUST.

**Pinotage** South African red grape, a cross between P NOIR and CINSAUT, useful for high yields and hardiness. Its wine is lush and fruity but never first-class.

**Premier Grand Cru** See Grand Cru.

**Rhine Riesling** Produces full-flavoured dry and off-dry wines. Generally needs two years or more of bottle age. See Weisser Riesling.

**Riesling** South African Riesling (actually Crouchen Blanc) is very different from RHINE RIESLING, providing neutral, fresh, easy drinking wines.

**Rietvallei ★★**
ROBERTSON estate producing excellent fortified Muscadel.

**Robertson** Small demarcated district e. of the Cape and inland. Mainly dessert wines (notably Muscat), but red and white table wines are on the increase. Includes Bonnievale. Irrigated vineyards.

**Roodeberg ★★**
High-quality brand of blended red wine from the k.w.v. Has good colour, body and flavour and ages well in bottle.

**Rustenberg ★★★**
Effectively, if not officially, an estate red wine from just n.e. of STELLENBOSCH. Rustenberg Dry Red is a good CAB/CINSAUT blend. The straight CAB is outstanding. P NOIR is promising.

**Sauvignon Blanc** Adapting well to warm conditions. Widely grown and marketed in "wooded" and "unwooded" styles.

**Schoongezicht ★★→★★★★★**
Partner of RUSTENBERG, one of S. Africa's most beautiful old farms and producer of agreeable white wine from STEEN, RIESLING and Clairette Blanche. CHAMP promising.

**Shiraz** Provides the base in many top red blends. Rich deep-coloured wine.

**Simonsig ★★★**
Estate owned by F.J. Malan, pioneering estate producer. Produces a wide range, incl. gewürz, Vin Fumé (wood-matured dry white) and a méthode champenoise. Quality improving.

**Simonsvlei** One of S. Africa's best-known cooperative cellars, just outside PAARL. A prize-winner with PINOTAGE.

**Spier ★→★★★**
Estate of five farms w. of STELLENBOSCH producing reds and whites. COLOMBARD and PINOTAGE are best.

**Steen** South Africa's commonest white grape, said to be a clone of the CHENIN BLANC. It gives strong, tasty and lively wine, sweet or dry, normally better than S. African RIESLING.

**Stein** Name often used for commercial blends of semi-sweet white wine. Not necessarily to be despised.

**Stellenbosch** Town and demarcated district 30 miles e. of Cape Town, extending to the ocean at False Bay. Most of the best estates, esp. for red wine, are in the mountain foothills of the region.

**Stellenbosch Farmers' Winery (S.F.W.)** South Africa's biggest winery (after the k.w.v.) with several ranges of wines, incl. NEDERBURG and ZONNEBLOEM. Wide range of mid- and low-priced wines. See Cape wine and distillers.

**Stellenryck ★★★**
Top-quality BERGKELDER range. RHINE RIESLING, Fumé Blanc, CABERNET and gewürz.

**Superior** An official designation of quality for wines of origin. The wine must meet standards set by the Wine & Spirit Board.

**Swartland** Demarcated district around MALMESBURY. ALLESVERLOREN is the best estate.

**Tassenberg** *
Popular and good-value red known to thousands as Tassie.

**Theuniskraal** ***
Well-known TULBAGH estate specializing in white wines, esp. RIESLING, GEWÜRZTRAMINER and Sémillon.

**Tulbagh** Demarcated district n. of PAARL, best known for the white wines of MONTPELLIER, THEUNISKRAAL and TWEE JONGEGEZELLEN, and the dessert wines from Drostdy. See also Boberg.

**Twee Jongegezellen** ** ←→ ***
Estate at TULBAGH. One of the great pioneers which revolutionized S. African wine in the 1930s, still in the family of its 18th-century founder. Mainly white wines, incl. "Schanderl" and "T.J. 39". Night harvesting has improved quality.

**Uiterwyk** **
Old estate w. of STELLENBOSCH making a good CAB SAUV and pleasant whites.

**Uitkyk** (***)
Old estate (400 acres) at STELLENBOSCH famous for Carlonet (big gutsy CAB) and Carlsheim (chiefly SAUV BLANC) white.

**Vergenoegd** (***)
Old family estate in s. STELLENBOSCH supplying high-quality sherry to the k.w.v. and offering deeply flavoured CABERNET and excellent SHIRAZ under the estate label. Not as good as before.

**Villiera** (***)
Paarl estate with Tradition top-class *méthode champenoise.* Winner of 1988 Gault et Millau Paris Olympiad with RHEIN RIESLING. Fine CAB and CAB/MERLOT blend.

**Vriesenhof** ***
Small-scale winery with vines high on Stellenbosch mountain slope. Highly rated CAB and CHARD.

**Weisser Riesling** Alias Rhine Riesling. Producing good wines in S. Africa. They need time to mature and are not really appreciated.

**Welgemeend** ***
Boutique PAARL estate producing Médoc-style blends, delicate CABER-net and Amadé, a Grenache, SHIRAZ and PINOTAGE blend.

**Weltevrede** * ←→ ***
Progressive ROBERTSON estate. Blended white and fortified wines.

**De Wetshof** ***
Pioneering estate in ROBERTSON district. CHARDONNAY, SAUVIGNON BLANC, RHINE RIESLING and a sweet noble-rot white. Edeloes. Won best wine of show trophy at '87 Bordeaux Vinexpo with CHARD.

**Wine of Origin** The S. African equivalent of Appellation Controlée. Demarcated regions are described on these pages.

**Worcester** Demarcated wine district round the Breede and Hex river valleys, e. of PAARL. Many cooperative cellars make mainly dessert wines, brandy and dry whites.

**Zandvliet** **
Estate in the ROBERTSON area making a fine light SHIRAZ.

**Zevenwacht** ***
Large Stellenbosch Estate with wines only available through share-holders and restaurants. CAB SAUV is impressive.

**Zonnebloem** **
Good-quality brand of CABERNET, RIESLING, PINOTAGE and SHIRAZ from the STELLENBOSCH FARMERS' WINERY. Recent SAUV BLANC and Blanc de Blancs whites have shown quality.

# A few words about words

In the shorthand essential for this little book (and sometimes in bigger books as well) wines are often described by adjectives that can seem irrelevant, inane – or just silly. What do "fat", "round", "full", "lean", and so on mean, when used about wine? Some of the more irritatingly vague are expanded in this list:

**Attack**
The first impression of the wine in your mouth. It should "strike" positively, if not necessarily with force. Without attack it is feeble.

**Attractive**
Means "I like it, anyway". A slight put-down for expensive wines; encouragement for juniors. At least a refreshing drink.

**Big**
Concerns the whole flavour, including the alcohol content. Sometimes implies clumsiness, the opposite of elegance. Generally positive, but big is easy in California and less usual in, say, Bordeaux. So the context matters.

**Charming**
Rather patronizing when said of wines that should have more impressive qualities. Implies lightness, possibly slight sweetness. A standard comment on Loire wines.

**Crisp**
With pronounced but pleasing acidity; fresh and eager.

**Deep/depth**
This wine is worth tasting with attention. There is more to it than the first impression; it fills your mouth with developing flavours as though it had an extra dimension. (Deep colour simply means hard to see through.) All really fine wines have depth.

**Easy**
Used in the sense of "easy come, easy go". An easy wine makes no demand on your palate (or intellect). The implication is that it drinks smoothly, doesn't need maturing, and all you will remember was a pleasant drink.

**Elegant**
A professional taster's favourite term when he is stuck to describe a wine whose proportions (of strength, flavour, aroma), whose attack, middle and finish, whose texture and all its qualities call for comparison with other forms of natural beauty, as in the movement of horses, the forms and attitudes of women . . .

**Fat**
With flavour and texture that fills your mouth, but without aggression. Obviously inappropriate in e.g. a light Moselle, but what you pay your money for in Sauternes.

**Finish**
See Length.

**Firm**
Flavour that strikes the palate fairly hard, with fairly high acidity or tannic astringency giving the impression that the wine is in youthful vigour and will age to gentler things. An excellent quality with high-flavoured foods, and almost always positive.

**Flesh**
Refers to both substance and texture. A fleshy wine is fatter than a "meaty" wine, more unctuous if less vigorous. The term is often used of good Pomerols, whose texture is notably smooth.

**Flowery**
Often used as though synonymous with fruity, but really means floral, like the fragrance of flowers. Roses, violets, etc., are sometimes specified.

**Fresh**
Implies a good degree of fruity acidity, even a little nip of sharpness, as well as the zip and zing of youth. All young whites should be fresh: the alternative is flatness, stale-ness . . . ugh.

**Fruity**
Used for almost any quality, but really refers to the body and richness of wine made from good ripe grapes. A fruity aroma is not the same as a flavoury one. Fruitiness usually implies at least a slight degree of sweetness.

| | |
|---|---|
| **Full** | Interchangeable with full-bodied. Lots of "vinosity" or wineyness: the mouth-filling flavours of alcohol and "extract" (all the flavouring components) combined. |
| **Hollow** | Lacking a satisfying middle flavour. Something seems to be missing between first flavour and last. A characteristic of wines from greedy proprietors who let their vines produce too many grapes. An extremely hollow wine is "empty". |
| **Lean** | A bit more flesh would be an improvement. Lack of mouth-filling flavours: often astringent as well. But occasionally a term of appreciation of a distinct and enjoyable style. |
| **Length** | The flavours and aromas that linger after swallowing. In principle the greater the length the better the wine. One second of flavour after swallowing = one "caudalie". Ten caudalies is good; 20 terrific. |
| **Light** | With relatively little alcohol and body, as in most German wines. A very desirable quality in the right wines. |
| **Meaty** | Savoury in effect with enough substance to chew. The inference is lean meat; leaner than in "fleshy". |
| **Oaky** | Smelling or tasting (or both) of fresh-sawn oak; e.g. a new barrel. |
| **Plump** | The diminutive of fat, implying a degree of charm as well. |
| **Rich** | Not necessarily sweet, but giving an opulent impression. |
| **Robust** | In good heart, vigorous, and on a fairly big scale. |
| **Rough** | Flavour and texture give no pleasure. Acidity and/or tannin are dominant and coarse. |
| **Round** | Almost the same as fat, but with more approval. |
| **Stylish** | Style is bold and definite; wears its cap on its ear. |
| **Supple** | Often used of young red wines which might be expected to be more aggressive. More lively than an "easy" wine, with implications of good quality. |
| **Well-balanced** | Contains all the desirable elements (acid, alcohol, flavours, etc.) in appropriate and pleasing proportions. |

## ... and a few words about numbers

Many wine-drinkers in the USA have become convinced recently that the differences in quality between wines can be accurately and adequately expressed in terms of points out of a hundred – starting at fifty, which is (apparently) the lowest mark given in American schools.

But the notion that e.g. Château Belair 1985 is a "90", while Beaune Clos des Mouches 1985 is an "88" not only makes direct comparisons between two wines which are intentionally totally unlike, it also gives a spurious air of scientific accuracy to a judgement that is really at least partly subjective.

Worse, if the scores are averaged from the results of a group tasting they can mislead a reader into thinking they represent a unanimous opinion.

Scores for wines are a useful, even essential, part of any competitive tasting. But without explanation and discussion they are a trap. Moreover, they tend to convey the impression that all wines are striving to be "good" in the same way, rather than stressing the greatest glory of wine: its infinite variety.

# The 1987 vintage

1987 will not be one of the easy vintages to remember when things went well in most of the wine-making world. Northern Europe had a generally poor summer, with rain at vintage time in many regions.

Southern Europe was generally more fortunate. California and Australia had very good vintages. Yet even within these generalizations there was a wide variety of results, with Burgundy, for example, being much more fortunate than the Rhône valley.

The only region where there is an urgent need to buy the 1987 vintage is Australia, where it ended a run of highly successful years. 1988 was the most difficult harvest for a long time; with Australian wines conquering world markets with their high quality/price ratio it is a piece of bad luck for us all.

Other regions where 1987 is a vintage to buy, though not to fill the cellar with, include burgundy for some highly promising red wines and Bordeaux for excellent dry whites (though not sweet ones). Piemonte had another very good vintage for Barolo and its kin and in Tuscany Montepulciano and Brunello are successes. Penadès in Spain reports one of its greatest red wine vintages.

Both Germany and Alsace are well pleased to have made lively and well-balanced Rieslings, if nothing exceptional. Muscadet of 1987 is extremely good. Wines from Provence, particularly Bandol, are very fine.

California's vintners are very happy with the overall quality of both reds and whites in 1987, if a little disappointed, in some cases, with the quantity they were able to make.

# What to drink in an ideal world

**Wines at their peak in 1989**

**Red Bordeaux:**

Top growths of 1980, 1979, 1976, 1975, 1970, 1966, 1962, 1961

Other Crus Classés of 1981, 1980, 1979, 1978, 1976, 1975, 1970, 1966, 1961

Petits châteaux of 1985, 1984, 1983, 1982, 1981, 1979, 1978

**Red Burgundy**

Top growths of 1982, 1980, 1979, 1978, 1976, 1973, 1971, 1969, 1966, 1964

Premiers Crus of 1984, 1983, 1982, 1980, 1979, 1978, 1976, 1971 . . .

Village wines of 1986, 1985, 1984, 1983

**White Burgundy**

Top growths of 1984, 1983, 1982, 1981, 1979, 1978 . . .

Premiers Crus of 1985, 1984, 1983, 1982, 1981, 1978 . . .

Village wines of 1987, 1986, 1985, 1983

**Sauternes**

Top growths of 1982, 1981, 1980, 1979, 1978, 1976, 1975, 1971, 1970, 1967 . . .

Other wines of 1985, 1983, 1982, 1981, 1980, 1979, 1978, 1976, 1975 . . .

**Sweet Loire wines**

Top growths of (Anjou/Vouvray) 1983, 1982, 1981, 1980, 1979, 1978, 1976, 1975, 1973, 1971, 1969, 1964 . . .

**Alsace**

Grands Crus and late-harvest wines of 1986, 1985, 1984, 1983, 1981, 1979, 1978, 1976 . . .

Standard wines of 1987, 1986, 1985, 1983 . . .

**Rhône**

Hermitage/top Northern Rhône reds of 1982, 1980, 1979, 1978, 1973, 1971, 1969

Châteauneuf-du-Pape of 1982, 1981, 1980, 1979, 1978 . . .

**German wines**

Great sweet wines of 1976, 1975, 1971 . . .

Ausleses of 1983, 1981, 1979, 1976 . . .

Spätleses of 1986, 1985, 1983, 1979, 1976 . . .

Kabinett and QbA wines of 1986, 1985, 1984, 1983 . . .

**Californian**

Top Cabernets, Pinot Noirs, Zinfandels of 1984, 1983, 1981, 1980, 1979, 1978, 1976, 1974

Most Cabernets, etc., of 1985, 1984, 1983, 1982, 1981, 1980 . . .

Top Chardonnays of 1985, 1984, 1983 . . .

Most Chardonnays of 1986, 1985, 1984 . . .

**Vintage Port**

1975, 1970, 1967, 1966, 1963, 1960 . . .

## Quick reference vintage charts for France and Germany

These charts give a picture of the range of qualities made in the principal areas (every year has its relative successes and failures) and a guide to whether the wine is ready to drink or should be kept.

| ↓ drink now | — needs keeping | ✓ can be drunk with pleasure now, but |
|---|---|---|
| 0 no good | 10 the best | the better wines will continue to improve |

Combinations of these symbols mean that there are wines in more than one of the categories.

| FRANCE | RED BORDEAUX | | WHITE BORDEAUX | |
|---|---|---|---|---|
| | MÉDOC/GRAVES | POM/ST-EM | SAUTERNES & SW. | GRAVES & DRY |
| 87 | 3–6 — | 3–6 — | 2–5 — | 7–10 — |
| 86 | 6–9 — | 6–8 — | 7–10 — | 7–9 ↓ |
| 85 | 6–8 ✓ | 7–9 ↓ | 6–8 ✓ | 5–8 ✓ |
| 84 | 4–7 ↓ | 2–5 ✓ | 4–7 ✓ | 5–7 ✓ |
| 83 | 6–9 ↓ | 6–9 ↓ | 6–10 ✓ | 7–9 ↓ |
| 82 | 8–10 ↓ | 7–9 ↓ | 3–7 ✓ | 7–8 ↓ |
| 81 | 5–8 ↓ | 6–9 ✓ | 5–8 ✓ | 7–8 ↓ |
| 80 | 4–7 ↓ | 3–5 ↓ | 5–9 ✓ | 5–7 ↓ |
| 79 | 5–8 ↓ | 5–7 ✓ | 6–8 ✓ | 4–6 ↓ |
| 78 | 6–9 ↓ | 6–8 ✓ | 4–6 ✓ | 7–9 ↓ |
| 77 | 3–5 ↓ | 2–5 ↓ | 2–4 ↓ | 6–7 ↓ |
| 76 | 6–8 ↓ | 7–8 ✓ | 7–9 ✓ | 4–8 ↓ |
| 75 | 7–9 ↓ | 8–9 ↓ | 8–10 ✓ | 8–10 ↓ |
| 74 | 4–6 ↓ | 3–5 ↓ | 0 | 4–6 ↓ |
| 73 | 5–7 ↓ | 5–7 ↓ | 0–4 ↓ | 7–8 ↓ |
| 72 | 2–5 ↓ | 2–4 ↓ | 2–4 ↓ | 4–5 ↓ |
| 71 | 5–8 ↓ | 6–8 ↓ | 8–9 ↓ | 8–9 ↓ |
| 70 | 9–10 ✓ | 9–10 ↓ | 9–10 ↓ | 9–10 ↓ |

| FRANCE | RED BURGUNDY | WHITE BURGUNDY | | |
|---|---|---|---|---|
| | CÔTE D'OR | CÔTE D'OR | CHABLIS | ALSACE |
| 87 | 6–9 — | 5–8 ✓ | 5–7 ✓ | 7–8 ✓ |
| 86 | 5–8 ✓ | 7–10 ↓ | 7–9 ↓ | 7–8 ↓ |
| 85 | 7–10 ✓ | 5–8 ✓ | 6–9 ↓ | 7–10 ↓ |
| 84 | 3–6 ✓ | 4–7 ↓ | 4–7 ↓ | 4–6 ↓ |
| 83 | 5–9 ↓ | 6–9 ✓ | 7–9 ↓ | 8–10 ↓ |
| 82 | 4–7 ↓ | 6–8 ↓ | 6–7 ↓ | 6–8 ↓ |
| 81 | 3–6 ↓ | 4–8 ↓ | 6–9 ✓ | 7–8 ↓ |
| 80 | 4–7 ↓ | 4–6 ↓ | 5–7 ↓ | 3–5 ↓ |
| 79 | 5–6 ↓ | 6–8 ↓ | 6–8 ↓ | 7–8 ↓ |
| 78 | 8–10 ✓ | 7–9 ↓ | 7–10 ↓ | 6–8 ↓ |
| 77 | 2–4 ↓ | 4–6 ↓ | 5 ↓ | 3–5 ↓ |
| 76 | 7–10 ✓ | 7–8 ↓ | 8 ↓ | 10 ↓ |

**Beaujolais:** 86 was good, 85 excellent. **Mâcon-Villages** (white): 86, 85, 84, 83 are good now. **Loire:** Sweet Anjou and Touraine. Best recent vintages: 85, 84, 83, 82, 79, 78, 76. **Upper Loire:** Sancerre and Pouilly-Fumé 86, 85 are good now. **Muscadet:** D.Y.A.

| FRANCE | RHÔNE | GERMANY | RHINE | MOSELLE |
|---|---|---|---|---|
| 87 | 3–6 ✓ | 87 | 4–7 ✓ | 5–7 ✓ |
| 86 | 5–8 ↓ | 86 | 4–8 ↓ | 5–8 ↓ |
| 85 | 6–8 ↓ | 85 | 6–8 ↓ | 6–9 ↓ |
| 84 | 5–7 ↓ | 84 | 4–6 ✓ | 4–6 ↓ |
| 83 | 6–9 ↓ | 83 | 6–9 ↓ | 7–10 ↓ |
| 82 | 5–8 ↓ | 82 | 4–6 ↓ | 4–7 ↓ |
| 81 | 5–7 ↓ | 81 | 5–8 ↓ | 4–8 ↓ |
| 80 | 6–8 ↓ | 80 | 4–7 ↓ | 3–7 ↓ |
| 79 | 6–7 ↓ | 79 | 6–8 ↓ | 6–8 ↓ |
| 78 | 8–10 ↓ | 78 | 5–7 ↓ | 4–7 ↓ |
| 77 | 4–6 ↓ | 77 | 5–7 ↓ | 4–6 ↓ |
| 76 | 6–9 ↓ | 76 | 9–10 ↓ | 9–10 ↓ |
| 75 | 0–5 ↓ | 75 | 7–9 ↓ | 8–10 ↓ |

N.B. Detailed charts will be found on pages 24, 25 (France). 103 (Germany).